INTEREST GROUP
POLITICS

INTEREST GROUP POLITICS

Sixth Edition

Edited by

Allan J. Cigler
Burdett A. Loomis
University of Kansas

CQ PRESS

A Division of Congressional Quarterly Inc.
Washington, D.C.

CQ Press
1255 22nd St. N.W., Suite 400
Washington, D.C. 20037

202-822-1475; 800-638-1710

www.cqpress.com

♾ The paper used in this publication meets the minimum requirements of the American National Standard for Information Sciences—Permanence of Paper for Printed Library Materials, ANSI Z39.48-1992.

Cover design: Debra Naylor

Composition: TSI Graphics

Printed and bound in the United States of America

06   05   04   03   02   5   4   3   2   1

Library of Congress Cataloging-in-Publication Data

Interest group politics / edited by Allan J. Cigler, Burdett A.
Loomis. — 6th ed.
    p.   cm
Includes bibliographical references and index.
   ISBN 1-56802-674-9 (alk. paper)
   1. Pressure groups—United States. I. Cigler, Allan J. II.
Loomis, Burdett A.
   JK1118.I565   2002
   322.4′3′0973—dc2

                                                    2002000838

Contents

Preface

About twenty years ago we began working with CQ Press to publish the first edition of *Interest Group Politics*. Six editions later, we're all still at it. And interest group politics is still around, too, as it has been since before the U.S. Constitution. This book has marked both the changes and the continuities in the study of organized interests. Our introductory essay has changed only modestly over the years, and our contributors continue to write perceptively about how groups organize, how they participate in electoral politics, and how they influence policies.

As we note in the concluding chapter, interest groups interject themselves into almost all aspects of American politics. But they stop short of going to the heart of political life. Rather than explore politics through an interest group–based theory, we've chosen to incorporate interest groups into broader perspectives of American politics. New organizations pop up to represent emerging interests; other groups die or change their missions. All in all, interest group politics remains a fascinating field.

One of the great joys of editing this book continues to be the quality and diversity of the contributed chapters. We always have more good authors and topics than we can publish, and it's been our good fortune to work with long-term contributors like M. Margaret Conway and Eric M. Uslaner, as well as fresh faces like David M. Hart and Maureen Casamayou. As with any edited volume, success depends on the quality of each article, and we have never been disappointed on this score.

At the same time, our association with CQ Press remains central to the staying power of *Interest Group Politics*. Our long-term associations, first with Joanne Daniels and Jean Woy, and then Brenda Carter, have proved productive and enjoyable. On this edition, Charisse Kiino and Molly Lohman have labored long and hard to make the project a success. We are truly grateful for the professionalism, support, and good cheer of the entire staff at CQ Press.

Once again, we owe a great debt to our families. Beth Cigler and Michel Loomis know that we'll soon return to our normal, jovial selves. And our children, Kirsten Cigler and Dakota Loomis, now have the luxury of maturity and distance from which to view our efforts. All in all an enjoyable process, and one that continues to be gratifying.

Allan J. Cigler
Burdett A. Loomis

Contributors

Frank R. Baumgartner is professor and head of the Department of Political Science at Pennsylvania State University, University Park. His books include *Policy Dynamics* (edited with Bryan D. Jones, 2002), *Basic Interests: The Importance of Groups in Politics and in Political Science* (with Beth L. Leech, 1998), *Agendas and Instability in American Politics* (with Bryan D. Jones, 1993), and *Conflict and Rhetoric in French Policymaking* (1989). His current research projects include a study of lobbying and public advocacy and an analysis of changes in American government since the Second World War.

Jeffrey M. Berry is professor of political science at Tufts University. His books include *Feeding Hungry People* (1984), *The Rebirth of Urban Democracy* (1993), and *The New Liberalism* (1999).

Christopher J. Bosso is associate professor of political science at Northeastern University, where he served as department chair from 1995 to 2001. His books include *Pesticides and Politics: The Life Cycle of a Public Issue* (1987), winner of the Policy Studies Organization award for best book in public policy, and the textbook *American Government: Conflict, Compromise, and Citizenship* (2000). He has also written on environmental politics, the tactics and strategies pursued by environmental organizations, and the dynamics of public policymaking generally.

Clyde Brown is associate professor of political science at Miami University. His research focuses on citizen participation in interest groups, elections and social movements, and interest group behavior. He has worked as a congressional staffer, campaign manager, and political organizer.

William P. Browne is professor of political science at Central Michigan University. His research interest is the process of making public policy. Most of his publications are about interest groups or agricultural policy. His most recent book is *The Failure of National Rural Policy: Interests and Institutions* (2001).

Maureen Casamayou is visiting assistant professor of American government at George Mason University. Her teaching and research interests include public administration and policymaking.

Allan J. Cigler is Chancellor's Club Teaching Professor of Political Science at the University of Kansas. He received his doctorate from Indiana University. His research and writing focus on parties and interest groups, particularly on the relationship between the two mediating institutions.

Michael Thomas Collins is the cofounder and chief technology officer of e-guana.net, an Internet consulting firm that works with nonprofit organizations. His research includes work on a Brookings Institution study on the economic potential of the Internet for government, and he has written or cowritten papers on the use of metadata and XML and the concept of return on investment in a nonprofit or academic setting. He has also studied database systems and Geographic Information Systems at the Harvard Graduate School of Design and done large-scale Web development work.

M. Margaret Conway is Distinguished Professor Emeritus of political science at the University of Florida. She has written several books on political participation, political parties, and women and politics. She has also published a number of articles in academic journals.

Marian Currinder is visiting assistant professor of American government at the College of Charleston. Her current research interests include party and interest group politics, Congress, political action committees, and congressional campaign committees.

Diana Dwyre is associate professor of political science at California State University, Chico. She is the coauthor of *Legislative Labyrinth: Congress and Campaign Finance Reform* (2001) and has published numerous journal articles and chapters on campaign finance, political parties, and interest groups. She served as the American Political Science Association's Steiger Congressional Fellow in 1998.

R. Kenneth Godwin is Marshall Rauch Professor of Political Science and Public Policy at the University of North Carolina at Charlotte. His research focuses on models of interest group activity and on education policy.

Joanne Connor Green is associate professor of political science at Texas Christian University. Her research interests include the dynamics of open-seat elections for the U.S. House of Representatives, with special attention to the impact of gender and money on elections and the political process. She is also researching the pedagogical concerns and considerations in quality Web-based instruction.

John C. Green is director of the Ray Bliss Institute of Applied Politics and professor of political science at the University of Akron. He has written extensively on religion and politics, campaign finance, and political parties. He is the coauthor of *Religion and the Culture Wars* (1996) and coeditor of *The State of the Parties* (2002).

James L. Guth is William R. Kenan Jr. Professor of Political Science at Furman University. He has written widely for professional and popular audiences on the role of religion in American politics.

David M. Hart is associate professor of public policy at the John F. Kennedy School of Government, Harvard University, and author of *Forged Consensus: Science, Technology, and Economic Policy in the U.S., 1921–1953* (1998). His research focuses on politics and policies that affect the development and diffusion of economically significant new technologies. He has also written on many other subjects related to technology, business, and politics; his essay "Making Technology Policy at the White House" appeared in *Investing in Innovation* (1998), edited by Lewis M. Branscomb and James H. Keller. He is a member of the Whitehead Institute's Task Force on Genetics and Public Policy.

Marie Hojnacki is associate professor of political science at Pennsylvania State University. Her research, which appears in several academic journals, investigates how the goals and capabilities of interest groups shape their tactics for affecting policy in governmental and nongovernmental venues. She is working on a collaborative project that investigates how communities of advocacy organizations shape the amount and type of attention given by the news media, Congress, and the president to diseases such as AIDS, Alzheimer's, heart disease, and cancer.

Mark Joslyn is assistant professor of political science at the University of Kansas. His research interests include how public opinion forms and changes; his work has appeared in *The Journal of Politics* and other professional publications.

Lyman A. Kellstedt is professor of political science at Wheaton College. He is the author and coauthor of numerous articles and books on religion and politics. His current research involves a reinterpretation of the role of religion in American politics and an examination of the role of contemporary religious activists.

Rogan Kersh is assistant professor of political science at the Maxwell School, Syracuse University. He is the author of *Dreams of a More Perfect Union* (2001) and has published articles on interest groups, Congress, and American political thought.

David C. Kimball is assistant professor of political science at the University of Missouri, St. Louis. His research focuses on interest group lobbying, voting, and elections. He is completing a book on split-ticket voting and divided government.

Beth L. Leech is assistant professor of political science at Rutgers University. She and Frank M. Baumgartner coauthored *Basic Interests: The Importance of Groups in Politics and in Political Science* (1998) and some articles on interest group lobbying. Her research interests include the roles of interest groups and the news media in policy formation.

Burdett A. Loomis is professor of political science at the University of Kansas. He received his doctorate from the University of Wisconsin. A former American Political Science Association congressional fellow and recipient of a Kemper Teaching Award, he has written extensively on legislatures, political careers, interest groups, and policymaking.

Kelly D. Patterson is associate professor and chair of the Department of Political Science at Brigham Young University. He is the author of *Political Parties and the Maintenance of Liberal Democracy* (1996) and numerous articles on campaigns and elections. His teaching and research interests include political parties, campaigns and elections, and theories of American politics.

Barry J. Seldon is professor of economics and political economy at the University of Texas at Dallas and a senior fellow at the National Center for Policy Analysis. He has published pieces on economics, public opinion, political support, and public administration.

Matthew M. Singer is a James Duke Fellow and graduate student at Duke University. His research interests include voting behavior and political campaigning from a comparative perspective.

Corwin E. Smidt is director of the Henry Institute for the Study of Christianity and Politics and is professor of political science at Calvin College. He is the editor of *In God We Trust? Religion & American Political Life* (2001) and has written and cowritten numerous articles and book chapters on religion and politics.

Eric M. Uslaner is professor of government and politics at the University of Maryland at College Park. In 1981–1982 he was a Fulbright professor of American studies at the Hebrew University in Jerusalem. His research interests include Congress, elections, civic engagement, and Canadian politics. He is the author of *The Moral Foundations of Trust* (2002).

Herbert Waltzer is professor emeritus of political science and a former academic administrator at Miami University. His research interests include political parties and elections, political communication, the news media and politics, and university governance and leadership. He has been a journalist and media political analyst, a U.S. Air Force public information officer, and a consultant on university governance and management.

INTEREST GROUP POLITICS

1

Introduction
The Changing Nature of Interest Group Politics
Burdett A. Loomis and Allan J. Cigler

The original version of this chapter appeared in the first edition (1983) of this book. It sought to convey what we saw as the most important trends in interest group politics from roughly the 1960s on. In subsequent editions we have modified this chapter in modest ways and have used our concluding chapter to consider the continuing evolution of interest group politics. For the most part, our initial generalizations have been true. Organized interests have proliferated over the past twenty years, and the trend toward increased representation of all kinds of interests continues. Despite some opposition, we still view the imbalance of influence that tilts toward moneyed interests as one of the cornerstones of the interest group system.

Some things we failed to anticipate. The almost complete breakdown of national campaign finance laws has been a surprise, as has parties' ability to take advantage of this failure. Although we understood the potential of outside lobbying strategies, we underestimated the extent to which grassroots, grasstops (local elites), public relations, and advocacy advertising would be used to set the policy agenda. Indeed, the intensity of organized interests' focus on agenda setting has been unexpected.

More than ever, however, we remain convinced that our original emphasis—on interest group representation and the overall responsiveness of the political system—is still valid. Government continues to respond to groups that clearly communicate their interests and have the funding to convey their message effectively. Still, representation is not simply a matter of responding to specific interests or citizens. Government must also respond to society's collective needs, and responsiveness to particular interests can reduce overall responsiveness. Indeed, the vibrancy and success of many organized interests contributes to a policymaking process that continues to struggle in formulating palatable solutions to complex societal problems.

From James Madison to Madison Avenue, political interests have played a central role in American politics. But this great continuity in our political experience has been matched by ambivalence from citizens, politicians, and scholars toward interest groups. James Madison's warnings of the dangers of faction echo in the rhetoric of reformers from Populists and Progressives near the turn of the century to the so-called public interest advocates of today.

If organized special interests are nothing new in American politics, can today's group politics nevertheless be seen as having changed fundamentally? Acknowledging that many important, continuing trends exist, we seek to place in perspective a broad series of changes in modern interest group politics. Among the most substantial of these developments are:

- A great proliferation of interest groups since the early 1960s.
- A centralization of group headquarters in Washington, D.C., rather than New York City or elsewhere.
- Major technological developments in information processing that promote more sophisticated, more timely, and more specialized communications strategies, such as grassroots lobbying and the message politics of issue-based campaigns.
- The rise of single-issue groups.
- Changes in campaign finance laws (1971, 1974) and the ensuing growth of political action committees (PACs), and more recently, the sharp increases in soft money contributions to parties and issue advocacy campaign advertisements for individual candidates.
- The increased formal penetration of political and economic interests into the bureaucracy (advisory committees), the presidency (White House group representatives), and the Congress (caucuses of members).
- The continuing decline of political parties' ability to perform key electoral and policy-related activities, despite their capacity to funnel soft money to candidates.
- The increased number, activity, and visibility of public interest groups, such as Common Cause and the Ralph Nader–inspired public interest research organizations.
- The growth of activity and impact of institutions, including corporations, universities, state and local governments, and foreign interests.
- A continuing rise in the amount and sophistication of group activity in state capitals, especially given the devolution of some federal programs and substantial increases in state budgets.

All these developments have antecedents in earlier eras of American political life; there is little that is genuinely new under the interest group sun. Political action committees have replaced (or complemented) other forms of special interest campaign financing. Group-generated mail directed at Congress has been a tactic since at least the early 1900s.[1] Many organizations have long been centered in Washington, members of Congress traditionally have represented local interests, and so on.

Still, the level of group activity, coupled with growing numbers of organized interests, distinguishes contemporary group politics from the politics of earlier eras. Group involvement trends lend credence to the fears of scholars such as political scientist Theodore Lowi and economist Mancur Olson, who have viewed interest-based politics as contributing to governmental stalemate and reduced accountability.[2] If accurate, these analyses point to a fundamentally different role for interest groups than those suggested by Madison and group theorists after him.

Only during the past thirty years, in the wake of Olson's pathbreaking research, have scholars begun to examine realistically why people join and become active in groups.[3] It is by no means self-evident that citizens should naturally become group members—quite the contrary in most cases. We are faced, then, with the paradoxical and complex question of why groups have proliferated when it can be economically unwise for people to join them.

Interest Groups in American Politics

Practical politicians and scholars alike generally agree that interest groups (also known as *factions, organized interests, pressure groups,* and *special interests*) are natural phenomena in a democratic regime—that is, individuals will band together to protect their interests.[4] In Madison's words, "The causes of faction . . . are sown in the nature of man." But controversy continues as to whether groups and group politics are benign or malignant forces in American politics. "By a faction," Madison wrote, "I understand a number of citizens, whether amounting to a majority or minority of the whole, who are united and actuated by some common impulse of passion, or of interest, adverse to the rights of other citizens, or to the permanent and aggregate interests of the community."[5]

Although Madison rejected the remedy of direct controls over factions as "worse than the disease," he saw the need to limit their negative effects by promoting competition among them and by devising an elaborate system of procedural "checks and balances" to reduce the potential power of any single, strong group, whether that interest represented a majority or minority position.

Hostility toward interest groups became more virulent in industrialized America, where the great concentrations of power far outstripped anything Madison might have imagined. After the turn of the century many Progressives railed at various monopolistic "trusts" and intimate connections between interests and corrupt politicians. Later, in 1935, Hugo Black, then a senator (and later a Supreme Court justice), painted a grim picture of group malevolence: "Contrary to tradition, against the public morals, and hostile to good government, the lobby has reached such a position of power that it threatens government itself. Its size, its power, its capacity for evil, its greed, trickery, deception and fraud condemn it to the death it deserves." [6]

Similar suspicions are expressed today, especially in light of the increased role of money in electoral politics. The impact of groups on elections has grown steadily since the adoption of the Federal Election Campaign Act of 1971 and its 1974 amendments—reform legislation originally intended to limit the impact of organized interests. Instead, such interests accelerated their spending on campaigns. Until the 1990s most concerns focused on PACs; indeed, direct PAC contributions to congressional candidates rose from less than $23 million in 1975–1976 to nearly $260 million in the 1999–2000 election cycle. The number of PACs has leveled off at about 4,000, and only a few are major players in electoral politics. Moreover, PACs encourage large numbers of contributors to pool their funds, a tactic that enhances Americans' political participation.

More worrisome over the past decade have been the growing amount and impact of essentially unregulated money from organized interests. "Soft money" contributions to national political parties totaled nearly $600 million in 2000, almost doubling the amount in the 1996 presidential year. Democrats received 98 percent more, and Republicans upped their totals by 81 percent. Even more troublesome may be issue advocacy advertising by organized interests, which does not fall under the expenditure limits and disclosure requirements of the Federal Election Commission. Thus in the 2000 campaign the drug industry group called Citizens for Better Medicare spent more than $40 million on advertisements designed to help congressional allies, both past and prospective.[7] At the time this group and many like it did not need to disclose where their funds came from. Nor was there any limit on the amount of expenditures, as long as they did not "expressly advocate" a preference for a candidate (that is, use the words *vote for* and similar words) or coordinate efforts with a candidate or party committee.

By focusing on "hard money" activity (largely reported contributions to candidates), "The [Federal Election Commission] . . . could no longer restrain most of the financial activity that takes place in modern elections."[8] Such an environment has renewed calls for additional campaign finance reform. So far, however, Congress has resisted changing laws that regulate group activity in national elections, and public cynicism about special interest influence will likely continue.

Pluralism and Liberalism

Despite popular distrust of interest group politics, political scientists and other observers often have viewed groups in a positive light. This perspective draws on Madison's *Federalist* writings, but is tied more closely to the growth of the modern state. Political science scholars such as Arthur Bentley, about 1910, and David Truman, forty years later, placed groups at the heart of politics and policymaking in a complex, large, and increasingly specialized governmental system. The interest group becomes an element of continuity in a changing political world. Truman noted the "multiplicity of co-ordinate or nearly co-ordinate points of access to governmental decisions" and concluded that "the significance of these many points of access and of the complicated texture of relationships among them is great. This diversity assures various ways for interest groups to participate in the formation of policy, and this variety is a flexible, stabilizing element."[9]

Derived from Truman's work and that of other group-oriented scholars is the notion of the pluralist state in which competition among interests, in and out of government, will produce policies roughly responsive to public desires, and no single set of interests will dominate.

> Pluralist theory assumes that within the public arena there will be countervailing centers of power within governmental institutions and among outsiders. Competition is implicit in the notion that groups, as surrogates for individuals, will produce products representing the diversity of opinions that might have been possible in the individual decision days of democratic Athens.[10]

In many ways the pluralist vision of American politics corresponds to the realities of policymaking and the distribution of policy outcomes, but a host of scholars, politicians, and other observers have roundly criticized this perspective. Two broad (although sometimes contradictory) critiques have special merit.

The first argues that some interests habitually lose in the policy process; others habitually win. Without endorsing the contentions of elite theorists that a small number of interests and individuals conspire together to dominate societal policies, one can make a strong case that interests with more resources (money, access, information, and so forth) usually will obtain better results than interests that possess fewer assets and employ them less effectively. The small, cohesive, well-heeled defense industry, for example, does well year in and year out in policymaking; marginal farmers and the urban poor produce a much less successful track record.[11] Based on continuing unequal results, critics of the pluralist model argue that interests are still represented unevenly and unfairly.

The second critique generally agrees that inequality of results remains an important aspect of group politics. But this perspective, most forcefully set out by Theodore Lowi, sees interests as generally succeeding in their goals of influencing government—to the point that government itself, in one form or another, provides a measure of protection to almost all societal interests. Everyone thus retains some vested interest in the structure of government and array of public policies. This does not mean that all interests get exactly what they want from governmental policies; rather, all interests get at least some rewards. From this point of view the tobacco industry surely wishes to see its crop subsidies maintained, but the small farmer and the urban poor also have pet programs, such as guaranteed loans and food stamps.

Lowi has labeled the proliferation of groups and their growing access to government "interest group liberalism." He argues that this phenomenon is pathological for a democratic government:

> Interest group liberal solutions to the problem of power [who will exercise it] provide the system with stability by spreading a *sense* of representation at the expense of genuine flexibility, at the expense of democratic forms, and ultimately at the expense of legitimacy.[12]

Interest group liberalism is pluralism, but it is sponsored pluralism, and the government is the chief sponsor. On the surface, it appears that the *unequal results* and *interest group liberalism* critiques of pluralism are at odds. Reconciliation, however, is relatively straightforward. Lowi does not suggest that all interests are effectively represented. Rather, there exists in many instances only the appearance of representation. Political scientist Murray Edelman pointed out that a single set of policies can provide two related types of rewards: tangible benefits for the few and symbolic reassurances for the many.[13] Such a combination encourages groups to form, become active, and claim success.

The Climate for Group Proliferation

Substantial cleavages among citizens are essential for interest group development. American culture and the constitutional arrangements of the U.S. government have encouraged the emergence of multiple political interests. In the pre-Revolutionary period, sharp conflicts existed between commercial and landed interests, debtor and creditor classes, coastal residents and those in the hinterlands, and citizens with either Tory or Whig political preferences. As the new nation developed, its vastness, characterized by geographical regions varying in climate, economic potential, culture, and tradition, contributed to a great heterogeneity. Open immigration policies further led to a diverse cultural mix with a wide variety of racial, ethnic, and religious backgrounds represented among the populace. Symbolically, the notion of the United States as a "melting pot," emphasizing group assimilation, has received much attention, but a more appropriate image may be a "tossed salad."[14]

The Constitution also contributes to a favorable environment for group development. Guarantees of free speech, association, and the right to petition the government for redress of grievances are basic to group formation. Because political organization often parallels government structure, federalism and the separation of powers—principles embodied in the Constitution—have greatly influenced large numbers of interest groups in the United States.

The decentralized political power structure in the United States allows important decisions to be made at the national, state, or local levels. Within each level of government there are multiple points of access. For example, business-related policies such as taxes are acted on at each level, and interest groups may affect these policies in the legislative, executive, or judicial arenas. In the case of federated organizations such as the U.S. Chamber of Commerce, state and local affiliates often act independently of the national organization. Numerous business organizations thus focus on the varied channels of access.

In addition, the decentralized political parties found in the United States are less unified and disciplined than parties in many other nations. The resulting power vacuum in the decision making process offers great potential for alternative political organizations, such as interest groups, to influence policy. Even in an era of strong legislative parties (mid-1980s on), many opportunities for influence remain.

Finally, American cultural values may encourage group development. As Alexis de Tocqueville observed in the 1830s, values such as individualism and the need for personal achievement underlie the propensity of citizens to join groups. Moreover, the large number of access points—local, state, and national—contributes to Americans' strong sense of political efficacy when compared with that expressed by citizens of other nations.[15] Not only do Americans see themselves as joiners, but they tend to belong to more political groups than do people of other countries.[16]

Theories of Group Development

A climate favorable to group proliferation does little to explain how interest groups organize. Whatever interests are latent in society and however favorable the context for group development may be, groups do not arise spontaneously. Farmers and a landed interest existed long before farm organizations first appeared; laborers and craftsmen were on the job before unions. In a simple society, even though distinct interests exist, there is little need for interest group formation. Farmers have no political or economic reason to organize when they work only for their families. Before the industrial revolution workers were craftsmen, often laboring in small family enterprises. Broad-based political organizations were not needed, although local guilds often existed to train apprentices and protect jobs.

David Truman has suggested that increasing societal complexity, characterized by economic specialization and social differentiation, is fundamental to group proliferation.[17] In addition, technological changes and the increasing interdependence of economic sectors often create new interests and redefine old ones. Robert Salisbury's discussion of American farming is instructive:

> The full-scale commercialization of agriculture, beginning largely with the Civil War, led to the differentiation of farmers into specialized interests, each increasingly different from the next.... The interdependence that accompanied the specialization process meant potential

conflicts of interests or values both across the bargaining encounter and among the competing farmers themselves as each struggled to secure his own position.[18]

Many political scientists assume that an expansion of the interest group universe is a natural consequence of growing societal complexity. According to Truman, however, group formation "tends to occur in waves" and is greater in some periods than in others.[19] Groups organize politically when the existing order is disturbed and certain interests are, in turn, helped or hurt.

It is not surprising, then, that economic interests develop both to improve their position and to protect existing advantages. The National Association of Manufacturers originally was created to further the expansion of business opportunities in foreign trade, but it became a more powerful organization largely in response to the rise of organized labor.[20] Mobilization of business interests since the 1960s often has resulted from threats posed by consumer advocates and environmentalists, as well as requirements imposed by the steadily growing role of the federal government.

Disturbances that trigger group formation need not be strictly economic or technological. Wars, for example, place extreme burdens on society, and lengthy conflicts lead to a growth of groups, whether based on support of (World War II) or opposition to (Vietnam) the conflict. Likewise, broad societal changes may disturb the status quo. The origin of the Ku Klux Klan, for example, was fear that increased numbers of ethnic and racial minorities threatened white, Christian America.

Truman's theory of group proliferation suggests that the interest group universe is inherently unstable. Groups formed from an imbalance of interests in one area induce a subsequent disequilibrium, which acts as a catalyst for individuals to form groups as counterweights to the new perceptions of inequity. Group politics thus is characterized by successive waves of mobilization and countermobilization. The liberalism of one era may prompt the resurgence of conservative groups in the next. Similarly, periods of business domination often are followed by eras of reform group ascendancy. In the 1990s health care reform proposals raised the stakes for almost all segments of society. Interest group politicking reached historic proportions as would-be reformers, the medical community, and business interests sought to influence the direction of change in line with their own preferences. And given the complexity of health care policymaking, the struggles among organized interests will surely continue for years.

Personal Motivations and Group Formation

Central to theories of group proliferation are the pluralist notions that elements of society possess common needs and share a group identity or consciousness, and that these are sufficient conditions for the formation of effective political organizations. Although the perception of common needs may be necessary for political organization, whether it is sufficient for group formation and effectiveness is open to question. Historical evidence documents many instances in which groups have not emerged spontaneously, even when circumstances such as poverty or discrimination would seem, in retrospect, to have required it.

Mancur Olson effectively challenged many pluralist tenets in *The Logic of Collective Action*, first published in 1965. Basing his analysis on a model of the "rational economic man," Olson posited that even individuals who have common interests are not inclined to join organizations that attempt to address their concerns. The major barrier to group participation is the "free rider" problem: "rational" individuals choose not to bear the participation costs (time, membership fees) because they can enjoy the group benefits (such as favorable legislation) without joining. Groups that pursue "collective" benefits, which accrue to all members of a class or segment of society regardless of membership status, will have great difficulty forming and surviving. According to Olson, it would be economically irrational for individual farmers to join a group seeking higher farm prices when benefits from price increases would be enjoyed by all farmers, even those who contribute nothing to the group. Similarly, it would be irrational for an individual environmentalist to become part of organized attempts to reduce air pollution, when all citizens, members of environmental groups or not, would reap the benefits of cleaner air. The free rider problem is especially serious for large groups because the larger the group the less likely an individual will perceive his or her contribution as having any impact on group success.

For Olson, a key to group formation—and especially group survival—was "selective" benefits. These rewards—for example, travel discounts, informative publications, and cheap insurance—go only to members. Organizations in the best positions to offer such benefits are those initially formed for some nonpolitical purpose and that ordinarily provide material benefits to their clientele. In the case of unions, for example, membership may be a condition of employment. For farmers, the American Farm Bureau Federation offers inexpensive insurance, which induces individuals to join even if they disagree with the group's goals. In professional circles, membership in professional societies may be a prerequisite for occupational advancement and opportunity.

Olson's notions have sparked several extensions of the rational man model, and a reasonably coherent body of incentive theory literature now exists.[21] Incentive theorists view individuals as rational decisionmakers interested in making the most of their time and money by choosing to participate in groups that offer benefits greater than or equal to the costs they incur by participation. Three types of benefits are available. Olson, an economist, emphasized *material* benefits—tangible rewards of participation, such as income or services that have monetary value. *Solidary* benefits are the socially derived, intangible rewards created by the act of association, such as fun, camaraderie, status, or prestige. Finally, *expressive* (also known as *purposive*) benefits derive from advancing a particular cause or ideology.[22] Groups formed on both sides of issues such as abortion or gun control illustrate the strength of such expressive incentives.

The examination of group members' motivations, and in particular the focus on nonmaterial incentives, allows for some reconciliation between the traditional group theorists' expectations of group development and the recent rational actor studies, which emphasize barriers to group formation. Nonmaterial incentives, such as fellowship and self-satisfaction, may encourage the proliferation of highly politicized groups and "have the potential for producing a more dynamic group context in which politics, political preferences, and group goals are more centrally determining factors than in material associations, linking political considerations more directly to associational size, structure, and internal processes."[23] Indeed, pure political benefits may attract members, and even collective benefits can prove decisive in inducing individuals to join large groups. Like elected officials, groups may find it possible to take credit for widely approved government actions, such as higher farm prices, stronger environmental regulations, or the protection of Social Security.[24]

Finally, several studies indicate that the free rider problem may not be quite the obstacle to participation that it was once thought to be, especially in an affluent society. Albert Hirschman, for example, has argued that the costs and benefits of group activity are not always clear; in fact, some costs of participation for some individuals, such as time and effort expended, might be regarded as benefits (in terms of personal satisfaction) by others.[25] Other researchers have questioned whether individuals even engage in rational, cost-benefit thinking as they make membership decisions. Michael McCann noted that "there seems to be a general threshold level of involvement below which free rider calculations pose few inhibitions for . . . commitment from moderately affluent citizen supporters."[26] In short, individuals may join and participate in groups for reasons beyond narrow economic self-interest or the availability of selective benefits.[27]

Contemporary Interest Group Politics

Several notable developments mark the modern age of interest group politics. Of primary importance is the large and growing number of active groups and other interests. The data here are sketchy, but one major study found that most current groups came into existence after World War II and that group formation has accelerated substantially since the early 1960s.[28] Also since the 1960s groups have increasingly directed their attention toward the center of power in Washington, D.C., as the scope of federal policymaking has grown, and groups seeking influence have determined to "hunt where the ducks are." As a result the 1960s and 1970s marked an explosion in the number of groups lobbying in Washington.

A second key change is evident in the composition of the interest group universe. Beginning in the late 1950s political participation patterns underwent some significant transformations. Conventional activities such as voting declined, and political parties, the traditional aggregators and articulators of mass interests, became weaker. Yet at all levels of government, evidence of citizen involvement has been apparent, often in the form of new or revived groups. Particularly impressive has been the growth of citizens' groups—those organized around an idea or cause (at times a single issue) with no occupational basis for membership. Fully 30 percent of such groups have formed since 1975, and in 1980 they made up more than one-fifth of all groups represented in Washington.[29]

In fact, a participation revolution occurred in the country as many citizens became active in an increasing number of protest groups, citizens' organizations, and special interest groups. These groups often comprise issue-oriented activists or individuals who seek collective material benefits. The free rider problem has proven not to be an insurmountable barrier to group formation, and many new interest groups do not use selective material benefits to gain support. Still, since the late 1970s, the number of these groups has remained relatively stable, and they are well established in representing consumers, environmentalists, and other public interest organizations.[30]

Third, government itself has profoundly affected the growth and activity of interest groups. Early in this century, workers found organizing difficult because business and industry used government-backed injunctions to prevent strikes. By the 1930s, however, with the prohibition of injunctions in private labor disputes and the rights of collective bargaining established, most governmental actions directly promoted the growth of labor unions. In recent years changes in campaign finance laws have led to an explosion in the number of political action committees, especially among business, industry, and issue-oriented groups. Laws facilitating group formation certainly have contributed to group proliferation, but government policy in a broader sense has been equally responsible.

Fourth, not only has the number of membership groups grown in recent decades, but a similar expansion has occurred in the political activity of many other interests, such as individual corporations, universities, churches, governmental units, foundations, and think tanks.[31] Historically, most of these interests have been satisfied with representation by trade or professional associations. Since the mid-1960s, however, many have chosen to employ their own Washington representatives. Between 1961 and 1982, for example, the number of corporations with Washington offices increased tenfold.[32] The chief beneficiaries of this trend are Washington-based lawyers, lobbyists, and public relations firms. The number of attorneys in the nation's capital, taken as a rough indicator of lobbyist strength, tripled between 1973 and 1983, and the growth of public relations firms was dramatic. The lobbying community of the 1990s is large, increasingly diverse, and part of the expansion of policy domain participation, whether in agriculture, the environment, or industrial development. Political scientist James Thurber has calculated that 91,000 lobbyists and people associated with lobbying were employed in the Washington, D.C., area in the early 1990s.[33] As of 2001, the *Encyclopedia of Associations* listed approximately 22,200 organizations, up more than 50 percent since 1980 and almost 400 percent since 1955.[34] And this number does not include hundreds of corporations and other institutions (such as universities) that are represented in Washington.

The Growth of Government

Although the government prompted the establishment of some agricultural interest groups in the nineteenth century, since the 1930s the federal government has become increasingly active as a spur to group formation. One major New Deal goal was to use government as an agent in balancing the relationship between contending forces in society, particularly industry and labor. One goal was to create greater equality of opportunity, including the "guarantee of identical liberties to all individuals, especially with regard to their pursuit of economic success."[35] For example, the Wagner Act (1935), which established collective bargaining rights, attempted to equalize workers' rights with those of their employers. Some New Deal programs did have real redistributive qualities, but most, even Social Security, sought only to ensure minimum standards of citizen welfare. Workers were clearly better off, but "the kind of redistribution that took priority in the public philosophy of the New Deal was not of wealth, but a redistribution of power."[36]

The expansion of federal programs accelerated between 1960 and 1980; since then, costs have continued to increase, despite resistance to new programs. In what political scientist Hugh Heclo termed an "Age of Improvement," the federal budget has grown rapidly (from nearly $100 billion in 1961 to $2.1 trillion in 2001) and has widened the sweep of federal regulations.[37] Lyndon Johnson's Great Society—a multitude of federal initiatives in education, welfare, health care, civil rights, housing, and urban affairs—created a new array of federal responsibilities and program beneficiaries. The growth of many of these programs has continued, although that growth was slowed markedly by the Reagan and Bush administrations, as well as by the Republican capture of Congress in 1994. In the 1970s the federal government further expanded its activities in consumer affairs, environmental protection, and energy regulation. It also redefined some policies, such as affirmative action, to seek greater equality of results.

Many of the government policies adopted early in the Age of Improvement did not result from interest group activity by potential beneficiaries. Several targeted groups, such as the poor, were not effectively organized during the period of policy development. Initiatives typically came from elected officials responding to a variety of private and public sources, such as task forces of academics and policy professionals.[38]

The proliferation of government activities led to a mushrooming of groups around the affected policy areas. Newly enacted programs provided benefit packages that encouraged interest group formation. Consider group activity in policy toward the aging. The radical Townsend Movement, based on age grievances, received much attention during the 1930s, but organized political activity focused on age-based concerns had virtually no influence in national politics. Social Security legislation won approval without the involvement of age-based interest groups. Four decades later, by 1978, roughly $112 billion (approximately 24 percent of total federal expenditures) went to the elderly population, and it was projected that in fifty years the outlay would amount to 40 percent of the budget.[39] By the early 1990s, however, the elderly population already received one-third of federal outlays, and long-term projections had been revised upward. The existence of such massive benefits has spawned a variety of special interest groups and has encouraged other organizations, often formed for nonpolitical reasons, to redirect their attention to the politics of aging.

Across policy areas two types of groups develop in response to governmental policy initiatives: recipients and service deliverers. In the sector devoted to policies affecting elderly individuals, recipient groups are mass-based organizations concerned with protecting—and if possible expanding—old-age benefits. The largest of these groups—indeed, the largest voluntary association represented in Washington—is the American Association of Retired Persons (AARP).

The AARP is well over twice the size of the AFL-CIO and, after the Roman Catholic Church, is the nation's largest organization. In 1998 it counted 33 million members, an increase of 23 million in twenty years.[40] Approximately half of Americans ages fifty or older, or one-fifth of all voters, belong to the group, in part because membership is cheap—$8 a year. Much of the organization's revenue comes from advertising in its bimonthly magazine, *Modern Maturity*. The organization's headquarters in Washington has its own zip code, a legislative/policy staff of 165; 28 registered, in-house lobbyists; and more than 1,200 staff members in the field. Charles Peters, editor of *Washington Monthly*, claimed that the "AARP is becoming the most dangerous lobby in America," given its vigorous defense of the elderly population's interests.[41] At the same time, because the AARP represents such a wide array of elderly individuals, it is often cautious and slow in its actions.

Federal program growth also has generated substantial growth among service delivery groups. In the health care sector, for example, these range from professional associations of doctors and nurses to hospital groups to the insurance industry to suppliers of drugs and medical equipment. Not only is there enhanced group activity, but hundreds of individual corporations have strengthened their lobbying capacities by opening Washington offices or hiring professional representatives from the capital's many lobbying firms.[42]

Federal government policy toward the aging is probably typical of the tendency to "greatly increase the incentives for groups to form around the differential effects of these policies, each refusing to allow any other group to speak in its name."[43] The complexity of government decision making increases under such conditions, and priorities are hard to set. Particularly troublesome for decisionmakers concerned with national policy is the role played by service delivery groups. In the area of aging, some service groups are largely organizational middlemen concerned with their status as vendors for the elderly population. The trade associations, for example, are most interested in the conditions surrounding the payment of funds to elderly individuals. The major concern of the Gerontological Society, an organization of professionals, is to obtain funds for research on problems of elderly individuals.

Middleman organizations do not usually evaluate government programs according to the criteria used by recipient groups; rather, what is important to them is the relationship between the program and the well-being of their organizations. Because many service delivery groups offer their members vitally important selective material incentives (financial advantages and job opportunities), they are usually far better organized than most recipient groups (the elderly population in this case, the AARP notwithstanding). As a result, service groups sometimes speak for the recipients. This is particularly true when recipient groups represent disadvantaged people, such as poor or mentally ill peoples.

Middleman groups have accounted for a large share of total group growth since 1960, and many of them are state and local government organizations. Since the late 1950s the federal government has grown in expenditures and regulations more than in personnel. Employment in the federal government has risen only 20 percent since 1955, whereas that of states and localities has climbed more than 250 percent. Contemporary federal activism largely involves overseeing and regulating state and local governmental units, which seek funding for a wide range of purposes. The intergovernmental lobby, which includes the National League of Cities, the International City Manager Association, the National Association of Counties, the National Governors' Association, the U.S. Conference of Mayors, and more, has grown to become one of the most important lobbies in Washington. In addition, many local officials, such as transportation or public works directors, are represented by groups, and even single cities and state boards of regents have established Washington offices.

Direct Intervention. Not only do public policies contribute to group proliferation, but government often directly intervenes in group creation. This is not an entirely new activity. In the early twentieth century officials in the Department of Agriculture encouraged the formation of the American

Farm Bureau Federation, and officials in the Commerce Department did the same for the U.S. Chamber of Commerce. Since the 1960s the federal government has been especially active in providing start-up funds and in sponsoring groups. One study found that government agencies have concentrated on sponsoring organizations of public service professions:

> Federal agencies have an interest in encouraging coordination among the elements of these complex service delivery systems and in improving the diffusion of new ideas and techniques. Groups like the American Public Transit Association or the American Council on Education . . . serve as centers of professional development and informal channels for administrative coordination in an otherwise unwieldy governmental system.[44]

Government sponsorship also helps explain the recent rise of citizens' groups. Most federal domestic legislation has included provisions requiring some citizen participation, which has spurred the development of various citizen action groups, including grassroots neighborhood associations, environmental action councils, legal defense coalitions, health care organizations, and senior citizens' groups. Such group sponsorship evolved for two reasons:

> First, there is the ever-present danger that administrative agencies may exceed or abuse their discretionary power. In this sense, the regulators need regulating. Although legislatures have responsibility for doing this . . . the administrative bureaucracy has grown too large for them to monitor. Therefore, citizen participation has developed as an alternative means of monitoring government agencies. Second, government agencies are not entirely comfortable with their discretionary power. . . . [T]o reduce the potential of unpopular or questionable decisions, agencies frequently use citizen participation as a means for improving, justifying, and developing support for their decisions.[45]

Citizens' groups thus have two sometimes inconsistent missions: to oversee an agency and to act as an advocate for the groups' programs.

Government funding of citizens' groups takes numerous forms. Several federal agencies—including the Federal Trade Commission, Food and Drug Administration, and Environmental Protection Agency—have reimbursed groups for participation in agency proceedings.[46] At other times the government makes available seed money or outright grants. Interest group scholar Jack Walker found that 89 percent of citizens' groups received outside funding in their initial stages of development.[47] Not all the money was from federal sources, but much did come from government grants or contracts. Government can also take away, however, and the Reagan administration made a major effort to "defund" left-leaning interests, especially citizens' groups. But once established, groups have strong instincts for survival. Indeed, the Reagan administration provided an attractive target for many citizens' groups in their recruiting efforts. This dance of defunding took place again, in 1995, after Republicans won control of the House of Representatives.

Citizens' groups, numbering in the thousands, continually confront the free rider problem because they are largely concerned with collective goods and rarely can offer the selective material incentives so important for expanding and maintaining membership. With government funding, however, the development of a stable group membership is not crucial. Many groups are essentially staff organizations with little or no membership base. In the world of interest group politics, resources are often more important than members.

Unintended Intervention.   Government policies contribute to group formation in many unintended ways as well. Policy failures can impel groups to form, as happened with the rise of the American Agriculture Movement in the wake of the Nixon administration's grain export policies. An important factor in the establishment of the Moral Majority was the perceived harassment of church-run schools by government officials. As for abortion, the 1973 Supreme Court decision in *Roe v. Wade* played a major role in the mobilization of antiabortion rights groups. And the 1989 *Webster* decision, which limited the availability of legal abortions, did the same for abortion rights groups. Even the lack of federal funding can play a role. The rise in the incidence of prostate cancer, coupled with a modest budget for research, helped lead to the formation of the National Prostate Cancer Coalition. This group has pressed the government to increase funding on prostate cancer toward levels that are spent on AIDs and breast cancer, given that the three diseases kill about the same number of individuals each year.

Finally, the expansion of government activity often inadvertently contributes to group development and the resulting complexity of politics. The development of the Bass Anglers Sportsman Society (BASS) is a good example. From the late 1940s through the 1960s the Army Corps of Engineers dammed enough southern and midwestern streams to create a host of lakes, thereby providing an inviting habitat for largemouth bass. Anglers arrived in droves to catch their limits, and the fishing industry responded by creating expensive boats filled with specialized and esoteric equipment. The number and affluence of bass aficionados did not escape the attention of Ray Scott, an enterprising soul who began BASS in 1967. In the early 1990s, with its membership approaching 1 million (up from 400,000 in 1982), BASS remained privately organized, offering its members selective benefits such as a slick magazine filled with tips on how to catch their favorite fish, packages of lures and line in return for joining or renewing their memberships, instant information about fishing hot spots, and boat owners' insurance. BASS also provided a number of solidary benefits, such as the camaraderie of fishing with fellow members in specially sanctioned fishing tournaments and the vicarious excitement of fishing with "BASS pros" whose financial livelihood revolved around competitive tournament fishing. The organization is an excellent example of Robert Salisbury's exchange theory approach to interest groups, because it provides benefits to both members and organizers in a "mutually satisfactory exchange."[48]

In fact, *members* may be a misnomer, in that the nominal members have no effective role in group decision making. In 1993 a federal district judge dismissed a $75 million suit filed against Scott by some BASS members. The judge reasoned that the organization was and always had been a for-profit corporation; its "members" thus had no standing to sue.

Although Scott sold the organization to a private corporation in 1986 (the ultimate expression of entrepreneurial success), he remained active in much of its work and wrote a column for the monthly publication, *BassMaster.* Never denying that the organization was anything but a profit-making entity, Scott stated, "Every time I see one of those BASS stickers I get a lump, right in my wallet."[49]

Like most groups BASS did not originate as a political organization, and for the most part it remains an organization for fishermen, with 600,000 members, even in the wake of its 2001 acquisition by the ESPN television network.[50] Yet BASS has entered politics. *BassMaster* has published political commentary, and in 1980, 1988, and 1992 endorsed George Bush for president. It also has called for easing travel restrictions to Cuba, where world-record catches may lurk.

Most groups claim that access is their major goal within the lobbying process, and here BASS has succeeded beyond its wildest dreams. Former president Bush has been a life member of BASS since 1978 and has claimed that *BassMaster* is his favorite magazine. Scott has used his relationship with Bush to lobby for the fishing community in general and BASS in particular. In March 1989 Scott visited the White House and, during a horseshoe match with President Bush, indicated his concern about rumors that the Office of Management and Budget (OMB) planned to limit the disbursement of $100 million in trust funds for fishery management projects. The next morning Bush informed Scott that "all of *our* monies are secure from OMB or anyone else."[51]

BASS increased its political activities by sponsoring Voice of the Environment, which lobbies on water quality issues, and filing class-action lawsuits on behalf of fishermen against environmental polluters. Although the organization can point to a number of conservation and environmental activities, it is distrusted by much of the mainstream environmental movement. BASS's connections to the boating industry often put it at odds with groups seeking to preserve a pristine natural environment or elite angling organizations whose members fish for trout in free-flowing streams rather than for the bass behind federally funded dams.

Indeed, regardless of Scott's entrepreneurial skills, there would probably be no BASS if it were not for the federal government and the Army Corps of Engineers. Fifty years of dam building by the Corps and the U.S.

Bureau of Reclamation have altered the nature of fish populations. Damming of rivers and streams has reduced the quality of fishing for cold-water species such as trout and pike and enhanced the habitat for largemouth bass, a game fish that can tolerate the warmer waters and mud bottoms of man-made lakes. Finally, because many of these lakes are located close to cities, the government has made bass fishing accessible to a large number of anglers.

From angling to air traffic control, the federal government has affected, and sometimes dominated, group formation. But many other forces have contributed to group proliferation, often in concert with increased public sector involvement.

The Decline of Political Parties

In a diverse political culture characterized by divided power, political parties emerged early in our history as instruments to structure conflict and facilitate mass participation. Parties function as intermediaries between the public and formal government institutions, as they reduce and combine citizen demands into a manageable number of issues and enable the system to focus on society's most important problems.

The party performs its mediating function primarily through coalition building—"the process of constructing majorities from the broad sentiments and interests that can be found to bridge the narrower needs and hopes of separate individuals and communities."[52] The New Deal coalition, forged in the 1930s, illustrates how this works. Socioeconomic divisions dominated politics from the 1930s through the 1960s. Less affluent citizens tended to support government provisions for social and economic security and the regulation of private enterprise. Those economically better off usually took the opposite position. The Democratic coalition, by and large, represented disadvantaged urban workers, Catholics, Jews, Italians, Eastern Europeans, and African Americans. On a variety of issues, southerners joined the coalition, along with a smattering of academics and urban liberals. The Republicans were concentrated in the rural and suburban areas outside the South; the party was made up of established ethnic groups, businesspeople, and farmers and was largely Protestant. Party organizations dominated electoral politics through the New Deal period, and interest group influence was felt primarily through the party apparatus.

Patterns of partisan conflict are never permanent, however, and since the 1940s social forces have contributed to the creation of new interests and the redefinition of old ones. This has destroyed the New Deal coalition without putting a new partisan structure in its place and has provided opportunities for the creation of large numbers of political groups— many that are narrowly focused and opposed to the bargaining and compromise patterns of coalition politics. The changes of recent decades reflect the societal transformation that scholars have labeled the "post-industrial society." Postindustrial society is centered on several interre-lated developments:

> affluence, advanced technological development, the central importance
> of knowledge, national communication processes, the growing promi-
> nence and independence of the culture, new occupational structures,
> and with them new life styles and expectations, which is to say new
> social classes and new centers of power.[53]

At the base is the role of affluence. Between 1947 and 1972 median family income doubled, even after controlling for the effects of inflation. During that same period the percentage of families earning $10,000 and more, in constant dollars, grew from 15 percent to 60 percent of the popu-lation.[54] A large proportion of the population began to enjoy substantial discretionary income and moved beyond subsistence.

The consequences of spreading abundance did not reduce conflict, as some observers had predicted.[55] Instead, conflict heightened, because affluence increased dissatisfaction by contributing to a "mentality of de-mand, a vastly expanded set of expectations concerning what is one's due, a diminished tolerance of conditions less than ideal."[56] By the 1960s the democratizing impact of affluence had become apparent, as an extraordi-nary number of people enrolled in institutions of higher education. It is not surprising that the government was under tremendous pressure to satisfy expectations, and it too contributed to increasing demands both in rhetoric and through many of its own Age of Improvement initiatives.

With the rise in individual expectations, class divisions and conflicts were drastically transformed. Political parties scholar Walter Dean Burn-ham noted that the New Deal's class structure changed, and by the late 1960s the industrial class pattern of upper, middle, and working class had been "supplanted by one which is relevant to a system dominated by advanced postindustrial technology." At the top of the new class structure was a "professional-managerial-technical elite . . . closely connected with the university and research centers and significant parts of it have been drawn—both out of ideology and interest—to the federal government's social activism." This growing group tended to be cosmopolitan and more socially permissive than the rest of society. The spread of affluence in postindustrial society was uneven, however, and certain groups were dis-advantaged by the changes. At the bottom of the new class structure were those "whose economic functions had been undermined or terminated by the technical revolution of the past generation . . . people, black and white, who tend to be in hard core poverty areas."[57] The focus of Presi-dent Lyndon B. Johnson's War on Poverty was to be on this class.

The traditional political party system found it difficult to deal effec-tively with citizens' high expectations and a changing class structure. The economic, ethnic, and ideological positions that had developed during the

New Deal became less relevant to parties, elections, and voter prefer-ences. The strains were particularly evident among working class Demo-crats. New Deal policies had been particularly beneficial to the white working class, enabling that group to earn incomes and adopt lifestyles that resembled those of the middle class. And although Age of Improve-ment policies initiated by Democratic politicians often benefited minori-ties, many white workers viewed these policies as attempts to aid lower class blacks at the expense of whites. By the late 1960s the white working class had taken on trappings of the middle class and conservatism, both economically and culturally.

At the same time, such New Deal divisions as ethnicity also had lost their cutting edge because of social and geographic mobility.

> It does not seem inaccurate to portray the current situation as one in which the basic coalitions and many of the political symbols and rela-tionships, which were developed around one set of political issues and problems, are confronted with new issues and new cleavages for which these traditional relationships and associations are not particularly rele-vant. Given these conditions, the widespread confusion, frustration, and mistrust are not surprising.[58]

Various conditions led to the party system's inability to *realign*—build coalitions of groups to address new concerns to adapt to changing societal divisions. For example, consider the difficulty of building coali-tions around the kinds of issues that have emerged over the past fifteen or twenty years.

Valence issues—general evaluations of the goodness or badness of the times—have become important, especially when related to the cost of liv-ing. Yet most such issues do not divide the country politically. Everyone is against inflation and crime. A second set of increasingly important issues are those that are highly emotional, cultural, or moral in character, such as abortion, euthanasia, AIDS, the death penalty, and drug laws. These sub-jects divide the electorate but elicit intense feelings from only a relatively few citizens. Opinion on such issues often is unrelated to traditional group identifications. Moreover, public opinion is generally disorganized or in disarray—that is, opinions often are unrelated or weakly related to one another on major issues, further retarding efforts to build coalitions.

There is some question about whether parties retain the capacity to shape political debate even on issues that lend themselves to coalition build-ing. Although the decline of political parties began well before the 1960s, the weakening of the party organization has accelerated in the postindustrial age. The emergence of a highly educated electorate, less dependent on party as an electoral cue, has produced a body of citizens that seeks out indepen-dent sources of information. Technological developments—such as tele-vision, computer-based direct mail, and political polling—have enabled candidates to virtually bypass political parties in their quest for public office.

The rise of political consultants has reduced even further the need for party expertise in running for office. The recruitment function of parties also has been largely lost to the mass media, as journalists now "act out the part of talent scouts, conveying the judgment that some contenders are promising, while dismissing others as of no real talent." [59]

Considerable evidence suggests that parties have adapted to this new political environment, but party organizations no longer dominate the electoral process. In an era of candidate-centered politics, parties are less mobilizers of a diverse electorate than service vendors to ambitious individual candidates. The weakness of political parties has helped to create a vacuum in electoral politics since 1960, and in recent years interest groups have moved aggressively to fill it. Indeed, in the 2000 election many interests bypassed the parties—and even the candidates' organizations—to advertise directly on behalf of particular candidates, all the while articulating their own positions on key issues such as Medicare, drug pricing, term limits, Social Security, and gun control. Simultaneously, organized interests such as labor, environmentalists, antiabortion rights groups, and some corporations have worked closely with parties both by contributing soft money and by implicitly coordinating the corporation's campaign activities with those of the parties.

The Growth of Interest Groups

Although it may be premature to formulate a theory that accounts for growth spurts, we can identify several factors fundamental to group proliferation in contemporary politics.[60] Rapid social and economic changes, powerful catalysts for group formation, have created new interests (for example, the recreation industry) and redefined traditional ones (for example, higher education). The spread of affluence and education, coupled with advanced communication technologies, further contributes to the translation of interests into formal group organizations. Postindustrial changes have generated many new interests, particularly among occupational and professional groups in the scientific and technological arenas. For instance, genetic engineering associations have sprung up in the wake of recent DNA discoveries, to say nothing of the growing clout and sophistication of the computer industry, from Microsoft's Bill Gates on down.

Perhaps more important, postindustrial changes have altered the pattern of conflict in society and created an intensely emotional setting in which groups rise or fall in status. Ascending groups, such as members of the new professional-managerial-technical elite, have both benefited from and supported government activism; they represent the new cultural liberalism—politically cosmopolitan and socially permissive. At the same time, rising expectations and feelings of entitlement have increased pressures on government by aspiring groups and the disadvantaged. The 1960s and early 1970s witnessed wave after wave of group mobilization based on causes ranging from civil rights to women's issues to the environment to consumer protection.

Threat as Motivation.   Abrupt changes and alterations in status, however, threaten many citizens. Middle America, perceiving itself as downwardly mobile, has grown alienated from the social, economic, and cultural dominance of the postindustrial elites, on one hand, and resentful of government attempts to aid minorities and other aspiring groups on the other. The conditions of a modern, technologically based culture also are disturbing to more traditional elements in society. Industrialization and urbanization can uproot people, cutting them loose from familiar life patterns and values and depriving them of meaningful personal associations. Fundamentalist elements feel threatened by various technological advances (such as use of fetal tissue for medical research) as well as by the more general secular liberalism and moral permissiveness of contemporary life. In the 1990s the growth of the Christian Coalition, both nationally and locally, has profoundly affected both electoral and legislative politics by mobilizing citizens and activists. In addition, the growth of bureaucracy, in and out of government, antagonizes everyone at one time or another.

Elites feel postindustrial threats as well. The nuclear arms race and its potential for mass destruction fostered the revived peace movement of the 1980s and its goal of a freeze on nuclear weapons. In addition, the excesses and errors of technology, such as oil spills and toxic waste disposal, have led to group formation among some of the most advantaged and ascending elements of society.

The growth of the animal rights movement since the mid-1980s illustrates interest groups' potential for enhanced participation and influence. Although traditional animal protection organizations such as the Humane Society have existed for decades, the past fifteen years have spawned a host of proanimal offspring, such as People for Ethical Treatment of Animals (PETA), Progressive Animal Welfare Society, Committee to Abolish Sport Hunting, and the Animal Rights Network. Reminiscent of the 1960s, there is even the Animal Liberation Front, an extremist group that engages in direct actions that sometimes include violence.[61] Membership in the organizations that make up the animal rights movement has increased rapidly; founded in 1980, PETA grew from 20,000 members in 1984 to 370,000 by 1994 and 600,000 in 2001. One estimate places the number of animal rights organizations at 400, representing approximately 10 million members.[62]

One major goal of these groups is to stop, or greatly retard, scientific experimentation on animals. Using a mix of protest, lobbying, and litigation, the movement has contributed to the closing of several animal labs, including the Defense Department's Wound Laboratory and a University of Pennsylvania facility involved in research on head injuries. In 1988 Trans-Species, a recent addition to the animal rights movement, forced the Cornell University Medical College to give up a $600,000 grant, which left unfinished a fourteen-year research project in which cats were fed barbiturates.[63]

As the most visible of the animal rights groups, PETA embarked on an intensive campaign in the early 1990s to influence children's attitudes and values toward society's treatment of animals. Using a seven-foot mascot, Chris P. Carrot, to spread its message, PETA organizers have sought to visit public schools throughout the Midwest. Although some of their message is noncontroversial (for example, children should eat their vegetables), they also argue aggressively against consuming meat. Chris P. Carrot thus carries a placard stating, "Eat your veggies, not your friends." More prosaically, PETA produces publications denouncing hunting, trapping, and other practices that abuse animals; PETA's *Kids Can Save Animals* even encourages students to

> call the toll-free numbers of department stores to protest furs and animal-test cosmetics, to call sponsors and object to rodeos, circulate petitions for "violence-free" schools that do not use frog corpses for biology lab, and to boycott zoos and aquariums, and marine parks.[64]

It is not surprising that PETA protests have spawned countermobilizations, as, for example, in the growth of an antianimal rights movement. In the forefront of such actions are organizations that support hunting as a sport. They must contend with a public that has become increasingly hostile to hunting; a 1993 survey reported that 54 percent of Americans were opposed to hunting, with the youngest respondents (ages eighteen to twenty-nine) expressing the most negative sentiments.[65] In addition, farm and medical groups have mobilized against the animal rights movements, and a number of new organizations have been formed. Such groups range from the incurably ill for Animal Research (iiFAR), representing those who hope for medical breakthroughs in biomedical research, to the Foundation for Animal Health, organized by the American Medical Association in hopes of diverting funds away from animal rights groups.

The most visible group in the animal rights countermobilization, Putting People First (PPF), claimed more than 35,000 members and one hundred local chapters within one year of its formation. PPF counted hunting clubs, trapping associations, rodeos, zoos, circuses, veterinary hospitals, kennels and stables, and carriage horse companies among its membership. Taking a page from animal rights' public relations activities, PPF has begun a Hunters for the Hungry campaign that has provided 160,000 pounds of venison to economically disadvantaged families in the South. To PPF, the animal rights movement has declared war on much of America and is "seeking to destroy a way of life—to tell us we can no longer believe in the JudeoChristian principles this country was founded on. They insist every form of life is equal: humans and dogs and slugs and cockroaches." PPF leaders see the organization as speaking for "the average American who eats meat and drinks milk, benefits from medical research, wears leather, wool, and fur, hunts and fishes, and owns a pet and goes to the zoo."[66]

The intensity of conflict between the animal rights advocates and their opponents typifies the deep cultural divisions of the postindustrial era. Similar differences affect many other key issues, from gun control to education (school choice) to immigration policy. Moreover, many of these conflicts do not lend themselves to compromise, whether because of vast policy differences or group leaders' desire to keep "hot" issues alive as a way to increase membership.

Affluent Members and Sponsors.   Although postindustrial conflicts generate the issues for group development, the spread of affluence also systematically contributes to group formation and maintenance. In fact, affluence creates a large potential for "checkbook" membership. Issue-based groups have done especially well. Membership in such groups as PETA and Common Cause might once have been a luxury, but the growth in discretionary income has placed the cost of modest dues within reach of most citizens. For a $15–25 membership fee, people can make an "expressive" statement without incurring other organizational obligations. Increasing education also has been a factor in that "organizations become more numerous as ideas become more important."[67]

Reform groups and citizens' groups depend heavily on the educated white middle class for their membership and financial base. A Common Cause poll, for example, found that members' mean family income was $17,000 above the national average and that 43 percent of members had an advanced degree.[68] Animal rights groups display a similar membership profile, although they are disproportionately composed of college-educated, urban, professional women.[69] Other expressive groups, including those on the political right, have been aided as well by the increased wealth of constituents and the community activism that result from education and occupational advancement.

Groups can overcome the free rider problem by finding a sponsor who will support the organization and reduce its reliance on membership contributions. During the 1960s and 1970s private sources (often foundations) backed groups. Jeffrey Berry's 1977 study of eighty-three public interest organizations found that at least one-third received more than half their funds from private foundations, and one in ten received more than 90 percent of its operating expenses from such sources.[70] Jack Walker's 1981 study of Washington-based interest groups confirmed many of Berry's earlier findings, indicating that foundation support and individual grants provide 30 percent of all citizens' group funding.[71] Such patterns produce many staff organizations with no members, raising major questions about the representativeness of the new interest group universe. Finally, groups themselves can sponsor other groups. The National Council of Senior Citizens (NCSC), for example, was founded by the AFL-CIO, which helped recruit members from the ranks of organized labor and still pays part of NCSC's expenses.

Patrons often are more than just passive sponsors who respond to group requests for funds. In many cases group mobilization comes from the top down, rather than the reverse. The patron—whether an individual such as General Motors' heir Stewart Mott or the peripatetic conservative Richard Mellon Scaife, an institution, another group, or a government entity—may initiate group development, to the point of seeking entre-preneurs and providing a forum for group pronouncements.

Postindustrial affluence and the spread of education also have con-tributed to group formation and maintenance through the development of a large pool of potential group organizers. This group tends to be young, well educated, and from the middle class, caught up in a movement for change and inspired by ideas or doctrine. The 1960s was a period of oppor-tunity for entrepreneurs, as college enrollments skyrocketed and powerful forces such as civil rights and the antiwar movement contributed to an idea orientation in both education and politics. Communications-based pro-fessions—from religion to law to university teaching—attracted social activists, many of whom became involved in forming groups. The govern-ment itself became a major source of what James Q. Wilson called "orga-nizing cadres." Government employees of the local Community Action Agencies of the War on Poverty and personnel from Volunteers in Service to America were active in forming voluntary associations, some created to oppose government actions.[72]

Technological Opportunities.   Compounding the effects of the growing number of increasingly active groups are changes in what organizations can do, largely as a result of contemporary technology. On a grand scale, technological change produces new interests, such as cable television and the silicon chip industry, which organize to protect themselves as inter-ests historically have done. Beyond this communications breakthroughs make group politics much more visible than in the past. Civil rights activists in the South understood this, as did many protesters against the Vietnam War. Of equal importance, however, is the fact that much of what contemporary interest groups do derives directly from develop-ments in information-related technology. Many group activities, whether fund-raising or grassroots lobbying or sampling members' opinions, rely heavily on computer-based operations that can target and send messages and process the responses.

Although satellite television links and survey research are important tools, the technology of direct mail has had by far the greatest impact on interest group politics. With a minimum initial investment and a reason-ably good list of potential contributors, any individual can become a group entrepreneur. These activists literally create organizations, often based on emotion-laden appeals about specific issues, from Sarah Brady's Handgun Control to Randall Terry's Operation Rescue.[73] To the extent that an entrepreneur can attract members and continue to pay the costs of direct mail, he or she can claim—with substantial legitimacy—to articulate the organization's positions on the issues, positions probably defined initially by the entrepreneur.

In addition to helping entrepreneurs develop organizations that require few (if any) active members, information technology also allows many organizations to exert considerable pressure on elected officials. Washington-based interests are increasingly turning to grassroots techniques to influence legislators. Indeed, after the mid-1980s these tactics had become the norm in many lobbying efforts, to the point that they were sometimes discounted as routine and "manufactured" by groups and consultants.

Communications technology is widely available but expensive. In the health care debate, most mobilized opinion has come from the best-financed interests, such as insurance companies, the drug industry, and the medical profession. Money remains the mother's milk of politics. Indeed, one of the major impacts of technology may be to inflate the costs of political action, whether for candidates engaged in increasingly expensive election campaigns or in public lobbying efforts that employ specifically targeted advertisements and highly sophisticated grassroots efforts.

Group Impact on Policy and Process

Assessing the policy impact of interest group actions has never been an easy task. We may, however, gain some insights by looking at two different levels of analysis: a broad, societal overview and a middle-range search for relatively specific patterns of influence (for example, the role of direct mail or political action committee funding). Considering impact at the level of individual lobbying efforts is also possible, but here even the best work relies heavily on nuance and individualistic explanations.

Although the public often views lobbying and special interest campaigning with distrust, political scientists have not produced much evidence to support this perspective. Academic studies of interest groups have demonstrated few conclusive links between campaign or lobbying efforts and actual patterns of influence. This does not mean that such patterns or individual instances do not exist. Rather, the question of determining impact is exceedingly difficult to answer. The difficulty is, in fact, compounded by groups' claims of impact and decisionmakers' equally vociferous claims of freedom from any outside influence.

The major studies of lobbying in the 1960s generated a most benign view of this activity. Lester Milbrath painted a Boy Scout–like picture of Washington lobbyists, depicting them as patient contributors to policy-making.[74] Rarely stepping over the limits of propriety, lobbyists had only a marginal impact at best. Similarly, Raymond Bauer, Ithiel de Sola Pool, and Lewis Dexter's lengthy analysis of foreign trade policy, published in

1963, found the business community to be largely incapable of influencing Congress in its lobbying attempts.[75] Given the many internal divisions within the private sector over trade matters, this was not an ideal issue to illustrate business cooperation, but the research stood as the central work on lobbying for more than a decade—ironically, in the very period when groups proliferated and became more sophisticated in their tactics. Lewis Dexter, in his 1969 treatment of Washington representatives as an emerging professional group, suggested that lobbyists would play an increasingly important role in complex policymaking, but he provided few details.[76]

The picture of benevolent lobbyists who seek to engender trust and convey information, although accurate in a limited way, does not provide a complete account of the options open to any interest group that seeks to exert influence. Lyndon Johnson's long-term relationship with the Texas-based construction firm of Brown & Root illustrates the depth of some ties between private interests and public officeholders. The Washington representative for Brown & Root claimed that he never went to Capitol Hill for any legislative help because "people would resent political influence."[77] But Johnson, first as a representative and later as a senator, systematically dealt directly with the top management (the Brown family) and aided the firm by passing along crucial information and watching over key government-sponsored construction projects.

> [The link between Johnson and Brown & Root] was, indeed, a partnership, the campaign contributions, the congressional look-out, the contracts, the appropriations, the telegrams, the investment advice, the gifts and the hunts and the free airplane rides—it was an alliance of mutual reinforcement between a politician and a corporation. If Lyndon was Brown & Root's kept politician, Brown & Root was Lyndon's kept corporation. Whether he concluded that they were public-spirited partners or corrupt ones, "political allies" or cooperating predators, in its dimensions and its implications for the structure of society, their arrangement was a new phenomenon on its way to becoming the new pattern for American society.[78]

Entering the twenty-first century, one could legitimately substitute Sen. Trent Lott's, R-Miss., name for Johnson's and that of defense and shipbuilding giant Northrup Grumman for Brown & Root; the basic set of links were very similar. Any number of events, such as the 1980s savings and loan scandal, show that legislators can be easily approached with unethical and illegal propositions; such access is one price of an open system. In addition, the growth of interest representation has raised long-term questions about the ethics of former government officials acting as lobbyists. Despite some modest reforms, many executive branch officials, members of Congress, and high-level bureaucrats leave office and eventually return to lobby their friends and associates. Access is still important, and its price is often high.

Contemporary Practices

Modern lobbying emphasizes information, often on complex and difficult subjects. Determining actual influence is, as one lobbyist noted, "like finding a black cat in the coal bin at midnight," but we can make some assessments about the impact of group proliferation and increased activity.[79]

First, more groups are engaged in more forms of lobbying than ever before—both classic forms, such as offering legislative testimony, and newer forms, such as mounting computer-based direct mail campaigns to stir up grassroots support.[80] As the number of new groups rises and existing groups become more active, the pressure on decisionmakers—especially legislators—mounts at a corresponding rate. Thus a second general point can be made: Congressional reforms that opened up the legislative process during the 1970s have provided a much larger number of access points for today's lobbyists. Most committee (and subcommittee) sessions, including the markups at which legislation is written, remain open to the public, as do many conference committee meetings. More roll call votes are taken, and congressional floor action is televised. Thus interests can monitor individual members of Congress as never before. This does nothing, however, to facilitate disinterested decision making or foster graceful compromises on most issues.

In fact, monitoring the legions of Washington policy actors has become the central activity of many groups. As Robert Salisbury has observed, "Before [organized interests] can advocate a policy, they must determine what position they wish to embrace. Before they do this, they must find out not only what technical policy analysis can tell them but what relevant others, inside and outside the government, are thinking and planning."[81] Given the volume of policymaking, just keeping up can be a major undertaking.

The government itself has encouraged many interests to organize and articulate their demands. The rise of group activity thus leads us to another level of analysis: the impact of contemporary interest group politics on society. Harking back to Lowi's description of interest group liberalism, we see the eventual result to be an immobilized society, trapped by its willingness to allow interests to help fashion self-serving policies that embody no firm criteria of success or failure. For example, even in the midst of the savings and loan debacle, the government continued to offer guarantees to various sectors, based not on future promise but on past bargains and continuing pressures.

The notion advanced by Olson that some such group-related stagnation affects all stable democracies makes the prognosis all the more serious. In summary form, Olson argued that the longer societies are politically stable, the more interest groups they develop; the more interest groups they develop, the worse they work economically.[82] The United

Automobile Workers' protectionist leanings, the American Medical Association's fight against intervention by the Federal Trade Commission into physicians' business affairs, and the insurance industry's successful prevention of FTC investigations all illustrate the possible link between self-centered group action and poor economic performance—that is, higher automobile prices, doctors' fees, and insurance premiums for no better product or service.

In particular, the politics of Social Security demonstrate the difficulties posed by a highly mobilized, highly representative set of interests. Virtually everyone agrees that the Social Security system requires serious reform; at the same time, many groups of elderly citizens (with the AARP among the most moderate) have resisted changes that might reduce their benefits over time. Moreover, many groups outside the traditional Social Security policy community have argued for the system's privatization, either partial or total. The system will have to be modified to maintain its viability, but groups will continue to frame the debate in ways that benefit their interests, perhaps at the expense of the general good.

Conclusion

The ultimate consequences of the growing number of organized interests, their expanding activities in Washington and in state capitals, and the growth of citizens' groups remain unclear. From one perspective, such changes have made politics more representative than ever. Although most occupation-based groups traditionally have been well organized in American politics, many other interests have not been. Population groupings such as African Americans, Hispanics, and women have mobilized since the 1950s and 1960s; animals and the unborn are well represented in the interest group arena, as is the broader "public interest," however defined.

Broadening the base of interest group participation may have opened the political process, thus curbing the influence of special interests. For example, agricultural policymaking in the postwar era was largely the prerogative of a tight "iron triangle" composed of congressional committee members from farm states, government officials representing the agriculture bureaucracy, and major agriculture groups such as the American Farm Bureau. Activity in the 1970s by consumer and environmental interest groups changed agricultural politics, making it more visible and lengthening the agenda to consider such questions as how farm subsidies affect consumer purchasing power and how fertilizers, herbicides, and pesticides affect public health.

From another perspective, more interest groups and more openness do not necessarily mean better policies or ones that genuinely represent the national interest. Government may be unable to process demands effectively, and openness may result in complexity. Moreover, the content of demands may be ambiguous and priorities difficult to set.

Finally, elected leaders may find it practically impossible to build the kinds of political coalitions necessary to govern effectively, especially in an era of partisan parity and the unrelenting demands of the permanent campaign, which requires continual fund-raising from organized interests.

This second perspective suggests that the American constitutional system is extraordinarily susceptible to the excesses of minority faction—in an ironic way a potential victim of the Madisonian solution of dealing with the tyranny of the majority. Decentralized government, especially one that wields considerable power, provides no adequate controls over the excessive demands of interest group politics. Decisionmakers feel obliged to respond to many of these demands, and "the cumulative effect of this pressure has been the relentless and extraordinary rise of government spending and inflationary deficits, as well as the frustration of efforts to enact effective national policies on most major issues."[83]

In sum, the problem of contemporary interest group politics is one of representation. For particular interests, especially those that are well defined and adequately funded, the government is responsive to the issues of their greatest concern. But representation is not just a matter of responding to specific interests or citizens; the government also must respond to the collective needs of a society, and here the success of individual interests reduces the possibility of overall responsiveness. The very vibrancy and success of contemporary groups contribute to a society that finds it increasingly difficult to formulate solutions to complex policy questions.

Notes

1. Kay Lehman Schlozman and John T. Tierney, "More of the Same: Washington Pressure Group Activity in a Decade of Change," *Journal of Politics* 45 (May 1983): 351–377. For an earlier era, see Margaret S. Thompson, *The Spider's Web* (Ithaca: Cornell University, 1985).
2. Theodore J. Lowi, *The End of Liberalism*, 2d ed. (New York: Norton, 1979); Mancur Olson, *The Rise and Decline of Nations* (New Haven, Conn.: Yale University, 1982).
3. Mancur Olson, *The Logic of Collective Action* (Cambridge, Mass.: Harvard University, 1971); Robert Salisbury, "An Exchange Theory of Interest Groups," *Midwest Journal of Political Science* 13 (February 1969): 1–32; and Terry M. Moe, *The Organization of Interests* (Chicago: University of Chicago, 1980).
4. David Truman's widely used definition of interest groups is "any group that, on the basis of one or more shared attitudes, makes certain claims upon other groups in the society for the establishment, maintenance, or enhancement of forms of behavior that are implied by the shared attitudes." Truman, *The Governmental Process*, 2d ed. (New York: Knopf, 1971).
5. James Madison, "Federalist 10," in *The Federalist Papers*, 2d ed., ed. Roy P. Fairfield (Baltimore: Johns Hopkins University, 1981), 16.
6. L. Harmon Ziegler and Wayne Peak, *Interest Groups in American Society*, 2d ed. (Englewood Cliffs, N.J.: Prentice-Hall, 1972), 35.
7. Michael Trister, "The Rise and Reform of Stealth PACs," *The American Prospect*, 11 (September 24, 2000), 32–35.
8. Anthony Corrado, "Financing the 2000 Elections," in *The Election of 2000*, ed. Gerald Pomper (New York: Chatham House, 2001), x.

9. Truman, *Governmental Process*, 519.
10. Carole Greenwald, *Group Power* (New York: Praeger, 1977), 305.
11. Leslie Wayne, "800-Pound Guests at the Pentagon," *New York Times*, March 15, 1998, section 5, 3.
12. Lowi, *End of Liberalism*, 62.
13. Murray Edelman, *The Politics of Symbolic Action* (Chicago: Markham, 1971).
14. Theodore J. Lowi, *Incomplete Conquest: Governing America* (New York: Holt, Rinehart & Winston, 1976), 47.
15. Gabriel Almond and Sidney Verba, *The Civic Culture* (Boston: Little, Brown, 1963), chs. 8 and 10.
16. Ibid., 246–247.
17. Truman, *Governmental Process*, 57.
18. Salisbury, "Exchange Theory of Interest Groups," 3–4.
19. Truman, *Governmental Process*, 59.
20. James Q. Wilson, *Political Organizations* (New York: Basic Books, 1973), 154.
21. Major works include Olson, *The Logic of Collective Action;* Peter Clark and James Q. Wilson, "Incentive Systems: A Theory of Organizations," *Administrative Science Quarterly* 6 (September 1961): 126–166; Wilson, *Political Organizations;* Terry Moe, "A Calculus of Group Membership," *American Journal of Political Science* 24 (November 1980): 593–632; and Moe, *Organization of Interests.* The notion of group organizers as political entrepreneurs is best represented by Salisbury, "Exchange Theory of Interest Groups," 1–15.
22. See Clark and Wilson, "Incentive Systems," 129–166; and Wilson, *Political Organizations*, 30–51. In recent years researchers have preferred the term *expressive* to *purposive*, because, as Salisbury notes, *purposive* includes what we call collective material benefits. *Material, solidary*, and *expressive* would seem to be mutually exclusive conceptual categories. See Salisbury, "Exchange Theory of Interest Groups," 16–17.
23. Moe, *Organization of Interests*, 144.
24. John Mark Hansen, "The Political Economy of Group Membership," *American Political Science Review* 79 (March 1985): 79–96.
25. Albert O. Hirschman, *Shifting Involvements* (Princeton: Princeton University, 1982).
26. Michael W. McCann, "Public Interest Liberalism and the Modern Regulatory State," *Polity* 21 (winter 1988): 385.
27. See, for example, R. Kenneth Godwin and R. C. Mitchell, "Rational Models, Collective Goods, and Non-Electoral Political Behavior," *Western Political Quarterly* 35 (June 1982): 161–180; and Larry Rothenberg, "Choosing among Public Interest Groups: Membership, Activism and Retention in Political Organizations," *American Political Science Review* 82 (December 1988): 1129–1152.
28. Jack L. Walker, "The Origins and Maintenance of Interest Groups in America," *American Political Science Review* 77 (June 1983): 390–406; for a conservative critique of this trend, see James T. Bennett and Thomas Di Lorenzo, *Destroying Democracy* (Washington, D.C.: Cato Institute, 1986). See also many of the articles in Mark P. Petracca, ed., *The Politics of Interests*, (Boulder, Colo.: Westview, 1992).
29. Walker, "Origins and Maintenance of Interest Groups," 16.
30. Robert H. Salisbury, "Interest Representation and the Dominance of Institutions," *American Political Science Review* 78 (March 1984): 64–77.
31. See Jeffery Berry, The New Liberalism: The Power of Citizen Groups (Washington, D.C.: Brookings Institution, 1999).
32. Gregory Colgate, ed., *National Trade and Professional Associations of the United States, 1982* (Washington, D.C.: Columbia Books, 1984).
33. Cited in Kevin Phillips, *Arrogant Capital* (Boston: Back Bay/Little, Brown, 1995), 43.
34. Encyclopedia of Associations, http://www.library.dialog.com/bluesheets/html/bl0114.html, December 5, 2001.

35. Samuel H. Beer, "In Search of a New Public Philosophy," in *The New American Political System*, ed. Anthony King (Washington, D.C.: American Enterprise Institute, 1978), 12.
36. Ibid., 10.
37. Hugh Heclo, "Issue Networks and the Executive Establishment," in King, *New American Political System*, 89.
38. Beer, "In Search of a New Public Philosophy," 16.
39. Allan J. Cigler and Cheryl Swanson, "Politics and Older Americans," in *The Dynamics of Aging*, ed. Forrest J. Berghorn, Donna E. Schafer, and Associates (Boulder, Colo.: Westview, 1981), 171.
40. The AARP offers free memberships to spouses, which artificially enlarges its ranks, but it remains—by any count—a huge group.
41. See John Tierney's articles, "Old Money, New Power," *New York Times Magazine*, October 23, 1988, 17; and "The Big Gray Money Machine," *Newsweek*, August 15, 1988, 47.
42. Tierney, "Old Money, New Power."
43. Heclo, "Issue Networks and the Executive Establishment," 96.
44. Walker, "Origins and Maintenance of Interest Groups," 401.
45. Stuart Langton, "Citizen Participation in America: Current Reflections on the State of the Art," in *Citizen Participation in America*, ed. Stuart Langton (Lexington, Mass.: Lexington Books, 1978), 7.
46. Ibid., 4.
47. Walker, "Origins and Maintenance of Interest Groups," 398.
48. Salisbury, "Exchange Theory of Interest Groups," 25.
49. Quoted in Ted Williams, "River Retrieval," *Fly Rod and Reel* 15 (January–February 1994): 17.
50. The April 2001 ESPN purchase both enhances and limits the potential political clout of BASS. It loses much of its independent political identity, but might well benefit from its position within the ABC-Disney corporate family.
51. Ray Scott, "Presidential Promises," *BassMaster*, May 1989, 7 (emphasis added).
52. David S. Broder, "Introduction," in *Emerging Coalitions in American Politics*, ed. Seymour Martin Lipset (San Francisco: Institute for Contemporary Studies, 1978), 3.
53. Everett Carll Ladd Jr. with Charles D. Hadley, *Transformations of the American Party System*, 2d ed. (New York: Norton, 1978), 182.
54. Ibid., 196.
55. See, for example, Daniel Bell, *The End of Ideology* (New York: Free Press, 1960).
56. Ladd and Hadley, *Transformations of the American Party System*, 203.
57. For all three quotes in this paragraph, Walter Dean Burnham, *Critical Elections and the Mainsprings of American Politics* (New York: Norton, 1970), 139.
58. Richard E. Dawson, *Public Opinion and Contemporary Disarray* (New York: Harper and Row, 1973), 194.
59. Everett Carll Ladd, *Where Have All the Voters Gone?* 2d ed. (New York: Norton, 1982).
60. But see Virginia Gray and David Lowery, *The Population Ecology of Interest Representation* (Ann Arbor: University of Michigan, 1996).
61. Kevin Kasowski, "Showdown on the Hunting Ground," *Outdoor America* 51 (winter 1986): 9.
62. Lauristan R. King and Kimberly Stephens, "Politics and the Animal Rights Movement" (paper presented at the annual meeting of the Southern Political Science Association, Tampa, Fla., November 7–9, 1991).
63. Sara Lyall, "Scientist Gives up Grant to Do Research on Cats," *New York Times*, November 21, 1988, A12.

64. John Balzar, quoted in Kit Harrison, "Animal 'Rightists' Target Children," *Sports Afield* 211 (June 1994): 12.

65. "Americans Divided on Animal Rights," *Los Angeles Times*, December 17, 1993, B3. This national survey of 1,612 adults also found that 50 percent opposed the wearing of fur.

66. Phil McCombs, "Attack of the Omnivore," *Washington Post*, March 27, 1992, B1, B4.

67. Wilson, *Political Organizations*, 201.

68. Andrew S. McFarland, *Common Cause* (Chatham, N.J.: Chatham House, 1984), 48–49.

69. King and Stephens, "Politics and the Animal Rights Movement," 15.

70. Jeffrey M. Berry, *Lobbying for the People* (Princeton: Princeton University, 1977), 72.

71. Walker, "Origins and Maintenance of Interest Groups," 400.

72. Wilson, *Political Organizations*, 203.

73. Sarah Brady, wife of former White House press secretary James Brady, organized Handgun Control after her husband was wounded in John Hinckley's 1981 attack on Ronald Reagan. Randall Terry formed Operation Rescue, which seeks to shut down abortion clinics through direct action (for example, blocking entrances), after concluding that other antiabortion rights groups were not effective in halting abortions.

74. Lester Milbrath, *The Washington Lobbyists* (Chicago: Rand-McNally, 1963).

75. Raymond Bauer, Ithiel de Sola Pool, and Lewis Dexter, *American Business and Public Policy* (New York: Atherton, 1963).

76. Lewis A. Dexter, *How Organizations Are Represented in Washington* (Indianapolis: Bobbs-Merrill, 1969), ch. 9.

77. See Ronnie Dugger, *The Politician* (New York: Norton, 1982), 273; and Robert A. Caro, *The Years of Lyndon Johnson: The Path to Power* (New York: Knopf, 1982) and *The Years of Lyndon Johnson: Means of Ascent* (New York: Knopf 1990).

78. Dugger, *Politician*, 286.

79. Quoted in Burdett A. Loomis, "A New Era: Groups and the Grass Roots," in *Interest Group Politics*, 2d ed., ed. Allan J. Cigler and Burdett A. Loomis (Washington, D.C.: CQ Press, 1983), 184.

80. Schlozman and Tierney, "Washington Pressure Group Activity," 18.

81. Robert H. Salisbury, "The Paradox of Interest Groups in Washington—More Groups and Less Clout," in *The New American Political System*, 2d ed., ed. Anthony King (Washington, D.C.: American Enterprise Institute, 1990), 225–226.

82. For an expansion of this argument, see Jonathan Rauch, *Democlerosis*, (New York: New York Times Books, 1994).

83. Everett Carll Ladd, "How to Tame the Special Interest Groups," *Fortune*, October 1980, 6.

I. GROUP ORGANIZATION

2

Groups, Social Capital, and Democratic Orientations

Allan J. Cigler and Mark Joslyn

What comes to mind when we think of the role of organized interests in politics? Perhaps the image of competing forces struggling for advantage in electoral or policy processes. Many of the chapters in this volume approach interest group involvement—including group expenditures and activities in elections, attempts to influence policymakers, and more—from this perspective. The consequences of group behavior are seen in electoral outcomes or the substance and direction of public policy.

In this chapter Allan J. Cigler and Mark Joslyn look at the consequences of group activity from a different point of view. They argue that citizen involvement in groups has a socialization effect that spurs growth of "social capital," with implications for the broader political system. The authors contend that extensive involvement in groups, especially a diverse array of groups, makes citizens more likely to have traits considered essential in a democratic polity.

Cigler and Joslyn examine their contention empirically using national survey data. The results link citizens' involvement in groups to attitudes that underpin and help sustain the larger democratic system. The authors find that involvement in a range of groups has a positive effect on political tolerance. And more extensive group involvement makes it more likely that voting in a presidential election will increase voters' feelings of political trust and efficacy. Cigler and Joslyn conclude, "groups may contribute far more to democracy than organizing supporters to seek advantage."

Throughout history the United States has been considered a nation of "joiners," and the political impact of citizen involvement in group activities has long been controversial. Some scholars, while recognizing that group formation is inevitable in a free and open society, regard such activity with suspicion or fear. More than two centuries ago James Madison warned in *Federalist No. 10* that "mischiefs of faction" may result in citizens engaging in group activity to pursue narrow and selfish interests, with little thought to the broader public interest.[1] Today media coverage reinforces perceptions that groups' involvement in politics is self-interested and divisive, at times seeming to thwart majority will and undermine democracy.

Alongside this negative perspective is another view, also with a long history, which celebrates citizen involvement in group life as the basis of a genuinely democratic society. This view focuses not on group involvement in public decisions per se, but on how immersion in the internal dynamics of group life helps prepare people for the tensions and conflicts inherent in a governing system where authority lies with a heterogeneous, often divided citizenry. From this viewpoint, citizens learning by experience in associational settings, both political and nonpolitical, are said to develop transferable skills, orientations, and behavioral patterns— "habits of the heart" in Alexis de Tocqueville's words, which have been deemed essential for a democratic polity.[2]

In this chapter we will examine the link between involvement in citizen groups and the acquisition of democratic orientations, such as political tolerance, political efficacy (a sense of influence over government decisions), and trust in government, that many believe to be core elements of a democratic system. In light of recent evidence that membership in voluntary organizations has declined, and the possible connection between this decline and deterioration in civic behaviors such as voting, interest in this relationship has increased in both scholarly and public circles. Using national survey data, we find a positive relationship between group involvement by citizens and the acquisition of orientations that are indispensable in a democratic political culture. People not involved in group activity are less likely than those who are involved to display many of the attitudes and behavior that ostensibly sustain the larger democratic system.

Linking Group Involvement to Democratic Orientations

More than a century and a half ago, Alexis de Tocqueville observed in *Democracy in America* that group life plays a pivotal role in a democratic political system.[3] Tocqueville argued that democratic institutions are most successful among a multitude of secondary associations or groups, those beyond an individual's primary circle that mediate between individuals and the state. From Tocqueville's perspective, involvement in such groups enables people to escape the isolating confines of primary groups, such as family, and learn about their mutual dependence on others, often strangers.

The social integration afforded by secondary group activity helps prepare citizens for their roles in the broader political system.

In the modern era the work of political scientist Robert Putnam and other "social capital" theorists has focused on the connection between group involvement and democratic values, behaviors, and policy outcomes.[4] Building on the earlier work of sociologist James Coleman, Putnam argues that "civic engagement" has an important connection to healthy, responsive democratic government.[5] Civic engagement is our associational connection to our communities in the broadest possible sense, from participating in a bowling league or a church to becoming active in a political party or other political group. Such activities help us develop what Putnam calls "social capital"—"features of social organizations such as networks, norms, and social trust that facilitate coordination and cooperation for mutual benefit."[6]

Putnam believes that groups and associations are society's mechanisms for forming social capital, and the keys to understanding the link between social capital and a democratic orientation lie in assessing how involvement in collective activities translates into orientations that affect the broader political system. Putnam is alarmed by the apparent decline of group involvement, the lost opportunities for social capital development as a consequence, and the resulting isolation of citizens from each other and from their government.

Putnam's observations on how social capital develops, its decline in recent decades, and its link to citizen orientations and actions have not gone unchallenged.[7] Some have argued that Putnam fails to understand the character of participation and social networks in the modern world, especially the increasing irrelevance of formal organizations to people's lives and the rise of new forms of networking and civic participation. Others have speculated that "perhaps . . . the picture of voluntary associations as the source of communitarian habits of the heart is too sweeping."[8]

Still, few would challenge the assumption that group involvement is a key component of political socialization, crucial to developing and transmitting democratic values and behaviors. In a manner similar to conventional education, group activity has the potential to shape an individual's attitudes through shared experiences and knowledge acquisition. As group theorist David Truman noted, "the group experiences and affiliations of an individual are the primary, though not the exclusive, means by which the individual knows, interprets, and reacts to the society in which he exists."[9] The role of shared group experiences is especially crucial. Norms of reciprocity, trust, and affiliation inculcated by the "little democracies" of voluntary groups are said to spill over into the larger political system. Theorist John Stuart Mill referred to the practices of voluntary associations as a means of "mental education," whereas Tocqueville thought associations to be "the great free school" of American democracy.[10] Political behavior is typically learned indirectly or inadvertently rather than directly through political education. Group experience is the great teacher.

Empirical research on group involvement and its potential consequences is surprisingly sparse. Although abundant research links group
membership to increased political participation, few studies examine
empirically the relationship between group involvement and the incul-
cation of democratic orientations, such as political tolerance. Interest
group scholars have preferred to focus on such concerns as why citizens
join groups, how groups mobilize members and maintain themselves,
and how groups affect electoral and policy processes; the question
of how group members turn micro experiences in group settings into
democratic orientations significant at the macro level has not been an
important research endeavor.[11] And although public opinion scholars
have been concerned with the factors that underlie democratic orientations, group involvement variables have rarely been considered as
key predictors.[12]

In the analysis that follows we attempt to assess how social capital
acquired through group experiences affects democratic orientations. We
contend that the more involvement citizens have in groups, especially a
diverse array of groups, the more likely they are to have such orientations.

Group Activity and Political Tolerance

At the core of a democratic ethos is citizens' willingness to recognize
and value the rights of others in the political process. Political theorists
from Jean Jacques Rousseau to Tocqueville to John Rawls have viewed
citizens' commitment to tolerance as a prerequisite for a stable and effective democratic system. As political scientist Paul Sniderman and his colleagues have observed, "The more tolerant citizens are of the rights of
others, the more secure are the rights of all, their own included; hence the
special place of political tolerance in contemporary conceptions of democratic values and citizenship."[13]

Political tolerance also figures prominently in the debate about the
desirability of widespread mass participation. If citizens are willing to
extend civil liberties to people with differing viewpoints, then mass participation is welcome and perhaps encouraged. But if citizens are intol-
erant and reluctant to accept the exercise of liberties by others, then
mass participation may endanger the political system. Though a government may have characteristics associated with democracy—competitive
elections, inclusive participation, political equality, and the like—if citizens are unwilling to tolerate individuals and groups they oppose, it is
doubtful that political institutions predicated on democracy would work
successfully.

People's experiences in associational settings would appear to be an
essential part of developing tolerant attitudes. Ideally, political tolerance
is both necessitated and enhanced by immersion in group life. The give-
and-take of group interaction, coupled with the typical organizational

imperative for cooperative endeavors, encourages reciprocity and trust. Compromise is often called for and willingness to respect the views and affiliations of others becomes necessary. Scholars argue that such orientations affect the larger political context, forming the basis of diffuse support for higher-level social and political institutions.[14]

But the positive correlation between group involvement and political tolerance is not nearly so obvious in practice and may be conditional. The ideal group environment may not reflect contemporary reality for many citizens, leading even Putnam to contemplate the potentially "dark side" of group activity.[15] Participation in a homogeneous group with an ideological orientation and hierarchical rather than democratic decision making style, like the American Nazi Party, the Ku Klux Klan, or even some churches, is not conducive to developing democratic orientations. Recent empirical studies demonstrate the importance of the structural dimensions of a group environment—hierarchical or horizontal, diverse or homogenous—to social capital growth.[16] Democratic orientations flourish when individuals participate in a range of groups with democratic decision making structures.

Also important to social capital growth is the strength of members' ties to a group. For example, many citizens involved in group activity today are not as directly involved as they were in the past. The tendency toward "checkbook participation," the decline of face-to-face interaction, and the trend toward group policymaking by staff rather than members may isolate rather than incorporate citizens, prohibiting the development of such democratic orientations as political tolerance.[17] For many, group "involvement" may be little more than token affiliation, more sponsorship than membership, with internal democracy rarely practiced. The proliferation of interest groups in recent decades has created a universe of associations with narrower and narrower interests, characterized by relatively homogeneous—not diverse—membership bodies.[18] Attracting members often requires emphasizing the threat of "collective bads" and demonizing opponents.[19] None of this appears compatible with groups contributing to important democratic orientations such as political tolerance. Indeed, under such circumstances, group experiences might lead to political intolerance.

But the proliferation of groups does afford citizens the opportunity to get involved in some way—from passive to active involvement—in a wider cadre of groups than ever before. From this vantage point, a key factor becomes the number of groups with which one is affiliated, and whether the set of groups is cumulative or overlapping in impact.[20] A cumulative pattern of group association, when one is a member only of religious organizations, for example, typically exposes members to people of similar backgrounds and viewpoints. This may encourage members to see people outside their groups as wrong, threatening, or evil. On the other hand, memberships in an overlapping, yet diverse, set of groups should have the opposite effect: exposure to different backgrounds and perspectives (or at least to various group literatures) could sensitize members to the views of others, perhaps creating empathy for, if not agreement with, other positions.

To examine the relationship between group involvement and political tolerance, we relied on data from the General Social Survey (GSS). The GSS typically interviews approximately 2,000 respondents every two years, generating a representative sample of U.S. citizens. Surveys have been administered since the early 1970s, yielding a valuable reservoir of data for countless research efforts. The GSS cumulative file of 1972–1996 offers a series of questions that can be combined into an index of political tolerance. Throughout this period respondents were asked fifteen questions that addressed three civil liberties typically associated with freedom of expression: making a public speech, teaching at a college or university, and allowing a controversial book to be in the public library. The GSS posed each question with reference to members of five nonconformist groups: atheists, communists, homosexual men, persons advocating military rule rather than rule by democratic election, and persons believing that blacks are genetically inferior. For example, respondents were asked whether they would allow an atheist to make a public speech against churches and religion in their communities. Would respondents remove a book from their public library written by a homosexual author advocating homosexuality?[21] Responses to all questions were combined for each respondent, yielding an additive index that ranged from zero (least tolerant) to fifteen (most tolerant). The average level of political tolerance for the approximately 16,000 respondents across the twenty-year period was 9.1.

Each respondent also was given a list of sixteen different categories of groups and asked whether he or she was a member of any of the groups in each category. The categories ranged from obvious political groups, such as those representing a political ideology or concerned with a political issue, to those not usually associated with political activity, such as service/fraternal or hobby or sports/leisure groups. The GSS then calculated the number of memberships across the group sectors for each respondent. Slightly more than 55 percent of respondents indicated membership in one or no group categories; nearly 16 percent indicated membership in four or more categories.

Based on these data, how does group membership influence political tolerance? The pattern is unambiguous. As the number of memberships across group categories increases, so does political tolerance (Figure 2.1). But it is likely that other politically relevant social characteristics, such as education, affect our measure of group membership. Education is thought to increase familiarity with diverse ideas and people while inculcating democratic principles that contribute to respect for differences. Age is another factor, and research has shown it has an

Figure 2.1.   Group Membership and Mean Level
            of Political Tolerance

Index of political tolerance

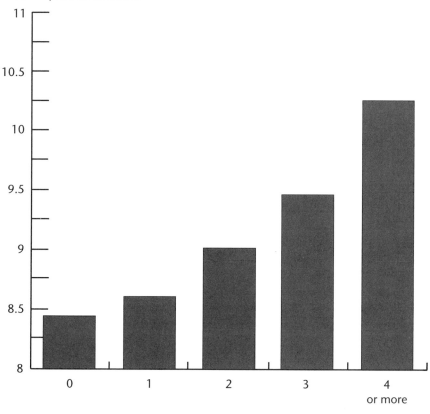

Number of group memberships

Source: GSS cumulative file, 1972–1996.

Note: The index scores political tolerance from zero (least tolerant) to fifteen (most tolerant).

inverse relationship with political tolerance. For example, increasing commitment to the civil rights of the poor, women, and blacks, especially among youth of the 1960s, is thought to have instilled in younger respondents a greater commitment to tolerance. Other researchers have discovered that people with strong religious beliefs are less likely to support civil liberties. Additional social variables that could affect political tolerance include gender, race, political ideology, and income. Over time the public has arguably become more tolerant, especially with regard to free speech for different groups.

What happens when these variables—education, age, and so on—and others are controlled for? Does extensive group involvement still have a separate and independent effect on political tolerance? To answer these questions we used ordinary least squares regression, a technique that provides an estimate of the effects—both in magnitude and direction—of each explanatory variable independent of the effects of the other variables (Table 2.1).[22] Inspection of the results shows that the standard controls—education, income, age, and religiosity—exhibit the expected direction and magnitude of association. Education is the most important predictor of political tolerance. More important for our purposes, the extensiveness of group involvement emerges as a statistically significant factor. The effect is not trivial, representing nearly half of the overall effects of income and ideology, and is more important than the effects of race and gender.

In sum, the socialization that occurs within groups apparently enhances tolerance for the civil liberties of nonconformist groups in society.[23] And tolerance grows when memberships across a range of group categories increase. From our results we infer that respondents' multiple group memberships are largely overlapping, exposing respondents to a diverse array of people, ideas, and organizational cultures. The broader the involvement of citizens in the association universe, the more likely that political tolerance will develop.

Table 2.1.   The Effect of Different Variables on Political Tolerance (N = 6,450)

Independent variable	Coefficient	t-statistic
Number of group memberships (0–4 or more)	.76 (.14)	5.2*
Gender (female)	.12 (.09)	1.3
Age	−3.87 (.20)	−18.9*
Education	4.66 (.18)	25.3*
Ideology	−1.35 (.21)	−6.3*
Religiosity	−2.83 (.15)	−18.5*
Race (black)	−.61 (.13)	−4.3*
Income	1.50 (.20)	7.3*
Time period	1.09 (.22)	4.8*
Constant	8.98 (.27)	7.2*
R^2	.27	
Adjusted R^2	.26	

Source: GSS cumulative file, 1972–1996.

* $p < .01$ or better.

Note: Standard error in parentheses.

Group Involvement and Postelection
Democratic Orientations

Elections empower citizens by giving them control over who serves in elected office. Elections also give citizens a way to affirm their faith in the validity and legitimacy of the political system through participation.[24] Elections can thus be viewed as a resource for democratic governments, providing legitimacy for the political system and latitude for elected authorities that work within it. By presenting social and political stimuli that generate and reaffirm confidence in the political system, the electoral experience contributes to the stock of public social capital.[25] In short, experiencing an election should enhance a citizen's democratic orientation. We contend that an important determinant of this enhancement, reflected in an increase in positive democratic orientations after an election, stems from the social capital citizens develop from their involvement in voluntary associations.

To empirically test our hypothesis, we used panel survey data collected by the American National Election Studies (ANES) from the same individuals before and after the 1996 presidential election (which pitted Republican Robert J. Dole against incumbent Democrat William Jefferson Clinton).[26] If group involvement influences attitudes associated with democracy, this should leave discernable empirical traces on pre- and postelection measures. That is, if successive pre- and postelection measures of democratic orientation differ, we simply ask whether group involvement may explain the differences.

Although many attitudes may be essential to the effectiveness and vitality of democratic institutions, several are regularly documented by ANES. Of the survey measures developed since the 1950s, citizens' trust in government and perceived political efficacy are among the most credible indicators of diffuse political support, representing sentiments relating to legitimacy and responsiveness of the political system and perceived fairness of process and outcome.[27] Although researchers have examined changes in political efficacy before and after elections,[28] documenting that elections contribute to enhanced feelings of efficacy and trust, these changes have never been linked to group involvement.

Efficacy attitudes were assessed by responses to the following statement before and after the 1996 election: "People like me don't have any say about what government does—agree strongly, agree somewhat, neither agree nor disagree, disagree somewhat, disagree strongly." Though there has been debate about the dimension of efficacy this question measures, recent research strongly concludes that the conventional "no-say-in-government" question is a good indicator of a respondent's attachment and loyalty to the political system.[29]

Respondents were also asked the following to assess political trust: "How much of the time do you trust government in Washington to do what is right—just about always, most of the time, some of the time, or none of the time?" This question was found to be a significant component of incumbent-based trust, a measure that taps the normative expectations of how elected officials and the government should operate.[30] This question thus solicits attitudes toward government and politicians generally rather than systemic attachments. By analyzing responses to these two questions, we obtain related yet conceptually and empirically distinct measures of respondents' support for the political system and the institutions and public figures that function in it.

We collapsed responses to both questions across pre- and postelection surveys into two categories, "1" for trusting and efficacious responses, "0" for distrusting and inefficacious responses. By subtracting preelection responses from postelection ones we found that approximately 17 percent of respondents felt more efficacious after the 1996 election, and 13.5 percent reported greater trust in government.

We then related our measures of efficacy and trust to a summated measure reflecting respondents' reported group involvement—the number of groups each respondent reported having some involvement with. In the ANES survey respondents were asked about their involvement in twenty-two groups. Some of these groups were overtly political, like political parties or liberal and conservative groups, whereas others were not, such as literary or hobby groups. Thirty-eight percent of respondents belonged to one or no groups; 40 percent belonged to three or more.

Do higher levels of group involvement translate into higher postelection levels of political trust and efficacy? We explored this using a statistical model called multiple logistic regression—commonly used when the dependent variable represents two distinct categories (for example, trust increased or trust decreased). The model enabled us to estimate the effects of group involvement while controlling for other variables commonly thought to predict postelection trust and efficacy, such as interest in the campaign, party identification, and a variety of standard demographic indicators. Our estimates were derived from the assumption that respondents reported no political trust or efficacy in the preelection period. Hence the probabilities are to be interpreted as the likelihood that respondents who felt inefficacious and distrusting of government before the election would feel efficacious and trusting after the election (Figure 2.2). For example, a respondent reporting no involvement in groups is less likely—by a probability of .11—to acquire postelection efficacy than an individual involved in four or more groups. In short, involvement in more groups increases the probability that respondents will develop postelection trust and efficacy. This is consistent with the notion that group involvement has a positive effect on orientations considered supportive of democratic processes.

Figure 2.2.   The Effect of Group Involvement on Postelection Trust and Efficacy

Probability of postelection trust

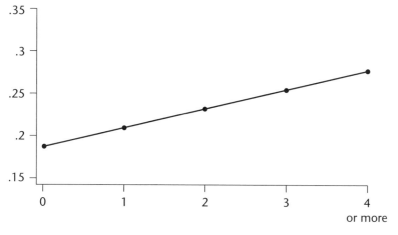

Number of groups involved with

Probability of postelection efficacy

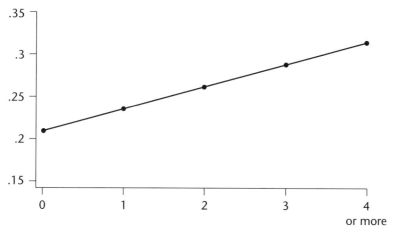

Number of groups involved with

Source: ANES 1996.

Postelection Depolarization

An important but seldom studied function of American electoral processes is the "depolarization" of partisan conflict immediately following a presidential election. Depolarization entails adjusting attitudes toward candidates in a way that diminishes the feelings of sharp conflict that often characterize preelection attitudes, such as when voters reconcile themselves to the fact that the candidate they voted for lost. Depolarization is critical not only for system support but also for establishing a political climate where decisionmakers can negotiate and compromise to reach and implement policy decisions. Depending on the partisan division in the electorate, excessive polarization could induce instability, political stalemate, or, in a worst case scenario, widespread political violence. Thus the manner in which the electorate accepts the election results and comes to regard the opposition in the postelection period could have important consequences.

Some evidence shows that voters "adjust" to the outcome of the election by changing their attitudes about the electoral contest in a manner that depolarizes the political climate.[31] For example, supporters of losing candidates perform psychological adjustments after an election, reconciling themselves to the defeat of their preferred choice.[32] We believe that voters who come to an election with extensive group involvement are more likely than citizens without such involvement to adjust to electoral outcomes by depolarizing their assessments of the electoral contestants after the election.

Our research strategy was again straightforward; we relied on the same 1996 ANES survey. The 1996 pre- and postelection surveys provide an evaluative measure of respondents' views of the candidates of the two major parties, making it possible to assess the degree of convergence or divergence in the comparative ratings of the candidates. The survey instrument, called a "feeling thermometer," asks respondents to rate each candidate on a scale of zero to one hundred "degrees," according to how "cold " or "warm" the respondent feels toward the candidate. The distance on the scales between the two major party candidates (Clinton and Dole) can be considered a measure of the degree of polarization, potentially ranging from zero (no polarization) to one hundred (maximum polarization). If the score on the comparative evaluation after the election is less than the score before the election, a respondent is said to have experienced depolarization. For example, assume a respondent's preelection evaluation of Clinton is seventy and of Dole, fifty. Also assume the same respondent records a postelection evaluation of Clinton at seventy and Dole at sixty. This represents a depolarization of ten points, which we label attitudinal depolarization.

The research question, therefore, is to what extent a respondent's group involvement affects the propensity to depolarize after the election. We found that as group involvement expands, attitudinal depolarization increases as well (Figure 2.3).

Figure 2.3.   Group Involvement and Postelection Depolarization, 1996

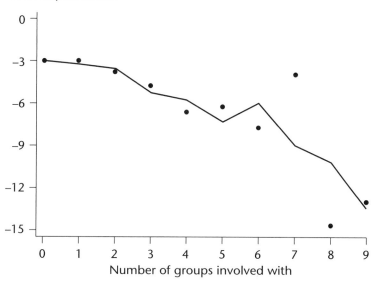

Source: ANES 1996.

Note: Data are the mean values of the absolute difference in postelection comparative evaluations minus the absolute difference in the same comparative evaluation in the preelection survey.

The impact of group involvement on postelection depolarization is perhaps most vividly illustrated when we compare noninvolved respondents with highly involved respondents (members of four or more groups). Before the election respondents involved in four or more groups exhibited considerable polarization, a mean difference of more than 41 points on the 100-point feeling thermometers, compared with 35.5 points for noninvolved respondents. After the election, however, the mean spread decreased by 7.3 points for the most involved; for uninvolved respondents the decrease was significantly smaller: 2.6 points (Figure 2.4). So citizens involved in many groups are more polarized before the election than their uninvolved counterparts, but group experiences contribute to a greater depolarization in the election's aftermath. The relationships depicted in Figures 2.3 and 2.4 remained significant even after more demanding multivariate statistical tests were applied, controlling for other determinants of postelection depolarization.[33] The extensiveness of people's group experiences matters in reducing tensions in electoral politics.

Figure 2.4.   Group Involvement and Mean Attitudinal
                   Polarization before and after the 1996 Election

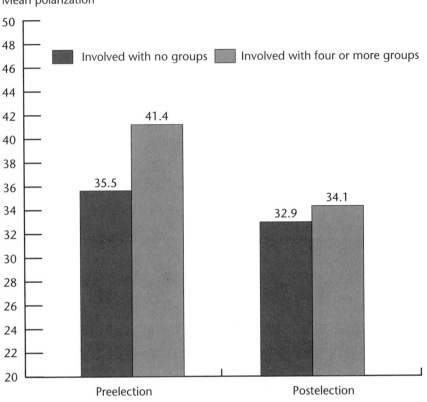

Mean polarization

Source: ANES 1996.

Note: Polarization data are "degrees" on a hundred-point "feeling thermometer" that measures respondents' feelings of "warmth" or "coldness" toward a candidate.

Conclusion

In this chapter we have attempted to find a connection between citizens' involvement in groups on the micro level and the development of macro-level political orientations that would seem crucial in a democratic political system. Our findings support the social capital proposition that links group involvement to important democratic orientations. Involvement in a range of groups appears to increase an individual's political tolerance, independent of such variables as education. Further, the more extensive a person's group involvement the more likely that person will feel increased political trust and efficacy after a presidential election.

Citizens with more extensive group involvement are also more likely to depolarize their feelings toward candidates after an election, adjusting their attitude toward the outcome. Overall, our research links the micro-level experiences of citizens within groups to attitudes that underpin and help sustain the democratic system.

But we have just scratched the surface. We need to know much more about the development of democratic orientations in particular types of group settings, and how people's involvement across different group categories affects their political attitudes. Conjecture about such matters abounds, but empirical investigation, especially by interest group scholars, has been infrequent.

A change in research priorities to address such issues would take the field of interest group politics back to its roots, reexamining issues raised by influential writers such as Tocqueville and Truman. It would also help connect the field to a major contemporary debate in political science surrounding the importance of social capital, a discussion that has extended well beyond the confines of our discipline. So far interest group scholars have not been major contributors to the debate. Perhaps the typical unit of analysis (an individual's degree of associational involvement) seems inappropriate because not all groups—bowling leagues, for example—are "interest groups" in any classic sense. On the other hand, involvement in so-called nonpolitical groups may have consequences for the whole political system and is worth further inquiry.

Political scientists' work on individuals and groups in recent decades has been dominated by an economic perspective, which focuses on individual incentives to join organized interests and how organizations induce collective action.[34] At the organizational level, the major concern has been about what individuals get from involvement or from being members, what groups get from their supporters, and what organizations can achieve in the public realm. The perspective emphasizes self-interest by both individuals and organizations.

But groups may contribute far more to democracy than organizing supporters to seek advantage. Social capital theorists like Putnam force us to consider the socialization experiences of group members and the possibility that even self-centered, micro-level activities within groups may lead to the growth of orientations considered favorable to democratic practices.

Notes

1. David B. Truman, *The Governmental Process* (New York: Alfred A. Knopf, 1951), 3–13.
2. Alexis de Tocqueville, *Democracy in America*, trans. George Lawence (New York: Doubleday, Anchor Books, 1969), 287.
3. Ibid. Most of the relevant material is found in volume two.
4. See, in particular, Robert P. Putnam's works, *Making Democracy Work* (Princeton: Princeton University, 1993); "Bowling Alone: America's Social Capital," *Journal of*

Democracy 6 (1): 65–78 (1995); "Tuning In, Tuning Out: The Strange Disappearance of Social Capital in America," *PS* 28 (4): 664–683 (1998); *Bowling Alone: The Collapse and Revival of American Community* (New York: Simon and Schuster, 2000).

5. James Coleman, "Social Capital in the Creation of Human Capital," *American Journal of Sociology* 94 (1988 supplement): S94–S120.

6. Putnam, "Bowling Alone," 65–66.

7. See, for example, Theda Skocpol and Morris P. Fiorina, eds., *Civic Engagement in American Democracy* (Washington: Brookings Institution, 2000); M. Margaret Conway, Sandra Bowman Damico, and Alfonso J. Damico, "Democratic Theory, Socialization in the Schools, and Democratic Outcomes," in *Democracy, Socialization, and Conflicting Loyalties in East and West*, ed. Russell F. Farnen, Henk Dekker, Rudiger Meyenberg, and Daniel B. German (New York: St. Martin's Scholarly Press, 1996), ch. 21.

8. Alphonso J. Damico, M. Margaret Conway, and Sandra Bowman Damico, "Patterns of Political Trust and Mistrust: Three Moments in the Lives of Democratic Citizens," *Polity* 32 (spring 2000): 397.

9. Truman, *The Governmental Process*, 21.

10. Kenneth Newton, "Social Capital and Democracy," *American Behavioral Scientist* 40 (5): 575–586 (1997).

11. Reviews of interest group literature by interest group scholars suggest that the role of groups in inculcating democratic orientations among members has not been a research priority. See Allan J. Cigler, "Interest Groups: A Subfield in Search of an Identity," in *Political Science: Looking to the Future*, vol. 4, ed. William Crotty (Evanston, Ill.: Northwestern University, 1991): 99–136; Frank Baumgartner and Beth L. Leech, *Basic Interests: The Importance of Groups in Politics and Political Science* (Princeton: Princeton University, 1998).

12. An illustration of the paucity of research linking group involvement to democratic orientations can be found in a survey of the literature on political tolerance. See Steven E. Finkel, Lee Sigelman, and Stan Humphries, "Democratic Values and Political Toleration," in *Measures of Political Attitudes*, ed. John P. Robinson, Phillip R. Shaver, and Lawrence Wrightsman (New York: Academic, 1999), 203–296. A noteworthy recent example of an effort to link group involvement to an important democratic orientation can be found in Damico, Conway, and Damico, "Political Trust and Mistrust," 377–410.

13. P. M. Sniderman, P. E. Tetlock, P. E. Glaser, J. M. Green, and M. Hout, "Principled Tolerance and the American Mass Public," *British Journal of Political Science* 19 (1): 25–45 (1989).

14. Gabriel A. Almond and Sidney Verba, *The Civic Culture* (Princeton: Princeton University, 1963); John Brehm and Wendy Rahn, "Individual Evidence for the Causes and Consequences of Social Capital," *American Journal of Political Science* 41 (September 1998): 999–1023.

15. Putnam, *Bowling Alone*, 350–363.

16. Dietlind Stolle and Thomas R. Rochon, "Are All Associations Alike?" *American Behavioral Scientist* 42 (1): 47–65 (1998); Travis N. Ridout and Rodolgo Espino, "What Is It About Joining a Group That Makes People Trust Others More?" (paper presented at the Midwest Political Science Association Meeting, Chicago, Ill., spring 2000).

17. Michael T. Hayes, "Interest Groups: Pluralism or Mass Society?" in *Interest Group Politics*, ed. Allan J. Cigler and Burdett A. Loomis (Washington: CQ Press, 1983), 84–109; Theda Skocpol, "Associations without Members," *The American Prospect* 45 (July–August 1999): 66–73.

18. Burdett A. Loomis and Allan J. Cigler, "The Changing Nature of Interest Group Politics," in *Interest Group Politics*, 5th ed., ed. Allan J. Cigler and Burdett A. Loomis (Washington: CQ Press, 1998): 1–34.

19. R. Kenneth Godwin, *One Billion Dollars of Influence* (Chatham, N.J.: Chatham House, 1998). Environmental groups, for example, tend to solicit support by emphasizing the negative—how everyone's clean air and water are threatened by polluting industries.

20. Truman, *The Governmental Process*, particularly 501–535; Sidney Verba, "Organizational Membership and Democratic Consensus," *Journal of Politics* 27 (summer 1965): 467–497.

21. The precise wording of the tolerance question was, "There are always some people whose ideas are considered bad or dangerous by other people. For instance, somebody who is against all churches and religions … (atheist): (1) If such a person wanted to make a speech in your (city/town/community) against churches and religion, should he be allowed to speak, or not? (2) Should such a person be allowed to teach in a college or university, or not? (3) If some people in your community suggested that a book he wrote against churches should be taken out of your public library, would you favor removing this book, or not?

22. For comparability purposes, we standardized the numerical scales, giving all variables a range of zero to one.

23. For a more detailed report of our research on group involvement and political tolerance, including how group type affects tolerance, see Allan J. Cigler and Mark Joslyn, "The Extensiveness of Group Membership and Social Capital: The Impact on Political Tolerance Attitudes," *Political Research Quarterly*, forthcoming.

24. Gerald M. Pomper, *Elections in America* (New York: Longman, 1980).

25. Wendy M. Rahn, John Brehm, and Neil Carlson, "National Elections as Institutions for Generating Social Capital," in Skocpol and Fiorina, *Civic Engagement in American Democracy*, 111–160.

26. Respondents in ANES survey are selected according to conventional probability sampling procedures. Interviews for the preelection period began in September and continued until election day. The postelection wave commenced immediately after the election, and except for a small proportion of respondents interviewed in December and January, was completed by late November. Our analysis is restricted to only those respondents who participated in both pre- and postelection surveys ($N = 1,460$).

27. Shanto Iyengar, "Subjective Efficacy as a Measure of Diffuse Support," *Public Opinion Quarterly* 44 (summer 1980): 249–256; Steven Weatherford, "Mapping the Ties that Bind: Legitimacy, Representation, and Alienation," *Western Political Quarterly* 44 (June 1991): 251–276.

28. Benjamin Ginsberg and Robert Weisberg, "Elections as the Mobilization of Popular Support," *American Journal of Political Science* 22 (March 1978): 31–55.

29. Stephen Craig, Richard Niemi, and Glenn Silver, "Political Efficacy and Trust: A Report on NES Pilot Study Items," *Political Behavior* 12 (3): 289–314 (1990).

30. Ibid.

31. V. O. Key Jr., *Public Opinion and American Democracy* (New York: Alfred A. Knopf, 1961), 478–79.

32. Allan J. Cigler and Russell Getter, "Conflict Reduction in the Post-Election Period: A Test of the Depolarization Thesis," *Western Political Quarterly* 30 (September 1977): 363–376; Donald Granberg and Tim Nanneman, "Attitude Change in an Electoral Context as a Function of Expectations Not Being Fulfilled," *Political Psychology* 7 (December 1986): 753–765.

33. See Mark R. Joslyn and Allan Cigler, "Group Involvement and Democratic Orientations: Social Capital in the Postelection Context," *Social Science Quarterly* 82 (June 2001): 357–368.

34. This research follows the tradition started by Mancur Olson, *The Logic of Collective Action* (Cambridge: Harvard University, 1965).

3

The National Rifle Association in the Face of the Clinton Challenge

Kelly D. Patterson and Matthew M. Singer

Perhaps no American interest group is regarded with greater affection or disdain than the National Rifle Association (NRA). Founded more than a century ago, the NRA in the past three decades has evolved into a high-profile advocate for the rights of gun owners. And it has opposed any attempt to compromise what group leaders argue is the unrestricted constitutional right to bear arms. The NRA has been largely successful in its policy goals, even though public opinion has supported strict gun control laws, especially after the 1999 shootings at Columbine High School in Colorado.

In this chapter Kelly Patterson and Matthew Singer examine the origin, development, and activities of the NRA from an organizational perspective. The NRA has evolved from an organization for sportspersons into a comprehensive political organization with a cadre of Washington lobbyists, a well-funded political action committee, a legal foundation, and grassroots political connections in every congressional district.

But size and success have not kept the NRA from its share of problems. Membership fluctuations have caused financial hardship, and the organization has been beset with factional difficulties as it tries to satisfy two types of members: Second Amendment fundamentalists and gun enthusiasts who join for sporting and shooting activities. The challenge for the NRA will be "to maintain its commitment to a goal that generates enthusiasm (and contributions) from its members while not alienating the moderate elements that enlarge its membership base."

The authors would like to thank those who assisted with this chapter, including Tanya Metaksa, executive director of the NRA's Institute for Legislative Action, for her interview; Bernie Hoerr, director of membership programs for the NRA, for providing membership data; Edward J. Land Jr., secretary of the NRA, for providing information about NRA charters; research assistants Carter Swift and Elizabeth Pipkin for their diligent work on earlier versions; and the Brigham Young University College of Family, Home, and Social Sciences for providing the resources that made this research possible.

Single-interest groups have become a prominent fixture in U.S. politics. The number of single-interest groups has increased dramatically in the United States, and the effects of this proliferation can be seen throughout politics.[1] But few single-interest groups have enjoyed the success and notoriety of the National Rifle Association (NRA).

The NRA's goals and national reputation revolve around promoting and protecting the rights of gun owners. The magnitude of the NRA, the size of its budget, and the intensity of its ideological commitment make the NRA a formidable force; very few single-interest groups can boast as much. The NRA participates in more than 10,000 campaigns in any given electoral cycle and raises millions of dollars for candidates committed to the goals of the organization.

But success does not come without a price. Organizations that grow rapidly and win political battles become difficult to manage and create bitter enemies. In the past decade the NRA has suffered attacks from presidents (Republican and Democrat), struggled through financial difficulties, and waged internecine battles that fractured the organization. It has survived a public and presidential onslaught in the wake of Columbine and other school shootings. Not only did the NRA survive—it thrived. In May 2001 *Fortune* named the NRA the most powerful lobby in America.[2]

How has the NRA gotten to this point? Are these challenges inevitable for any single-interest group that grows to the size and prominence of the NRA? In this chapter we look at the NRA's history and development, focusing on leadership, growth, and campaign activities. Like most large enterprises, the NRA faces tradeoffs as it expends resources in pursuit of the multiple, often conflicting goals in its charter.

History and Purpose

David Truman theorized that groups form to meet the needs of individuals in an increasingly complex society. His Disturbance Theory contends that groups form in response to changes in society and the economy.[3] Disturbances such as war, recessions, or depressions stimulate the creation of groups to restore balance in society. In the wake of the Civil War, Union officers sought a remedy for the poor marksmanship and rifle skills that Union soldiers exhibited throughout the conflict. The original charter of the NRA stated that

> The object for which [this organization] is formed is the improvement of its members in marksmanship, and to promote the introduction of the system of accuracy drill and rifle practice as part of the military drill of the National Guard of this and other states, and for those purposes to provide a suitable range or ranges in the vicinity of the City of New York.[4]

Through proper training and facilities, the NRA hoped to avert another poor performance by Union soldiers.

The organization grew slowly until the Militia Act of 1903. This act authorized a National Board for the Promotion of Rifle Practice. One of the board's first acts was to sell surplus weapons and ammunition to rifle clubs around the United States. Customers often became NRA members.[5] Through the first half of the 1900s the NRA grew modestly. It had fewer than 300,000 members in the 1950s and focused on meeting their shooting and sporting needs.[6]

Although Truman's theory may explain the origin of groups, it fails to account for how groups evolve over time, prosper, or fail. Robert Salisbury posited that groups prosper if the leadership makes a "profit" and provides a proper mix of incentives to members.[7] Over time the NRA built on the mandate in the original charter to adjust to the changing political climate. Where the organization once provided only "material" incentives to its members (access to ranges, gun training, and so on), it gradually began to play an active role in efforts by the federal government to regulate firearms.

In the 1930s Congress passed three main gun control acts. The Uniform Firearms Act of 1930 forbade the delivery of pistols to "convicts, drug addicts, habitual drunkards, incompetents, and minors under the age of 18." Karl T. Frederick, then president of the NRA, served as a special consultant in the framing of this act. The NRA also supported the National Firearms Act of 1934, which taxed and required registration of such firearms as machine guns, sawed-off rifles, and sawed-off shotguns, although some controversy surrounded Congress's definition of a machine gun. The NRA also supported the Federal Firearms Act of 1938, which imposed regulations on interstate and foreign commerce in firearms and pistol ammunition and restricted the use of sawed-off shotguns and machine guns.[8] In all of these attempts at regulation, the NRA worked as an insider and supported some restrictions on gun ownership without the ideological zeal that characterizes today's organization.

A crucial moment for the NRA came when Congress passed the Gun Control Act of 1968 in response to the assassinations of Martin Luther King Jr. and Robert F. Kennedy. The act prohibited unlicensed persons from buying, selling, or otherwise transferring rifles, shotguns, handguns, or ammunition outside of their home state or in any form of interstate commerce. Viewing these regulations as serious infringements on Second Amendment rights, the NRA opposed the act, but as a group of hunters and gun owners interested mainly in sport, it was ill prepared for the rough-and-tumble world of politics. According to Neal Knox, the NRA's former first vice president, "the leadership lacked a taste for [politics]. They considered lobbying beneath them."[9] The NRA had less than a million members at the time and could not prevent the act from passing. Indeed, some viewed the act as a slap in the organization's face. To succeed the NRA needed to provide ideological—or what are often called "purposive"—incentives to its members. The incentives came to be defined primarily around the constitutional right "to keep and bear arms."

The expansion of incentives led to changes in the NRA's charter in July 1977. The certificate of amendment states that one of the purposes of the NRA is "generally to encourage the lawful ownership and use of small arms by citizens of good repute; and to educate, promote, and further the right of the individual of good repute to keep and bear arms as a common law and constitutional right both of the individual citizen and of the collective militia." The grafting of this additional purpose on to the original goal of educating citizens and promoting firearm safety places the organization in a precarious position. Although the NRA can try to fulfill its original purpose, the addition of a new mission can alter the mix of members, making it easier for conflicts to occur. What happens when members dedicated to hunting and sport disagree with the single-minded pursuit of Second Amendment freedoms? Over the past decade the NRA has faced just such a dilemma.

Membership Has Its Privileges

The NRA is a full-service interest group. It attracts and retains a large and faithful membership through a range of benefits and plans. It services that membership with a gleaming new building in Fairfax, Virginia, and a full-time staff of about 300. The NRA appeals to two types of gun owners: sportspersons, including hunters and competitive shooters, and Second Amendment fundamentalists.[10] Tanya Metaksa, former director of the NRA's political action committee, the Institute for Legislative Action, explained that the NRA changed in the late 1970s from a small, tightly knit group of people interested in target shooting and supporting the military to include more diverse interests.[11] To entice these different groups of gun owners to join the NRA, the organization offers benefits of three types: material, solidary, and purposive.[12]

Material incentives involve actual goods, such as insurance, training, and discounts. The NRA has cultivated a relationship with police departments by offering police training sessions that include police and security firearm training and law enforcement instructor certification. And the organization provides as much as $25,000 in life insurance to the families of NRA–member police officers killed feloniously in the line of duty. The NRA also sponsors and trains shooters going to the Olympics and funds research on the causes of violent crime. The NRA offers selective benefits that appeal to all its members, including gun loss insurance, accidental death insurance, and discounts on car rentals, hotels, and airline tickets.

The NRA also offers opportunities for members to develop relationships with each other. These solidary incentives can make a large group seem more like a community. Because the NRA comprises more than 10,000 state associations and local clubs, it provides specialized benefits to its different membership groups.[13] For sportspersons, the NRA offers safety and training programs and recreational and competitive shooting.

For its general membership, the "Friends of the NRA" (a grassroots fund-raising organization) hosts periodic dinners and auctions to raise money for local activities that support NRA goals. The annual NRA national convention gives members a chance to mingle, see the latest in gun technology, and hear speeches by NRA leaders and government officials. More than 47,000 members attended the 2001 convention in Kansas City.[14] Finally, the NRA publishes several different magazines.[15]

The NRA also provides purposive benefits. A purposive benefit is the ideological satisfaction of seeing your group's goals accomplished. Citizens concerned with Second Amendment rights join the NRA because they expect the organization to protect their rights to own guns. In pursuit of this goal, the NRA has gained a reputation for effectiveness and influence matched by few single-interest groups.

Tenuous Public Standing

But the NRA has also earned a reputation for being fanatical and uncompromising. Critics claim that the NRA "resist[s] any gun controls on the fear that it will lead inexorably to confiscation of all guns owned by private citizens."[16] Some contend that the tactics and goals of the NRA have distanced it from its rank-and-file membership. For example, former president George Bush resigned his membership in 1995 when an NRA fund-raising letter referred to federal agents as "jackbooted government thugs."[17] In 1995 Senate majority leader and soon-to-be presidential candidate Robert Dole quipped that the association could stand "a little image repair job."[18] The NRA retaliated by refusing to endorse Dole during the 1996 presidential election campaign.

Public opinion is hostile toward the all-or-nothing approach. Dependable and long-term trend data about Americans' preferences for stricter gun control are not available, but the data we do have tend to reveal widespread support for firearms regulation. Since 1972 more than 70 percent of citizens have said they would favor a law that requires a person to obtain a police permit before he or she could buy a gun. Similar if not greater support has been expressed for waiting periods before a gun may be purchased and for laws that would require the registration of all purchased guns.[19]

Although most Americans favor stricter gun laws, recent polls show that support falling off. Since 1990 Gallup has periodically asked if people believe laws covering the sale of firearms should be made more strict, less strict, or kept as they are. In the early 1990s more than 70 percent of Americans felt that gun laws needed to be tougher. By 2000 that figure had declined to 60 percent. And polls reveal a distinct gender gap: 72 percent of women want tighter gun restrictions; only 52 percent of men feel the same.[20]

Not surprising, NRA members have very different opinions about gun control measures than the general population. In a poll of Utah voters in 1998, 44 percent of NRA members said there should be no restrictions on gun ownership; only 11 percent of non–NRA members had the same opinion. The same poll showed that 42 percent of voters who did not belong to the NRA believed that gun control laws reduce violent crime, but only 12 percent of NRA members believed that tougher laws would have that effect.[21]

With the public willing to support gun control measures, the aggressive tactics and uncompromising positions of the NRA seem to have eroded its standing in public opinion polls. In 1989, 58 percent of people said they had a "very favorable" or "mostly favorable" opinion of the NRA. By 2000 only 51 percent evaluated the NRA favorably.[22] A large difference was discerned in how gun owners and nongun owners evaluated the NRA; 71 percent of gun owners viewed the NRA favorably, compared with 36 percent of nongun owners.[23]

The NRA has further attenuated its public standing by landing at the center of controversies it did not create. The 1995 bombing of the Murrah Federal Building in Okalahoma City came only a week after the release of the NRA's fund-raising letter describing federal agents as "jack-booted government thugs." Membership declined as mainstream gun owners grew concerned that the organization had become too antigovernment and ideologically extreme. It took several years and changes in the organization's leadership for the NRA to project a more positive image.[24]

The Columbine Shootings

The NRA's largest challenge came in the wake of the Columbine school shooting. On April 20, 1999, two students at Columbine High School in Littleton, Colorado, killed twelve students and a teacher before committing suicide. An additional twenty-three students were injured in the worst school shooting in U.S. history. The NRA's 1999 convention was scheduled to be held in nearby Denver the first week in May. Denver Mayor Wellington Webb asked the NRA to cancel the convention.[25] The NRA scaled back its convention to one day and canceled a gun show, but refused to cancel the convention completely. Eight thousand people, including students and parents from Columbine, marched in protest. Only 2,500 NRA members attended the meeting.

During the convention's keynote address, NRA President Charlton Heston asked the audience to take a moment of silence for the victims. He praised members of the SWAT teams and police departments involved in the rescue as "heroes who risked their lives to rescue the students of Columbine from evil, mindless executioners."[26] But Heston also defiantly explained the organization's decision not to cancel the convention:

> We will not be silent or be told, "Do not come here, you are not welcome in your own land.". . . What saddens me most [about Webb's request] is how that suggests complicity. It implies that 80 million honest

gun owners are somehow to blame, that we don't care as much as they, or that we don't deserve to be as shocked and horrified as every other soul in America mourning for the people of Littleton. . . .We cannot, we must not let tragedy lay waste to the most rare, hard-won right in history.[27]

The public responded to the shooting by increasing pressure for more restrictions on gun sales. Polls taken the week after Columbine showed a 9 percent increase in the number of Americans who consider tougher gun laws the best way to prevent violence.[28] The day after the shooting, the Colorado legislature postponed action on three gun bills that would have reduced restrictions on concealed weapons, an action that more than a dozen state legislatures soon followed. That same week the U.S. Senate passed a gun control bill restricting gun sales at gun shows and pawnshops, with Vice President Al Gore casting the deciding vote. Following the Senate vote, minority leader Tom Daschle said, "What you just saw was the [National Rifle Association] loosing its grip on the U.S. Senate."[29]

Following the shootings President Clinton proposed a waiting period for all gun purchases. He also proposed holding parents responsible for some gun crimes committed by their children.[30] He hosted a meeting on youth violence that included most major gun producers but not the NRA. The gun manufacturers agreed to support increased restrictions on gun ownership, breaking with the NRA. Industry experts agreed that the NRA's constituency was becoming increasingly divided by public controversy.[31]

But the NRA and its Republican allies in the House passed a much more lenient gun control measure than the Senate did. The NRA spent some $3 million to prevent the Senate bill from being enacted by the House, sending mailings to its members encouraging them to contact their legislators.[32] Clinton pressured the House to act on the Senate bill by reminding them of Columbine and other school shootings.[33] Despite this pressure, including an explicit reference in the 2000 State of the Union Address to how Columbine demonstrated the need for increased gun control, the conference committee never presented a compromise bill to the full Congress.

As clashes between President Clinton and the NRA multiplied, the attacks became increasingly personal. In a national news magazine the week after a school shooting in Michigan, President Clinton said the NRA was "ruthlessly brutal" in its campaigns against legislators who vote for increased gun control. NRA Executive Vice President Wayne LaPierre responded that President Clinton "needs a certain level of violence in this country. . . . He is willing to accept a certain level of killing to further his political agenda, and his vice president too."[34] This built on a previous accusation by LaPierre that "there is a deliberate effort by this administration and by the Department of Justice not to enforce any of the [gun] laws on the books and not to prosecute any of these cases."[35]

Theories of Membership Growth and Decline

Despite these challenges, or perhaps because of them, the NRA has grown tremendously over the past twenty years, especially since 1999. Although membership fell to 2.8 million in May of 1999 following Columbine, one year later it had grown to 3.7 million. By the end of 2000 membership had reached 4.2 million, an all time high.[36]

Various theories seek to account for the growth or decline in interest group memberships. Some theories emphasize the benefits members receive for their dues.[37] If members receive ample material benefits, then membership figures should remain stable and perhaps even increase. Other theories emphasize the policy environment in which the groups operate. If the policy environment is hostile toward the goals of the organization, then the threats should stimulate a growth in membership.[38] Single-interest groups routinely trumpet, if not exaggerate, the consequences of particular initiatives or policies to attract new members and to rally the faithful. Finally, some theories emphasize the economics of group membership. Recessions or increases in dues adversely affect membership because of damage to a member's or potential member's disposable income. We examine each of these theories below.

As an ideological organization, the NRA faces three problems related to membership dues. First, demand for ideological benefits is income elastic, meaning that small fluctuations in income will result in large changes in how much individuals want what interest groups provide. If the economy is doing well and people are making money, then they feel more able to back up their ideological beliefs through membership in ideological organizations. Second, demand for ideological benefits will be price elastic, meaning the organization will be sensitive to the level of dues. Third, demand for ideological benefits is sensitive to changes in fashion. When it is fashionable to belong to the NRA, membership will flourish. When the public sees members as extremists or radical, it becomes unfashionable to belong to the NRA. Under such circumstances recruiting and retaining members becomes difficult.[39]

Which theory best accounts for the fluctuations and growth in NRA membership? Since 1977 membership has quadrupled (Figure 3.1) despite increases in dues and cutbacks in member benefits. Before 1977 a one-year membership in the NRA cost $10. Dues have steadily increased to $35 for a one-year membership (Table 3.1). In 1981 a membership in the NRA fetched a year's subscription to the *American Rifleman,* $300 in firearm insurance, $10,000 accidental death and dismemberment insurance, $300,000 of shooter's liability insurance, and an NRA cap.[40] The NRA has altered the benefit package through the years, eventually reducing and finally dropping the shooter's liability insurance. The group still offers $10,000 in personal accident insurance, the magazine subscription, and the NRA cap, but it has replaced the hunter's liability insurance with $1,000 worth of ArmsCare firearm insurance.

Figure 3.1.   NRA Membership, 1977–2000

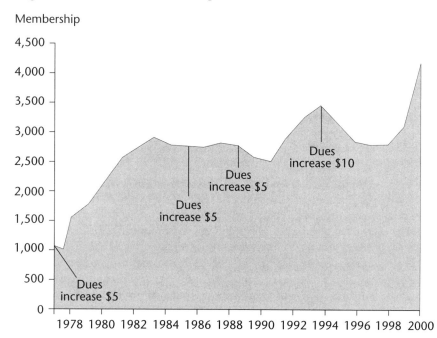

Source: For membership data from 1977 to 1996, Membership Division of the NRA; for 1997, "NRA Chief Overcomes Criticism from Ranks," *Lubbock Avalanche Journal,* February 12, 1997, http://www.lubbockonline.com/news/021097/nrachief.htm, March 13, 2001; for 1998, Michael Janofsky, "Enthusiastic NRA Gives Mandate to Charlton Heston," *New York Times,* June 8, 1998, A12; for 1999, Nancy Kletecka, "NRA Banquet Draws Large Crowd," *Southwest Daily Times,* February 8, 2000, http://204.233.65/swdtimes/htm/index.html, December 4, 2001; for 2000, Institute for Legislative Action, National Rifle Association, "General Information," http://www.nraila.org/research/19991123-generalinfo-001.shtml, February 1, 2001. Membership dues are from *American Rifleman* 1977, 1986, 1989, 1994.

Although membership has increased over time, it dropped temporarily following each dues increase. In 1991 acting Executive Vice President Gary Anderson said "a $5 rise in annual dues to $25 in July of 1989 had a major effect on membership."[41] But when dues and benefits remained constant from 1994 to the present, membership fluctuated greatly.

Another theory contends that membership fluctuates according to the threats a group experiences.[42] Like other single-interest groups, the NRA relies on people's expectations of certain political benefits. People have a notion of what the NRA's benefits are worth to them. They also have an idea of the likelihood that those benefits will disappear if people do not cooperate through membership in the organization. When gun ownership is threatened, free riders are motivated to join the organization. This argument maintains that people's risk attitudes change when a threat becomes too great. Normally risk-averse, people are slow to invest

Table 3.1. Changes in NRA Membership Dues (in dollars)

Membership	Before 1977	Oct. 31, 1977	April 1, 1986	July 1, 1989	July 1, 1994	Jan. 1, 2001
One year	10	15	20	25	35	35
Two years	19	27.50	n.a.	n.a.	n.a.	60
Three years	27	40	55	68	90	85
Five years	42.50	60	85	100	140	125
Lifetime	200	300	500	500	750	750

Source: American Rifleman 1977, 1986, 1989, 1994, 2001.

their money in ideological organizations like the NRA. When the potential costs for inaction increase in the face of such large potential risks as the regulation of firearms, people become risk seeking. In other words, threats increase awareness of the collective benefits of group membership. From this perspective, leaders of ideological interest groups tend to emphasize threats over benefits in their membership campaigns.[43]

Some indirect evidence supports this theory. NRA Executive Vice President LaPierre claimed that growth in membership since 1991 can be traced to the hostility of the Clinton administration toward gun owners. "People respond when there's a threat. I think Clinton is mobilizing gun owners at record rates," he said.[44] In 1999 former U.S. representative Gerald B.H. Solomon predicted that the increase in pressure for gun control after Columbine would mobilize people sympathetic to the NRA. "This [challenge] is a rallying cause. . . . [NRA members] rally together just like the Serbs support Milosevic, because they think their country is being attacked." [45]

Highly visible and controversial gun control legislation, such as the Brady Bill, seems to mobilize those who see the legislation as a threat. Some argue that in the wake of the Brady Bill, membership in the NRA increased dramatically.[46] After the passage of the Gun Control Act of 1968 and the Omnibus Crime Control and Safe Streets Act of 1968, the NRA began its metamorphosis from mainly a sporting organization into a politically motivated giant. NRA leaders looked at past failures and hoped to make up for lost ground by reversing components of the congressional acts of the late 1960s. A large percentage of bills presented to Congress during the 1970s dealt with the repeal of different aspects of the Gun Control Act of 1968. From 1977 to 1984 NRA membership increased steadily from 1,059,682 to 2,924,488 (see Figure 3.1).[47] During this time about 200 bills that dealt with gun control were presented to Congress.[48]

During 1984–1991 membership growth stagnated near 2,700,000, reaching a low of 2,516,908 in 1991. During these same years approximately one hundred bills were presented to each Congress. Most of these bills attempted to repeal various aspects of gun control legislation. The focus of Congress and of the country no longer revolved around gun control issues. The lack of some external threat, shown by the decline in the number of bills seeking to regulate firearms and the presence of a Republican in the White House, probably contributed to the stall in membership growth.

Beginning with the Brady Bill in 1990 the number of gun control bills before Congress began to increase. Gun control once again became a hot topic in Washington and around the nation. With this increase in gun control bills and the election of a pro-gun control president in 1992, NRA membership soared from 2,516,908 in 1991 to 3,454,430 in 1994. The NRA also began to more actively campaign against certain pieces of legislation in its monthly magazines, *American Rifleman* and *American Hunter*. The NRA's political renaissance leading up to the congressional elections of 1994 convinced old members to renew their memberships and attracted new members. The NRA campaigned actively for Republican congressional candidates, with great success. The victory brought an unexpected cost, however; with the gun control threat reduced, membership dropped from 3.4 million in 1994 to 2.8 million in 1995.

Membership continued to decline until 1999, when threats to the NRA resumed. In the 1997–1998 Congress, 128 bills were introduced that would have regulated the sale or use of firearms; in 1999–2000, 158 bills were introduced.[49] For gun owners, the greatest threat was the potential for licensing handguns. An NRA opponent said after the 2000 campaign that for gun owners, "licensing equals registration; registration equals confiscation."[50]

These fluctuations in membership seriously affect the budget of the NRA, whose largest source of revenue (55 percent) is membership dues. The other sources of revenue are contributions (15 percent), advertising in NRA magazines (9 percent), interest and dividends (9 percent), and other sources (13 percent).[51] Increased emphasis on membership drives and fund-raising before the 2000 elections left the NRA with an operating budget of more than $168 million.[52] These membership drives are not cheap, and the NRA has invested heavily in them. According to former NRA leaders and outside analysts, in 1995 it cost the NRA an average of $46 to recruit a new member.[53] The NRA also attracts members through brief promotions with manufacturers of hunting and shooting equipment.

Organization: Problems and Possibilities

The organizational structure of interest groups can be categorized from the simple and centralized to the complex and federated. Structure determines everything from the time it takes to make a decision to the kind of input enjoyed by rank-and-file members. Groups with a complex decision making structure, such as the NRA, generally receive more communication from rank-and-file members and actually solicit these opinions.[54] Allowing such input makes organizations more susceptible to challenges from members and key constituencies within the group. For example, Executive Vice President LaPierre survived a challenge from Neal Knox at the 1997 annual convention.

Knox served as executive director of the NRA's Institute for Legislative Action from 1978 to 1982. During this time he built a coalition of politically active hard-liners who saw the future of the organization in promoting Second Amendment rights through influence in Washington. Fired in 1982 for lobbying efforts that conflicted with NRA policies, Knox remained involved with the organization by supporting candidates for the board of directors that shared his hard-line political views. Because the number of members who participate in the nomination of directors is normally less than 5 percent, Knox was able to orchestrate the nominations of new directors and control the votes of board members whom he had helped elect. In 1995 Knox was elected to the position of second vice president by board members he had supported.

Appealing to the hard-liners in the organization, Knox attempted to overthrow Executive Vice President LaPierre, who advocated a more moderate image for the organization. Knox not only failed but also lost his new post as first vice president. Members who supported a more "family oriented" NRA reelected LaPierre and elected actor Charlton Heston as first vice president. In supporting Heston, LaPierre stated that he didn't intend to "stand by and let the NRA be turned into the John Birch Society." [55] Supporters of LaPierre and Heston hoped that the elections would finally put to rest the fanatical Knox, silence the rumors of an organization disabled with divisions, and wipe away the unhealthy image mainstream Americans seemed to have of the NRA.[56]

The NRA is governed by a board of directors made up of seventy-five NRA members elected by mail ballot by the membership at large. One director is elected by members at the annual meeting. The right to hold the office of director is limited to NRA lifetime members who are eighteen years or older and U.S. citizens. Directors serve a renewable term of three years, with the exception of the director elected at the annual meeting of members, who serves a renewable term of one year. The terms of office of one-third of the board expire each year.[57] Directors can be elected by their peers to the executive committee, which oversees a complex system of thirty-six standing and special committees.

Part of the NRA's success can be attributed to stability in major leadership positions. The NRA is a multimillion-dollar enterprise with operations throughout the United States. It is not easy to find talented individuals capable of managing such far-flung enterprises. The executive vice president is the most powerful office in the organization because it oversees day-to-day operations. Only five people have filled this position in the past twenty years, and two of those served for only one year.[58] LaPierre has held the office since 1992. Before that he served for six years as executive director of the Institute for Legislative Action (ILA), the political action committee and lobbying wing of the NRA. This upward mobility within the leadership is not uncommon. Gary L. Anderson served as executive director of operations before becoming executive vice president. J. Warren Cassidy, like LaPierre, served as executive director of the ILA before becoming executive vice president.

NRA members can influence the organization and the candidates it supports through a variety of means. Leaders encourage members to write, email, and fax their opinions to the national office, because most of the money that supports candidates and sustains the organization comes from member dues. Therefore, the national office solicits advice about which candidates to support, polls the membership, and tries to keep members informed about campaign activities. The willingness of an organization to listen to its members contributes to the organization's well being; members are less likely to contribute to unresponsive organizations.[59]

And when candidates for office know that the national organization listens to its rank-and-file members, the candidates become more responsive to members in their state or district. For this reason the ILA oversees the Political Victory Fund, the NRA's political action committee.[60] When the NRA talks to an elected official about a policy, it wants the official to understand that the members in the district or state can influence the official's electoral fortunes.[61] The NRA uses this strategy of combining lobbying and campaign activities at both the state and federal levels.

Representation and Political Influence

The NRA supports only candidates who support the NRA's objective: to staunchly defend the Second Amendment. Who is deemed faithful to this objective depends in part on the assessment of local members. The NRA recruits election volunteer coordinators to assess the candidates in each congressional district and pass along the findings to the national office. Members are also free to lobby the national office on behalf of particular candidates. Disagreements between the national office and the rank-and-file members sometimes arise over who should receive electoral support. But because most of the money that the NRA gives to candidates comes from its members, the organization tolerates these disagreements.

Giving money to candidates is only one way in which the NRA gets involved in campaigns. The NRA has developed five levels of involvement.[62] First, it grades candidates and publishes those grades in *American Rifleman*. Candidates for Congress can receive grades from "A" to "F." Candidates who most actively help the NRA receive an "A." Candidates who actively oppose the NRA receive an "F." The important dimension of the grade is activity. Candidates who lead the charge for NRA principles receive the higher grades. Some candidates vote in favor of the NRA's positions but do not lead on the issues. These candidates receive "average" grades.

Endorsement of a candidate is the second level of involvement. Only faithful allies of the NRA receive its endorsement. An endorsement is better than a good grade because of the signal it sends to local members. Longtime friends of the NRA receive endorsements even when local members vehemently oppose it. The national organization believes that loyalty should be rewarded, even if the incumbent or candidate may not be popular in local areas. The names of endorsed candidates in each district are printed on the cover of the November edition of *American Rifleman*, along with contact information for the local grassroots coordinator. Endorsed candidates also receive a letter from the NRA outlining the reasons for their endorsement, which the candidates can distribute to constituents.

The next three levels of involvement pertain to material support. At the third level the NRA contributes money to the candidate's campaign. Some political action committees give only to incumbents, hoping to gain access after the election. Other political action committees carefully target their donations, seeking to turn the tide in a close race.[63] The NRA's wealth allows it to do both. But the organization rarely gives the full legal amount to any candidate and gives only to candidates who ask.[64] At the fourth level the NRA uses in-kind contributions, such as fund-raising and meet-and-greet events, to help the candidate. The national office involves local members in many of these functions to make the candidate aware of NRA rank-and-file members.

At the fifth level the NRA uses independent expenditures to help its candidates. These expenditures run the gamut from radio and television ads to telephone banks, and often rely on the work of local members. In *American Rifleman*, Tanya Metaksa urged local members to help local candidates in the 1996 election by "making the phone calls, stuffing the envelopes, canvassing the neighborhoods."[65] Local member involvement maximizes the NRA's effectiveness. It harnesses members' ideological zeal and translates it into a language candidates for any office can understand: campaign resources. Jim Wilkinson, a spokesman for the Republican Congressional Campaign Committee, said that one reason the committee likes working with the NRA is that it "does a great job of educating their members, especially in the battleground congressional districts."[66]

From 1978 to 2000 the NRA spent more than $26 million in elections to support or oppose presidential and congressional candidates. Over this time the NRA gave much more to Republicans ($22.5 million) than to Democrats ($4.3 million; Figure 3.2). This preference has deepened over time; 94 percent of NRA expenditures and contributions in 2000 were to Republican candidates (Tables 3.2 and 3.3). The total amount spent by the NRA gradually expanded from $383,690 in 1978 to more than $16.8 million in 2000, including more than $8 million in contributions to candidates from both parties for national office.

The 1996 presidential campaign stands out as a glaring failure among NRA successes. NRA leaders urged members to work to defeat Clinton and also refused to endorse his main opponent, Republican Bob Dole.

Figure 3.2.   NRA Contributions to Campaigns for
National Office, 1978–2000

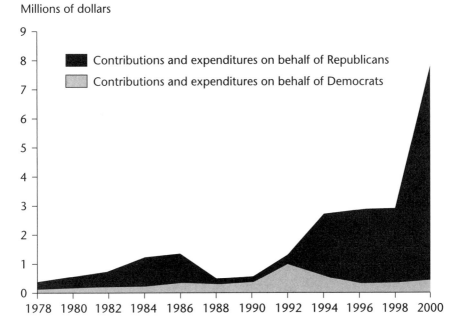

Millions of dollars

Contributions and expenditures on behalf of Republicans
Contributions and expenditures on behalf of Democrats

Source: Federal Election Commission, "Committee Index of Candidates Supported/Opposed 1978–1996 and 1997–2000," http://herndon1.sdrdc.com/cgi-bin/com_supopp/C00053553.htm, July 1, 2001.

The NRA believed that Dole could have been a more faithful supporter. The actions of the NRA in this election show how far some single-interest groups will go to preserve their ideological purity. Rather than compromise principles, the NRA worked to defeat incumbent president Clinton but did not fully rally the faithful to Senator Dole. This preserved the principles of the organization—not supporting any candidate that did not enthusiastically protect the Second Amendment—but produced what members perceived as a less than optimal electoral outcome.

The NRA faced a very different environment in 2000. Both candidates for the Democratic Party's presidential nomination made gun control a central issue of their campaigns. Key NRA supporters in the House and Senate were also vulnerable, which left the possibility of a Congress and President that would support increased gun control. Gun opponents also sensed the opportunity; the organization Handgun Control spent more than 10 times on candidate contributions and issue advocacy in 2000 than it had in 1996.

It is not surprising then that the NRA approached the 2000 election with unprecedented vigor. LaPierre and current ILA head James Jay Baker called the 2000 election "the most important election in the history

Table 3.2.   NRA Contributions and Expenditures on Behalf
of Republicans (in dollars)

Year	Contributions	Expenditures	Total
1978	272,035	15,745	287,780
1980	336,035	201,190	537,225
1982	540,207	193,761	733,968
1984	500,215	721,287	1,221,502
1986	643,740	693,030	1,336,770
1988	488,487	4,370	492,857
1990	456,285	81,222	537,507
1992	1,098,354	202,969	1,301,323
1994	1,442,519	1,205,189	2,647,708
1996	1,288,371	1,537,580	2,825,951
1998	1,249,911	1,618,860	2,868,771
2000	1,213,844	6,578,476	7,792,320

Source: Federal Election Commission, *Committee Index of Candidates Supported/Opposed 1978–1996 and 1997–2000*, http://herndon1.sdrdc.com/cgi-bin_suppopp/C00053553.htm., July 1, 2001.

of the Second Amendment. We're telling people, if they value the freedom to own a firearm, this is the election you'd better get out and vote." [67] The NRA endorsed George W. Bush and encouraged all its members to work for his election. [68] The NRA spent more than $16.8 million, more than double any previous election cycle. [69] Of this, only $1.5 million was given directly to candidates. [70] Most of the NRA's spending in candidate races (some $6.5 million) was as independent expenditures on behalf of candidates, including more than $2.2 million in support of Bush.

The NRA's largest expenditures were on issue advertisements that encouraged voters to "vote freedom first." The NRA aired a series of infomercials, half hour television programs featuring Charlton Heston speaking about the impact of gun control measures in other countries. Heston argued that gun control advocates, including the Clinton administration, have the ultimate goal of confiscating firearms. The program vigorously encouraged gun owners to join the NRA and to register to vote. [71]

The Bush–NRA relationship created a controversy in May 2000. At an NRA meeting in Los Angeles in February 2000, NRA First President Kayne Robinson had said that if George W. Bush were to win in November, "we'll have . . . a president where we work out of their office." [72] Handgun Control obtained a video of the speech and by May the clip was featured in a nationwide ad campaign. Gore spokesman Chris Lehane called the Robinson video "the proverbial smoking gun that proves once and for all that George W. Bush is in the hip holster of the gun lobbyists." [73] Bush was forced to respond that he had never been a member of the NRA and that "I

Table 3.3.   NRA Contributions and Expenditures on Behalf
of Democrats (in dollars)

Year	Contributions	Expenditures	Total
1978	93,626	2,284	95,910
1980	98,268	63,796	162,064
1982	170,695	38,589	209,284
1984	200,109	49,442	249,551
1986	254,824	60,790	315,614
1988	284,269	0	284,269
1990	293,208	61,898	355,106
1992	632,642	329,861	962,503
1994	410,519	152,626	563,145
1996	262,600	44,572	307,172
1998	283,750	58,188	341,938
2000	472,000	19,362	441,326

Source: Federal Election Commission, *Committee Index of Candidates Supported/Opposed 1978–1996 and 1997–2000*, http://herndon1.sdrdc.com/cgi-bin_suppopp/C00053553.htm, July 1, 2001.

don't want to disappoint the man [Robinson], but I'll be setting up shop in the White House. It will be my office. I'll make the decisions."[74]

After this controversy the NRA's public statements placed less emphasis on the organization's relationship with Bush. Instead the NRA focused on attacking Gore's record on guns and motivating NRA voters to vote. NRA campaign messages often tied Gore to Clinton, building on the strongest threat perceived by NRA members. The NRA also emphasized local races and its independent expenditure campaign encouraging voters to "vote freedom first." But as the election neared Heston and LaPierre campaigned for George W. Bush in such key battleground states as Michigan and Missouri. The NRA was especially active in courting the vote of union members who were gun owners.[75] Meanwhile, in the weeks before the election, Gore backed off from making guns an issue, much to the displeasure of several of his allies.[76]

The NRA was also active in congressional campaigns and in initiative campaigns in several states, using a wide range of tactics and resources to support its favored candidates. For example, in the race for Virginia's Senate seat, the NRA sent out mailings, ran 378 television advertisements and 155 radio advertisements, and set up a network of members to mobilize support for Republican George Allen.[77] The NRA also reported spending more than $500,000 in support of Allen. The NRA used a similar mix of television and radio advertising with grassroots organization in other states, reflecting its strength in providing both types of campaign resources: money and people power.

The 2000 elections were a mixed success for the NRA. It accomplished its most important goal: preventing Al Gore from being elected president and placing an ally in the White House. Observers have concluded that the NRA played a decisive role in the Bush victories in Arkansas, Tennessee, and West Virginia.[78] Eighty-six percent of the candidates for federal office endorsed by the NRA won.[79] Even President Clinton ended the election praising his rivals. "I don't think that there's any doubt that, in at least five states I can think of, the NRA had a decisive influence. . . .You've got to give it to them, they've done a great job. They probably had more to do than anyone else in the fact that we didn't win the House this time. And they hurt Al Gore."[80]

But Gore and NRA opponents won in Michigan and Missouri even though the NRA spent more time and energy in these states than in any other except Virginia. Additionally, the number of "pro-gun" senators decreased by two. But an additional five NRA allies were elected to the House, leaving ILA Federal Affairs Director Chuck Cunningham to conclude that the House "will serve as our backstop for potential anti-gun actions in the Senate."[81] This leaves the NRA in a precarious position for 2002.

Conclusion

The NRA is clearly one of the most powerful single-interest groups in the United States. Its influence is the result of a sustained and deliberate attempt to attract and retain a large and enthusiastic membership base. The NRA spends large sums to recruit new members and satisfy current ones. It offers incentives from social benefits for sportspersons to ideological satisfaction enjoyed largely by hard-core proponents of Second Amendment liberties.

The NRA enjoyed a remarkable year in 2000. Though the year began with vivid memories of school shootings, a popular president, and nearly a million moms marching in Washington for gun reform legislation, it ended with no new major gun laws, much to the chagrin of President Clinton.[82] A school shooting in Santee, California, in March 2001 elicited few congressional calls for tougher legislation. Many Democrats believe that gun control costs them more swing votes than it gets them.[83] Meanwhile, in March 2001 a gun control group called the Million Mom Organization laid off all but five of its employees due to financial restraints and low attendance at the 2001 Mother's Day March (about one hundred people attended).[84] The NRA did not hide its glee. Speaking of gun control advocates and Democrats, LaPierre said, "they spent years building up for what they planned to be a referendum on guns. By the end of the campaign, the air was completely out of that balloon."[85]

But the large membership and perceived power of the group do not mean that all is well in the NRA. Most complex organizations face tradeoffs as they allocate resources among goals. The NRA must satisfy two distinct types of members: those who resist any attempt to regulate firearms or ammunition and those who join for the sporting and shooting activities. The sportspersons are much less politicized and do not see some restrictions on the "right to bear arms" as unreasonable. Internal tension will continue so long as the NRA pursues the different goals in its charter and so long as the organization allows all members access to the decision making processes in the national office.

Single-interest groups can fall prey to their own success. Membership and fund-raising declined in the wake of the Republican revolution in 1994. The NRA will have to maintain its commitment to a goal that generates enthusiasm (and contributions) from its members without alienating the moderate elements that enlarge its membership base. Although NRA leaders have said that "if one word describes the state of the NRA today, it is *unity*," the combination of divergent constituencies and the NRA's responsive organization always leave the potential for disagreements and conflicts.[86] Only time will tell how the NRA will respond to these challenges.

A final challenge facing the NRA is to avoid gaining a reputation as strictly a partisan organization. According to some observers, "the NRA, which used to be a fairly bipartisan lobby, has become just another fundamentally GOP constituency group with lots of money."[87] The NRA has been in this situation before. In 1994 it used its resources and endorsements to defeat several Democratic leaders in Congress for their support of the Brady Bill. Although at the time the NRA considered this a victory for gun rights, ILA head James Jay Baker says, in hindsight, this strategy was shortsighted. "It was a huge mistake. There was too much emphasis on one vote in a career and ruining people who opposed us. We need Democratic friends. Our survival depends upon the gun issue not becoming a strictly partisan issue."[88]

In the wake of the terrorist attacks on the World Trade Centers and the Pentagon on September 11, 2001, a Boston columnist argued that federal authorities need to close loopholes at gun shows where terrorists might purchase guns.[89] The NRA reacted swiftly. It accused a recently formed group called Americans for Gun Safety of planting the story and exploiting the tragedy.[90] It disputed the facts of the story and then reiterated the NRA's support for instant background checks at gun shows. The response ended with an attack on Americans for Gun Safety and its founder. Although the events of September 11 have altered much of what American politicians do these days, the NRA shows no sign of ceding ground to its opponents. Indeed, if Truman's Disturbance Theory is correct, the NRA should find itself competing with new and old groups to establish its relevance in this new policy environment. With supporters in the White House, the Justice Department, and Congress, the NRA seems poised to promote and protect the agenda of gun owners.

Notes

1. For a discussion of the reasons for the growth in the number of interest groups, see Jeffrey M. Berry, "Citizen Groups and the Changing Nature of Interest Group Politics," *The Annals of American Academy* 528 (July 1993): 30–41. Unlike other interest groups, which may advocate several issues, single-interest groups advocate only one.

2. Jeffrey H. Birnbaum, "Fat and Happy in D.C.," *Fortune Magazine*, May 28, 2001, 94–103.

3. David Truman, *The Governmental Process*, 2d ed. (New York: Alfred A. Knopf, 1971).

4. "Original Charter of the National Rifle Association," 1871, available from the Office of the Secretary of State in New York.

5. This also seems to be an example of what Graham K. Wilson refers to as encouragement of the growth of interest groups by their proximity to such institutions as political parties and the state. Wilson has argued that the NRA is an example of a group that exists because of early beneficial government policies. Graham K. Wilson, *Interest Groups* (Oxford: Basil Blackwell, 1990). Burdett A. Loomis and Allan J. Cigler make a similar argument in "The Changing Nature of Interest Group Politics," in *Interest Group Politics*, ed. Allan J. Cigler and Burdett A. Loomis (Washington, D.C.: CQ Press, 1986).

6. For an excellent discussion of the history of the NRA, see Robert Spitzer, *The Politics of Gun Control* (Chatham, N.J.: Chatham House, 1995), 99–115.

7. Robert H. Salisbury, "An Exchange Theory of Interest Groups, *Midwest Journal of Political Science* 13 (February 1969): 1–32.

8. Alan C. Webber, "Where the NRA Stands on Gun Legislation," *American Rifleman*, March 1968, 22–23.

9. Michael Powell, "Call to Arms," *Washington Post Magazine*, August 6, 2000, W8.

10. David Brock, "Wayne's World; In May the NRA Will Decide Whether It Wants to Be a Modern Political Organization or an 'Extremist' Group Sprung from a Liberal's Worst Nightmare," *American Spectator*, May 1997, 38.

11. Charles Madigan and David Jackson, "NRA in the Cross Hairs: Lobby Battles Foes, Itself," *Chicago Tribune*, August 3, 1995, N1.

12. Peter B. Clark and James Q. Wilson, "Incentive Systems: A Theory of Organizations," *Administrative Science Quarterly* 6 (September 1961): 129–166.

13. Institute for Legislative Action, *General Information*, 2001, http://www.nraila.org/research/1999 1123-generalinfo-001.shtml, February 22, 2001.

14. Rick Alm, "NRA Convention Was a Bonanza, in a Few Places." *Kansas City Star*, May 29, 2001, D14.

15. *American Rifleman* is for general members, *American Hunter* for hunters, *America's First Freedom* for those interested in second amendment issues, *Shooting Sports USA* for competitive shooters, and *Insights* for junior members.

16. Brock, "Wayne's World," 38.

17. Scott Shepard, "National Convention; NRA's Message: 'The Gun Lobby Is People,'" *Atlanta Constitution*, May 19, 1995, 12A.

18. Peter Stone, "The NRA's Been Shaken, Too," *National Journal*, May 6, 1995, 1133.

19. John T. Young, David Hemenway, Robert J. Blendon, and John M. Benson, "Trends: Guns," *Public Opinion Quarterly* 60 (winter 1996): 634–649.

20. Gallup Organization, "Gallup Poll Topics: Guns," http://www.gallup.com/poll/indicators/indguns2.asp, March 16, 2001.

21. Data collected in the 1998 KBYU Television/Utah College Exit Poll. This exit poll is designed and conducted by students and faculty at Brigham Young University.

22. Ibid.

23. Gallup Organization, "Majority of Americans Have Favorable Opinion of the National Rifle Association," May 19, 2000, http://www.gallup.com/poll/releases/pr000519.asp, March 20, 2001.

24. Matthew Kauffman, "Can Heston Be a Silver Bullet for the NRA? As President, Actor Gives Group Chance to Cure Ailing Image," *The Hartford Courant*, June 14, 1998, A1.
25. CNN, "8,000 Protest NRA Convention in Denver," 1999, http://www.cnn.com/ US/9905/01/nra.protest.02/, April 10, 2001.
26. Charlton Heston, "Opening Remarks to Members," 1999, http://www.nrahq.org/ transcripts/denver_open.asp, May 16, 2001.
27. News Services, "Heston, NRA Take Stand at Denver Convention," *St. Louis Post Dispatch*, May 2, 1999, A6.
28. Associated Press, "Gun Control Bolstered: Americans Want Tougher Gun Laws, Poll Says," *Newsday New York*, May 6, 1999, A20.
29. Dan Luzador, "Politicians Distance Themselves From Guns: Concealed Weapons Measures Just Too Hot," *Denver Rocky Mountain News*, May 6, 1999, 5A; David Olinger, "Tide Turing on Gun Control," *Denver Post*, May 17, 1999, A1.
30. Lorraine Woellert, "Gun Control: Even After Littleton, the NRA Will Keep It at Bay," *Business Week*, May 10, 1999, 47.
31. James Dao, "After Littleton, Gun Industry Sees Wider Gap with the NRA," *New York Times*, May 25, 1999, A21.
32. "Inside Washington for August 14, 1999," *National Journal*, August 14, 1999, 2343.
33. CNN, "Clinton Slams House on Guns," http://www.cnn.com/allpolitics/stories/ 1999/06/09/gun.control/index.html, June 9, 2000.
34. Joe Hallett, "Clinton, NRA Official Continue Skirmishing over Gun Control," *Columbus Dispatch*, March 14, 2000, A1.
35. "I Think the Real Target Is the Second Amendment," *Newsweek*, August 23, 1999, 30.
36. For 1999 data, see Woellert, "Gun Control." For 2000 data see Powell, "Call to Arms" and http://www.nraila.org/research/19991123-generalInfo-001.shtml.
37. Salisbury, "An Exchange Theory of Interest Groups."
38. Truman, *The Governmental Process*.
39. John Mark Hansen, "Political Economy of Group Membership," *American Political Science Review* 79 (March 1985): 79–96.
40. Shooter's liability insurance started at $300,000 and increased $100,000 for each year of membership, with a cap of $1,000,000.
41. Steven Holmes, "Rifle Lobby Torn by Dissidents and Capitol Defectors," *New York Times*, March 27, 1991, A20.
42. Truman, *The Governmental Process*.
43. Hansen, "Political Ecology of Group Membership," 81.
44. Peter H. Stone, "Showing Holes: The Once-Mighty NRA Is Wounded, but Still Dangerous," *Mother Jones* 19 (1994): 39, http://www.motherjones.com/mother_jones/ JF94/nra.html, November 20, 2001.
45. James Dao and Don Van Natta, "NRA is Using Adversity to Its Advantage." *New York Times*, June 12, 1999, A10.
46. Charles Mahtesian, "Firepower," *Governing Magazine* 8 (March 1995): 16.
47. The membership figures were provided by Bernie Hoerr, director of Membership Programs in the Membership Division of the NRA.
48. I determined the number of bills relating to gun control by using the *Thomas Bill Summaries and Status, Previous Congresses, Index*. The index includes a brief discussion of the subject of the bill, the bill number, and its sponsor. Any bill listed that mentioned any issue relating to the regulation or deregulation of firearms was included in this analysis.
49. Search in the THOMAS database under the CRS Subject term "firearm control" in the 105th and 106th Congresses.
50. Jonathan Weisman, "For Pro-Bush Interest Groups, It's Wish List Time," *USA Today*, December 15, 2000, 6A.
51. J. Warren Cassidy, "Here We Stand," *American Rifleman*, January 1991, 7.
52. Michael Powell, "Call to Arms," *Washington Post*, August 6, 2000, W8.

53. Peter Stone, "From the K Street Corridor," *National Journal*, July 8, 1995, 1774.
54. Philip A. Mundo, *Interest Groups: Cases and Characteristics* (Chicago: Nelson-Hall, 1992).
55. Powell, "Call to Arms." The John Birch Society is an ultraconservative interest group formed to stop the spread of communism. Many perceive it as too extreme to influence policy debate.
56. Katherine K. Seelye, "Gun Lobby in Bitter Power Struggle," *New York Times*, January 30, 1997, B6.
57. E. G. Bell Jr., ed., "Exercise Your Rights: Assist in the Nomination of Directors," *American Rifleman*, July 1995, 56–57.
58. Harlon B. Carter served from 1977 to 1984, G. Ray Arnett in 1985, J. Warren Cassidy from 1986 to 1990, Gary L. Anderson in 1991, and Wayne LaPierre has served since 1992.
59. Anthony Nownes and Allan J. Cigler, "Public Interest Groups and the Road to Survival," *Polity* 27 (spring 1995): 379–404.
60. Kelly Patterson, "Political Firepower: The National Rifle Association," in *After the Revolution: PACs and Lobbies in the Republican Congress*, ed. Robert Biersack, Paul Herrnson, and Clyde Wilcox (Boston: Allyn and Bacon, 1998).
61. Tanya Metaksa, interview by the author, July 18, 1996.
62. For a full discussion of how the NRA makes its decisions to allocate these resources, see Patterson, "Political Firepower."
63. Paul S. Herrnson, *Congressional Elections: Campaigning at Home and in Washington* (Washington, D.C.: CQ Press, 1995), 109–110.
64. Metaksa interview.
65. Tanya Metaksa, "Memorandum: Election of Pro-Gun Candidates," *American Rifleman*, September 1996, 33.
66. Peter Stone, "In the NRA's Sights," *National Journal*, July 22, 2000, 2366
67. Wolf Blitzer and Brian Cabell, "Gun Lobby Targets Gore, Democrats," CNN.com, May 23, 2000, http://www.cnn.com/2000/us/05/23/nra.politics/index.html.
68. See Charlton Heston, "The President's Column," *American Rifleman*, November/December 2000, 16.
69. Federal Election Commission, "Top 50 Pacs' Disbursements," http://www.fec.gov/press/053101pacfund/tables/pacdis00.htm, June 18, 2001; Juliet Eilperin, "A Pivotal Election Finds NRA's Wallet Open," *Washington Post*, November 1, 2000, A16.
70. Federal Election Commission, *Committee Index of Candidates Supported/Opposed 1999-2000*, 2001, http://herndon1.sdrdc.com/cgi-bin/com_supopp/C00053553, July 1, 2001.
71. Stone, "In the NRA's Sights"; Eilperin, "A Pivotal Election"; Annenberg Public Policy Center at the University of Pennsylvania, "Issue Ads: The National Rifle Association," *Issue Ads@APPC*, 2000, www.appcpenn.org/issueads/national%20rifle%20association.htm, February 27, 2001.
72. "Bush Victory Ensures Entrée, NRA Says," *Los Angeles Times*, May 4, 2000, www.latimes.com/news/politics/elect2000/pres/money/20000504.htm, February 27, 2001.
73. Ibid.
74. Blitzer and Cabell, "Gun Lobby Targets Gore, Democrats."
75. Chris Mondics, "NRA Targets Union Members Who Are Leery of Gun Control," *Milwaukee Journal Sentinel*, November 5, 2000, 13A; Julian Borger, "Race for the White House: Gun Lobby Takes Aim at White Working Class," *The Guardian of London*, November 4, 2000, 19.
76. Mondics, "NRA Targets Union Members."
77. Bob Dudley, Harry Wilson, Robert Holsworth, Scott Keeter, and Stephen Medvic, "The 2000 Virginia Senate Race," in *Election Advocacy: Soft Money and Issue Advocacy in the 2000 Congressional Elections*, ed. David B. Magleby (Provo, Utah: Center for the Study of Elections and Democracy), 106–120.

78. See Weisman "For Pro-Bush Groups"; Susan Page, "The Changing Politics of Guns—Democrats Back off on Firearms," *USA Today*, August 13, 2001, A1.
79. James Jay Baker, "Voting Freedom First," *American Rifleman*, January 2001, 78–80.
80. Institute for Legislative Action, "Rating the NRA on the 2000 Elections," http://www.nraila.org/research/20010215-electioninformation-001.shtml, February 22, 2001.
81. Baker, "Voting Freedom First." Cunningham quoted in Fred Barnes, "How the House Was Won," *The Weekly Standard*, November 20, 2000, 19.
82. For example, see the interview of President Bill Clinton by *Newsweek's* Debra Rosenberg and Matt Bai, "Caught in the Gun Culture," *Newsweek*, May 15, 2000, 29.
83. James Dao, "New Gun Control Politics: A Whimper, Not a Bang," *New York Times*, March 11, 2001, http://www.nytimes.com/2001/03/11/weeki.../11DAO.html.
84. Ibid.
85. Weisman, "For Pro-Bush Interest Groups."
86. Wayne R. LaPierre, "Standing Guard," *American Rifleman*, February 2001, 12.
87. Larry Sabato quoted in Stone, "In the NRA's Sights," 2366.
88. Powell, "Call to Arms."
89. Thomas Oliphant, "Lax Gun Laws Help Terrorists," *Boston Globe*, September 25, 2001, A19.
90. James Jay Baker, "NRA Response to Boston Globe," September 27, 2001, http://www.nraila.org/NewsCenter.asp?FormMode=Detail&ID=1020&T=print.

4

Collective Entrepreneurialism and Breast Cancer Advocacy

Maureen Casamayou

Where do interest groups come from? We often assume that some prominent and longstanding groups have always just existed—the Chamber of Commerce, the American Farm Bureau Federation, the National Rifle Association—but every group has had a founding experience. It is worthwhile to think about how groups organize, especially when they appear to have few resources.

In this chapter Maureen Casamayou examines how the first breast cancer advocacy groups began. Founders often came from the ranks of those diagnosed with the disease. As medical technology advanced, many articulate, active women received diagnoses in their 40s and 50s, and turned to their peers for support. Across the country these women came together in doctors' offices and breast cancer support groups. Out of these informal groups emerged a "collective entrepreneurialism" that produced first local advocacy groups, then national ones. Through the continuing efforts of the National Breast Cancer Coalition, enhanced funding for breast cancer research and treatment remains near the top of the national health policy agenda.

On a lecture tour across the United States in 1990, Dr. Susan Love, breast cancer surgeon and cofounder of the National Breast Cancer Coalition in May 1991, was astounded by the anger and frustration among women in her audiences.[1] The women were "fed up with the fact that this virtual [breast cancer] epidemic was being ignored."[2] Dr. Love noted that, "It wasn't just in the big centers like San Francisco and Boston and Washington, D.C., where I'd expect to see political movements springing up. It was everywhere—everywhere women were ready to fight for attention to breast cancer."[3]

These exhilarating days of the early movement were characterized by small, loosely connected pockets (or cadres) of individuals who advocated unprecedented changes in funding for breast cancer research. Social science literature on interest groups would suggest two theories to explain why these small groups formed: The groups were either the direct result of a "disturbance"—"any significant event or series of events other than leadership activity" in the environment. Or the groups were started by a highly motivated, goal-oriented entrepreneur whose decision to organize was independent of social changes.[4] Neither theory offers a satisfactory explanation for breast cancer mobilization. Instead, portions of both provide the basis for a new paradigm of multiple leadership that I call "collective entrepreneurialism."

Like single entrepreneurs, collective entrepreneurs have a vision, initiative, and willingness to take risks as they invest their time, energy, and other types of capital to form an organization. Collective entrepreneurs offer incentives similar to those offered by a lone entrepreneur seeking to attract members to his or her organization. Incentives could include the opportunities to fight for a cause (purposive benefits), enjoy the companionship and friendship of likeminded people (solidary benefits), and even to receive material benefits. But here the similarities end. The differences between the collective and the single entrepreneurial models for breast cancer are substantial. Instead of focusing on the experiences that galvanize the lone entrepreneurial risk-taker, the collective model focuses on the shared experiences of a new generation of baby boomer women.[5] This context helped produce the organizational spark from which multiple leadership emerged. Equally important is the contribution of Disturbance Theory to this model. Certain social disturbances or changes play a critical, if indirect, role in providing the preconditions for collective entrepreneurialism.

Social Changes and
Collective Entrepreneurialism

This study draws from many informal personal and telephone interviews and primary and secondary materials to examine the social and cultural trends originating in the late 1970s that provided fertile ground for collective entrepreneurship. These trends include a greater willingness to discuss breast cancer, increased patient advocacy, technological changes, and a more highly educated body of women, many of whom emphasized quality of life issues.

Breast Cancer Comes out of the Closet

Breast cancer has historically been associated with fear, dread, and shame. Aside from being a deadly disease, breast cancer conjured up a powerful symbol of female identity tied both to the nurturing nature of women and to female sexuality. Indeed, for some women the male-engendered "breast-vaunting" culture of the United States added to the emotional and psychological pain of losing a breast.[6] As a consequence, many women suffered in silence and even kept their diagnosis secret from family and friends.

This began to change in the mid-1970s. When female public figures announced their diagnosis and, on occasion, described their personal journey with the disease, some obstacles to open discussion began to break down, and the social stigma lessened. In 1974, for example, First Lady Betty Ford went public with descriptions of her diagnosis and surgeries; another political wife, Happy Rockefeller, soon followed suit. The resulting media coverage produced a fountain of new information on the disease and on surgical alternatives to the Halsted radical mastectomy.[7] In the next decade First Lady Nancy Reagan, journalist Bette Rollins, and actress Jill Ireland, among others, made similar public declarations of their direct experience with the disease and further softened the taboo on open and frank discussion. The female breast was being talked about in a context other than *Playboy* or *Penthouse*. In this gradually changing environment, the courage of these public women was an example and inspiration to others.

Patient Advocacy and Breast Cancer

Patient advocacy was rooted in the women's health movement, an important component of the second women's liberation movement of the 1960s. In the words of one scholar, the women's health movement grew from an

> awareness [among women] of not only how little they knew about their own bodies but how much of the health system to which they must turn for care was controlled by male professionals who showed little concern for or understanding of women's health and lives. . . .Women's health activists, meeting in conscious-raising groups across the country in the late 1960s and the early 1970s, soon shared with each other the realization that male physicians and male-created stereotypes of women controlled how women felt and looked at their bodies.[8]

Such attitudes fostered the principle of patient control, which led to patient advocacy in breast cancer diagnosis and treatment. Women's health groups and some health care professionals promoted this approach to patient care, which challenged the heavily paternalistic attitudes of medical professionals. Traditional attitudes encouraged treating women as passive entities with no control over their treatment decisions. Information and decision making about breast cancer treatment belonged to a woman's team of (usually male) doctors.

In contrast, patient advocacy, as noted by Amy Langer, a cofounder of the National Breast Cancer Coalition (NBCC), involved "getting the best care for yourself, through your own efforts and with the help of others." The patient advocacy movement urged women to become informed about their bodies and about medical treatments and to become equal partners in decision making.[9] In other words, women had a justifiable claim to participate in the procedures through which they were diagnosed and treated.[10]

In concrete terms, women were encouraged to become more assertive with their doctors by requesting clear and understandable explanations of their diagnosis and treatment and by seeking second opinions. Most important, patient advocacy presumed that the woman diagnosed with breast cancer was an informed consumer, "to be treated as a full member of the team caring for her, with respect, honesty, and dignity."[11]

As a consequence of this idea's spreading influence, the psychosocial care of women with life-threatening diseases began to change. A crucial tool for sustaining a partnership between doctor and patient was the availability of information on state-of-the-art treatments. This information was a primary instrument for managing and minimizing the fear and anxiety associated with a breast cancer diagnosis. Also important was getting emotional and psychological support from women going through similar experiences. Some physicians began to encourage women to form breast cancer support groups affiliated with hospital and breast care centers. Many oncology nurses took up the cudgel of patient advocacy, doing what they could to share information with women whose doctors displayed traditional, paternalistic behavior.[12] At the same time the American Cancer Society already had a Reach to Recovery program that sent former breast cancer patients to visit women after their mastectomy, offering emotional support and certain accoutrements (such as a prosthesis) for their physical recovery. In addition, the National Cancer Institute had begun a national toll-free hotline in the mid-1970s.[13]

Not surprising, other organizations gradually emerged to meet women's needs for information and peer support. Some of them were national nonprofit organizations, such as the National Alliance for Breast Cancer Organizations, located in New York City. These national organizations, along with local support groups affiliated with cancer centers and breast care facilities, became important resources and breeding grounds for the political advocacy that erupted in 1991. According to Amy Langer, these organizations epitomized one stage along a continuum of awareness that may lead to the ultimate act of political advocacy, which occurred in the evolution of the movement as a whole, but is also a process that repeats itself daily as women who are newly diagnosed with breast cancer work through the challenges of their own treatment and recovery, and then turn to the "bigger picture"—the process of changing the face of breast cancer for others.[14]

Technological Changes

The proportion of women diagnosed with breast cancer in the late 1980s was larger than ever before due to technological changes associated with improved mammography facilities, as well as new governmental and private initiatives to screen women age forty and older. During 1982–1991, 1,315,000 women were diagnosed and 404,300 died. Between 1987 and 1991 almost a third of all new breast cancer cases were in women ages thirty-five to fifty-four. Many of the leaders of the newly emerging breast cancer advocacy groups fell within this age range and were diagnosed with breast cancer (Table 4.1).[15] Still, the disease is most prominent among women older than sixty.

Table 4.1. Breast Cancer Occurrence and Recurrence among Early Movement Entrepreneurs

Entrepreneurs	First diagnosis (all stages of disease) 25–55 years	Recurrence 25–55 years	"Caring others" of those dead or living with the disease
National Breast Cancer Coalition	1	1	2
California/Breast Cancer Action	2	1	
California/Bay Area Breast Cancer Network	2		
California/Save Ourselves	2		
Massachusetts group	1		
Arizona group	1		
Kentucky group	2		1
Virginia group	4		
New York group	2		1
Vermont group	1		

Source: Author's data.

Note: The early movement happened before May 1991.

College-Educated and Politically Savvy Women

How did these newly diagnosed women feel? Having gone to college in significantly higher numbers than previous generations and as beneficiaries of the liberating changes for women and minorities of the 1960s, the breast cancer advocates were more politically assertive and skilled than their counterparts of earlier eras. By the 1980s women were voting in increasing numbers and showing signs of independence in their electoral behavior and in their attitudes on such issues as social welfare. Moreover, women's political assertiveness went beyond changes in voting behavior to a willingness to run for public office, especially at the state level. Journalists labeled the election of 1992 "The Year of the Woman" because of the record number of women seeking elective office.[16]

Apart from politics, the growing service sector offered women many new career opportunities after the 1960s. Indeed, the activists who spearheaded the breast cancer movement at the local and national levels were professionals—teachers, doctors, nurses, administrators, accountants, senior and mid-level managers, writers, salespersons, and business owners.

Quality of Life and the Rise in Living Standards

The women who spearheaded the movement were part of a generation that had an unprecedented amount of economic and physical security and a broader professional middle class oriented to the growing service sector of an advanced industrial society. Accompanying this broad cultural change were new values that deemphasized material and defense issues and emphasized quality of life.[17]

These major social and cultural changes were shaping a new breed of woman. Still, the most immediate impetus for collective entrepreneurialism came from women's reaction to their own diagnosis of breast cancer. Most important, these social changes shaped women's perception and reaction to their diagnosis. All the grassroots leaders, plus one of the three who planned and organized the national coalition, had been diagnosed with breast cancer.

The Role of Experience in Forming Collective Entrepreneurs

Personal experiences with diagnosis and treatment produced intense anger from the self-confident and professionally well-connected baby boomer women who organized the first breast cancer advocacy groups. Their lives were in jeopardy—a reality especially horrifying to younger women and younger families. Although treatments had become more refined since the 1970s, they did not guarantee a cure. Some of the movement's prominent activists died before seeing the fruit of their political efforts. The late Sherry Kohlenberg of the Virginia

Breast Cancer Foundation is remembered for her fiery and eloquent speech on the Washington Mall in 1992. In Massachusetts Susan Shapiro died shortly after providing the impetus for an advocacy and support organization.

Breast cancer treatments had not changed much over the years, and they were to varying degrees disfiguring, toxic, and debilitating. The psychological and physical suffering these women endured made them feel let down by the political system. NBCC President Fran Visco, a lawyer and antiwar activist during the 1960s who had been diagnosed in 1987, summed up their reaction:

> I was shocked and I was angry. Before my diagnosis, it never occurred to me that I should fear breast cancer—I had no family history of the disease and believed that I was safe. When I discovered [that] the number of women who died of breast cancer in the last ten years exceeds the number of Americans killed in combat in all wars from World War I through the Persian Gulf War, I could not understand why this country was not up in arms about this disease.[18]

Organizational Spark and the Shared Experience

These women had anger in common, but what brought them together to organize a national advocacy movement? What was the spark that fired up small groups of women in different parts of the country? One of the activists from those heady days characterized the spark as "something that just erupted in women's souls about this time," or as "an unrelated collection of events and an explosive moment."[19] In any event, strong feelings did ripple through these groups of women as they agreed that the government did not take their health condition seriously enough. The women gradually began to interact with one another and to share their experiences with the disease, their treatment traumas, and their anxieties. From this shared powerful experience emerged the collective impulse to organize.

Shared Experience and Collective Entrepreneurialism

Although limited in number, the breast cancer advocacy cases help us understand how the grassroots leaders came together. Christopher Foreman's research shows that the entrepreneurial creators of what he terms "grassroots victim organizations" were mostly women who had suffered a traumatic experience in the context of a personal health problem. And these leaders exhibited "a very strong, even consuming, personal stake in a health or safety-related issue."[20]

An even more illuminating study shows that one of several "trigger events" for AIDS activism occurred when roughly a dozen infected men attended an AIDS forum and met as a group in a hotel hospitality suite set aside for them. They realized they had "experienced similar patronizing treatment" and decided to take political action, appointing two spokespersons to "give voice to their collective discontent." [21]

Similar stages can be identified in the development of a multiple leadership for breast cancer advocacy; risk-takers had already gathered for some common interest or concern that did not ostensibly involve political organizing. Such a meeting, however, raises a level of awareness that steers some to political action. Collective entrepreneurial risk-taking thus originates in the interaction of individuals with a shared concern: their diagnosis of breast cancer. The social opportunities for this interaction took place, with one exception, in settings related to the disease. For example, some of the women met one another by virtue of their professional interest in the disease; some through a chance meeting at the doctor's office; and some, most important, through attending breast cancer support groups affiliated with hospitals or operating independently in the community. In these cases women came together to seek psychosocial support for their health condition and were propelled down the road to political advocacy.

Most of these "sparks" that ignited a movement were geographically concentrated along the West and East Coasts, and most of them occurred between 1989 and May 1991. But there were a few exceptions. Kentucky was home to one of the earliest support groups, started in 1975 by an English nurse affiliated with the University Hospital of Kentucky in Lexington. This group became politicized when Doris Rosenbaum, with the help of her husband (a radiation oncologist), helped form a breast cancer coalition of health organizations as early as 1988. The coalition's first political undertaking was to lobby the state legislature for insurance coverage for mammography screening.[22]

In New York the grassroots group "1 In 9" was formed when two lifetime friends and coworkers, Francine Kritchek and Marie Quinn, joined a support group sponsored by Cancer Care. After attending meetings for a year, they determined that "breast cancer must be addressed at the political level." [23] Quinn, who "had never been involved in political action," called Barbara Balaban, director of the Adelphi Breast Cancer Support Program on Long Island. Quinn wanted Balaban to put her in touch with others "to help women become empowered." [24] Upon receiving crucial initial support, Balaban's organization was the home for the group until it had enough resources to find a place of its own. Fifty women attended a November 1990 meeting that resulted in New York's first organized breast cancer advocacy group.[25]

Similarly, a support group planted the seeds for the San Francisco advocacy group, Breast Cancer Action (BCA). Two of the cofounders, Elenore Pred and Belle Shayer, attended a retreat under the aegis of an organization (Commonweal) that offered group therapy sessions to help people deal with life-threatening illnesses. According to Shayer, the first treasurer of BCA, the group consisted of six women and one man who had bonded, "liv[ing] very closely together, talking about their fears, their anger at their misdiagnoses, and their ultimate fear of life and death. [They also] talked a lot about needing to do something."[26]

Pred and Shayer joined a metastatic breast cancer support group that met every Saturday morning at the Cancer Support Community in San Francisco. This group was already thinking about "doing something" more than merely talking about their feelings and treatment options.[27] In July of 1990 twelve women gathered at a friend's house to form BCA. The women chose a name for the organization, elected officers, offered donations, and discussed strategies and goals. Pred was the president, and others in the founding group played a crucial, though less visible, role. Susan Claymon, who excelled in administrative matters, served as the vice president, while Shayer, an accountant by profession, was the treasurer (Table 4.2).

Within this context of collective decision making, Pred was exceptionally successful in garnering media attention. She made television appearances on the *Today Show* and *20/20* and gave interviews to magazines such as *US News & World Report*.[28] Local newspapers also focused on her story, while other print media included Pred with other activists in broader articles on breast cancer and women's health.[29] By telling her own story and representing a small organization, Pred brought attention to the disease and shared her concerns with women who read about her or saw her on television. In this way she provided the spark for other women to take political action. For example, Donna Horn from Phoenix, Arizona (who later initiated a local advocacy group), contacted Pred after reading a newspaper article about her.[30]

Table 4.2.   Founders' First Interaction and the Collective Decision to Organize

Founders' first interaction	National Breast Cancer Coalition	Virginia group	Save Ourselves California	Breast Cancer Action California	Bay Area Breast Cancer Network, California	New York group	Kentucky group
Support group		X	X	X		X	X
Doctor's office					X		
Professional or personal interest	X						

Source: Author's data.

In Virginia a chance viewing of Elenore Pred on the *Today Show* by a Richmond support group member became the catalyst for action. Mary Jo Kahn, a former president of the Virginia Breast Cancer Foundation, recalls the early beginnings of her advocacy group:

> One of our newest members, Patti Goodall, was in the hospital getting chemo when she heard on the *Today Show* that Elenore Pred was a San Francisco activist saying that she was planning a Mother's Day rally in California to protest. She was so taken by this woman and what she was doing that she came back to the support group meeting the following week really red faced and angry, saying that there's not enough money for breast cancer research; we need to protest, too. Let's do a Mother's Day rally. This was in April 1991. We said we had four weeks 'til Mother's Day. Well we can't do a big rally; we can do what we can do, and we said, okay, let's do it. It was a small support group—it probably had twelve members max. And we asked the hospital to help us, and the American Cancer Society to help us, and we put the rally on at the capitol, and we got ourselves, our friends, our families, and a few other people to come, and it wasn't big and it was probably eighty people. But we were pleased for a first foray into activism, we thought we were successful.[31]

Physicians' Offices

Although breast cancer support groups were pivotal in advancing the advocacy initiative, other places proved important, too. In San Jose, for example, the Bay Area Breast Cancer Network organized in response to the initiative of Sheila Swanson, a registered nurse and breast cancer patient, and her friend Beth Ellis. In 1987 these women met at a clinic when they had to decide what to do about surgery options after having bilateral mastectomies. Ellis came up with the idea of forming a support group, which began in a rented room in Los Gatos, meeting once a week for six weeks. As more women cycled through the group, there began to develop a network of informed people who were upset with the breast cancer diagnosis and mortality rates, as well as with the little progress that had been made in finding a cure.[32]

Swanson and Ellis joined a national breast cancer support organization called Y-ME in 1990, which "empowered them."[33] They held their first advocacy meeting in Swanson's living room. Fifteen of the twenty-five attendees became members of the new organization, the Bay Area Breast Cancer Network, a chapter of Y-ME.

In Sacramento a young nurse, Ellen Hobbs, was diagnosed with breast cancer in October 1990 and told that in addition to her mastectomy she should have a bone marrow transplant. This led her into battle with her insurance company over financing the operation. A friend suggested that Hobbs get politically involved, so she contacted the headquarters of

Y-ME in Chicago to see if there was a local group. There was not, but the organization gave her the name of a nearby woman named Cathy Ferris, and the two of them got together and decided to demonstrate on the west steps of the capitol in Sacramento. At the same time, Ferris had read an article in *Time* on breast cancer that mentioned Swanson. Ferris called Swanson and told her about the idea of organizing a peaceful demonstration in Sacramento (Hobbs suggested Mother's Day for the demonstration). Swanson liked the idea and arranged for other groups to meet, including BCA, the National Organization for Women, and ACTUP.

The two exceptions to this collective entrepreneurial decision making model were Vermont and Boston, which had single entrepreneurial initiatives.[34] The Boston advocacy group, for example, got started in early fall 1989 as a result of the initiative of thirty-eight-year-old Susan Shapiro. Shapiro wrote a thoughtful article on breast cancer in the local feminist newspaper, *Sojourner,* asking why there was no woman's community for helping breast cancer patients through their diagnosis and treatment. She also drew attention to the lack of a cure, rising breast cancer rates, and the inadequate amount of research money compared with the amount spent on AIDS.

> The number of breast cancer deaths in a single year is greater than the total of all AIDS deaths to date. Yet there has been no commemorative effort, no organized demand for education and increased funding, little public attention.[35]

Near the end of the article, Shapiro, who had lost her mother to cancer and had recently been diagnosed herself, sounded a rallying cry for political organization. Though stating categorically that she had no desire to take funds away from AIDS, she argued:

> There is a lot we can learn from the inspiring work and commitment of AIDS activists and the gay community. We can do more than make occasional donations to the American Cancer Society. We must tap into the wealth of human resources at the local level and begin to organize. Cancer is clearly a feminist issue. We need an organization—of women, for women—that will encompass political action, direct service, and education . . . We must look at cancer research and funding: how much is going toward prevention or alternatives to chemotherapy and how much towards slightly improving the same old drugs that are never going to be very effective. In addition to political action, we must provide widespread education about cancer prevention as well as treatment.[36]

At the very end of the article in fine print was an announcement of a meeting at the Cambridge YMCA. This ultimately led to the founding of the Women's Community Cancer Project, a cancer information, education, support, and advocacy group. Shapiro attended two further meetings before she became very ill and succumbed to the disease. Still, she "left behind a legacy of an energized and enraged group of women." [37]

Interacting Face-to-Face and Forming the National Organization

At the national level, shared experience resulted from professional and personal interest in the disease. The entrepreneurial players at this level were Dr. Susan Love, Susan Hester, and Amy Langer. When the first edition of Love's book was published in 1990, she toured the country to market and promote it.[38] That tour made her fully aware of the grassroots groups that had organized on the East and West Coasts. As the tour progressed, Love began to realize how deep women's anger was, and how ready they were to do something.

> The key moment for me was in Salt Lake City in June 1990, when I gave a talk for 600 women. It was the middle of the afternoon, during the week, and the audience was mostly older women. It was a pretty long talk, and at the end I said, 'We don't have the answers, and I don't know what we have to do to make President Bush wake up and do something about breast cancer. Maybe we should march topless on the White House.' I was making a wise crack, hoping to end a somber talk with a little lightness.[39]

The audience's response was amazing. "Women came up to [her] asking when the march was, [and] how they could sign up for it and what they could do to help organize it." Love saw the opportunity to form an umbrella advocacy movement "to give these women the hook they needed to begin organizing." [40] After further consultations with leaders of women's health groups, planning meetings took place in New York and included Amy Langer from the National Alliance for Breast Cancer Organizations; Sharon Greene, executive director of Y-ME; Ann Maguire of the Women's Community Cancer Project; Kim Calder from Cancer Care; Elenore Pred from Breast Cancer Action; and a representative from New York's Can Act.[41]

In Love's words, "We set up several task forces to figure out how we'd go about it and what our goals would be." [42] A May meeting was arranged, with the resources of each organization tapped to recruit interested parties and to raise money for operating expenses. Langer, for example, contacted several hundred groups and individual members from her organization's national mailing list to alert them to the upcoming meeting. At the same time, she raised $8,000.[43] The other organizations followed suit. As Hester stated, "We did a huge mailing and everyone interested in health came." [44]

At the May meeting Love and Langer pitched their ideas to approximately 150 representatives of seventy-five organizations across the country. The fundamental issue was "the goal of eradicating breast cancer, and doing this in an intelligent way [with a] focus on the causes and cure not [through] new chemotherapy drugs." [45] In attendance were representatives from the American Cancer Society, a longtime presence on Capitol Hill; the Linda Creed Foundation from Baltimore; SHARE:

Support Services for Women with Breast or Ovarian Cancer from New York; the Adelphi Breast Cancer Support Program; and newly formed support and advocacy organizations such as the Virginia Breast Cancer Foundation.[46]

The response was hugely encouraging. Love stated, "We were over-whelmed, and we started the National Breast Cancer Coalition on the spot."[47] Fran Visco, the first and current president of the NBCC, de-scribed the meeting as one where "the energy, commitment, and resolve in that room were electrifying. From that meeting came the first Board of the Coalition—and a movement that has defied even our expectations."[48]

The coalition grew at a startling pace, attracting an increasing num-ber of nonprofit organizations to the cause while developing a substantial grassroots base. Within four months the NBCC had organized a 600,000-person letter writing campaign that highlighted the ravages of breast can-cer and urged legislators to increase funding for research. The next two years witnessed sympathetic media coverage of an impressive lobbying agenda that included press conferences on Capitol Hill, congressional testimony, Mother's Day rallies and marches in thirty-eight states, 1 mil-lion petitions delivered to the White House, as well as letters to and visits with members of Congress.

A New Political Environment and Collective Entrepreneurialism

There is a critical link between social factors and collective entrepre-neurialism. Indeed, this study supports a hybrid theory of interest group formation.[49] Neither social changes nor entrepreneurial efforts alone can explain the formation of the NBCC. In other words, gradual social changes during the 1970s and 1980s set the stage for both the grassroots movement and the collective leadership of the precoalition days. These changes included the increased use of mammography by women in their forties and fifties, a more open social climate for public discussion and ex-pression of the disease, and the growth of breast cancer information and support groups. Baby boomer women with similar medical problems were able to find each other and share their experiences. Most important, pro-fessional, politically assertive, and college-educated women became in-tensely dissatisfied with breast cancer treatment options and expressed their discontent. Even though many breast cancer patients were older women, there were enough patients in the baby boomer cohort to pro-duce the initial leadership that mobilized the movement.

Breast cancer support groups were the venue for this interaction and collective leadership. Women met and talked, absorbing norms that pro-moted nonhierarchical ways of relating. Sharing, collaborating, and cooper-ating became the new norms that were readily transferable during the process of forming political advocacy groups. Inherent gender differences, reinforced by socialization, may incline women rather than men to use a collective leadership pattern in this manner.

The NBCC has shown no signs of slowing down. Building on its fragile base of May 1991, it has added considerable numbers of new recruits (both organizational and individual) to its ranks. The NBCC mounted several national petition drives during the 1990s, with a grassroots presence in at least forty-five states by 2000. Moreover, when activists dropped out, either from exhaustion or death, their natural replacements came from those newly diagnosed. Thus the organization has a continual fresh pool of potential recruits—critical for its favored lobbying strategy of peaceful marches, petition drives, rallies, press conferences, and visits with members of Congress.

Led by President Fran Visco and working board members, the NBCC has conformed to a more typical hierarchical organizational structure. At the same time, grassroots groups have mirrored the national organization, many of which have evolved into nonprofit organizations with tax-exempt status. Broadening its legislative agenda to include such things as increased access to breast cancer health care, the principle of a patients' bill of rights, and safeguards against genetic information discrimination in health insurance and employment, the NBCC's primary goal remains more funding for breast cancer research. The organization is firmly entrenched in the cancer research policy arena, running at full throttle, an organizational expression of the passionate obduracy of the late Sherry Kohlenberg, an early activist who declared: "I will not go silently. I will go shouting in the dark night; enough is enough." [50]

Notes

1. This was initially known as the Breast Cancer Coalition. See Maureen Hogan Casamayou, *The Politics of Breast Cancer* (Washington, D.C.: Georgetown University, 2001), 7.
2. Susan M. Love with Karen Lindsey, *Dr. Susan Love's Breast Book*, 2d ed. (Reading, Penn.: Addison Wesley, 1995), 518.
3. Ibid.
4. Jeffrey M. Berry, "On the Origins of Public Interest Groups: A Test of Two Theories," *Polity* 10 (spring 1978): 382; see David B. Truman, *The Governmental Process: Political Interest and Public Opinion* (New York: Alfred Knopf, 1951) for the original source of "Disturbance Theory"; Robert H. Salisbury, "An Exchange Theory of Interest groups," *Midwest Journal of Political Science* 13 (spring 1969): 1–32.
5. Berry, "On the Origins of Public Interest Groups."
6. Roberta Altman, *Waking Up, Fighting Back: The Politics of Breast Cancer* (Boston: Little, Brown and Company, 1996), 242.
7. Rose Kushner, *Alternatives: New Developments in the War Against Breast Cancer* (New York: Warner, 1984), xii.
8. Anne S. Kasper, "Rose Kushner: Breast Cancer As a Personal and Professional Issue," in *Rose Kushner Papers 1929–1990 Collection* (Cambridge: Harvard University, 1983), folder 2, 4.
9. *Our Bodies Ourselves* (Cambridge: Boston Women's Health Book Collective, 1973).

10. This concept is adapted from Patricia Siplon, "Action Equals Life: The Power of Community in AIDS Political Activism" (Ph.D. diss., Brandeis University, 1997), 91.
11. Amy S. Langer and Karen Hassey Dow, "The Breast Cancer Advocacy Movement and Nursing," *Oncology Nursing* 1 (3): 2 (1994).
12. Ibid., 3.
13. Ibid.
14. Ibid., 3.
15. Judith A. Johnson, "Breast Cancer Research," *CRS Report for Congress* (Washington, D.C.: Congressional Research Service, Library of Congress, February 8, 1996), 2.
16. Elizabeth Adell Cook, Sue Thomas, and Clyde Wilcox, eds., *The Year of the Woman: Myths and Realities* (Boulder, Colo.: Westview, 1994).
17. Ronald Inglehart, *Culture Shift in Advanced Industrialized Society* (Princeton: Princeton University, 1990).
18. National Breast Cancer Coalition, *The National Breast Cancer Coalition: A Grassroots Advocacy Effort, Annual Report: 1991–1993* (Washington, D.C.: NBCC, 1993), 4.
19. Quotations from interviews with breast cancer advocates.
20. Christopher H. Foreman Jr., "Grassroots Victim Organizations: Mobilizing for Personal and Public Health," in *Interest Group Politics*, 4th ed. (Washington D.C.: CQ Press, 1992), 36.
21. Siplon, "Action Equals Life," 179.
22. Doris Rosenbaum, interview by the author, July 1995.
23. Francine Kritchek, interview by the author, October 1998.
24. Barbara Balaban, interview by the author, June 1995.
25. Ibid.
26. Belle Shayer, interview by the author, May 1995.
27. Marilyn McGregor, interview by the author, October 14, 1998; also see Altman, *The Politics of Breast Cancer,* 302–303.
28. Erica E. Goode, "Fighting for their Lives," *U.S. News and World Report,* August 26, 1991, 70.
29. Katherine Fong, "Fighting Breast Cancer," *San Francisco Weekly,* March 13, 1991, 1; Janny Scott, "Women's New Push for Health," *Los Angeles Times,* April 30, 1991, A1; Jane Gross, "Turning Disease into Political Cause: First AIDS, and Now Breast Cancer," *New York Times,* October 2, 1991, final edition, B1.
30. Donna Horn, interview by the author, June 1995.
31. Mary Jo Kahn, interview by the author, May 1995.
32. Sheila Swanson, interview by the author, May 1995.
33. Ibid.
34. Ellen Crowley and Ginny Soffa, interview by the author, June 1995.
35. Susan Shapiro, "Cancer As a Feminist Issue," *Sojourner: The Women's Forum,* September 1989, 18.
36. Ibid.
37. Ellen Crowley, "Grassroots Healing," in *Confronting Cancer, Constructing Change: New Perspectives on Women,* ed. Midge Stockter, vol. 2 (Chicago: Third Side, 1993), 201–206.
38. Love with Lindsey, *Dr. Susan Love's Breast Book,* 518.
39. Ibid.
40. Ibid.
41. Ibid., 519.
42. Ibid.
43. Meeting with Amy Langer, May 1995.
44. Ibid.
45. Fran Visco, interview by the author, November 1993.
46. NIH staff person, interview by the author, November 1993.

47. Love with Lindsey, *Dr. Susan Love's Breast Book*, 519.
48. National Breast Cancer Coalition, *The National Breast Cancer Coalition, A Grassroots Advocacy Effort*, 4.
49. Berry, *On the Origins of Public Interest Groups*, 384.
50. Susan Ferraro, "You Can't Look Away Anymore: The Anguished Politics of Breast Cancer," *New York Times Magazine*, August 15, 1993, 27.

5

Just Another Tool?
How Environmental Groups Use the Internet
Christopher J. Bosso and Michael Thomas Collins

Since the mid-1990s the Internet has offered the potential to revolutionize American politics. Candidates, consultants, organizers, and lobbyists envision seamless communication between policy-makers and carefully identified sets of citizens. Large membership groups in particular have been eager to harness the Internet's power, seeing it as a way to create individual communications tailored to 535 members of Congress. But as with many Web-based strategies, results have not always met expectations. Still, email is a powerful tool, and particularly important for Congress in the wake of 2001's anthrax attacks through the U.S. Postal Service.

In this chapter Christopher J. Bosso and Michael Thomas Collins present some much-needed data on interest groups and Internet usage. After assessing the many possible ways that interest groups can use the Internet, the authors examine actual Web use by eighteen major environmental groups. Among the most notable findings is that distinctions between traditional, inside strategies of person-to-person lobbying and outside approaches of grassroots lobbying may be unimportant, given groups' ability to deliver timely and specialized electronic messages to targeted congressional offices.

Bosso and Collins cannot offer any definitive answer to the question of how Web strategies and practices will affect interest representation in American politics. But the authors are confident that Internet usage will grow more sophisticated among both policy-makers and citizens. Given the rapid evolution of Internet communication in the 1990s, predictions are hard to make. Nevertheless, the authors see the makings of a revolution in communications, one—like all revolutions—that has no preordained outcome.

Christopher J. Bosso thanks Northeastern University graduate students Sabine Schutte-Morris, Brendan Cullen, Wendy Surinach, and Sheilagh Scollin for their assistance. Michael Thomas Collins extends special thanks to Cary Coglianese from the John F. Kennedy School of Government, Harvard University. Michael Collins's views are not necessarily those of e-guana.net.

The Promise

It's a cliché by now: the Internet is a revolution. As Microsoft founder Bill Gates wrote, "We are watching something historic happen, and it will affect the world seismically, rocking us the same way the discovery of the scientific method, the invention of printing, and the arrival of the Industrial Age did."[1]

But, as with any revolution, nobody really knows how or how much the Internet will change our lives. For example, how will it change democratic politics? It could, as Anthony Wilhelm observes, usher in a cyber-democracy that finally fulfills the "democratic values (equity, access, and diversity, to name a few) in the social practices of everyday life."[2] Conversely, as Robert Putnam suggests, the Internet could accelerate erosion of the relationships among individuals that make up the nation's "social capital," the reservoir of civic participation essential to maintaining democracy.[3] It could empower the powerless, or it could simply reinforce existing inequities in resources, access, and leverage. Every scenario commands some plausibility.

Our goal here is to look at a modest part of this puzzle: How the Internet may shape the organizational life of established interest groups. We do so by assessing how the nation's major environmental organizations are using their websites to convey information, communicate with supporters and members, raise money, and, perhaps, foster communities of action. Though our scope is constrained, the broader issues we raise are important inasmuch as the Internet promises, or threatens, to fundamentally change how interests—those already organized and those yet to be—aggregate, mobilize, and wield influence.

Given the current debate about social capital, we are intrigued most by the Internet's potential to invigorate the role of dues-paying members of major national public interest organizations, who today seem little more than a passive source of funds for organizational maintenance and numerical backdrops for conventional lobbying tactics.[4] At the very least, the Internet gives organizations the technological capacity to communicate with and disseminate information to members and supporters more quickly, more conveniently, and at a lower cost than ever. Such lower transaction and distribution costs could enhance the connection between groups and supporters, create more convenient and perhaps more meaningful forms of participation for members, and, as a result, aid in member recruitment and retention. Lower barriers to the exchange of information and ideas, paired with the way the Internet can enhance a group's technical capacity to direct and target such information, could also increase the efficacy of grassroots action. Naturally, such profound changes will also pose challenges to the groups, whether in their relationship with members or in increased competition among groups to be heard in the vast sea of electronic information.

We focus here on those major groups that Bosso elsewhere labeled the "flagships of American environmental activism" because they exemplify the organizational challenges facing all established public interest groups.[5] To do so, we lay out purposes for which the Internet might be used and then assess how it is actually being used by major environmental groups to further organizational goals. Given space constraints, this assessment is broad and somewhat impressionistic, but it is a start. Revolutions take time to figure out.

How Groups Might Use the Internet

Money aside, information is the currency of the realm for the average interest group. It can be used to mobilize believers, educate policymakers, or influence the terms of policy debate. In this regard, the "information superhighway" provides a heretofore unavailable mechanism by which groups of all sizes and types can transmit vast amounts of information to more people more quickly, at a lower cost, and with greater convenience to both the sender and recipient.

For groups, the Internet dramatically lowers per-unit distribution costs, whether information is delivered directly by email or is placed on a website. The Internet also makes transmission almost instantaneous, enabling groups to capitalize better on breaking issues. For potential and actual supporters, the Internet offers speed and convenience. Search engines and directories make it easy to find an organization by name or by issue—much more convenient than finding an address or phone number in the phone book, requesting information, and waiting for it to arrive by mail. Well-designed websites enable people to gather information more easily, make a contribution, and contact policymakers. As a result, any organization, regardless of membership size or resource base, should be able to offer a more attractive range of benefits in the form of timely and content-rich information, relevant services, and even mechanisms by which members can interact with one another.

According to Cliff Landesman, organizations can use the Internet for eight general purposes—publicity, public education, communication, research, fund-raising, advocacy, volunteer recruitment, and service provision.[6] We have collapsed his list into a few overarching themes as a starting point for discussing the possibilities for organized interests.

Getting the Word Out

For any group the easiest and most obvious use of the Internet is to publicize the group and its activities. Of course, as Landesman observes, there is "a fine line between grabbing the public's attention and educating the public about an important social problem."[7] The first must come before the second. And unlike most other forms of outreach, a well-designed website can grab attention, publicize, educate—even mobilize—all at the same time and in a far subtler way than through direct mail, newspaper advertising, or curbside proselytizing.

To pose but one scenario, a high school student doing a research project on recycling may be directed by a search engine like Google to the website of the Natural Resources Defense Council (www.nrdc.org), which contains extensive data on the topic as well as links to related information. At minimum, the website makes it easier—too easy, more than a few teachers might grouse—for the student to put the research paper together. Along the way, perhaps the student also comes to care more about recycling and maybe about the environment in general. The ideal outcome, at least from the organization's perspective, is that this nascent commitment also translates into a new dues-paying supporter. For any organization, the promise of such multiple outcomes makes the website look like a pretty good bang for the buck.

Such a multiplier effect is found in Scorecard (www.scorecard.org), a website created by Environmental Defense (formerly the Environmental Defense Fund). Scorecard pairs a powerful database with mapping technology provided by the Geographic Information System (GIS) to enable residents to find out about local pollution threats down to the neighborhood level, a "right to know" element deemed necessary for energizing local interest and action.[8] Beyond this informational role, Scorecard also provides email action alerts, moderated discussion boards—organized by issue and geography—and directories of local environmental groups. Environmental Defense also offers an interface that allows these local groups to set up their own gateways to the tools on Scorecard, a way of enabling smaller and less resource rich organizations to feature these powerful interactive features on their own websites. Scorecard is but a technologically rich example of the ways in which a website can enable an organization to communicate with a large and diverse audience.

Groups also can get the word out in more direct ways, most obviously through email to members and other supporters. "It would be hard to overemphasize the advantages, cost savings, or numerous virtues of email," Landesman notes. "It is as fast and as reliable as the phone, while compensating for the frailties of human memory by preserving a written record, as does the mail."[9] In this regard, email encourages clarity of expression by remaining a form of "written" communication, in contrast to the fleeting, sometimes muddled messages conveyed by telephone, television, or even direct conversation.

Email also allows *asynchronous* communication; that is, you can read your email on your own time and at your own pace, rather than playing telephone tag, attending a meeting, or responding to a canvasser's doorbell at dinnertime. Moreover, unlike such mass media as television and radio, which are typically unidirectional and less easily targeted "broadcast" technologies, the Internet makes it possible to "narrow-cast"—to target media and information to discrete audiences, with individualized adjustments made according to the stored electronic profile of the recipient. A group thus can customize its email messages to different subsets of its supporters depending on particular issues and areas of concern.

The Web's multimedia capabilities are particularly intriguing. Unlike most forms of communication—television is an arguable exception—Internet communication can occur simultaneously in audio, video, graphical, and text formats, the efficacy of which should increase as broadband technologies advance and gain greater coverage. For example, organizations can now offer targeted visual and text information on local pollution hazards, real-time images such as the World Wildlife Fund's links to "Panda-cams," and video presentations on current controversies like the Bush administration's proposal to allow oil exploration in the Arctic National Wildlife Refuge. To use a market analogy, the savvy interest group regards a website as a unified multimedia platform capable of delivering a wide array of products directly to discrete elements of its diverse customer base.

The Internet also offers qualitative advantages to groups in the form of bidirectional communication. That is, an organization's leaders and members can more easily communicate with *one another* either through chat rooms or in real time using mechanisms akin to AOL Instant Messenger. These forms of communication are second only to face-to-face contact, which requires geographical and temporal proximity. Other electronic forms of bidirectional communication, such as the telephone, can connect only two people. And conference calls present technological and cognitive problems. After all, how many people can realistically take part in a conference call without causing confusion?

By contrast, the Internet acts as a one-to-many channel or even a many-to-many channel. Interaction among individuals through the Internet can be either synchronous or asynchronous, local or global, thus holding promise for a revolution in interest group dynamics. For example, the solidary benefits so difficult to provide in large groups could potentially exist in online communities, even with large numbers of people. These many-to-many communication channels, backed by robust database-powered websites, might make it easier to mobilize group members and supporters.

Of course, nothing so new and big comes without a price, and the Internet can create new pressures on organizations and their leaders. With the exception of direct email, the Internet is a rather passive form of communication. After all, contact usually has to be initiated by the user, so an organization's website is useless until someone makes an effort to visit it. An email newsletter can enable a group to make its own overtures, but concerns over privacy, Internet "spam," and viruses have made people wary about direct email, even from trusted sources. Thus interest groups, like their for-profit brethren, must find innovative ways to attract and hold lots of eyeballs. And these methods can get expensive now that the free or low-cost banner advertisements common during the Web's infancy are fading memories.

Additionally, the ability to store and categorize massive amounts of information online might raise members' and donors' expectations about organizational transparency. Supporters know more about the group and have a convenient channel through which to voice opinions about its activities and operations; this access could erode the relative insulation from member interference that group leaders typically enjoy when making decisions. Lowering these barriers to access also offers greater choice and convenience to potential supporters, forcing groups within a single policy or issue sector to compete harder for members' resources and loyalty. In such a context, organizations that rely on members' dues but that fail to adopt effective Internet strategies will fall behind.

Mobilizing Supporters

The Internet's lower technological barriers to the exchange of information and ideas, as well as its potential for enabling a group to effectively target recipients of this information, theoretically should enhance a group's capacity to mobilize members and supporters. The benefits should be greatest for organizations that promote grassroots, or "outside," activities, such as demonstrations or product boycotts, which logically will focus on deploying interactive tools such as action alerts, online petitions, and chat rooms for local members.[10] Organizations that depend on volunteers and local activists would find these tools especially useful for nurturing the grassroots.

For groups that do not traditionally use grassroots tactics, the Internet can enable the groups to start doing so without extensive cost or major immediate changes in organizational culture. For example, for most of its thirty-five-year history Environmental Defense relied almost exclusively on lawsuits, cost-benefit analyses, and negotiated settlements with corporations, not the kinds of grassroots activism long promoted by the Sierra Club or Greenpeace. With the Internet, however, Environmental Defense can develop its own grassroots of sorts. For example, its email Action Network purportedly has enrolled thousands of supporters to contact Congress and other policymakers on fast-breaking issues.[11] As noted earlier, Environmental Defense also allows other environmental and population groups to piggyback on its Scorecard website, making coalition building that much easier. These cyber-activities aren't going to turn Environmental Defense into the Sierra Club any time soon—Environmental Defense still has no local chapters—but with the Internet it can energize its grassroots in a political context where such mobilization is a necessary, albeit not sufficient, condition to claim any clout with policymakers.

Beyond the major organizations, the Internet enables new groups to grow in size and impact more quickly than would have been possible earlier. For example, the Rainforest Action Network (RAN), established in 1985, has transformed its "off-line" campaigns to influence policymakers and corporate leaders into online electronic alerts that generate faxes to corporate executives. "By tapping into a worldwide network of free fax servers," argues Tom Price, "RAN is able to deliver faxes to the targeted executives at essentially no cost. The messages are forwarded as email to fax servers within the local calling area of the targeted executive. The fax then is sent to its final destination as a toll-free telephone call." [12]

The ease with which RAN can use the Internet for such tactics, combined with the group's focus on targeting the brand images of companies whose actions or products generate environmentally controversial practices, has been an apparent success for the organization, which purportedly deployed more than 3,500 electronic activists in mid-2000. [13] This does not seem like a large number, but the probability that each of these individuals sent email copies of RAN's messages to friends and fellow activists magnifies the group's potential outreach—and impact—beyond what numbers alone imply. [14] For example, RAN used its email campaign to organize concerted protests against Home Depot, the nation's largest home-improvement store, until the store agreed to stop selling lumber harvested from endangered forests in the United States and abroad. [15]

A much-examined example of the Internet's potential for grassroots purposes was the organization of the Million Mom March against gun violence on Mother's Day 2000. The effort started with a website created by a single individual, Donna Dees-Thomases, dedicated to fostering stronger gun control. It quickly grew into a national configuration of local groups of involved mothers based largely on the information and tools available on the website. [16] Organizers of the march built a network of national and local websites to facilitate communication between organizers and participants in the demonstration in Washington, D.C., and also used the Internet to generate widespread television and newspaper coverage. The website contained interactive tools such as a registration form, online housing and transportation options, local organizing guides, and a feature for purchasing t-shirts. Afterward, organizers used this network to transform the movement into a "normal" advocacy group. Though the apparent success of the march was not due entirely to the Internet, Price notes that the march "could not have succeeded to the extent that it did without [the Internet]." [17]

Of course, rapid response email lists and website features that offer groups the capacity to mobilize their respective supporters raise important questions about impact, both on policy outcomes and on the organizations themselves. For example, whether the kinds of Internet-derived grassroots organized by Environmental Defense are "real" or simply a new variation on Astroturf (that is, artificial grass) is a topic worth study. Indeed, although what Jeff Berry calls "high-tech lobbying" has "quickened the pace of politics," he wonders whether it has really changed the fundamental equation:

> Impressive as this is, it's important to remember that such lobbying is a variation on a theme, not a whole new symphony. In the last analysis, faxes and email are simply letters that constituents send to their members of Congress—they just get there faster. . . . Ironically, the capabilities of high-tech tactics for mobilizing public opinion may have actually raised the threshold that . . . must be crossed before someone . . . begins to pay attention.[18]

Fund-raising

Not surprising, the Internet tantalizes all interest organizations with its promise of an easier and less expensive way to raise funds. Compared with direct mail, for example, the cost of a website is minuscule. In the early 1990s—that primitive era just before the emergence of the World Wide Web—Burdett Loomis and Allan Cigler noted that information technology was already fast becoming vital to a group's capacity to "target and send [direct mail] and to process the responses." But given the relatively high costs of information technology at that time, it seemed that only larger and more resource rich groups could benefit from such technological advances.[19]

Today, of course, the costs of computers and Internet access have dropped dramatically. Now even small groups—or individuals, for that matter—can establish an interactive Web presence at a reasonable investment of time and money, sometimes aided by foundations (such as the Benton Foundation) that support the extensive use of the Web by public interest groups.[20] Translating direct mail practices to the Internet will enable organizations to reach out to and target users like never before. Email lists, like direct mail lists, are available for purchase, many containing detailed user preferences that enable organizations to customize messages and target the constituency they feel will respond best to entreaties. Not only are such Internet-based solicitations relatively inexpensive, but the recipient can immediately take action just by going to the specified part of the website.

The high cost of traditional fund-raising partly explains the lure of Web-based efforts. An analysis of the for-profit sector by *eMarketer* found that traditional direct mail typically generates a 1–1.5 percent response at a cost of 75 cents to $2 per piece. By contrast, "permission based" email, messages to individuals who have directly signed up for email on the organization's website, costs about 25 cents per unit and results in a 11.5 percent rate of participation, defined in the study as the completion of some type of transaction on the organization's website. Unsolicited email is even less expensive, costing about 1 cent per unit, but is of dubious efficacy because of growing hostility to spam.[21]

The World Wildlife Fund (WWF) is a useful example of how an organization can employ permission-based email for both fund-raising and member communications. Its "Panda Passport" feature enables participants to construct personalized lists of species and issues of interest, data that the WWF uses to send customized information and targeted email alerts. Participants get online "passports" that are "stamped" whenever they volunteer, donate money, or send emails or faxes to policymakers. Moreover, the WWF sends out a thank-you email each time a participant takes action. Such regular interaction enables the WWF to maintain a list of active and interested supporters, essential to cultivating donations.[22]

Despite these apparent advantages, for most groups Internet-based fund-raising may not displace traditional direct mail appeals any time soon. First, despite rapid growth in Internet penetration, access to and use of the Web is not universal. There may be more than 160 million Internet users in the United States today, but only a little more than one-third seem to use it with any frequency.[23] An Internet-based strategy would surely miss a large number of potential supporters, particularly among older cohorts who constitute the financial backbone for many established environmental groups. Second, as noted earlier, concerns over Internet spam and viruses make users increasingly hostile to unsolicited email of any kind. Even permission-based email may have limited effectiveness. As the *eMarketer* study noted, nearly twice as many emails were sent as postal letters in 1999, and "as more and more email floods in-boxes, the tendency of the user to delete or ignore email will increase."[24]

Second, the technological challenge of guaranteeing the privacy of credit card numbers and other personal information on the Web has complicated this form of online fund-raising.[25] For example, the much-touted use of candidate websites to raise funds during the 2000 presidential election obscured the fact that most of the online pledges were subsequently fulfilled over the telephone or through traditional mail.[26] Related privacy concerns have led most large environmental groups to post policies outlining what they will and will not do with personal information, including email addresses. Better encryption technology may ease such concerns over time, but direct credit card-based donations over the Web are still relatively modest.

Finally, current tax implications will complicate Web-based fund-raising, at least until Congress and the Internal Revenue Service align law with technology. For example, tax-exempt organizations that link their websites to other websites, particularly those with overt political intent, risk running afoul of IRS prohibitions against 501(c)(3) groups endorsing candidates or engaging in openly partisan political activity. A related problem occurs when an organization links its site to a commercial site, such as when a tax-exempt group provides a link to Amazon.com in return for a small portion of the sales price if a member uses that link to purchase a book. The IRS at this time is pondering a range of issues related to how tax-exempt organizations can use the Web to generate funds.[27] Until those issues are sorted out, tax-exempt groups are wise to be cautious about Web-based fund-raising.

How Groups Do Use the Internet

Based on this overview, we assessed how major environmental organizations use the Internet for conveying information, recruiting members, raising money, and fostering communities.[28]

We were particularly interested in how organizational traits shape Internet use. In theory, an organization's website should reflect the group's membership recruitment, grassroots, lobbying, and litigation activities. For example, groups that traditionally rely on member support should logically deploy the most current information technology they can afford. Their websites should stress individual giving and interactive features to create website "stickiness" that keeps potential donors on the site as long as possible. Indeed, the capacity of the Internet for providing material, purposive, and solidary benefits to supporters should induce membership groups to invest heavily in the widest range of website features.

By contrast, organizations that rely on institutional support or on a few large donors may not be as motivated to implement powerful Internet systems or feature-rich websites. In the same vein, organizations that promote grassroots activism should logically have websites that contain more informational features, grassroots tools, and community-maintenance applications (such as chat rooms) than those that rely traditionally on litigation and lobbying tactics.

Data Collection and Methods

Our focus here is on groups large and established enough to be able to execute planned Internet strategies around a coherent set of political objectives. Thus the organizations selected belonged to the Green Group, a loose coalition of eighteen major organizations formed in the late 1980s to promote a unified national environmental agenda (Box 5.1).[29] Its members are what Ron Shaiko has called "full-service" environmental organizations, groups that pursue their objectives through a variety of tactics, including litigation, lobbying, and grassroots mobilization.[30] This definition excludes organizations like the Nature Conservancy or Greenpeace, which typically have a narrower scope of activities through which they pursue

Box 5.1.   Green Group Organizations

Children's Defense Fund	www.childrensdefense.org
Defenders of Wildlife	www.defenders.org
Earthjustice Legal Defense Fund[a]	www.earthjustice.org
Environmental Defense[b]	www.environmentaldefense.org
Friends of the Earth	www.foe.org
Izaak Walton League	www.iwla.org
National Audubon Society	www.audubon.org
National Parks Conservation Association	www.npca.org
Natural Resource Defense Council	www.nrdc.org
National Wildlife Federation	www.nwf.org
Native American Rights Fund	www.narf.org
Planned Parenthood	www.plannedparenthood.org
Population Action International	www.populationaction.org
Sierra Club	www.sierraclub.org
Union of Concerned Scientists	www.ucsusa.org
Wilderness Society	www.wilderness.org
World Wildlife Fund	www.worldwildlife.org
Zero Population Growth	www.zpg.org

Source: Authors' compilation.

[a]Formerly the Sierra Club Legal Defense Fund.
[b]Formerly the Environmental Defense Fund.

goals, as well as more purely Internet-based organizations like the Rain Forest Action Network.

Guiding this analysis was our question as to how organizational characteristics affect the organization's website. In particular, we wanted to see if groups that relied traditionally on members' dues and activism would be more effective builders of Web features related to recruitment of and overt provision of material (information, for example) and solidary (community building, for example) benefits to supporters. The organizations under study thus were divided roughly into "member" and "nonmember" groups, with the latter comprising the Children's Defense Fund, Earthjustice Legal Defense Fund (formerly the Sierra Club Legal Defense Fund), Native American Rights Fund, Planned Parenthood, and Population Action International. This distinction is not precise, because nonmember groups use many of the same recruitment and retention practices with their donors as membership groups use with their members. Even so, this distinction does reflect the relative importance that members play in an organization's overall plans.

The major features of group websites were divided into five categories—informational, membership, fund-raising, grassroots, and community—using a system of content analysis developed by Christopher Weare and Wan-Ying Lin. Content analysis of the Web, they note, is complicated by the Web's sheer size and chaotic structure, the integration of multimedia content, the use of hyperlinks to guide users through content, and the public's lack of the "combined 'societal' experience" in recognizing core structures and genres that we have for books and newspapers.[31] This said, the approach offers a reasonable way to systematically assess group websites (Box 5.2).

Informational features tested whether a site offered a site search and site map, a consistent graphical interface, effective navigational tools, contact information and email addresses for staff members and leaders, and information about the organization (such as an annual report). The purpose of this category was to provide a measure of whether the website met basic design and information-provision expectations.

Membership features tested the ability and ease of signing up as a group member online, as well as the provision of online material benefits to new and continuing members. Specific features include membership signup and renewal forms, lists of membership benefits, online credit card transaction, and members-only Web pages. A few of the features in this category pertained to the ability of organizations to contact, track, and target potential members, such as through Web cookies and a referral or egreeting card application. These features may not relate directly to the provision of benefits to members, but their presence gives the organization the capacity to gather information, monitor user behavior, and disseminate targeted recruitment solicitations.

Fund-raising features pertained to nonmembership dues giving or other fund-raising activities. Features in this category included online event ticket sales, online merchandise sales, and donations other than membership dues.

Grassroots features examined the capacity of a group's site to foster some type of grassroots activism. These features aim to enable individuals or groups of supporters to act on issues of concern to them. With "action alerts" for example, a group may post notices on a controversy, accompanied by a button that automatically generates a form to email or fax to a specified corporate executive or government official. The user clicks on the button, customizes the letter, and sends it. Other grassroots features include interactive Geographic Information System applications such as those found on Scorecard, local organizing and volunteering collaboration tools (an online forum or scheduling system to coordinate activities), and contact information for companies or government offices.

Box 5.2.   Website Features

Informational features
Multiple forms of feedback
    —requests and complaints
"What's new?" section on
    homepage
Privacy policy
Site search
Listed in Yahoo! directory
Site map
Consistent graphical interface
    —navigation bar
Contact form
Webmaster email address
Multiple email addresses with
    names
Department contact
    information
Board contact information
Organizational history
Organization description
    —mission statement
Activities
IRS 501(c) status
Annual report
Multimedia
Photographs and artwork
External links and Web
    resources

Membership features
HTML email
Cookies
Membership signup
Membership renewal
Campaign-specific giving
Gift memberships
Referral and ecard system
List of benefits
Online transaction
Members-only site
Personalized page
Newsletter or magazine online

Fund-raising features
Workplace giving
Ecommerce partners
Affiliate membership sales
    program
Matching gift programs
    —combined federal
    campaigns
Affinity credit card
Ecommerce merchandise and
    publications
Fund-raising event ticketing
Monthly donations
Other types of donations
SSL encryption (security)
Trips and events with online
    signup

Grassroots features
Geographic Information
    System applications
Research materials and reports
Action alerts
Campaign and candidate
    information
Activism tools, guides, and
    resources
Poll
Local chapter and affiliate sites
Local organizing guides
Local organizing and volunteer-
    ing collaborative tools
Elected representative contact
    information

Community features
Threaded discussion boards
Live chat rooms
Hosted chats
Calendar
Event management system
Email listserv

Source: Based on Christopher Weare and Wan-Ying Lin, "Content Analysis of the World Wide
Web: Opportunities and Challenges," *Social Science Computer Review* 18 (fall 2000): 272–292.

Community features measured the online solidary benefits offered by groups. These include features like live chat rooms, threaded discussion boards, an online calendar of events, and other site features that could be expected to provide at least a modicum of social interaction among members.

Of course, simply coding for the presence or absence of such website features does not indicate the importance the organization places upon them. For example, counting the number of grassroots features on a website tells us relatively little about how important or prevalent these features are relative to recruitment features on the same website. Therefore, three "emphasis tests" were used to assess the relative prevalence of these different categories of features on a website. A "feature proportion test" tracked the number of features found in a particular category as a proportion of the total number of features on that website. A "links test" used a software program to calculate the percentage of links on the homepage that went to specified categories of features on the website.

Finally, an "area test" measured the percent of space on the homepage dedicated to the specified category of features. This last test was performed by taking a screenshot of the homepage and analyzing it with a pixel-counting graphics software (Macromedia Fireworks) to measure the percentage of that homepage's area covered by a specific feature. Included in this measure were any actual features (signup forms) placed on the homepage, links to those features, or graphics advertising those features.

Prevailing Website Features

Not surprising, the straightforward provision of information is the most prevalent feature on all websites, which on average contained 70 percent of the possible informational features listed in Box 5.2. All of the groups assessed use the Web as a convenient way to publicize themselves and to convey a great deal of information on themselves and their issues to a broad and diverse audience. In this regard, there was no meaningful distinction between membership and nonmembership groups.

More interesting, features in the grassroots category showed up the next most frequently, with the average website offering 54 percent of relevant features in this category. Features related to membership recruitment came third (48 percent), followed by fund-raising (37 percent). Least frequent were those features comprising what could be considered relevant to community building, with the average website containing only 7 percent of the possible features.

In comparing types of organizations, membership groups are more likely than nonmembership groups to use their websites to entice and enable individuals to provide support in the form of regular donations or dues. The tests indicate a strong relationship between a group's dependence on membership support and the number, emphasis, and importance of membership recruitment features on its website. Indeed, as expected, membership groups are more likely than nonmembership groups to provide a broader and richer range of overall features on their websites.

On the other hand, the analysis did not support the hypothesis that organizations with a traditional commitment to grassroots activism (for example, the Sierra Club) display more informational features, grassroots tools, and community-building applications than groups that rely more on "inside" tactics such as lawsuits and direct negotiations with regulators (for example, the Natural Resources Defense Council). In this regard, there was no apparent correlation between the "offline" grassroots practices of an organization and the website features it deploys. Grassroots features were common on all sites, and present in higher percentages than recruitment, fund-raising, or community-building features.

If this is so, the Web may render meaningless the distinction between "grassroots" and "insider" groups—*at least online.* Organizations that once relied exclusively on lobbying may be using the Internet to expand the scope of their practices. Grassroots tools such as action alerts are now ubiquitous on public interest group websites because of the tools' perceived effectiveness in advocacy and, more important, because of their relatively low implementation costs.

Indeed, groups no longer need to develop these tools themselves. The emergence of application service providers and information technology consultants that exclusively serve public interest groups has enabled even relatively small groups to develop a Web presence. Companies like Locus Pocus (an Environmental Defense spin-off), e-guana.net, and Grassroots.com offer hosted Web services and turnkey applications for many of these features. In the specific case of action alerts, Environmental Defense runs the Action Network, a service for environmental groups that want to create email- and Web-based action alerts but do not have the capacity to do it themselves. In contrast to community-building applications, which require high levels of technical capability and concerted, organization-wide efforts to jump-start the community, grassroots applications can simply be launched on a site and expected to grow organically. Thus it seems nearly every organization has added some of these tools, whether or not grassroots activity is one of its core paths to influence.

This blurring of traditional organizational characteristics in grassroots activism was also true for recruitment features. Several of the nonmembership organizations offered the same online signup forms for individual donations and the same range of material benefits of "membership" as more traditional membership groups. For example, the Native American Rights Foundation has a donation page on its website with a pledge that begins "Yes! I want to become a member of the Native American Rights Fund."[32]

Just as with grassroots features, the Internet may obviate the need for a group to develop the expected organizational capacity directed at membership development. The website has all those "eyeballs" peering around already, why not try to convert them into donors? And if the best way to get donations is to offer a package of benefits and call the donor a member, why not do so? The definition of what makes a "member" was fuzzy enough before the Web, so an organization using this bit of logic might not have to make any major internal changes to carry out such a conversion.

Overall, however, member groups exhibit a stronger Web presence than nonmember groups, and their sites are more oriented toward fundraising and recruitment. The Internet's "quantitative" advantages as a communications medium—its speed, lower transaction costs, and convenience—enable groups to recruit members and provide a range of benefits to them more cheaply and efficiently than before. Information, which Jeff Berry calls the "most common material reward one can get from contributing to an interest group," is easily provided over the Web or via email.[33]

A website's text, sound, images, and animation can appeal to a person's values and thereby advertise the group's purposive benefits. For example, a group can use multimedia content to better stress the perception of threat—be it to polar bears, whales, or sick children—so key to recruiting supporters. Finally, once the potential member has been attracted to the group, the ability to finalize the transaction immediately online overcomes a key hurdle to traditional direct-mail recruitment. The Internet, in short, may make it easier for public interest groups to overcome some longstanding obstacles to member recruitment and retention.

The "qualitative" advantages of the Internet do not seem to be as well utilized. In theory, the Internet is not just faster and cheaper than other modes of communication, but is fundamentally different. For example, large public interest groups have traditionally found it difficult to foster social and political interaction among members. With the Internet, however, it seems plausible that even national groups could offer solidary benefits through the use of chat rooms, discussion forums, interactive calendars, and organizing tools for real-world events. Yet the data indicate this has not happened. For example, although groups on average offered 48 percent of the recruitment features tested for, few offered a personalized page delivering targeted content for members. Likewise, though the grassroots features tested were found 54 percent of the time, an online poll—an *interactive* grassroots feature—was found only 28 percent of the time. For these major groups, at least, the online conversation seems to go one way.

Community-building features were the least prevalent of all categories tested. The few chat rooms and bulletin boards were not well populated or active. Indeed, most of the groups avoided community features altogether. It is possible that the groups lacked the resources to invest in the necessary technology, but it is more likely that, recognizing the difficulty of maintaining an active community online, they either decided against it or put it off. An online community has the potential to thrive in a public interest setting, as was noted by the example of the Million Mom March, but it is not a certainty. Merely providing online tools will not create vibrant online communities.[34]

Another possibility is that organizations may actually find it to their advantage to *limit* members' social interaction. Shaiko argues that as members learn more information on the policy stances or operating procedures of the organization, they generate feedback that group leaders may not want to hear or implement.[35] Leaders of even the most grassroots-oriented groups still might not want to enable members to use the organization's website to debate the group's leadership or latest policy position. After all, allowing open online debate might undercut the organization's effort to present a unified public face or the effectiveness of its website for new member recruitment.

For example, in the 1990s the leaders of the Sierra Club faced strong dissent from members who felt that the organization had sold out to timber interests for the sake of compromise. These "John Muir Sierrans" successfully drew national attention to their cause, took several seats on the Sierra Club board of directors, and won an initiative that put the club in opposition to all commercial logging on public lands. Key to this insurgency was its use of the Internet to spread its message, both on bulletin boards and on the Sierra Club's website.[36] Chad Hanson, one of the insurgents elected to the board, stated that they "couldn't have done it without the Internet."[37] Leaders at other major environmental organizations undoubtedly took note of that claim.

In sum, this assessment of the Internet offerings of major environmental organizations shows that prevailing organizational practices shape much of what will be deployed on a group's website. Organizations that depend on membership dues posted websites with a wider and richer range of features, an indication of their need to present a package of meaningful benefits to current and prospective members. Grassroots features were far more common than expected, while community-building features were markedly underused. In this regard, at least, the Internet seems to be a medium in which an organization does not need to adhere closely to its established offline operating practices and can, for example, deploy grassroots action items online even if it does little else to foster such activism.

How Will the Internet Transform Organizations, and Whom Will It Benefit Most?

The admittedly tentative conclusions produced by this assessment offer clues to important issues that may arise as groups' Web presence becomes more integral to their operations. The study also raises intriguing questions.

One question is the Internet's impact on the transparency, account-ability, and competition of environmental and other public interest groups. The Internet has the potential to open up the internal workings of organizations to the general public as Internet users become accus-tomed to finding all the information they want immediately. Such de-mands for transparency may force more groups to put more financial and operating information online. The availability of such information, com-bined with the ease of changing loyalties made possible by Internet search engines and the like, may force greater organizational accountabil-ity to keep members from going to competitors.

For example, why should a member stick with the Defenders of Wildlife if it is seen as closed to scrutiny or unresponsive to input when that member can join the National Parks Conservation Association or the Sierra Club? Members have always been able to express dissatisfaction with leaders by leaving a group, but with the Internet demands for organi-zational accountability are likely to intensify. In this regard, the Internet may enable new and Web-savvy organizations to challenge established ones for policy primacy and member support. Or, conversely, the Internet could produce such a contagion of groups that only the already established "brand names" will survive.

A particularly compelling question is how established groups such as the National Audubon Society or Environmental Defense differ in Inter-net usage patterns from more "radical" groups like Earth First! or more Web-based groups like the Rain Forest Action Network. Current work by Lori Brainard and Patricia Siplon on competition between established health advocacy groups, such as the Muscular Dystrophy Association, and a new breed of "radical" cyber-advocates suggests such a divergence.[38] This question alone is worth a major study.

And, of course, the biggest question of all: Will the Internet pro-foundly change the nature of interest representation and political ac-tivism, creating a cyber-democracy where the voices of the many will match the wealth and leverage of the few? In this sense, some activists have hailed the Internet as "the strongest tool for re-invigorating democ-racy of anything we've ever seen."[39] To these observers, the Internet has the potential to energize issue advocacy across the board and, more specifically, connect established organizations more closely to their rank-and-file members. Robert Putnam, for one, isn't so sure that the Internet will be the panacea such activists proclaim, but it will be important. As Putnam concludes, "the Internet will not *automatically* offset the decline in more conventional forms of social capital, but it has that potential. In fact, it is hard to imagine solving our contemporary civic dilemmas with-out computer-mediated communication."[40]

Or will the Internet be just another tool in the hands of the already established and well positioned? As Jeffrey Berry observes, "Nothing about the Internet makes lawmaking any less arcane and public policy any less complicated. . . . High-tech tactics empower the same people who have always been empowered by interest group politics: those who are educated and have the necessary financial resources."[41]

Many questions, few answers. Revolutions take time to figure out.

Notes

1. William Gates, *The Road Ahead* (New York: Viking, 1995), 273.
2. Anthony G. Wilhelm, *Democracy in the Digital Age* (New York: Routledge, 2000), 154.
3. See Robert D. Putnam, *Bowling Alone: The Collapse and Revival of American Community* (New York: Simon and Schuster, 2000), 19.
4. See Ronald G. Shaiko, *Voices and Echoes for the Environment* (New York: Columbia University, 1999), and Christopher J. Bosso, "The Color of Money: Environmental Groups and the Pathologies of Fundraising," in *Interest Groups Politics*, 4th ed., ed. Allan J. Cigler and Burdett A. Loomis (Washington, D.C.: CQ Press, 1994), 101–130.
5. Christopher J. Bosso, "Environmental Groups and the New Political Landscape," in *Environmental Policy in the 1990s*, 4th ed., ed. Norman Vig and Michael Kraft (Washington, D.C.: CQ Press, 1999), 55–76.
6. Cliff Landesman, "Nonprofits and the World Wide Web," Internet Nonprofit Center, 2000, http://www.nonprofits.org/website.htm.
7. Ibid.
8. See Frank Fischer, *Citizens, Experts, and the Environment: The Politics of Local Knowledge* (Durham: Duke University, 2000).
9. Landesman, "Nonprofits."
10. Thomas Gais and Jack L. Walker, "Pathways to Influence in American Politics," in Jack L. Walker, ed., *Mobilizing Interest Groups in America: Patrons, Professions, and Social Movements*, (Ann Arbor: University of Michigan, 1991), 103.
11. Environmental Defense, *Annual Report*, 1999, at http://www.environmental-defense.org/pubs/AnnualReport/1999/a_finding.html.
12. Tom Price, *Cyber-Activism* (Washington, D.C.: Foundation for Public Affairs, 2000), 18.
13. Ibid.
14. An observation made by Sabine Schutte-Morris in an internship paper, "On the Use of Technology in Environmental Nonprofit Organizations," Department of Political Science, Northeastern University, October 2000.
15. Emily Schwartz, "Activists Now Have Corporate Attention," *Chicago Sun-Times*, February 13, 2000, MoneyLife Section, 40.
16. Price, *Cyber-Activism*, 8.
17. Ibid., 7.
18. Jeffrey Berry, *The Interest Group Society*, 3d ed., (New York: Longman, 1997), 136–137.
19. Burdett A. Loomis and Allan J. Cigler, "The Changing Nature of Interest Group Politics," in *Interest Group Politics*, 3d ed., ed. Allan J. Cigler and Burdett A. Loomis (Washington, D.C.: CQ Press, 1991), 24.
20. Monica Williams, *Planning for the Web: American Rivers*, Benton Foundation, April 2000, http://www.benton.org/Practice/Features/americanrivers.html.
21. Cathleen Santosus, "Email Everywhere," *Business 2.0*, June 27, 2000, 308.
22. Sandra Stewart, "Not for Profit," *Industry Standard*, December 6, 1999, at http://thestandard.net/article/0,1902,7809,00.html.
23. "Internet at a Glance," *Business 2.0*, March 20, 2001, 136.
24. Santosus, "Email Everywhere," 308.

25. Bruce R. McBrearty, "Are Non Profit Fund Raisers Ready for the Internet?" *Fund Raising Management*, 29 (October 1998): 28.
26. Ben Green, Director of Internet Operations, Gore 2000 Campaign, interview by Christopher J. Bosso, April 2000.
27. Rebecca Fairley Raney, "Charities Find a Gray Area on the Net," *New York Times*, February 12, 2001, C4.
28. This section is based on Michael T. Collins, *The Green Internet: Environmental Public Interest Groups on the World Wide Web* (Cambridge: Harvard University, 2001).
29. Shaiko, *Voices and Echoes for the Environment*, 58.
30. See Ron Shaiko, "More Bang for the Buck: The New Era of Full-Service Public Interest Organizations," in *Interest Group Politics*, 3d ed., ed. Allan J. Cigler and Burdett A. Loomis (Washington, D.C.: CQ Press, 1991), 109–130. In the same volume, see also Christopher J. Bosso, "Adaptation and Change in the Environmental Movement," 151–176.
31. Christopher Weare and Wan-Ying Lin, "Content Analysis of the World Wide Web: Opportunities and Challenges," *Social Science Computer Review* 18 (fall 2000): 272–292.
32. Native American Rights Fund, http://narf.securesites.com/contact/membershihtml.
33. Berry, *The Interest Group Society*, 71.
34. Kim Daus and Drew Banks, "Are We There Yet? The Long and Winding Road to Online Community," *Business 2.0*, June 27, 2000, 317.
35. Shaiko, *Voices and Echoes*, x.
36. On this internal dispute see Leora Broydo, "Mutiny at the Sierra Club," *Mother Jones*, November 3, 1998, http://www.motherjones.com/news_wire/sierra.html.
37. Price, *Cyber-Activism*, 31.
38. Lori A. Brainard and Patricia D. Siplon, "Cyperspace Challenges to Mainstream Non-Profit Health Organizations," *Administration and Society*, forthcoming.
39. Price, *Cyber-Activism*, 6.
40. Putnam, *Bowling Alone*, 180 (emphasis in original).
41. Berry, *The Interest Group Society*, 137.

II. GROUPS IN THE ELECTORAL PROCESS

6

Interest Group Money in Elections

M. Margaret Conway, Joanne Connor Green, and Marian Currinder

Federal election politics today rely on high-tech information gathering and timely communication with the electorate—all of which cost money. Candidates and parties seeking funds have found organized interests willing to contribute to those who share their policy views. Campaign spending by interest groups has escalated in recent years, and federal campaign finance laws have been largely ineffective in limiting the role of special interest money in campaigns.

In this chapter M. Margaret Conway, Joanne Connor Green, and Marian Currinder examine the role of interest group money in federal elections, documenting some of the most significant trends. The authors focus on the rise of political action committees (PACs) as potent political forces, with PACs contributing both "hard" money directly to candidates and "soft" money to political parties. Although hard money contributions have increased during each election cycle, the most spectacular increases have been in soft money (up more than 500 percent from 1991 to 2000). Unlike hard money contributions, soft money can be contributed in unlimited amounts, and six-figure contributions by companies, interest groups, or individuals are not unusual.

Finally, the authors examine some criticisms of campaign finance laws, evaluate the potential of suggested reforms, and highlight the increase in the amount of funds raised and spent outside the limits of federal law, especially spending by undisclosed donors. The authors doubt that proposed reforms, such as banning soft money, will be effective: group money could simply be channeled into those activities likely to remain outside of federal legal scrutiny.

In a democratic government, how do we help citizens communicate their policy preferences fairly and effectively? And how do we ensure that political parties and candidates can communicate their policy views to the electorate and mobilize supporters? Voting in elections and lobbying elected officials are two ways that citizens can articulate their preferences. Because of the key role of elections in democratic political systems, the electoral structure must prevent undue influence from any one set of groups or interests. And parties and candidates must have enough money to communicate and mobilize properly.

Running for office is expensive. In the early years of the republic, candidates tended to be part of the local elite and usually funded their own campaigns. Thus when George Washington ran for office in 1757, he used a standard electoral practice of that time and used his own money to purchase liquor for potential voters. Two decades later future president James Madison lost reelection to the Virginia legislature when he refused to follow that custom.[1]

After 1824 the creation of political parties that encompassed regular citizens led to other methods of funding campaigns. Elected officials and parties used patronage (appointment of supporters) to fill nonelective public offices, with the understanding that a certain percentage of all officeholders' salaries would be contributed to the party to help fund the next campaign. Government contracts were also distributed on the basis of past and promised future support of the governing party, with the contract recipient expected to contribute to the officeholders and the party that granted the contract.

Objections to what the public viewed as political corruption led to federal and state laws limiting the use of patronage and preferments. The Civil Service Reform Act of 1883 and subsequent laws limited patronage first at the federal level and then in any state program receiving federal funding. One consequence was increased dependence on prominent business leaders and interest groups to fund campaigns. The Tillman Act, enacted in 1907 after a congressional investigation revealed large contributions from insurance companies to officeholders and candidates over several elections, prohibited corporations and national banks from contributing part of their income directly to candidates for federal office.

In the 1920s people began calling for new federal legislation after a Pennsylvania senatorial contest exceeded federal spending limits, Congress investigated candidate and party spending practices, and the Supreme Court ruled that limits on expenditures by federal candidates in primary elections were illegal. Demands for campaign finance reform increased during the 1924 Teapot Dome scandal, in which the secretary of the interior granted oil drilling rights on federal lands to a private company while receiving illegal contributions of $400,000. So in 1925 Congress enacted the Corrupt Practices Act. The act continued the ban on campaign contributions from banks and corporations, strengthened reporting requirements for campaign contributions and expenditures by federal candidates and party organizations, and raised the limit on how much could be spent in a campaign to a maximum of $5,000 for House of Representatives candidates and $25,000 for Senate candidates unless state law set lower limits. But enforcement was weak and candidates' reports (filed with the Clerk of the U.S. House) were hard to access and were retained for only two years.[2]

Federal legislation to limit the influence of labor unions in federal elections, enacted temporarily by the Smith-Connally Act of 1943 and then permanently by the Taft-Hartley Act of 1947, prohibited union contributions to federal-level political organizations and candidates and expenditures from union dues on behalf of candidates for national office. The unions responded by creating political action committees (PACs), to which members donated money to support political candidates. The unions' desire to have political action committees legitimized by federal law was a major force behind the Federal Election Campaign Act of 1971.

Federal Regulations after 1971

The Federal Election Campaign Act of 1971 (FECA) and its amendments of 1974, 1976, and 1979, as well as the Revenue Act of 1971, govern campaign finance primarily at the federal level. Also important are several court decisions interpreting federal laws, as well as regulations and advisory opinions of the Federal Election Commission (FEC), which administers and enforces federal campaign finance laws. These laws have created several mechanisms for individuals and groups to fund federal campaigns.

To limit undue influence, individuals and most organizations are restricted in the amount of money they can give directly to a candidate or a political party in any year or two-year election cycle. These direct contributions are referred to as federal contributions or "hard money," as they pertain to the hard limit outlined in the statutes. The contribution limits for an individual are $1,000 per election to a candidate for federal office, $20,000 per year to the national political party committees, and $5,000 per election to a campaign committee. An individual may contribute no more than $25,000 in hard money in any one year to political action committees regulated by the Federal Election Commission, national party organizations, and candidates for federal office.

Federal campaign finance laws give multicandidate committees— those contributing to five or more candidates for federal office—an advantage, whether they are independent or affiliated. A multicandidate committee (generally called a PAC) may give no more than $5,000 per candidate per election. So a PAC may give a candidate up to $5,000 for a primary election, $5,000 for a run-off primary election if one is required, and $5,000 for a general election contest. There is no limit on how much a PAC may spend on "independent expenditures"—campaign efforts that are not coordinated in any way with the candidate, representatives of the candidate, or the candidate's campaign committee. Because PACs are able to raise and funnel large amounts to campaigns for federal office and to spend unlimited amounts of money in independent expenditures, the number of PACS has grown. Public concern about their influence on members of Congress has grown as well.

The 1974 FECA amendments permitted government contractors to establish PACs, thus greatly expanding the universe of businesses and labor unions eligible to use this form of political expression. The FEC's decision in April 1975 to permit corporations and labor unions to use their treasury funds to create PACs and to administer their activities, including soliciting funds from employees and stockholders, facilitated the establishment and operation of more PACs.[3] Authorization of the use of payroll deductions to channel funds to PACs was another boost.

Supreme Court decisions also stimulated the creation of PACs and PAC activities. In *Buckley v. Valeo* (1976) the Supreme Court indicated that the 1974 FECA amendments did not limit the number of local or regional PACs that unions or corporations and their subsidiaries could establish.[4] That decision also clarified the right of PACs to make independent expenditures on behalf of a candidate. The use of *issue advocacy*, in which a group or individual communicates about issues, is not regulated and need not be reported to the FEC. *Buckley* permits unlimited spending on issue advocacy so long as the ads do not explicitly advocate election or defeat of a candidate. Words such as *vote for, support, vote against*, and *defeat* attached to a candidate's name are not permitted.[5] The Court made a clear distinction between discussing issues and candidates and advocating electoral victory or defeat.[6] PACs now prefer issue advocacy ads to independent expenditures on behalf of a candidate (remember that independent expenditures are reported to the FEC, but issue advocacy ads are not).

In 1976 further amendments to FECA restricted labor union and corporation PAC contributions to one $5,000 contribution per election, regardless of the number of PACs created by a corporation's divisions or subsidiaries or a labor union's locals. The process of clarifying what is permissible continues, with the FEC and other interested parties proposing amendments to laws and FEC advisory opinions.

Although PACs existed before 1974, their numbers were limited and most were affiliated with labor unions. The first notable effect of changed laws and the FEC's interpretation of the laws was explosive growth in the number of corporate PACs (Table 6.1). Although labor union and corporate PACs have multiplied significantly, most do not raise and contribute large amounts of money. During the 1999–2000 campaign cycle, only sixty-six corporate PACs spent more than $500,000, but only twenty-five contributed that much to candidates from funds raised. In fact 22 percent

Table 6.1.   Number and Type of Political Action Committees, Selected Years from 1974 to 2000

Year	Corporate	Labor	Trade, membership, health	Independent	Cooperative	Corporation without stock	Total
1974	89	201	318				608
1976	433	224	489				1,146
1978	785	217	453	162	12	24	1,653
1980	1,206	297	576	374	42	56	2,551
1982	1,469	380	649	723	47	103	3,371
1984	1,682	394	698	1,053	52	130	4,009
1986	1,906	417	789	1,270	57	157	4,596
1988	2,008	401	848	1,345	61	169	4,832
1990	1,972	372	801	1,321	60	151	4,677
1992	1,930	372	835	1,376	61	153	4,727
1994	1,875	371	852	1,318	56	149	4,621
1996	1,836	358	896	1,259	45	134	4,528
1998	1,821	353	921	1,326	45	133	4,599
2000	1,725	350	900	1,362	41	121	4,499

Source: Federal Election Commission, press release, January 25, 2001, http://fecweb1.fec.gov/press/ 012501/count.htm.

Note: For 1974 and 1976 the data for trade, membership, and health PACs include independent, cooperative, and corporation-without-stock PACs. On November 24, 1975, the FEC issued its "SUNPAC" advisory opinion. On May 11, 1976, FECA (Public Law 94-283) was enacted. All data are from the end of the year indicated.

of all corporate PACs made no contributions to candidates in the 2000 election. Together the sixty-six PACs spent some $59.5 million. Fifty-three labor union PACs each spent $500,000 or more, and thirty-four contributed at least $500,000 to candidates. The fifty-three wealthiest labor PACs spent a remarkable $111.1 million.[7] These PAC expenditures, primarily unregulated (soft money), represent a dramatic increase from previous years.

Types of PACs

One basic distinction among political action committees is between independent and affiliated PACs.

Affiliated PACs

Labor unions, corporations, cooperatives, and trade, health, and professional organizations create affiliated PACs. Each PAC is a separate, segregated fund that collects money to contribute to political campaigns, to use in independent expenditures for or against a candidate, or to sponsor campaign ads supporting or opposing a policy. Affiliated PACs get their funds from donations from individuals associated with the sponsoring organization. Corporations and labor unions are not allowed to make direct campaign contributions to their PACs from their treasuries, but they can use treasury funds to establish and administer a PAC and to communicate with people associated with the organization. For example, an affiliated corporate PAC may contact the corporation's employees or shareholders and an affiliated labor union PAC may contact labor union members for such activities as communicating candidate endorsements or supporting voter registration drives.

The number of affiliated PACs has increased substantially since the 1970s. The largest increase occurred in corporate PACs, which jumped from 89 in 1974 to 1,725 in 2000, or 1,938 percent (see Table 6.1). In contrast, PACs affiliated with trade associations, membership organizations, or health-related organizations grew more modestly, increasing from 318 in 1974 to 900 in 2000 (283 percent). PACs sponsored by labor unions increased from 201 in 1974 to 350 in 2000 (174 percent).[8]

Independent PACs

After clarification of federal campaign finance law in 1976, independent (also called nonconnected) PACs were created. The number of independent PACs increased from 162 in 1978 to 1,362 in 2000, an increase of 841 percent. Officially independent of any organization, independent PACs include leadership PACs and issue, ideological, and type-of-candidate PACs.

Leadership PACs.   Some federal politicians head leadership PACs independent of those politicians' individual campaign committees. Like other PACs, leadership PACs receive donations from individuals and groups and then contribute to political candidates. Politicians can give candidates up to $1,000 per election out of their personal campaign committees and up to $5,000 per election out of their leadership PACs. Politicians with leadership PACs thus can give $12,000 to candidates facing primary and general elections; politicians without leadership PACs can give only $2,000. The number of leadership PACs registered with the FEC has grown considerably over the past two decades, as has the amount of money these PACs raise and contribute. In 1978 fewer than 10 leadership PACs contributed a total of $62,485; during the 2000 election cycle 141 leadership PACs gave $15.8 million.[9]

Most leadership PACs are connected to members of Congress. Members typically use their leadership PAC funds to support both personal and party goals. Funds are used to pay for travel, political consultants, overhead, and other activities that may indirectly benefit the member's political fortunes. Leadership PAC funds also support party-building and party-maintenance activities. By contributing money to incumbent colleagues, promising nonincumbent candidates, and party campaign committees, members with leadership PACs assist in party efforts to gain or maintain majority status.

Members interested in keeping or securing a formal leadership post are more likely to give heavily to their colleagues across the board. Rep. Nancy Pelosi, D-Calif., who was vying to be the Democrats' whip in the 107th Congress (2001–2003), gave more leadership PAC money to her colleagues than any other member of Congress during the 2000 election cycle. In the subsequent Democratic House caucus election to replace Whip David Bonior, D-Mich., Pelosi defeated Rep. Steny Hoyer, D-Md., by twenty-three votes.[10]

Even when there is little or no competition in leaders' home districts, most leaders are able to consistently raise millions of dollars. The ability to attract huge amounts of campaign money allows leaders to help other candidates and foster colleague support and loyalty. During the 1999–2000 election cycle House Majority Whip Tom DeLay, R-Texas, House Majority Leader Dick Armey, R-Texas, and Speaker of the House Dennis Hastert, R-Ill., contributed more leadership PAC money to Republican candidates than any of their Republican House and Senate colleagues.[11] Other members may contribute on a more selective basis and give to candidates who can help them achieve their specific leadership goals. For example, committee and subcommittee chairpersons who face leadership challenges may give to members of their own panels to secure their support.

Issue, Ideological, and Type-of-Candidate PACs.   Another category of independent PACs has increased dramatically in the past decade—one that supports a particular ideology, type of candidate, or issue. Examples include the Americans for a Republican Majority, the Campaign for Working Families, the Human Rights Campaign Fund Political Action Committee, and EMILY's List. EMILY's List is the most successful of the PACs supporting female candidates. The name is an acronym derived from "Early Money Is Like Yeast"—it makes the dough rise. Founded in 1985 by Ellen Malcolm to fund Democratic, abortion rights female candidates, the PAC has raised lots of money. Its endorsed candidates have high rates of electoral success, in part because EMILY's List is very careful in choosing who to endorse. Perhaps not unexpectedly, EMILY's List has been criticized for not endorsing more candidates who might have lower probabilities of electoral success.

Supporters of EMILY's List are expected to contribute $100 per year to the organization and to make at least two $100 contributions to female candidates for Congress or for statewide office who have been endorsed by EMILY's List. The contribution checks are made out to the candidate's campaign fund and mailed to EMILY's List headquarters, which bundles the checks for each candidate together and forwards them to the candidate. This practice, known as "bundling," is widely used by PACs. Therefore when PACs practice bundling, the amount of money contributed to a candidate by a political action committee may significantly underrepresent the hard money contributions stimulated by the PACs' activities.

In 1986 EMILY's List raised more than $350,000 for two Senate candidates. In 1990 PAC members, using the bundling technique, donated $1.5 million to fourteen candidates. During the 1999–2000 election cycle EMILY's List bundled $9.2 million for women candidates. According to reports filed with the Federal Election Commission, EMILY's List spent $14.7 million in hard money during the 1999–2000 election cycle. A substantial part of that ($10.8 million) was spent to educate and mobilize women voters in states where EMILY's List had endorsed Democratic female candidates seeking election as governor, U.S. senator, or U.S. representative. EMILY's List ranked second in hard money expenditures only to the National Rifle Association (NRA) PAC (the Political Victory Fund), which disbursed $16.8 million.[12]

Funneling and Bundling

PACs are very creative in allocating resources. One strategy is bundling, discussed above, where PACs collect checks made out to particular candidates and then send each candidate the checks all at once. Another type of bundling is hosting a fund-raiser for a candidate. These fund-raisers bring together groups interested in the politician's future. One example is the Insurance Industry's Meet and Greet event for congressional challenger Greg Walden in 1998. The event took place at an exclusive French restaurant near Capitol Hill. Another example is the breakfast sponsored by Florida Citrus Growers for Rep. Dan Miller, R-Fla., the week after Walden's fundraiser. The list of such events is long.[13]

In addition to bundling money, PACs also funnel money by giving money to other PACs or to the political parties, from which they also can receive money. A few PACs have begun steering other PACs' contributions. These so-called "lead PACs" analyze elections and candidates and provide information to other PACs with similar goals.[14] PACs also give money to other PACs with similar policy agendas. For example, in the 2000 election cycle the Democratic Republican Voter Education PAC funneled $270,000 to other PACs, Democratic and Republican alike.

By examining the PACs that spent the most money in the 2000 election cycle (the NRA Political Victory Fund and EMILY's List), we can see different patterns in resource allocation. The NRA Political Victory Fund spent $16.8 million in the 1999–2000 election cycle. Of this, $6.46 million was independent expenditures and $1.78 million was donated to candidates, party organizations, and other PACs. The group spent more than $2 million on behalf of George W. Bush and more than $500,000 on behalf of John Ashcroft (then a Republican Senate candidate in Missouri, who after losing the election was appointed attorney general in the Bush administration). The PAC donated $97,350 to Republican Party committees (both state and local) and $10,150 to Democratic Party organizations. It donated varying amounts to 284 candidates of both parties in 2000. Additionally, $115,300 went to other PACs.

EMILY's List expenditures were very different.[15] This PAC disbursed $14.7 million in hard money, contributing almost $1.6 million to candidates, parties, and other PACs. Unlike the NRA's Political Victory Fund, which spent $6.46 million on independent expenditures, EMILY's List allocated only $21,478 to independent expenditures. EMILY's List targeted direct contributions to only thirty-four candidates, all of them abortion rights Democratic women. Furthermore, EMILY's List donated more money to the Democratic Party committees ($150,000) than the NRA's PAC gave to both parties ($107,500). EMILY's List transferred less than the NRA Political Victory Fund to other PACs ($26,000 compared with $115,300) but spent more than $6.7 million in nonfederal (soft money) expenditures; the NRA's PAC spent none. EMILY's List typically engages in issue advocacy, spending more than $3 million in twenty-six targeted states in 1998 on 8 million direct mailings and 2 million telephone calls to 3.4 million women.[16]

Patterns of PAC Contributions

During the 1999–2000 election cycle, political action committees operating at the federal level raised $604 million and contributed $259 million to candidates for federal office. Of the $259 million, 75 percent went to incumbents, almost 11 percent went to candidates challenging incumbents, and the rest went to candidates for open seats. PACs' overwhelming financial support for incumbent members of Congress is one reason why they are rarely defeated in their bids for reelection.

Representatives are much more dependent on PAC contributions than senators are. In the 1999–2000 election cycle, contributions from PACs represented 32 percent of money received by House candidates and 12 percent of money received by Senate candidates. Of the $259 million that PACs contributed in the 1999–2000 election cycle, House candidates received almost $196 million, three-fourths of the total.

PAC Decision Making

Influences on PAC decisions regarding campaign contributions include the PAC's:

- Goals.
- Contributors' expectations.
- Decisionmakers' official positions.

- Location (in Washington, D.C. versus elsewhere).
- Strategy.
- Competitive position.[17]

Interest groups have several strategies available to them, and the impact of these strategies may be difficult for outside observers to assess.[18]

An organization may follow a "maintaining strategy" to preserve access to certain legislators. Or, it may follow an "expanding strategy" to gain access to additional legislators. These legislators would not normally be receptive to the PAC's interests because of the demographic characteristics of the legislators' constituencies. The results of the limited research on this topic suggest that PACs generally emphasize a maintaining strategy, with only a third of contributions representing an expanding strategy.[19] PACs also tend to be more responsive to the needs of vulnerable representatives and senators who have befriended the PACs' interests.[20]

PAC decision making patterns vary. If the PAC has staff based in Washington, that staff tends to play a greater role in deciding who gets contributions and how much they get. Contributions are also more likely to occur through a Washington-based fund-raising event.[21] PACs whose local affiliates raise most of the money tend to follow the locals' more parochial concerns. But that may not be the most rational allocation strategy. PACs should allocate funds either to strengthen or broaden access or to replace opponents, but parochialism may require that an already supportive member of Congress receive substantial locally raised funds.[22] The degree of parochialism appears to vary by type of PAC—for example, defense-interest PACs are more locally oriented than labor-interest PACs.[23]

Partisanship and ideology also may influence PAC decision making—for example, defense PACs tend to be less ideological in their contribution decisions than labor, oil, and auto PACs.[24] Business PACs vary in the extent to which they pursue a partisan support strategy; usually this is associated with the vulnerability of a political party's incumbents. When political tides appear to be favoring Republicans, business PACs may contribute more to Republican challengers than when the political climate is less favorable.

Incumbents' voting records may be another major factor in contribution decisions. An incumbent who voted against legislation that a PAC considered vitally important would be unlikely to receive a campaign contribution. But there are exceptions. Some PACs will contribute to candidates who oppose them in the hope of minimizing the intensity or frequency of the opposition. F. L. Davis found this factor to be statistically significant; R. L. Hall and F. W. Wayman also suggest some PACs attempt to minimize the opposition.[25] One study of PACs affiliated with *Fortune 500* companies found voting records on key legislation to be the second most frequently cited criterion in making contribution decisions; the most frequently cited was the candidate's attitudes toward business.[26]

Some research suggests that corporate PACs' decisions about whether and to whom to contribute are also influenced by the size of the company's federal contracts, the company's size, and whether the federal government regulates the company's business.[27] The jurisdictions of committees on which incumbent members serve influence contribution decisions by both corporate and labor PACs,[28] but some research indicates committee jurisdiction is more relevant in decisions regarding House incumbents than Senate incumbents.[29] Some PACs also must be concerned about competition for supporters. Contributions that would leave the PAC open to criticism and thus endanger future support from donors must be avoided. Independent PACs that raise funds through mass mail solicitations must be particularly wary.[30]

Another factor that influences PAC contributions is concern about influence with key holders of power. If PAC "Y" gives to a member of Congress and PAC "X" does not, will that affect PAC X's access to that member? Although some PACs act as though it would, others could pursue a different strategy: giving to the challenger, with the hope that the incumbent might become more attentive. The effectiveness of that strategy, however, would be limited by the extent to which the PAC's preferred policy outcomes conflict with the strength of a contrary ideology held by a member of Congress or the intensity of support for a different policy position in that member's constituency.

Independent Expenditures

Remember that independent expenditures are expenditures made by individuals, organized interests, and party committees to support or oppose candidates for federal office, but are in no way coordinated with candidates' campaigns. The first widely documented use of independent spending was in 1980 when the National Conservative Political Action Committee (NCPAC) spent more than $1 million to defeat several Democratic senators. Democrats who supported the 1978 Panama Canal Treaty were targeted specifically and subject to negative advertising. Four of the targeted senators lost their bids for reelection, allowing NCPAC to claim credit for helping the Republicans secure a Senate majority for the first time since 1954. Other PACs followed suit and independently spent millions of dollars during the 1982 and 1984 elections to support or oppose candidates for federal office.[31]

Since the 1980 elections the amount of independent spending related to federal elections has varied considerably. In 1990 independent expenditures in House races were just less than $2 million. Two years later independent expenditures in House races totaled more than $4 million. In 1994 this figure dropped to $2.1 million, then jumped to $4.8 million in 1996. Since 1996 these expenditures have increased, with totals for the 2000 election cycle coming in at just less than $8 million. When independent spending in

Senate campaigns during the 2000 cycle is added to the total for House races, the figure rises to some $20 million.[32]

Why is independent spending erratic from one election to the next? Because it can backfire. Political advertisements paid for with independent money tend to be more negative and thus can work against the candidates the ad supports. In 1982 NCPAC ran 1,000 "attack" television ads against Sen. John Melcher, D-Mont. Melcher responded by running an ad accusing NCPAC of coming in from out of state and trying to influence the Montana vote. Being the subject of attack ads helped Sen. Paul Sarbanes, D-Md., raise money nationwide for his 1982 campaign. Both senators were reelected.[33]

Another way for groups to advocate the election or defeat of a federal candidate is through internal communications. Labor unions, membership organizations, and other associations can spend unlimited amounts on communicating political messages to their members. Only communications that directly endorse a candidate must be disclosed to the FEC, so it is difficult to determine exactly how much groups spend communicating with their members. David Magleby reports that in 2000 groups dedicated $10.2 million to internal communications, more than half of which was spent (mostly by labor unions) advocating for the election of presidential candidate Al Gore. For groups with large membership bases, internal communications can be particularly effective. The U.S. Chamber of Commerce, for example, joined forces with local and state chambers of commerce in 2000—a move that provided access to 3 million businesses for internal communications. Much of the $15 million in expenditures the chamber reported for 2000 was for member communications.[34] Internal communications play an increasingly important role in political campaigns mainly because they come from trusted sources and can reach large numbers of potential voters.

Another relatively recent trend in interest group spending is to endow academic chairs at universities in honor of members of Congress—or, even more prestigious, name an institute after a politician. The law allows interest groups to make tax-deductible donations, which often garner attention. One example is the Trent Lott Institute at the University of Mississippi (his alma mater). MCI WorldCom was a large donor to the institute. When Congress considers telecommunication legislation, MCI has a large vested interest (such legislation remains on the legislative agenda). Following MCI's contribution to the institute, Senator Lott (Republican majority leader at the time) named an MCI representative to a commission considering taxing the Internet.[35] Giving "favors" to contributors is not limited to members of Congress; the executive branch has a long tradition of rewarding political supporters with appointed positions. Ambassadorships are perhaps the most notorious rewards for loyal service. In fact, of President George W. Bush's ambassadors, 38 percent (fourteen of thirty-seven) donated more than $100,000 to the Republican Party or to Republican candidates.[36]

All these strategies have triggered concern among scholars, journalists, and many political leaders about the role of PACs in federal campaign funding. PACs may have enormous influence, affecting who is viewed as a viable candidate, the outcomes of elections, and access to policymaking. Because PACs have become a major source of campaign funds for congressional candidates, an inability to obtain PAC support may mean a candidate cannot afford to run an effective campaign. If elected, the successful candidate must be ever mindful of campaign funding sources, both past and future. The escalating costs of congressional and senatorial campaigns force incumbent legislators to be watchful of how policy positions and votes might affect their campaign fund-raising.

Soft Money

Soft money, also referred to as nonfederal money, falls beyond the FECA's statutory limitations and is thus very controversial. Although the money is officially raised to support party building, there is no denying that the expenditures affect individual candidacies and campaigns. Issue advocacy is perhaps the most popular use of soft money. Although issue advocacy is supposed to be distinct from electioneering, the line is blurry.

The U.S. District Court in the western district of Virginia ruled that interest groups can spend soft money on issue advocacy so long as they don't violate the *Buckley* standard (which mandates that the ads must not explicitly try to influence voting).[37] In this case, two weeks before the 1992 presidential election the Christian Action Coalition ran ads that negatively and forcefully opposed Democratic candidate Bill Clinton's "militant" stance on homosexual rights. The court ruled that the ads were advocating an issue position, not explicitly trying to defeat Clinton's candidacy.

In *Colorado Republican Federal Campaign Committee v. FEC* (1996), the Supreme Court ruled that political parties were allowed to spend money on behalf of candidates without using hard money.[38] That same year the FEC charged the Christian Coalition with violating federal law by using issue ads to benefit the Republican Party and its candidates. The case was dismissed. The Court ruled that advocacy was only considered illegal when a group substantially negotiates with the candidate or party. This ruling opened the door to the growing use of soft money to fund issue advocacy.[39] The clear pattern in federal court decisions is to apply a very strict standard for issue advocacy, in which the ads must unambiguously and explicitly urge voters to vote for or against a candidate to be considered a coordinated expense.[40]

As a direct consequence of these rulings, the use of soft money for issue advocacy in elections has grown at an incredible rate. In 1996 organized labor engaged in interest group election advocacy in forty-four congressional elections. Business groups countered with issue advocacy.[41]

The groups targeted their support based on candidates' issue stances. Steve Forbes, a candidate for the Republican presidential nomination, established Americans for Hope, Growth, and Opportunity in 1997 to generate grassroots support for his flat tax and school choice proposals. The PAC raised more than $13 million to spend on issue advocacy. In 1998 PACs began to allocate their resources more strategically, targeting districts with very competitive races.[42]

Groups also spend soft money on television and radio advertisements for or against candidates. In addition, groups generate grassroots support by contacting individuals directly and using phone banks and direct mail to mobilize voters.[43] For example, the AFL-CIO spent between $18 million and $19 million on issue advocacy in 1998 to defeat Republican candidates. The group mailed 9.5 million pieces of direct mail, made 5.5 million telephone calls, and spent a reported $5 million on television and radio issue advocacy.[44] The Business Roundtable, an organization of large U.S. companies, spent a reported $5 million to generate opposition to the Patients' Bill of Rights, managed care reforms, and environmental regulations in 1998.[45] U.S. Term Limits spent $11.6 million to build support for term limits in 1998.[46]

Some PACs are also spending money on campaign services, much like political parties offer, by providing extensive in-kind contributions. Paul Herrnson reports that some PACs provide polling, media, and research services to candidates.[47] Some PACs are even providing campaign consultants. The National Committee for an Effective Congress provided Democrats in a few marginal districts advice on voter mobilization and targeting. Issue PACs sometimes train workers and "loan" them to candidates. The Human Rights Campaign holds campaign-training seminars to train volunteers, then sends the volunteers out to work for specific candidates.[48] The Realtors' PAC, American Medical Association's PAC, and the AFL-CIO's PAC often give polling data to candidates.[49]

Interest groups are also funding parties' national conventions. The Center for Responsive Politics reports that eight corporations donated $1 million each to fund the Republican Convention in 2000.[50] The American International Group donated $2 million for the Democratic convention (they gave $500,000 to the Republicans.) House whip Tom DeLay raised $1 million to lavish Republican House members with chauffeured cars, concierge service, hospitality lounges, and lush parties.[51] One corporate party at the Republican National Convention cost $500,000; three others cost $400,000. At the Democratic Convention the NRA, Philip Morris Corporation, and UST Inc. sponsored a party for Blue Dog Democrats (an organization of conservative Democrats in Congress) at the Santa Monica Pier amusement park that had musical entertainment by Patty Loveless, food, and rides. Bristol-Myers Squibb Company and Merck and Co. (both drug makers) were gold sponsors of Sen. John Breaux's, D-La., $400,000-plus party, "Mardi Gras Goes

Hollywood."[52] The corporate sponsors of these parties have or will have policy concerns before Congress.[53]

Although soft money has received considerable attention in the press and in discussions of campaign finance reform, we must not forget the substantial amounts PACs spend in direct contributions (hard money). In fact, some PACs do not give soft money at all. David Rehr (from the National Beer Wholesalers Association) stated,

> We don't do soft money. It's a bottomless pit. It's never enough. Both sides play you against each other. Hard money is much more valuable, because it actually goes for electing someone. Giving a candidate ten thousand dollars directly is much more useful. Soft money is amorphous. . . . The only way you get attention with soft money is it has to be really big: three hundred, four hundred, five hundred thousand, a million—that gets people's attention.[54]

In 1998 the amount of soft money raised by both parties declined (Table 6.2.) More interest groups in 1998 spent money on issue advocacy than on soft money. Hard money contributions remained high because they are considered important in influencing individual races.[55] Record amounts of soft and hard money were raised in the 2000 election cycle. In fact the two major political parties raised a total of $495 million in soft money in 1999–2000.

Unless a future campaign finance bill eliminates soft money, there is no reason to anticipate a reversal in its popularity. In May 2001 Republicans raised $24 million in soft money from a dinner sponsored by their national committee. In June they held the President's Dinner, raising more than $20 million in soft money from $2,500-a-plate dinners. Republican leaders in Congress pressured companies and individuals to participate to raise as much money as possible before any reform bills were passed barring soft money. The Republican leaders in the House circulated lists of the pledges each member had solicited from interest group representatives and others around Capitol Hill.[56]

Table 6.2.   Hard and Soft Money Contributions, 1991–2000 (in millions of dollars)

	1991–1992	1993–1994	1995–1996	1997–1998	1999–2000
Hard money	445	384.7	438.1	445	741
Soft money[a]	86.1	101.6	262.1	224.4	495.1

Source: Federal Election Commission, January 12, 2001, http://fecweb1.fec.gov/press/011201 partyfunds.htm.

[a] Includes only national party soft money.

Relations between Political
Parties and Interest Groups

The relationship between parties and PACs is complex. On one hand parties see PACs as competing with them for scarce resources—campaign dollars. The parties have reacted with concern to the large amounts interest groups spend on issue advocacy. Parties appeal to donors by claiming the need to "offset" interest group expenditures.[57] On the other hand parties often see PACs as allies to help advance party causes. For example, Americans for Tax Reform (which has ties to former Republican National Committee chair Haley Barbour) received $4.6 million from the Republican National Committee during the 1996 election to articulate the Republican tax reform policies. The Democratic National Committee donated several hundred thousand dollars to the Rainbow Coalition and the A. Philip Randolph Institute to generate interest among their supporters for the committee's policy agenda.[58] Interest groups contributed $495 million in soft money to federally registered party organizations in 2000 ($245.2 million to Democrats and $249.8 million to Republicans).[59]

In the mid-1990s several Republican leaders invoked an aggressive, and sometimes hostile, relationship with PACs and lobbyists as retribution for what the leaders felt were unfairly high contributions from PACs to Democrats when that party was in power. In 1994 House whip Tom Delay refused to meet with any lobbyists that didn't contribute money to Republicans. His hardball approach was termed the "K Street Strategy" (many large lobbying firms are on K Street in Washington, D.C.).[60] In 1998 Republican leaders in the House refused to meet with lobbyists from the Electronic Alliance after a Democrat took the helm of the organization. John Linder (then chair of the National Republican Congressional Committee) confirmed to *Roll Call* (a newspaper on Capitol Hill) that GOP leaders were blocking legislation important to the Electronic Alliance.[61] Linder also reported that the leadership was not pleased that the Association of Home Builders (a large and powerful organization) had hired a Democrat as president.

Criticisms of the 1974 Campaign Finance Law

Criticisms of FECA and its implementation in the 1990s and 2000 are numerous. One is that large sums have benefited candidates and parties in ways that evade legal limits. This evasion is seen as corrupting to the American political system, giving undue influence to wealthy individuals, corporations, labor unions, and organized groups (social, economic, and ideological) able to raise lots of money.

The amount of soft money collected by both the Democratic and Republican parties' federal-level campaign committees increased enormously between the 1991–1992 and 1999–2000 election cycles—$86.1 million to $495.5 million (see Table 6.2). As a proportion of the total amounts (both hard and soft money) received by the national party committees, soft money increased from 17 percent to 40 percent. This sharp increase generated demands for reform.

The federal law's limits on hard money contributions to a candidate of $1,000 from an individual and $5,000 from a political action committee can be easily evaded by contributing soft money and independent expenditures. Some interest groups fund issue advocacy ads designed to support or oppose a candidate or party. An additional problem is that the identity of an ad's sponsors has been easy to conceal under the 1974 law, especially if the group is registered in a state such as Virginia, which facilitates nondisclosure of a group's sponsors and contributors. Using a loophole in the 1974 law, several PACs (known as 527 committees) collected and spent unlimited amounts of money. Even after Congress enacted a law in 2000 requiring disclosure through filings with the Internal Revenue Service, 527 committees continued to operate (see Chapter 7 in this volume).[62]

Another criticism of campaign finance laws is that the limits on the size of campaign contributions created by the 1974 Federal Election Campaign Act were not automatically adjusted for inflation, while the costs of campaigns increased at a rate exceeding the consumer inflation rate, primarily because of increased use of the mass media and the high rate of inflation in such costs. Also, the law favors wealthy candidates, as any candidate can spend unlimited amounts on their campaigns.

Related to that is the time legislators must allocate to raising money for reelection. If a reelection campaign for the House costs an incumbent $1.5 million, that incumbent must raise an average of $14,423 per week over the 104 weeks of the two-year term. Time spent fund-raising significantly reduces the time incumbents can devote to their legislative and constituency service obligations. Increasing the size of contributions allowed from an individual or a PAC might alleviate this pressure. With Senate campaigns averaging $5.3 million in 2000, and those in large states such as California, Florida, New York, and Texas costing much more, the time demands of Senate campaign fund-raising are much larger, even if spread over six years.[63] This enormous need for campaign funds gives an advantage to interest groups that have PACs and further advantages to those that bundle contributions from individuals.

Proposals for Campaign Finance Reform

What major proposals for campaign finance reform has Congress considered? What are the criticisms of the proposed reforms? How would these reforms affect interest groups, candidates, and political parties if they were enacted?

Several members of Congress—most notably Sen. John McCain, R-Ariz.; Sen. Russell Feingold, D-Wis.; Rep. Christopher Shays, R-Conn.; and Rep. Martin T. Meehan, D-Mass.—led the fight through several recent sessions of Congress to revise campaign finance laws, including reducing or eliminating the use of soft money in federal election campaigns. The House of Representatives passed the Shays-Meehan bill in July 1998, but the bill died in the Senate.[64] The Senate passed the McCain-Feingold bill in April 2001. One provision of the McCain-Feingold bill would ban the raising of soft money by federal-level political party and congressional committees and contributions by those committees to nonprofit organizations. State parties would be required to use hard money for any federal election activities, such as get-out-the-vote or voter registration drives, in the 120 days before a general election or 60 days before a primary election, with the exception that state parties may spend up to $10,000 of soft money if that is permitted under state law. Candidates for federal office would also be banned from raising soft money for federal election activities and from raising it for nonprofit organizations to use in federal election activities.

Other proposed changes to the 1974 law include banning corporations and labor unions from broadcasting electioneering communications on television or radio (those which clearly identify a candidate for Congress) within sixty days of a general election or thirty days of a primary election. An exception would be made if the corporations' or unions' PACs funded these communications with hard money. This proposal raises substantial free speech issues.

As for the inflation problem, some argue that increasing the amount that individuals and political parties may contribute to a candidate would weaken interest groups' influence over elected officials, provided that candidates receive substantially more funds from these two sources. The McCain-Feingold bill proposed increasing the limits on:

- Individual contributions to candidates from $1,000 to $2,000.
- Aggregate individual contributions to candidates from $25,000 to $37,500.
- Political party contributions to Senate campaigns from $20,000 to $25,000.
- Individual contributions to national party organizations from $20,000 to $25,000.
- Individuals' hard money contributions to state parties from $5,000 to $10,000.

All these limits would be indexed to inflation.

Another proposal is to reduce the maximum size of PAC contributions to candidates—for example, from $5,000 per election per candidate to $1,000 per election per candidate. One goal is to equalize the relative impact of individual contributions (which under the 1974 law are limited to $1,000) and PAC donations. But we must take caution in limiting the amount of hard money PACs are allowed to contribute. If PACs are not allowed to donate regulated money, they will probably turn to unregulated issue ads. Additionally, reducing hard money contributions could lead to an environment where PACs are making other kinds of donations to gain access and favor (for example, creating endowed chairs at universities or donating tax-deductible money to a member's favorite organization or charity). These alternative forms of contributions are difficult to regulate and track. Reducing the maximum size of PAC contributions would also increase the amount of time that candidates for Congress (including incumbent legislators) would have to devote to campaign fund-raising.

Another proposal is to cap the proportion of money candidates can receive in PAC contributions (for example, 20 percent of all expenditures for House candidates and 25 percent for all Senate candidates). But this could have the unintended consequence of encouraging candidates to spend more time raising money and benefiting PACs that are well entrenched, able to donate money at the beginning of the election cycle, and that can more easily raise and bundle individual contributions to candidates.

Advocates for reform also encourage limiting the contributions candidates can receive from outside their state. The idea is that local money ties candidates more directly to future constituents. This proposal could hurt challengers, who rely on out-of-state contributors to compete with well-entrenched incumbents. Furthermore, women and minority candidates also often need money from contributors in other states to conduct effective campaigns, as do candidates in smaller or less affluent states.[65] Other proposals for campaign finance reform include more clearly defining what constitutes coordinated expenditures and requiring more prompt disclosure of independent expenditures when a group or individual's total spending exceeds $10,000.

Criticisms of Reform Proposals

Reform proposals face a variety of criticisms. One is that some proposals violate the U.S. Constitution's First Amendment protections of free speech. The Supreme Court has consistently limited states and Congress from enacting campaign finance laws that infringe on an individual's or group's political expression, as expression is equated with free speech. In *Buckley v. Valeo* the Supreme Court clearly distinguished between campaign contributions and expenditures. Contributions are money given directly to a party, candidate, or PAC, who have complete control over how the money is used. An expenditure, on the other hand, is money spent directly by a person or entity to influence an election. Donors have full control of the money. Federal law can regulate and limit direct contributions and coordinated expenditures, but not independent expenditures. The Court's rationale is that expenditures are forms of political expression that show who donors support and why. As such, independent expenditures are strictly protected as a form of free speech. In contrast, the government can regulate contributions because they have the potential for corruption or quid pro quo (exchanging contributions for votes, for example). The government does not have as compelling an interest in limiting independent expenditures because the potential for corruption is smaller and the benefit for communication of political beliefs (free speech) is great.[66]

Another aspect of the *Buckley* decision is equality. Many believe it is important to equalize the relative impact of individuals' and groups' election financing and political expression. The Court, however, ruled that any attempt to influence the relative voice of some is not permissible under the First Amendment. Hence any plan to maximize the voice of some group relative to others appears to be unconstitutional.

The second criticism is that federal regulation of some aspects of campaign finance violates the Constitution's establishment of a federal system, with regulation of elections left primarily to the states. But Article 1, Section 4 of the Constitution permits Congress to enact laws that affect all aspects of congressional elections, except the manner in which senators are elected, which can be changed only by constitutional amendment.

Another criticism is that a ban on soft money would cripple the ability of federal-level political party organizations to influence the federal government's policy agenda. But the extent to which party organizations today play such a role is debatable. In contrast, soft money does greatly increase the importance and, many would argue, the influence of interest groups, corporations, labor unions, and wealthy individuals in federal policymaking. The effect of soft money on political party organizations at both the federal and state levels is to enable them to regain a role in the organization and conduct of campaigns. The parties' efforts in voter registration and get-out-the-vote drives have been important in mobilizing potential voters.[67] The parties have also sponsored and paid for issue advocacy and generic advertising campaigns. The argument can be made that party organizations will vigorously raise hard money if soft money is banned. Given the limits on hard money contributions, however, more effort will be needed to raise as many hard money dollars as have been raised in soft money in recent elections, because hard money must be raised in smaller amounts from more donors.

The Effects of Campaign Finance Reform

How would new campaign finance laws change the role of interest groups in federal politics and policymaking? Although it is difficult to say—there are so many unintended and unpredicted consequences—a critical examination of the reform proposals is essential.

Central to recent reform efforts is the call to ban soft money. Many believe that soft money has great potential for abuse and corruption because it is unregulated. Any discussion of banning soft money must consider why soft money is spent in campaigns in the first place. Soft money funds party-building activities, independent expenditures, and issue advocacy. Eliminating soft money will dramatically limit resources for activities such as get-out-the-vote drives, voter registration, and advertising that promotes the political party. Such bans, however, would be ineffective in limiting independent expenditures and issue advocacy advertisements, as both of these activities are given strong First Amendment protections. So eliminating soft money would probably increase independent expenditures by parties and interest groups. These independent expenditures are difficult to regulate, as is money spent on issue advocacy. The parties must report soft money; interest groups and the wealthy have far less stringent requirements for disclosure.

Another reform proposal that could help incumbents more than challengers or open seat candidates is voluntary spending limits. But unless all candidates for an office would agree to accept such limits, it would be irrational for any one candidate to accept them. Whether limits are voluntary or mandated by law, they must be high enough not to constrain challengers and open seat candidates in their communication to voters. Research demonstrates that high campaign expenditures are needed for most challengers to increase their name recognition.[68] Without the ability to spend sufficient amounts of money to mount a viable campaign, challengers would be hard pressed to unseat incumbents.

One last consideration is to examine what the reform proposals won't address. They can't address self-financing of campaigns. The Supreme Court ruled (in *Buckley*) that self-financing is a form of individual free speech and was absolutely protected. In 1998 candidates spent more than $91.8 million on their own candidacies. Rather than promote equality of influence, we are creating a millionaire's club in Congress. All of these concerns mean we must be cautious in revising our system of campaign finance. Any proposals to limit access by a multitude of potential candidates must be resisted.

Lessons from the States

States frequently act as laboratories for policy development, and that term is appropriate in considering state efforts at campaign finance reform. Interest groups strive to influence public policy at the state level, and one way to achieve this is to influence the outcome of elections. States have tried several methods to control campaign finance activities, including disclosure requirements, spending limits tied to public funding, and limits on contributions to candidates from individuals, political parties, labor unions, corporations, and PACs. Twelve states in the 1990s had spending limits and public funding, but in nine of the twelve this applied only to gubernatorial candidates or to all statewide elected constitutional officers. Only three states—Hawaii, Minnesota, and Wisconsin—extended this form of campaign finance regulation to state legislative candidates. Public funds were to replace large contributions, with the goal of matching funds increasing the importance of small contributions and inducing candidates to accept spending limits. It was assumed that this would reduce the amount of money candidates spent on campaigns and would enable challengers to compete more effectively.

The state programs vary, but in general their success has been limited. Most provide for a matching fund fueled by citizen check-off on the state income tax, with citizens designating a small amount of their taxes to go to the fund. But citizen participation in the matching fund check-off has declined over time. The fund has not been effective in reducing the role of interest groups or in equalizing access to funding between incumbents and challengers.[69]

Conclusion

Efforts to regulate and limit the role of interest groups in campaign finance have met with limited success. The group most affected by the laws—members of Congress—must enact them. Both personal and partisan concerns make change difficult, as was evident in the inability of the House and Senate to agree on a campaign finance reform bill in the first session of the 107th Congress.

Notes

1. George Thayer, *Who Shakes the Money Tree?* (New York: Simon and Schuster, 1973), 25.
2. Robert K. Goidel, Donald A. Gross, and Todd G. Shields, *Money Matters* (Lanham, Md.: Rowland and Littlefield, 1999), 24; Frank J. Sorauf, *Money in American Elections* (Glenview, Ill.: Scott, Foresman and Company, 1988), 30; Thayer, *Who Shakes the Money Tree?* 62–65.
3. See Edwin Epstein, "The Emergence of Political Action Committees," in *Political Finance*, ed. Herbert Alexander (Beverly Hills, Calif.: Sage, 1979), 159–179.
4. *Buckley v. Valeo*, 424 U.S. 1 (1976).
5. *FEC v. Massachusetts Citizens for Life*, 479 U.S. 238 (1986).
6. Anthony Corrado, Thomas E. Mann, Daniel R. Ortiz, Trevor Potter, Frank J. Sorauf, eds., *Campaign Finance Reform: A Sourcebook* (Washington, D.C.: Brookings Institution, 1997); see also Chapter 7 in this volume.
7. FEC, "PAC's Grouped by Total Spent, 1999–2000," press release, May 31, 2001, http://www.fec.gov/press/05301pacfund/tables/pacsp00.html.
8. FEC, "FEC Issues Semi-Annual Federal PAC Count," press release, January 25, 2001, http://fecweb1.fec.gov/press/012501count.htm.
9. Center for Responsive Politics, http://www.opensecrets.org; Ross K. Baker, *The New Fat Cats* (New York: Priority Press Publications, 1989): Clyde Wilcox, "Member to Member Giving," in *Money, Elections, and Democracy*, ed. Margaret Latus Nugent and John R. Johannes (Boulder, Colo.: Westview, 1990).
10. Juliet Eilperin, "Democrats Pick Pelosi as House Whip," *Washington Post*, October 11, 2001, A1.
11. Larry Makinson, "Opening Statement," http://www.opensecrets.org/pressreleases/oct18_00_statement.htm.

12. FEC, "Top 50 PACs by Disbursements, 1999–2000," press release, May 31, 2001, http://www.fec.gov/press/05301pacfund/tables/pacdis00.htm; EMILY's List, "EMILY's List Women Vote Project," http://www.emilyslist.org/el-womenvote/default.asp.

13. For a good discussion of this phenomenon see Elizabeth Drew, "The Money Culture," in *Principles and Practice of American Politics*, ed. Samuel Kernell and Steven S. Smith (Washington, D.C.: CQ Press, 2000), 718–740.

14. Paul S. Herrnson, "The Money Maze: Financing Congressional Elections," in *Congress Reconsidered*, 7th ed., ed. Lawrence C. Dodd and Bruce I. Oppenheimer (Washington, D.C.: CQ Press, 2001), 103.

15. All data obtained from FEC, http://www.fec.gov.

16. Herrnson, "The Money Maze," 117.

17. Theodore J. Eismeier and Philip H. Pollock III, "An Organizational Analysis of Political Action Committees," *Political Behavior* 7 (2): 192–216 (1985).

18. Richard A. Smith, "Interest Group Influence in the U.S. Congress," *Legislative Studies Quarterly* 20 (February 1995): 89–139.

19. John R. Wright, "PAC Contributions, Lobbying, and Representation," *Journal of Politics* 51 (August 1989): 713–729.

20. J. David Gopoian, "What Makes PACs Tick? An Analysis of the Allocation Patterns of Economic Interest Groups," *American Journal of Political Science* 28 (May 1984): 259–281.

21. Larry J. Sabato, *PAC Power: Inside the World of Political Action Committees* (New York: Norton, 1985), 42–43.

22. John R. Wright, "PACs, Contributions, and Roll Calls: An Organizational Perspective," *American Political Science Review* 79 (June 1985): 400–414.

23. Gopoian, "What Makes PACs Tick?" 279.

24. Ibid., 271.

25. See F. L. Davis, "Sophistication in Corporate PAC Contributions: Demobilizing the Opposition," *American Politics Quarterly* 20 (October 1992): 381–410; R. L. Hall and F. W. Wayman, "Buying Time: Moneyed Interests and the Mobilization of Bias in Congressional Committees," *American Political Science Review* 84 (September 1990): 797–820.

26. Ann B. Matasar, *Corporate PACs and Federal Campaign Financing Laws* (New York: Quorum, 1986), Table 13, 58.

27. R. B. Grierand and M. C. Munger, "Committee Assignments, Constituent Preferences, and Campaign Contributions," *Economic Inquiry* 29 (January 1991): 24–43.

28. J. W. Endersby and M. C. Munger, "The Impact of Legislator Attributes on Union PAC Campaign Contributions," *Journal of Labor Research* 13 (winter 1992), 79–97; M. C. Munger, "A Simple Test of the Thesis that Committee Jurisdictions Shape Corporate PAC Contributions," *Public Choice* 62 (2): 181–186 (1989).

29. K. B. Grier, M. C. Munger, and G. M. Torrent, "Allocation Patterns of PAC Monies: The U.S. Senate," *Public Choice* 67 (2): 111–128 (1990).

30. Eismeier and Pollock, "Organizational Analysis," 207–208.

31. Robert K. Goidel, Donald A. Gross, and Todd G. Shields, *Money Matters*, (Lanham, Md.: Rowman and Littlefield, 1999).

32. FEC, "Independent Expenditures by PACs during 1999–2000," May 31, 2001, http://www.fec.gov/ press/053101pacfund/tables/pacie00.htm; David B. Magleby, *Outside Money: Soft Money and Issue Advocacy in the 1998 Congressional Elections* (Boulder, Colo.: Rowman and Littlefield, 2000).

33. See Magleby, *Outside Money*.

34. Ibid.

35. Drew, "The Money Culture," 728.

36. Center for Responsive Politics, http://www.opensecrets.org.

37. *FEC v. Christian Action Coalition*, 894 F. supp. 946 (W.D. Va. 1995).

38. *Colorado Republican Federal Campaign Committee v. FEC*, 116 Sup. Ct. 2309 (1996).

39. Marianne Holt, "The Surge of Party Money in Competitive 1998 Congressional Elections," in Magleby, *Outside Money*, 25.
40. Corrado and others, *Campaign Finance Reform*, 235.
41. See Magleby, *Outside Money*, for a good discussion of this phenomenon.
42. Ibid.
43. Ibid.
44. Herrnson, "The Money Maze," 116; see Allan J. Cigler, "The 1998 Kansas Third Congressional District Race," in Magleby, *Outside Money*, 77–92, for a good discussion of specific tactics employed in one such district.
45. Drew, "The Money Culture," 739.
46. Herrnson, "The Money Maze," 116.
47. Ibid., 103.
48. Mark Rozell and Clyde Wilcox, *Interest Groups in American Campaigns* (Washington, D.C.: CQ Press, 1999).
49. Herrnson, "The Money Maze," 111; Mark Rozell and Clyde Wilcox, *Interest Groups in American Campaigns* (Washington, D.C.: CQ Press, 1999).
50. The Center for Responsive Politics, http://www.opensecrets.org.
51. Dana Milbank, "On the Outside Looking in as Tom DeLay Whips Up Some Fundraisers," *Washington Post*, August 2, 2000, C1.
52. Ruth Marcus and Juliet Eilperin, "Party's Targets among Sponsors of Social Events," *Washington Post*, August 17, 2000, A13.
53. Mike Allen, "For Some, Party Was Just Too Grand," *Washington Post*, August 4, 2000, A16.
54. Quoted in Drew, "The Money Culture," 738.
55. Ibid., 739.
56. Philip Shenon, "Worried Over Soft Money, GOP Readies Major Gala," *New York Times*, June 20, 2001; George Lardner Jr., "Eight 'Underwriters' Fill Hill Republican Coffers," *Washington Post*, July 1, 2001, http://www.washingtonpost.com/ac2/wp-dyn/A538-2001Jun29.
57. Magleby, *Outside Money*.
58. Herrnson, "The Money Maze," 105.
59. The Center for Responsive Politics, www.opensecrets.org/parties/index.asp.
60. Drew, "The Money Culture," 724.
61. Ibid., 735.
62. Public Law 106-230, 106th Cong., 2d sess., July 1, 2000.
63. FEC, "Financial Activity of General Election Senate Candidates, 1988–2000," May 15, 2001, http://www.fec.gov/press/051501congfinact/tables/gesenate.htm.
64. For a discussion of the efforts to pass campaign finance reform during the 105th and 106th Congresses, see Diana Dwyre and Victoria A. Farrar-Myers, *Legislative Labyrinth* (Washington, D.C.: CQ Press, 2001).
65. See Ronald J. Hrebenar, Matthew J. Burbank, and Robert C. Benedict, *Political Parties, Interest Groups, and Political Campaigns* (Boulder, Colo.: Westview, 1999).
66. See Corrado and others, *Campaign Finance Reform*, 61–63, for a clear discussion of this topic.
67. M. Margaret Conway, "Political Mobilization in America," in *The State of Democracy in America*, ed. William Crotty (Washington, D.C.: Georgetown University, 2001); M. Margaret Conway, "Political Participation in the 2000 Election," in *America's Choice*, ed. William Crotty (Boulder, Colo.: Westview, 2001).
68. See Gary C. Jacobson, *The Politics of Congressional Elections*, 5th ed. (New York: Addison-Wesley Educational Publishers, 2001) and Paul S. Herrnson, *Congressional Elections: Campaigning at Home and in Washington*, 3d ed. (Washington, D.C.: CQ Press, 2000).
69. See Michael J. Malbin and Thomas L. Gais, *The Day After Reform—Sobering Campaign Finance Lessons from the American States* (Albany, N.Y.: Rockefeller Institute, 1998).

7

Campaigning outside the Law
Interest Group Issue Advocacy
Diana Dwyre

The large role of organized interests in the 1999–2000 election cycle continued interest groups' extensive involvement in federal elections. As Chapter 6 documents, the 2000 elections were the most expensive on record. (Detailed records have been kept only since the early 1970s.) Even more impressive, and some would argue more worrisome, than the reported increases in money raised and spent were expenditures on election activities that were not reported to the Federal Election Commission. Groups have learned to take advantage of loopholes in the law that allow them to spend money to influence elections without reporting either their funding sources or the amounts of their expenditures.

Diana Dwyre argues that campaign finance law had almost no constraining effect on organized interests in the 2000 federal elections. In *Buckley v. Valeo* (1976) the Supreme Court ruled that only campaign communications that "expressly advocate" the election or defeat of a candidate for federal office—for example, by using such terms as "vote for" or "vote against"—can be regulated by the Federal Election Campaign Act. According to Dwyre, organized interests, from formal interest groups to parties to wealthy individuals, have learned to design communications that avoid these terms, relying instead on "issue advocacy" messages that serve the same purpose as regulated campaign ads. Thus the messages create the impression that a candidate does or does not deserve voters' support while avoiding contribution limits and reporting requirements. Although issue advocacy ads on television have received the most scrutiny, undisclosed and unlimited expenditures also pay for direct mail, person-to-person contact, voters' guides, and telephone calls.

Dwyre argues that the increasing use of issue advocacy advertising to circumvent campaign finance laws may alter the landscape of campaigns. The "balance between candidate-sponsored and noncandidate-sponsored communications may shift significantly away from the candidates themselves," possibly enabling interest groups to "define the issues of a campaign and shape the debate." Holding candidates accountable, already a formidable task, would be much more difficult under such circumstances.

Some interest group activities are constrained by rules intended to curb corruption in the financing of federal elections. For example, political action committees' (PACs) direct contributions to candidates and parties must be disclosed to the public and cannot exceed a certain dollar amount. The amount a PAC may allot to independent spending in favor of or against some candidate has no cap but must be fully disclosed. But other interest group activities fall outside the law and have created controversy. These activities include issue advocacy advertising and the use of non-profit tax status, which allow interest groups to avoid campaign finance regulations such as contribution limits and disclosure requirements. The 2000 elections show that scores of interest groups use these methods to circumvent campaign finance laws. And the number of groups using these activities increases every election cycle. In this chapter I examine these extralegal interest group activities during elections and their implications.

Why Do Interest Groups Want to Get around the Law?

The financial activities of interest groups in federal elections are governed by the 1971 Federal Election Campaign Act (FECA); its amendments of 1974, 1976, and 1979; tax code provisions; regulations and decisions issued by the Federal Election Commission (FEC); and a few key court decisions. This regulatory patchwork was designed to limit and make public the campaign finance activities of candidates, parties, individuals, and interest groups (operating through their PACs). Generally, the law limits the sources of the funds and the amounts that may be raised and spent on campaign activities.

For example, corporations, labor unions, national banks, and foreign nationals are not allowed to participate financially in federal elections. Corporations and labor unions must form separate PACs to contribute to candidates and parties and to spend money independently for or against a candidate. Corporations and unions cannot use their corporate profits or union treasury funds for election activities. PACs are allowed to accept contributions of up to $5,000 a year from individuals and make limited contributions to federal candidates and political party organizations.

FECA limits on the amount that PACs may contribute to candidates and their parties have not changed since the 1970s. So although PACs may raise an unlimited amount of money in $5,000 increments for electoral activities, they can spend it only in bits and pieces. Political action committees may give no more than $5,000 to a House or Senate candidate for each election (primary, run-off, and general election). PACs can contribute up to $5,000 to a candidate in a presidential nomination contest, and an additional $5,000 may be contributed for the general election, but only if the candidate does not accept presidential matching funds. However, inflation has eroded the value of a PAC contribution to a candidate: $5,000 in 1974 was worth only $1,400 in 2001. PACs may also give up to $15,000 of this regulated money (or "hard" money) to the national party committees, but that is only about $4,200 in 2001 dollars. So not only are PAC contributions worth less today than they were in 1974, but because modern campaigns cost far more now, a contribution from a single PAC constitutes far less of a candidate's overall receipts than it did in the 1970s.

The ever-diminishing value and impact of PAC contributions has encouraged interest groups to look for other ways to influence election outcomes. The only other regulated and disclosed means of PAC campaign giving is independent expenditures, which are unlimited expenditures in favor of or against a candidate and which cannot be coordinated with the favored candidate or his or her representatives.[1] Independent expenditures are generally used for some form of communication, such as a campaign ad, a mail piece, or a telephone communication. Although PACs' independent expenditures have risen in recent elections (see Chapter 6 in this volume), they have not replaced direct contributions to candidates and parties. Nor do independent expenditures rival the extralegal and less visible ways that interest groups now spend money.

Indeed, although PACs' independent expenditures are unlimited, PACs (and parties and individuals) must fully disclose these expenditures and report donors' identities to the FEC. Interest groups and parties would rather *not* disclose this information, and some would prefer their identities not be revealed when they, for example, help run negative ads against a candidate for office. Fund-raising would be easier if contributors knew their identities and occupations would not be disclosed to the FEC and broadcast on the Internet. Thus it is not surprising that interest groups are finding ways to raise and spend money that do not require disclosure of contributors or of expenditures and that allow otherwise prohibited funds (such as labor union treasury funds and corporate profits) to be used in unlimited amounts.

How Do Interest Groups Get around the Law?

Interest groups take advantage of loopholes in the law to spend unlimited amounts on elections without having to fully report their expenditures or the sources of their funding. One way to do this is by giving "soft" money to political parties (see Chapter 6 in this volume). Soft money is money given to parties in unlimited amounts by otherwise prohibited sources, such as corporations and labor unions, or by PACs and individuals in amounts higher than the contribution limits. Soft money activities have less stringent disclosure requirements than regulated, hard money campaign finance activities. But interest groups have little say over how their soft money contributions are spent. Interest groups gain more control by conducting issue advocacy activities (defined below) during campaigns and shielding their activities behind the protection of non-profit, tax-exempt organizations.

Congress intended the Federal Election Campaign Act of 1971 and its amendments to regulate all spending in connection with or for the purpose of influencing a federal election or "relative to" a federal candidate.[2] But this broad language did not specify exactly which activities are election-related activities and which are not. So even nonpartisan communications by groups that were not political committees would have been subject to limits and public disclosure. Consequently, the FECA was challenged on constitutional grounds. In *Buckley v. Veleo* (1976), the Supreme Court held that it was necessary to be precise and clear when specifying exactly which communications the FECA would govern, particularly because criminal penalties could be imposed for violating the law. The Court sought to specify what would be considered an election-related communication (and therefore subject to FECA limits and disclosure requirements) and what would not. But this desire for specificity in the law and the complexity of applying the First Amendment to political communications have created loopholes that allow interest groups (as well as parties and individuals) to legally escape regulation and public disclosure.

Express and Issue Advocacy

In *Buckley v. Valeo* the Supreme Court ruled that only communications that "expressly advocate" the election or defeat of a clearly identified candidate for federal office are campaign communications governable by the FECA. The Court held that "*explicit* words of advocacy of election or defeat" are required to avoid unconstitutional vagueness and provide First Amendment protection to political speech that does not expressly advocate the election or defeat of a candidate. In a footnote, the Supreme Court indicated that the following terms satisfied their strict "express advocacy" test: *vote for, elect, support, cast your ballot for, Smith for Congress, vote against, defeat, reject.*[3] These have become known as the "magic words" of express advocacy. If a communication does not contain them and is not produced in coordination with a candidate or his or her campaign, then it is an "issue advocacy" communication (that is, a discussion of some policy issue). Issue advocacy communications are not subject to FECA regulations, and sponsors may pay for them however they want, including from sources (such as corporations and labor unions) and in amounts prohibited by the FECA.

Interest groups, labor unions, corporations, political parties, and wealthy individuals take advantage of this narrow definition of express advocacy to design communications that avoid words of express advocacy but that are similar to conventional campaign pieces in nearly every other way. Many issue advocacy ads convey the same message as regulated campaign ads—namely, that some candidate does or does not deserve support—while avoiding the contribution limits and reporting requirements stipulated for official campaign communications. Even campaign commercials paid for with regulated dollars and disclosed to the public in recent elections did not contain words of express advocacy.

When run during an election, issue advocacy ads that mention or feature a candidate for office create controversy because they potentially influence the outcome of the election without being subject to the campaign finance rules that govern federal elections. Box 7.1 contains some of the issue advocacy ads run by interest groups during the 2000 election. Although none of them use words of express advocacy, they were all run after Labor Day, the traditional start of the campaign season. The mention of a candidate for office and the timing of these ads make their intent clear—to influence the outcome of the upcoming election.

An invitation to telephone a representative is a common feature of issue advocacy ads. This call to action seems to indicate that the ad's sponsor wants citizens to pressure an elected official to vote a particular way or do a particular thing. Yet the timing and generally negative tone of these ads suggest they are really intended to influence voters, not elected officials.

Two Sides of the Same Coin

Regulated campaign communications (express advocacy) do not differ much from unregulated ones (issue advocacy). It is not difficult to make a hard-hitting and effective advertisement that benefits a favored candidate without using words of express advocacy. Most voters in the television audience would interpret these ads as conventional campaign ads. David Magleby reports that citizens tested in focus groups were not able to distinguish between advertisements sponsored by candidates and candidate-centered issue advocacy ads sponsored by interest groups and political parties. In fact, respondents "saw candidate-focused issue ads as more about the election or defeat of a candidate than the candidates' own commercials."[4] Jonathan Krasno and Daniel Seltz found that in 1998 only 4 percent of ads run by candidates used words of express advocacy, with such words becoming only slightly more prominent in the final weeks of the campaign.[5] Because neither regulated nor unregulated ads use words of express advocacy, the Court's attempt to draw a clear line between campaign communications that should be regulated and issue advocacy communications that should not appears to have failed. Thus the distinction between express advocacy and issue advocacy is fiction.

Issue advocacy ads that mention candidates also use many of the same techniques as conventional campaign television ads.[6] Negative issue advocacy ads often feature ominous background music, code words such as *liberal* and *radical,* and grainy, unflattering black-and-white pictures common in campaign attack ads. Positive issue ads use cheery music, code words such as *trust* and family-values pictures, all while

Box 7.1.   Interest Group Issue Advocacy Ads
              Run during the 2000 Election

"Yankee Baby," American Conservative Union, began running September 12, 2000

[Shots of babies]

Announcer [voice over]: "In New York, all babies like these have something in common."

[Shot of baby wearing Yankee baseball cap]

"They've lived here longer than Hillary Rodham Clinton."

[On screen: Learn more http://www.conservative.org; Paid for by the one million members and supporters of the American Conservative Union]

Source: "Hilary, Don't Be a Baby," *National Journal's Ad Spotlight*, September 13, 2000, http://www.nationaljournal.com.

"Job," AFL-CIO, began running September 13, 2000

John Nalepinski: "Well, when you're lifting 70,000 pounds of castings a day and you do this for 24 years, you're gonna hurt yourself. I had surgery on both hands, but I'll be in pain for the rest of my life."

Announcer [voice over]: "Every year, tens of thousands of Americans suffer permanent and crippling repetitive motion injuries on the job. Yet Congressman Robin Hayes voted to block federal safety standards that would help protect workers from this risk."

[On screen: Source: H.R. 4577, H. Amdt. 760, R.C. #250, 6/8/00]

"Tell Hayes that his politics causes pain."

[On screen: Call Congressman Hayes: 704.786.1612]

John Nalepinski: "We're all human beings. We need to help each other so that this stuff doesn't happen to us."

[On screen: Paid for by the working men and women of the AFL-CIO]

Source: "AFL-CIO Uses TV to Fight Its Fights," *National Journal's Ad Spotlight*, September 26, 2000, http://www.nationaljournal.com.

"Stinks," Kentucky Sierra Club, began running late September 2000

Announcer [voice over]: "Some days the air in Louisville's west end smells like chemicals burning. Some days it smells like an overheated vacuum cleaner. But every day, the air stinks. And we don't know why.

What we do know is that we live in a neighborhood with a lot of chemical plants. And what gets pumped into our air is breathed in by

(continued)

Box 7.1.   *(continued)*

our children. Scientists have found evidence of strong links between air pollution and asthma, but Congresswoman Anne Northup has voted against strengthening clean air standards and enforcement. She even voted to stop the government from telling people when the air is unhealthy.

Call Anne Northup in Louisville at 582-5129. Tell her to vote in upcoming budget bills to fund Environmental Protection Agency efforts to clean up our air—for our families, for our future."

Paid for by the Kentucky Sierra Club

Source: "Sierra Club, NAACP Hit Three Hopefuls," *National Journal's Ad Spotlight*, September 20, 2000, http://www.nationaljournal.com.

praising some policy position of a candidate or party.[7] Moreover, issue ad sponsors hire the same media consultants who produce regulated campaign advertisements.[8]

The one significant difference between candidate and issue advocacy ads is that issue ads tend to be more attack oriented.[9] The Annenberg Public Policy Center at the University of Pennsylvania reports that some 81 percent of interest group issue advocacy ads aired after Super Tuesday 2000 (March 7) were either attack ads, which communicate harmful information about a candidate, or contrast ads, which communicate helpful information about one candidate and harmful information about another.[10] The NAACP Voter Fund ran one of the most highly criticized issue ads in 2000. The spot ran in late October and attacked GOP presidential nominee George W. Bush's position on a hate crime bill. The daughter of the late James Byrd Jr. narrated the ad, which recalls Byrd's murder by three white men (Byrd was black) who dragged him from a truck. The ad shows a truck pulling a chain with the view Byrd would have had as he was dragged.

> I'm Renee Mullins, James Byrd's daughter. On June 7, 1998, in Texas, my father was killed. He was beaten, chained, and then dragged three miles to his death, all because he was black. So when Governor George W. Bush refused to support hate crimes legislation, it was like my father was killed all over again. Call George W. Bush and tell him to support hate crimes legislation. We won't be dragged away from our future.[11]

Although most issue advocacy ads are not so graphically negative, they are more negative than candidate-sponsored ads.

Interest Group Spending on Issue Advocacy Communications

A few scholars have tried to estimate the amount interest groups spend producing and distributing issue advocacy communications. Researchers at both the Annenberg Public Policy Center and the Brennan Center for Justice at the New York University School of Law tracked spending on issue ads nationwide during the 2000 election. The Annenberg Center estimates that at least 123 interest groups spent approximately $347 million on issue advocacy television and radio ads during the 1999–2000 election cycle, a big increase from the 1996 election.[12] After Super Tuesday, interest group spending on television issue ads in the top seventy-five media markets was $91 million.[13] The Brennan Center estimates that between June 1 and election day interest groups spent almost $57 million on radio and television issue ads in the nation's seventy-five largest media markets, which cover only a small number of House and Senate races.[14]

David Magleby and a team of scholars took another approach to the study of issue ads. They used a case study method to track communications in twelve competitive House races and five close Senate races in 2000, attempting to collect information on all candidate-focused communications in those districts and states. The scholars estimate that interest groups accounted for $20 million of the $95 million spent on television and radio ads in these competitive races.[15] But the true cost of issue advocacy advertising in 2000 may have been considerably larger than any of these researchers estimated. The researchers were not able to account for the cost of fees for consulting and production and placement of the ads, nor for the fact that television stations often increase the cost of an ad spot as election day approaches.

Moreover, interest groups and parties also conduct issue advocacy activities through the mail, on the phone, through email, in voters' guides, and through person-to-person contact—campaign activities commonly referred to as the "ground war." These communications are even more difficult to detect because mail, phone calls, and emails are all targeted to individuals and not broadcast widely like television ads. And voters' guides are distributed at meetings, church services, work places, and other gatherings.

Magleby and his team of scholars tracked both the air war (television and radio) and the ground war in the seventeen competitive congressional races in 2000. The ground war was intense. In interviews with interest groups, Magleby found that a number of them—the National Education Association, the National Rifle Association, the National Federation of Independent Businesses, and the National Abortion Rights Action League—increased their use of mail and telephone communications from the previous election. He also notes that interest group issue advocacy mail appears to be more negative than candidate mail, as is the case with issue advocacy television and radio ads.[16]

We can see that interest groups spend huge sums on candidate-focused issue advocacy communications. The estimates reveal the magnitude of spending outside FECA regulations and illustrate why there is increasing support for reforms that would require limits on and disclosure of issue advocacy advertising during campaign season.

Who Makes Issue Advocacy Ads, and Where Do These Ads Appear?

Although the number of groups sponsoring issue ads has increased steadily in recent election cycles, only a handful of groups run most of the ads. At least seventy-four groups spent about $91 million on television issue ads between Super Tuesday and Election Day 2000. Yet a mere nine groups account for 73 percent ($66.7 million) of that spending:

- Citizens for Better Medicare (a pharmaceutical industry group).
- AFL-CIO.
- Planned Parenthood.
- Chamber of Commerce.
- Business Roundtable.
- League of Conservation Voters.
- Americans for Job Security (a Section 527 tax-exempt group backed by former Senate majority leader Trent Lott).
- EMILY's List (a group that supports Democratic, abortion rights female candidates).
- Coalition to Protect America's Healthcare (a coalition of hospitals, hospital associations, and business groups for increased Medicare funding for hospitals).

Citizens for Better Medicare spent 38 percent ($25.4 million) of the $66.7 million.[17] Among these nine groups, the five representing business interests spent 64 percent of the group total ($42.7 million), the AFL-CIO spent 14 percent ($49.5 million), and the remaining groups (most of them left-leaning) spent 22 percent ($14.5 million)—hardly the level playing field Congress intended to encourage when it created the FECA, or the plurality of voices the Supreme Court believed would result from *Buckley v. Valeo*.[18]

Most interest group advocacy is not only conducted by a small number of groups, but is directed at a few competitive congressional races and a few states in the presidential contest.[19] This is the same pattern we see with regulated campaign contributions and independent expenditures, whereby true competition for office occurs in only a few contests. Since the early 1990s, fewer and fewer congressional races have been seen as competitive by informed observers and by the political parties and interest groups that fund campaigns.[20] The reshuffling of districts through reapportionment will no doubt make more races competitive at first. Yet after one or two election cycles the number of competitive contests is likely to shrink, and the increasing influx of millions of dollars in issue advocacy spending into these few competitive districts is likely to exacerbate the concentration of electoral competition.

Partisan leanings also seem to influence the distribution of issue advocacy activity. Interest groups affiliated with the Democratic and Republican Parties appear to pursue different spending strategies. In 2000 GOP-leaning groups (the Business Roundtable, Citizens for Better Medicare, the U.S. Chamber of Commerce) directed most of their ad dollars (75 percent or $20.5 million of the $27.5 million spent by Republican groups) to House races, with only $2.1 million in ads for GOP presidential hopeful George W. Bush. Democratic-leaning groups (Planned Parenthood, the AFL-CIO, Handgun Control) spent some $29 million on ads to help Democratic candidates, and almost half of that ($14 million) on ads related to the presidential contest to help Al Gore.[21] Why Democratic interest groups were more inclined than Republican groups to support their presidential candidate is unclear. In the 2002 midterm elections, issue advocacy spending will likely concentrate on competitive congressional races, although redistricting may make for a wider distribution. If the 2004 presidential contest is as competitive as the 2000 one, we might see issue advocacy money distributed in similar ways, but it is too early to tell if the partisan differences that emerged in 2000 will form a pattern.

The Secretive Nature of Issue Advocacy

If sponsors of issue advocacy communications do not have to disclose their identities, activities, or donors to the Federal Election Commission, how do we know who is behind these communications? Just days before Super Tuesday in the 2000 presidential primary, a group no one had heard of—Republicans for Clean Air—ran television ads in targeted states that criticized Sen. John McCain's (R-Ariz.) environmental credentials and promoted Texas Governor George W. Bush. This spot ran in New York:

[On screen: Paid for by Republicans for Clean Air]

Announcer: Last year, John McCain voted against solar and renewable energy. That means more use of coal-burning plants that pollute our air.

New York Republicans care about clean air. So does Governor Bush. He led one of the first states in America to clamp down on old coal-burning electric power plants.

Bush clean air laws will reduce air pollution by more than a quarter million tons a year. That's like taking five million cars off the road.

Governor Bush: leading so each day dawns brighter.[22]

The political media scrambled to find out who was behind Republicans for Clean Air. Just one day before the pivotal Super Tuesday primaries, it was reported that the mystery group was the creation of Dallas businessman and friend of George W. Bush, Sam Wyly and his family. Wyly spent approximately $2.5 million on the ad campaign and nearly went undetected. Moreover, the Wyly ads had factual flaws.[23] John McCain cried foul and filed an official complaint with the FEC, but the damage was already done. Wyly's identity was revealed too late for the FEC to take any meaningful action or for McCain's campaign to respond effectively.

Another previously unknown group, Citizens for Better Medicare, ran some $40 million worth of issue advocacy ads before Super Tuesday 2000 and $25 million after. Early in the election season no one knew who the group was. Citizens for Better Medicare sounds like it might have been a group of senior citizens advocating for prescription drug coverage under Medicare. Actually, the group was a coalition of drug companies, hospitals, and health care providers that opposed the Democrats' plan to expand Medicare to include prescription drug coverage, preferring instead the GOP plan for government reimbursement to private insurance firms for prescription coverage.

Citizens for Better Medicare spent millions of dollars opposing the Democrats' plan. The group ran negative issue ads against Democratic incumbents who supported President Clinton's Medicare expansion plan and positive issue ads supporting Republicans who fought against the plan. Citizens for Better Medicare aired more issue ads than any other interest group both after Super Tuesday (27 percent of all interest group issue ads) and after Labor Day (20 percent).[24] This volume helped to shift the focus of the 2000 election toward the prescription drug issue, and in the final months of the campaign more was spent on issue ads about health care than any other topic.[25] Moreover, health care was the most frequent theme of Republican-affiliated interest group communications and the second most frequent theme (after the environment) of Democratic interest group communications during the 2000 election.[26]

The Citizens for Better Medicare issue advocacy campaign had a significant and often unwelcome effect on candidates' campaigns. The group ran attack ads against Democratic Senate challenger Brian Schweitzer from Montana. Schweitzer had captured national media attention for organizing bus trips for senior citizens to purchase U.S.-manufactured prescription drugs in Canada at much lower cost. One ad accused Schweitzer of supporting "Canadian-style government controls on medications here in America." In response, Schweitzer began television advertising earlier than he had planned, and with little money in the bank to respond to the attack.[27] Schweitzer's opponent, GOP incumbent Conrad Burns, even tried unsuccessfully to get Citizens for Better Medicare to suspend its advertising in Montana because the ads had focused so much attention on Schweitzer and the prescription drug issue. It is not unusual for interest group and party issue advocacy ads to backfire by hurting the candidates they mean to help.[28]

Like Citizens for Better Medicare, many issue advocacy groups have mysterious names, and voters often do not know who funds them and whom they represent. Sometimes the groups' names are misleading. A name like Citizens for Better Medicare gives no hint that the pharmaceutical industry funds the group, and Republicans for Clean Air sounds more like an affiliate of the Sierra Club than two Texas businesspeople who supported GOP presidential candidate George W. Bush. Here is a sampling of other groups with mysterious names:

- American Family Voices, a group set up with money from a large labor union called the American Federation of State, County, and Municipal Employees to promote progressive public policies.
- Americans for Job Security, a conservative, business-backed organization that supports Republican candidates.
- Coalition for the Future American Worker, an umbrella organization of anti-immigration, professional trade, population, and environmental groups.
- Citizens for a Better America, a group led by a New Jersey businessman, which ran an ad attacking New Jersey Democratic Senate candidate Jon Corzine for refusing to release his tax returns.
- Coalition to Protect Americans Now, a group supporting creation of a national missile defense system, which ran ads attacking Democratic presidential candidate Al Gore's lack of support for the system and praising his opponent George W. Bush.
- Shape the Debate, a conservative, free-market group formed by allies of former California governor Pete Wilson, a Republican, which ran ads against Al Gore in California, New York, and Washington.[29]

Even a group such as EMILY's List, which is well known among those who follow politics closely, would not be easily recognized by most voters. Moreover, the issue advocacy ads run by groups with innocuous names are even more harshly negative than ads run by more familiar groups.[30]

The secretive nature of issue advocacy advertising raises serious questions about accountability and influence in elections. Disclosure rules were established in part to identify who was trying to influence an election and allow the public to take that information into account when voting. When unfamiliar groups conduct undisclosed activities, voters do not have enough information to judge those activities and vote accordingly. David Magleby has found that most voters "could not differentiate the source of political communications (including mail), and ... assume that communications come from the candidate" and that voters saw issue advocacy communications as "even more election centered than the candidate ads."[31] Kathleen Hall Jamieson notes, "Issue advocacy masks the identity of some key players and by so doing, it deprives citizens of information about the source of messages which research tells us is a vital part of assessing message credibility."[32]

Taking Cover in the Tax Code

Groups that sponsor issue advocacy advertising have found a safe haven in the tax code. Registering as a nonprofit, tax-exempt group rather than as a political action committee allows groups to communicate issue advocacy messages to voters without disclosing their donors or spending. So-called "527 committees," named for section 527 of the tax code, are not required to report their donors or spending to either the FEC or the Internal Revenue Service (IRS). As long as 527 groups confine their activities to issue advocacy and do not expressly advocate the election or defeat of candidates, do not engage in any hard money activity, and keep their funds in noninterest bearing accounts, they are exempt from federal taxation and from FECA regulations.

Moreover such groups can accept money from sources, including foreign corporations and individuals, prohibited from participating in federal elections under the FECA.[33] Indeed, the biggest 527 group that operated in 2000, Citizens for Better Medicare, received funding through the Pharmaceutical Research and Manufacturers Association from U.S. subsidiaries of European pharmaceutical companies, including Bayer A.G. and Glaxo Wellcome.[34] During a June 2000 House debate over a bill to regulate the political activities of 527 groups, Rep. Greg Ganske, R-Iowa, commented that "these stealthy political action committees could be getting money from the Communist Chinese, Columbian drug lords, the Mafia, who knows."[35] The secrecy surrounding 527 committees earned them the title of "Stealth PACs" during the 2000 election.

Unlike PACs, 527 groups have no cap on how much they can spend or accept. Although donations to a 527 committee are not tax deductible, there is no IRS gift tax on them, so donors may contribute unlimited amounts without any tax consequences. Donors to other forms of nonprofit organizations that may engage in certain political activity face a steep federal gift tax if their donations exceed $10,000. Thus 527 groups essentially "receive a public subsidy for their activities to influence elections.[36] Democratic presidential candidate Al Gore called Section 527 organizations "the equivalent of Swiss bank accounts for campaigns."[37]

In 1996 the Sierra Club was one of the first nonprofit organizations to establish a 527 committee, and the League of Conservation Voters followed the next year.[38] A significant increase in the number and variety of 527 committees during the 1999–2000 election cycle caught the attention of the media and reform advocates in Congress. Following an IRS ruling in 1999 that clarified the law in a way that essentially endorsed the use of

527 tax-exempt status for issue advocacy organizations, groups of all political stripes began pouring millions of dollars into newly established 527 committees. These groups did not have to report their existence to the FEC or the IRS, so it is impossible to say how many there were during the 2000 elections. Greg Colvin, a lawyer who set up some of the first 527 organizations for liberal groups, noted that donors "were looking for a way to put large, anonymous money into organizations that would have a political effect."[39] Van Gosse, organizing director of Peace Action, which set up the 527 committee Peace Voter Fund for the 2000 election, said this about Section 527: "It's a thing of beauty from an organizing perspective. It gives one a lot of freedom and fluidity."[40] Other 527 committees that operated during the 2000 election included:

- Republicans for Clean Air.
- Americans for Equality, established by the NAACP in addition to its National Voter Fund, the non-527 group that ran the "Byrd" ad (see Box 7.1).
- Republican Majority Issues Committee, established by Rep. Tom DeLay, R-Texas.
- Business Leaders for Sensible Priorities, led by Ben Cohen, founder of Ben & Jerry's ice cream, to advocate for less spending on weapons and more on education.
- Million Mom March, which created a 527 committee to help end gun violence.

Congress and the president placed limits on 527 committees during the heat of the 2000 election. On July 1, 2000, President Clinton signed a new law requiring any group that organizes as a 527 committee to register with the IRS within twenty-four hours, to disclose the identities of its senior officers, and to report its receipts and disbursements every three months during an election year. Section 527 groups that spend more than $25,000 a year must disclose contributors who give more than $200 and report any expenditures greater than $500. The information is to be made public and posted on the Internet.

Will the new law close the 527 committee loophole? Or will the attraction of favorable tax treatment outweigh the negative effects of disclosure? There is at least one other place in the tax code for issue advocacy groups to hide, and many 527 committees will no doubt refile as 501(c)(4) committees, named after a provision in the tax code that provides for "social welfare organizations."[41] Like 527 committees, 501(c)(4) committees are permitted to engage in such political activities as issue advocacy advertising, polling, and lobbying as long as political functions constitute less than 50 percent of their activities. The disclosure requirements for 501(c)(4) committees are less restrictive than the new requirements for 527 committees, and 501(c)(4) committees are not required to report the identity of their donors.

Less than six weeks after Clinton signed into law the new restrictions on 527 groups, at least one group created a new 501(c)(4) organization. The American Federation of State, County, and Municipal Employees set up American Family Voices and began running a television attack ad against George W. Bush the second week of August. The NAACP's National Voter Fund was established as a 501(c)(4) committee, as was the Christian Coalition and the Democratic Leadership Council.

Interest groups will seek the most favorable conditions under which to operate. Veteran campaign finance reformer Fred Wertheimer recently called 501(c)(4) committees "another example of interests conducting blatant electioneering activities and hiding behind their donors. . . . This conduct is an evasion of the spirit of disclosure laws and will be a growing problem that will have to be solved just like the Section 527 groups were."[42]

Conclusion

Interest groups conduct a lot of election activity outside campaign finance laws, using issue advocacy to influence the outcome of an election without expressly advocating the election or defeat of a candidate. These groups have found shelter in the tax code, which allows them to register as nonprofit, tax-exempt organizations and therefore avoid contribution and spending limits without disclosing their donors. Interest groups' unregulated and undisclosed activities have increased tremendously in recent elections, and without further reforms are likely to increase even more. What are the implications of these activities for the health of our electoral system?

As the number of groups conducting issue advocacy campaigns during election season increases, the balance between candidate-sponsored and noncandidate-sponsored communications may shift significantly away from the candidates themselves. Indeed, there have already been several races where the number of noncandidate communications exceeded those sponsored by the candidates. As these other voices drown out candidate messages, interest groups may be able to define the issues of a campaign and shape the debate.

> Many observers are concerned that future campaigns will be conduced by shifting alliances of interest groups—some of which, backed by unknown funding sources and designed to further unknown agendas, will be created solely to spend money in a particular campaign.[43]

We've seen these groups already in the 2000 election. Moreover, because voters do not easily differentiate the source of political communications and often assume they all come from candidates, the prominence of noncandidate communications in contemporary campaigns poses an accountability problem.[44] Only candidates and their party affiliations appear on the ballot on election day, thus only they can be held accountable for the campaign. Interest groups that run attack ads in the final days of the campaign face few if any consequences. And if the group has a mysterious or innocuous sounding name, voters may be unable to attribute the ad at all.

Of course, candidates do not always approve of interest groups' power to define the issues and shape the debates of candidates' campaigns, as the Montana Senate race example illustrates. Whether candidates suffer or benefit from issue advocacy, they lose some control over the campaign dialogue, making contests for office much less predictable than they used to be.

Issue advocacy activity has affected the tone of campaign dialogue. Because noncandidate issue advocacy communications are more attack oriented than candidate communications, the more noncandidate communications there are relative to candidate-sponsored ones, the more negative the tone of the campaign is likely to be. Scholars disagree on the effect of negative advertising in campaigns. Some think that negative campaigning depresses turnout and polarizes the electorate.[45] Others think that voters get useful information from comparative ads that contain both attack and advocacy claims.[46] But comparative ads lack legitimacy when they are not delivered by candidates: "The key element in legitimate oppositional discourse is the accountability that comes from personal utterance of the message."[47] Indeed, there have been congressional proposals to mandate that attacks be spoken by the attacking candidate. Interest group attack-oriented issue advocacy ads, particularly those run by unknown groups, offer perhaps the lowest potential for legitimacy and accountability.

Another possible consequence of the increase in interest group issue advocacy is a growing inequality of voices in the campaign debate. During the 2000 elections business interests sponsored most of the interest group television issue advocacy ads, labor groups trailed far behind, and all other groups ran only a small portion of the ads. Interest groups with more resources have always had more influence in American politics than those with fewer resources. Congress created the FECA to adjust this imbalance by banning direct political activity by corporations and labor unions and by forcing these groups to conduct activities through PACs and to disclose all those activities to the public.

Now that interest groups have found ways around those FECA regulations, unequal influence is again the norm. "When significant portions of campaign funds are drawn from interest group treasuries [rather than from regulated PACs that must be funded with limited contributions], there is a potential for tremendous imbalances, as wealthier groups can easily outspend those with fewer financial resources."[48] Unless Congress can find a way to bring interest group issue advocacy activities under the jurisdiction of campaign finance laws, these imbalances will grow.

After the 2000 election there was renewed interest in achieving real campaign finance reform. Much of the momentum for reform in the Senate resulted from Sen. John McCain's, R-Ariz., presidential run and the positive public response to his calls for campaign finance reform with a ban on party soft money and limits on issue ads by parties and interest groups. McCain called attention to the tremendous influence of wealthy special interests in the policy process, and he offered campaign finance reform as a way to temper this influence. Although the leading reform bill (the McCain-Feingold bill) passed the Senate on April 2, 2001, sponsors of the House measure (the Shays-Meehan bill) chose to withdraw it that summer (through a defeat of the rule) rather than watch it face almost certain death on the House floor.

As this book goes to press, the nation is still reeling from terrorist attacks on the World Trade Center and the Pentagon. Most domestic policy issues, such as campaign finance reform, will move to the back burner for some time. Thus in 2002 and 2004 even more campaign finance activity is likely to occur outside the confines of the law and hidden from public scrutiny.

Notes

1. Independent expenditures are communications expressly advocating the election or defeat of a clearly identified federal candidate, are paid for with regulated and limited "hard" money, and are publicly disclosed. Independent expenditures may not be coordinated with any candidate or campaign committee.
2. *Federal Election Campaign Act*, Public Law 92-225.
3. *Buckley v. Valeo*, 424 U.S. at 44 n. 52 (1976). Although the Court did not indicate whether this list was exhaustive, most legal, political, and scholarly observers do not regard it as so.
4. David Magleby, "Dictum Without Data: The Myth of Issue Advocacy and Party Building," Brigham Young University, The Center for the Study of Elections and Democracy, November 13, 2000, http://www.byu.edu/outsidemoney/dictum, 13.
5. Jonathan S. Krasno and Daniel E. Seltz, *Buying Time: Television Advertising in the 1998 Congressional Elections* (New York: The Brennan Center for Justice at New York University School of Law, 2000), 9.
6. For analysis of conventional, regulated campaign ads, see Darrell M. West, *Air Wars: Television Advertising in Election Campaigns, 1952–1996*, 2d ed. (Washington, D.C.: CQ Press, 1997), 4–9; Kathleen Hall Jamieson, *Dirty Politics: Deception, Distraction and Democracy* (New York: Oxford University, 1992).
7. Paul S. Herrnson and Diana Dwyre, "Party Issue Advocacy in Congressional Elections," in *State of the Parties*, 3d ed., ed. John C. Green and Daniel M. Shea (Lanham, Md.: Rowman and Littlefield, 1999), 86–104.
8. David A. Dulio and Robin Kolodny, "Political Parties and Political Consultants: Creating Alliances for Electoral Success" (paper presented at the Western Political Science Association Annual Meeting, Las Vegas, Nev., March 15–18, 2001).
9. Annenberg Public Policy Center of the University of Pennsylvania, *Issue Advertising in the 1999–2000 Election Cycle*, http://www.appcpenn.org/issueads, 2001, 15; see also Herrnson and Dwyre, "Party Issue Advocacy in Congressional Elections."
10. Annenberg Public Policy Center, *Issue Advertising in the 1999–2000 Election Cycle*, 19; Herrnson and Dwyre, "Party Issue Advocacy in Congressional Elections," 17.

11. "Ads of the Year," *National Journal*, November 11, 2000, 3628.
12. Annenberg Public Policy Center, *Issue Advertising in the 1999–2000 Election Cycle*, 4, 27–28.
13. Ibid., 6.
14. Brennan Center, "2000 Presidential Race First in Modern History Where Political Parties Spend More on TV Ads Than Candidates," http://www.brennancenter.org/tvads2000, December 11, 2000 (see Tables 1, 6, and 9). This figure reflects ads aired between June 1 and election day.
15. David B. Magleby, ed., *Election Advocacy: Soft Money and Issue Advocacy in the 2000 Congressional Elections* (Provo, Utah: Brigham Young University, Center for the Study of Elections and Democracy, 2000), 2.
16. Ibid.
17. Annenberg Public Policy Center, *Issue Advertising in the 1999–2000 Election Cycle*, 20.
18. Ibid.
19. Ibid., 5; Magleby, *Election Advocacy*, 8–9; Brennan Center, "2000 Presidential Race First in Modern History."
20. Charlie Cook, "How Big Will the Republican Gains Be?" *National Journal*, September 26, 1998, 2251; Charlie Cook, "National Overview," *The Cook Political Report*, June 23, 2000, 6.
21. Brennan Center, "2000 Presidential Race First in Modern History," 2.
22. "GOP Enviro Ad Mystery Solved," *National Journal's Ad Spotlight*, March 7, 2000, http://www.nationaljournal.com.
23. Ibid.
24. Annenberg Public Policy Center, *Issue Advertising in the 1999–2000 Election Cycle*, 20.
25. Ibid., 9.
26. Magleby, *Election Advocacy*, 28.
27. Craig Wilson, "The 2000 Montana Senate Race," in Magleby, *Election Advocacy*, 99.
28. Diana Dwyre and Robin Kolodny, "Throwing Out the Rule Book: Party Financing of the 2000 Elections," in *Financing the 2000 Election*, ed. David B. Magleby (Washington, D.C.: Brookings Institution, forthcoming).
29. Annenberg Public Policy Center, "Index of Advocacy Groups," http://www.appcpenn.org/issueads/gindex.htm, September 10, 2001.
30. Magleby, *Election Advocacy*, 8.
31. Ibid., 48; see also Magleby, "Dictum Without Data."
32. Annenberg Public Policy Center, *Issue Advertising in the 1999–2000 Election Cycle*, 2.
33. John M. Broder, "Clinton's Drug Plan Attacked by Industry," *New York Times*, June 28, 2000, A22.
34. Ibid.
35. Eric Schmitt, "House Rejects Bill Requiring Donor Disclosure," *New York Times*, June 10, 2000, A11.
36. Allan J. Cigler, "Interest Groups and Financing the 2000 Elections," in Magleby, *Financing the 2000 Election*.
37. John M. Broder and Raymond Bonner, "The 2000 Campaign: The Money Factor; A Political Voice, Without Strings," *New York Times*, March 29, 2000, A1.
38. Ibid.
39. Ibid.
40. Ibid.
41. See Trevor Potter, "Where Are We Now: The Current State of Campaign Finance Law," in *Campaign Finance Reform: A Sourcebook*, ed. Anthony Corrado, Thomas Mann, Daniel Ortiz, Trevor Potter, and Frank Sorauf (Washington, D.C.: Brookings Institution, 1997), 18.
42. John M. Broder, "The 2000 Campaign: The Labor Effort; Finding Another Loophole, a New Secretive Group Springs Up," *New York Times*, August 11, 2000, A14.

43. Mark J. Rozell and Clyde Wilcox, *Interest Groups in American Campaigns: The New Face of Electioneering* (Washington, D.C.: CQ Press, 1999), 164.

44. Magleby, "Dictum Without Data."

45. Stephen Ansolabehere and Shanto Iyengar, *Going Negative: How Political Advertisements Shrink and Polarize the Electorate* (New York: Free Press, 1995).

46. Jamieson, *Dirty Politics: Deception, Distraction and Democracy*, 220.

47. Ibid., 227.

48. Rozell and Wilcox, *Interest Groups in American Campaigns*, 164.

8

A Distant Thunder?
Religious Mobilization in the 2000 Elections

James L. Guth, Lyman A. Kellstedt, John C. Green,
and Corwin E. Smidt

The past quarter century has witnessed a resurgence of political activity among the nation's religious interests. Religious activists on the political right believe that government action is needed to reverse what they see as a nationwide moral decline. Christian right mobilization has been widely credited for reenergizing the Republican Party and helping it gain control of both houses of Congress in 1994. Churches on the liberal end of the political spectrum have increased their political activities as well, often to counteract the perceived influence of the religious right.

In this chapter James L. Guth and his colleagues examine the tactics and targets of religious interest groups in the 2000 elections. Using the results of a national poll of more than 2,900 potential voters, the authors find that religious contacting during the 2000 elections was extensive, though not as widespread as it was in 1996. Christian right political messages reached their primary target, traditional Evangelicals, and also found other listeners, such as Catholics and members of mainline Protestant churches. The African-American church, especially the clergy, also played a central role in voter mobilization.

The authors conclude that "religious contacting still favors Republicans, although perhaps by a smaller margin than in recent elections." Contacting by Evangelicals was particularly effective in increasing Republican voter turnout. The countercampaign by liberal religious groups reached some voters, and "did not match, but may have constrained, Christian right activities."

Organized interest groups influence American elections in many ways. They support candidates financially, try to shape party platforms, recruit activists to staff campaigns, encourage citizens to run for office, and urge sympathizers to go to the polls to vote for favored candidates. Business organizations, labor unions, farmer associations, and other economic groups are veterans of such activities, and now work alongside a host of ideological and "cause" organizations.[1]

In recent years religious interest groups have also entered the world of campaign politics, engaging in every aspect of electioneering. This chapter addresses religious groups' role in electoral mobilization: getting likeminded citizens to the polls to vote for favored candidates. Christian right organizations are especially active, and liberal religious forces have participated in recent elections to counter them. Religious groups were more visible than ever during the 2000 presidential election campaign, when religion burst into the limelight after George W. Bush named Jesus as his favorite political philosopher and Sen. Joseph I. Lieberman, D-Conn., joined the Democratic ticket quoting the Book of Chronicles. And as many observers noted later, the electoral divisions of 2000 were grounded in religious, moral, and cultural values rather than social class or economic issues. If this is true, religious interest groups may well have reinforced these alignments.[2]

Religious Groups' Targets and Techniques

Over the past two decades Christian right organizations have emerged as perennial participants in U.S. electoral politics. Despite years of experience, these groups are still divided over the most effective means of participation. Christian right groups often argue about their "natural constituency." The first organizations in the early 1980s focused on specific Evangelical Protestant communities, such as fundamentalists or Pentecostals. Beginning in the 1990s, however, the Christian Coalition and newer groups not only broadened their targets to include all Evangelicals, but also sought alliances with religious conservatives in the Mainline Protestant, Roman Catholic, and even African-American Protestant traditions. Before the 1996 elections, for example, the Christian Coalition sponsored a "Catholic Alliance," and courted conservative black churches.[3] Neither venture was very successful, but as 2000 approached the Christian Coalition prepared to repeat these efforts, hoping to reinforce George W. Bush's assiduous wooing of these groups.

Whatever the target audience, the Christian right has also continually experimented with mobilizing techniques. Clergy dominated the pioneer organizations, such as the Moral Majority, and, not surprising, saw clergy as the key to action. As Jerry Falwell told fundamentalist pastors, "What can you do from the pulpit? You can register people to vote. You can explain the issues to them. And you can endorse candidates, right there in church on Sunday morning."[4] By the late 1980s some Christian right leaders had decided this approach didn't work: most clergy shunned overt electioneering and, in any event, many parishioners seemed unwilling to follow their lead.[5] As a result second-generation Christian right groups, such as the Christian Coalition, preferred to contact religious voters directly, relegating clergy to supportive roles as individual citizens.

In this approach laity would handle both church-based and more conventional electoral tasks. Recognizing that conservative congregations were still a "happy hunting ground" for sympathetic voters, lay activists would place voter guides in church bulletins or engage parishioners in political conversations. Others would use standard campaign tactics, contacting voters directly through phone calls, faxes, personal visits, or email, taking advantage of the dense communication networks among church people.[6]

Despite the shift in emphasis from church-based to conventional tactics and from clergy to laity, the 2000 election saw both old and new approaches. For example, Jerry Falwell ran "People of Faith 2000," a pastor-centered electoral effort endorsed by prominent religious conservatives, while the Christian Coalition relied on laity to distribute millions of voter guides, send postcards, and make phone calls. Groups such as the Traditional Values Coalition, the Campaign for Working Families, and Concerned Women for America used a mix of church-based and conventional strategies.[7]

Of course, the Christian right was not the only religious force active in 2000. A melange of liberal groups campaigned with different goals. Some, such as Americans United for Separation of Church and State, People for the American Way, and the Interfaith Alliance attacked the Christian right's "politicizing of religion" and its alleged violation of the separation of church and state. Americans United, in particular, sought to "disable" the Christian right by threatening (and occasionally instigating) legal action against churches "violating" their tax-exempt status by participating in the campaign. Americans United's most ambitious effort, however, involved mailing 285,000 letters to Protestant churches warning of the dire legal consequences of electoral activities. This threat was especially credible after a U.S. Court of Appeals decision, *Branch Ministries v. Rossotti* (2000), upheld the revocation of a New York church's tax exemption for buying newspaper ads in 1992 attacking Bill Clinton.

Although Christian right organizations quickly sought to reassure churches that the Americans United threat was hollow, anecdotal evidence hints that the campaign did frighten some conservative congregations, reducing the availability of voter guides and prompting clergy to be more cautious, especially in making political statements from the pulpit. Still, voter guides were widely available, especially in Evangelical churches. For example, the authors' study of the Southern Baptist Convention, the nation's largest Protestant denomination, showed that almost half of these congregations used such guides, with most provided by conservative interest groups. Similarly, more than two-thirds of the congregations in the Assemblies of God, a large Pentecostal group, used these voter guides.

Some liberal groups were interested not only in limiting Christian right incursions into politics but also in mobilizing more "progressive" forces. The Interfaith Alliance, led by clergy from many religious traditions, took a page from the Christian Coalition playbook in the late 1990s by expanding the number of grassroots organizations it sponsored and preparing materials to help religious citizens make electoral decisions. These materials focused less on candidates and more on fundamental values and appropriate forms of religious action. In most cases Interfaith Alliance values were much more compatible with Democratic policies than Republican ones. Similarly, Call to Renewal, a rather eclectic group of progressive Christian clergy, produced a guide stressing the fight against poverty, espousing federal programs for fair incomes, decent housing, and universal medical care. Although the document called on Christians to support candidates of any party who agreed with these principles, no Republican aspirant to national office would find the platform palatable. In any case, if we find that pro-Democratic religious sources contacted religious liberals, we may credit these religious interest groups with reaching their targets.[8]

While the Christian right and Christian "left" waged battle in white Protestant churches, other religious actors were deeply involved in the campaign. Just as the presidential race got underway, the National Conference of Catholic Bishops (NCCB) issued a statement on the political responsibilities of Catholics called "Faithful Citizenship," and followed this with "Political Activity Guidelines for Catholic Organizations." Although Faithful Citizenship spoke cautiously about religious involvement, it stressed support for antiabortion rights issues and candidates as the key to "faithful" Catholic voting. And though the "Political Activity Guidelines" reviewed the legal constraints on church groups, the text also described how Catholic activists could legally and effectively influence the electoral process, especially through registration and get-out-the-vote activities. During the campaign many Catholic bishops followed the advice of Faithful Citizenship by preparing voter guides for their dioceses. Furthermore, several prominent bishops made only slightly veiled pronouncements favoring antiabortion rights candidates, such as George W. Bush, and issued pastoral letters to be read in Catholic parishes. Some Catholic clergy spoke out explicitly against abortion rights Democrats, activated in part by Priests for Life, led by Father Frank Pavone. And throughout the campaign the Bush entourage never lacked a supportive priest for photo opportunities.[9]

Still, not all the cues for Catholics were conservative. Some priests used voter guides prepared by Catholic social agencies that stressed the church's liberal social welfare stances rather than its rejection of abortion, providing comfort for Democrats. In addition, progressive groups inside and outside the church, such as Catholics for a Free Choice, Catholics Speak Out, and Call to Action, sponsored full-page newspaper ads in urban areas to support liberal policies and candidates.[10] So with the potential for members of the same parish to be pulled in opposite political directions, the impact of religious mobilization among Catholics may have been mixed.

Some black churches were targets of the Christian right, but parishioners still generally favored Democrats. Although George W. Bush showcased an endorsement by a prominent black clergyman during the GOP national convention, Al Gore and Democratic candidates for Congress took the award for politicking in black churches. Gore's campaign began with a blessing from the pulpit by Floyd Flake, a former Democratic congressman and pastor of the Allen African Methodist Episcopal Church, and culminated with President Bill Clinton's conference call to hundreds of black ministers late in the campaign, urging them to mobilize their congregations. All this seems to have worked: two-thirds of African-American pastors ran voter registration programs and more than half transported parishioners to the polls. Experts concluded that African-American clergy were a vital piece of Democratic machinery.[11]

To assess all this religious mobilization, we used a poll of 2,925 Americans interviewed in the spring of 2000 and again right after the election.[12] We addressed four key questions about religious group activities:

- Which religious communities were most heavily targeted?
- Which mobilization techniques reached the largest audiences?
- What factors influenced the likelihood of contact?
- Did contacting increase the vote for favored candidates and enhance turnout?

Religious Traditions and Theological Subgroups

To simplify our inquiry, we focused on the four major Christian traditions in the United States: white Evangelical Protestants, white Mainline Protestants, black Protestants, and white Roman Catholics.[13] These communities encompass most U.S. voters and most of the targets for both the Christian right and the liberal countercampaign.[14] As ethnocultural historians have argued, these four traditions have also supplied the critical building blocs for party coalitions. From the turn of the twentieth century until recently, Evangelical Protestants were a major component of the Democratic electorate, joined by most Roman Catholics and, by the 1960s, most black Protestants. Mainline Protestants, on the other hand, constituted the core of the GOP, or as the old adage had it, the "Republican Party at prayer."

In contemporary politics, however, these historic alignments have shifted. Evangelicals—growing in numbers, upwardly mobile, and ideologically conservative—have become the biggest religious constituency of the GOP, while Catholics have become a "swing group." On the other hand, Mainline Protestants have not only declined in number, but some have also drifted away from their ancestral Republican home, shaking its old religious foundation.[15] Black Protestants remain a Democratic bastion.

As religious traditions shift their partisan loyalties, vital crosscutting changes are occurring within each tradition. In sociologist James Davison Hunter's vivid depiction, "culture wars" are polarizing religious communities with battles over abortion, gay rights, and other social issues. Mainline Protestants, Roman Catholics, and even Evangelicals are divided into competing theological factions, with the "orthodox" aligning with the Republicans and the "progressives" with the Democrats.[16]

We used insights from both perspectives to pinpoint targets of religious mobilization. To classify voters, we placed them in one of the four religious traditions (Evangelical, Mainline, black Protestant, or Roman Catholic), based on their denominational affiliation. Then we assigned them to a theological subgroup ("traditionalist," "centrist," and "modernist") within each tradition, using the "three Bs"—beliefs, belonging, and behavior.[17] Traditionalists are most committed to orthodox doctrines, tend to affiliate with theologically conservative religious movements, and are deeply enmeshed in religious life. Centrists are somewhat less orthodox on the historic tenets of their faith, tend not to adopt movement affiliations, and are somewhat less active religiously. Modernists adopt heterodox beliefs, often identify with theologically liberal religious movements, and typically exhibit less religious involvement.[18] Because the number of black Protestants in the postelection survey is relatively small (276), and because this group exhibits little evidence of theological polarization, we did not divide it into theological subgroups.

We asked respondents five questions:

- Did you discuss the election with friends at your place of worship?
- Was information on parties and candidates made available in your place of worship before the election?
- Were you contacted by a moral or religious group?
- Did the clergy or other leaders at your place of worship urge you to register and vote?
- Did the clergy or other leaders at your place of worship urge you to vote a particular way?

In addition, we ascertained whether church "friends" or the "moral or religious group" urged them to vote for a Republican or a Democrat. Thus we have information about most techniques used by religious groups and, because we asked identical or similar questions in 1996, we can also assess changes in religious contacting over time.[19]

The Contours of Religious Contacting

Many Americans received some form of religious contact regarding voting: for example, one in five discussed the election with a friend in church and almost a third heard a religious leader urging them to vote. Only 3 percent, however, reported that their pastor endorsed a candidate (Table 8.1). Compared with 1996, political talk in church increased, voter guides were fewer, religious group contacts declined, and the already small number of clergy endorsements dwindled.

The proportion of religious citizens contacted was higher than the proportion of nonreligious citizens, of course, but contacts varied substantially by religious tradition and subgroup. Political discussion in church was common, with black Protestants most involved, followed closely by Evangelicals. Both talked more in 2000 than in 1996, with black Protestants rising from 26 percent to 32 percent and Evangelicals from 28 percent to 30 percent. Talk among Mainliners declined substantially, however, from 24 percent in 1996 to only 18 percent in 2000. Catholics were again the least "vocal," reporting the same figure as in 1996—15 percent.

Table 8.1.   Share of Religious Contact Sources in the 2000 Election (in percent)

	Talk in church	Voter guides	Interest group	Clergy talk	Clergy endorse	At least one contact
Mass public	22	13	7	31	3	47
Evangelical Protestant	30	18	10	35	2	56
Traditionalist	47	25	19	55	4	80
Centrist	20	14	4	23	1	41
Modernist	12	4	8	14	2	28
Mainline Protestant	18	7	6	27	3	42
Traditionalist	22	13	8	42	0	63
Centrist	17	8	5	23	2	38
Modernist	19	1	5	23	5	29
Black Protestant	32	27	4	50	4	68
Roman Catholic	15	12	11	37	6	51
Traditionalist	15	29	11	63	16	71
Centrist	16	10	13	38	4	54
Modernist	17	6	6	22	2	36

Source: Authors' data.

Why Catholics have fewer political discussions in church is not clear. Perhaps Catholic worship services lack the "free time" that riddles the schedules of most black, Evangelical, or even Mainline Protestant churches. Adult Sunday school hours, coffees between Sunday school and church, postservice meals, mid-week prayer meetings, choir practice, and so on may offer Protestants more opportunities for political talk. Some scholars have also suggested that Catholicism's historic lack of emphasis on the role of laity may have parallel political effects, discouraging such conversations. Or perhaps the large size of the typical Catholic parish inhibits discussion.[20]

Political conversations varied by subgroup as well, with traditionalists generally talking the most, especially among Evangelicals. Almost half of traditionalist Evangelicals reported having political exchanges, compared with only 15 percent of Catholics. Interestingly, much of the decline in political discussion among Mainline Protestants occurred among traditionalists (from 39 percent to 22 percent), whereas talk actually increased among Mainline modernists (from 6 percent to 19 percent), perhaps reflecting greater liberal mobilization. Centrists in both white Protestant traditions also had fewer political conversations in 2000 than they had in 1996. Taken together, these changes over time almost wiped out differences among Mainline subgroups, and did erase the very small internal variation among Catholics in 1996. Among Evangelicals, however, political discussion once again declined sharply as we move from traditionalists to modernists, as the denser social networks of Evangelical traditionalists no doubt helped sustain such conversations. On the whole, then, political discussion occurred most often among traditionalist Evangelicals and black Protestants.

Because political discussion in religious settings is hard to observe, it is neglected in accounts of religious mobilization. Nevertheless, Christian right groups directly encourage electoral proselytizing; it is also a byproduct of other campaign activities. And the growing focus of religious groups on mobilizing laity in target congregations no doubt reflects their recognition of the critical nature of such political communications. We also know that these informal exchanges can shape the political attitudes and activities of religious communities, especially conservative ones.[21] Indeed, the findings support Verba, Schlozman, and Brady's emphasis on church as a place where all sorts of political orientations are fostered.[22]

If press accounts neglect the strategic role of informal discussions within congregations, they have often spotlighted the Christian right's controversial provision of "voter guides" at houses of worship. These materials have become almost canonical, having been used by antiabortion rights groups as early as the 1970s.[23] In 2000, as in previous elections, the Christian Coalition and other Christian right groups claim to have distributed millions of guides, primarily in Evangelical and traditionalist Mainline congregations, but also in some black Protestant and Catholic churches. That all these materials reached the people for whom they were intended is dubious, but some evidence suggests widespread use.[24] As always, these documents were criticized for their transparent Republican bias, and Interfaith Alliance and other liberal groups counterattacked, denigrating the guides and, implicitly, the candidates endorsed therein. As we noted earlier, many Catholic parishes also used voter guides produced by either church agencies or Catholic interest groups.

How many citizens received electoral materials? Thirteen percent reported seeing candidate information available in church, down slightly from 15 percent in 1996 (see Table 8.1). Availability by tradition and subgroup also changed. In 2000 traditionalist Catholics reported the highest usage, with 29 percent seeing a guide, up from 24 percent in 1996, no doubt reflecting considerable diocesan activity. Black Protestants reported the next highest level, increasing from 23 percent in 1996 to 27 percent in 2000. Traditionalist Evangelicals were a close third at 25 percent, but down from 31 percent four years earlier. Indeed, this decline occurred across all the white Protestant subgroups, suggesting either that the Christian right was not as effectively organized in 2000 or that fewer church leaders were willing to distribute the guides. Perhaps the Americans United campaign had some effect among white Protestants, but it seems not to have deterred black Protestants, with their long tradition of politics in church, or Catholics, veterans of some earlier legal skirmishes over clerical politics.

Christian right groups did not rely entirely on voter guides, but also used conventional techniques, such as contacting voters through phone banks, door-to-door canvassing, mail, fax, and email. But in 2000 leaders often limited these efforts to critical states in the presidential race and some close congressional contests. Direct contacts reached only half as many citizens as voter guides did, a substantial change from 1996 when direct contacts were just as numerous. Traditionalist Evangelicals still led the way with 19 percent reporting direct contacts, down from 26 percent in 1996. Of the remaining religious folks, only Catholics—primarily traditionalists and centrists—reported many contacts.

Religious interest groups also encouraged clergy to urge their congregations to register and vote, recognizing the electoral impact of higher turnout. If traditionalist Evangelicals or Catholics swarmed to the polls, Bush benefited; if black Protestant pastors galvanized their churches, Gore gained. Clergy efforts to get parishioners registered and voting were common: half the black Protestants, almost two-fifths of Catholics, and more than one-third of Evangelicals reported such blandishments. Furthermore, in all three white Christian communities, traditionalists reported many more clergy reminders to vote than did centrists or modernists. Traditionalist Catholics, for example, were almost three times as likely as a modernist Catholic to hear a priest urge them to register and vote. Thus a politically savvy pastor might make a real contribution to a favored party by mobilizing the congregation, especially where the people shared a common political stance, as in many Evangelical, traditionalist Catholic, or black Protestant churches.

Finally, there was even less effort than in 1996 to provide explicit pastoral guidance for parishioners' political choices. Although Christian right enthusiasm for this tactic had waned long before 2000, a few groups still urged ministers to tell parishioners how a good Christian should vote—reportedly a custom in black Protestant congregations as well. Despite some highly publicized endorsements by prominent ministers and priests, however, the practice was rare, with every subgroup scoring in single digits except for traditionalist Catholics: 16 percent of this group heard a priest endorse a candidate (usually a Republican).

Because the theological, organizational, legal, and constituency factors long constraining pastoral endorsements were still relevant, most clergy adhered to old adages against mixing religion and politics; a few may have feared the Internal Revenue Service. But keep in mind that although explicit endorsements were rare, many clergy no doubt found subtle ways of conveying their preferences, especially outside of religious services.[25]

What can we conclude, then, about religious activity in 2000? It was different than it was in 1996. Political discussion in church prospered but varied greatly by tradition, rising among black and Evangelical Protestants, declining sharply among Mainliners, and holding steady among Catholics. Voter guides were fewer than in 1996, especially among Protestant centrists and modernists, but held their ground among traditionalist Evangelicals and gained among Catholics and black Protestants. Interest group contacts generally declined, perhaps reflecting the organizational malaise of the Christian Coalition, while clergy endorsements almost disappeared. At the same time, black Protestant and traditionalist white clergy vigorously encouraged parishioners to cast their ballots.

Overall, then, religious contacting remained fairly extensive. Though not all contacts imparted partisan messages, those that did had a conservative and Republican bent. When we asked the "direction" of a contact (from an interest group, friend in church, or pastor), the answers pointed to Republicans by a nine to four margin. This varied somewhat by technique, with a bigger GOP edge (three to one) in interest group contacts and a narrower one (two to one) in church conversations and pastoral endorsements. These ratios also fluctuated by subgroup. Interest group contacts among traditionalist Evangelicals favored the GOP by ten to one, and conversion attempts by friends in church by six to one. Republican influence was more moderate in Mainline and Catholic traditionalist churches (in both cases about four to one). Only for black Protestants (and incidentally, Jews) did Democrats have a larger presence than Republicans. Of course, this does not capture the more amorphous partisan impact of friendly conversations or clerical cues not explicitly designed to convert, but which may have a similar partisan bias.

The role of religious contacts should be put in broader perspective. In an era when party organizations have either atrophied or find it difficult to locate and activate sympathetic voters, religious interests have become significant competitors (and sometimes adjuncts) to party committees, candidate organizations, and traditional interest groups. Indeed, the 47 percent of the public that received religious messages compares quite favorably with the proportion contacted by party organizations (26 percent), political candidates (24 percent), labor unions (8 percent) and business groups (4 percent). And among traditionalists, especially Evangelicals, religious contacts often outnumbered all secular ones put together.[26]

Determinants of Religious Contacting

There is significant variation in how often religious groups contact members of different faiths. To explore this issue further we calculated an index of religious contacting by summing the five types of contact—discussion in church, voter guides, interest group contacts, clergy talk, and clergy endorsement—and then considered several factors that might influence this score (Table 8.2). Evangelical traditionalists were the most likely to receive religious contacts, followed at some distance by black Protestants and Catholic traditionalists. These findings basically summarize the group patterns in Table 8.1.

As we might predict, people who regularly engage in religious practices (such as private prayer and Scripture reading), attend religious services, give generously to church, and participate in small groups all received more communications.[27] Presumably the religiously committed should be most open to religious contacts. Church attendance also facilitates contact: regular worshippers are more apt to have informal political discussions in church, be present to pick up a voter guide, or be put on the mailing list of a religious group. In a similar way, financial contributions enhance the probability of appearing on the phone-tree lists shared by religious organizations.

Of course, religious people are most likely to be involved in politics if they have a social theology that connects religious values to public life. In the twentieth century and today the dominant ethos in most Mainline and black Protestant churches has encouraged political activity, as has the American Catholic Church. On the other hand, many conservative Christians in all traditions, especially Evangelicals, have often abjured politics, preferring to concentrate on religious life alone. In recent years, however, the Christian right has promoted what we call the "civic gospel" to justify a new religious insurgency, urging conservative Christians to link their faith to political choices, fight attacks on the rights of religious people, and mobilize churches to advance these objectives.[28]

To measure adherence to this new social theology, we asked four questions. The first asked respondents how important religious beliefs

Table 8.2. Influences on Religious Contacting Correlation and Regression Coefficients ($N = 2,925$)

	Religious contacts	
	r	b
Religious tradition and theological subgroup		
Evangelical		
Traditionalist	.25**	.10**
Centrist	−.06**	−.03
Modernist	−.05**	−.02
Mainline		
Traditionalist	.02	−.02
Centrist	−.06**	−.03
Modernist	−.05*	.01
Catholic		
Traditionalist	.10**	.06*
Centrist	.02	.02
Modernist	−.05*	−.01
Black Protestant	.14**	.08**
Religious commitment		
General religious activity	.36**	.09*
Church attendance	.34**	.13**
Financial contributions	.30**	.02
Small group activity	.27**	.06**
Social theology		
Faith vital for political decisions	.22**	.01
Religious groups must stand for beliefs	.11**	.00
Government should protect religion	.11**	.00
The religious must protect rights	.09**	.04*
Organizational accessibility		
Religious media important	.24**	.14**
Identification with Christian right	.18**	.01
Christian right membership	.18**	.05*
Strong GOP identification	.13**	.09**
Strong Democratic identification	.00	.08**
Social and demographic variables		
Education	.11**	.07**
Income	.12*	.07**
Southern residence	.05*	−.01
Midwestern residence	.00	.01
Age	−.02	−.03
Male	.01	.03
$R^2 =$		.21

Source: Authors' data.
r = Pearson product moment correlations; b = standardized ordinary least squares coefficients.
* Coefficient significant at $p < .05$.
** $p. < 001$.
Note: This table reports both bivariate correlation coefficients between the index and the independent variables and standardized regression coefficients from a regression. This analysis includes the four religious traditions as well as other respondents, the omitted comparison group in the regression. We incorporated religious tradition and theological subgroup as dummy variables. For each tradition, those who fell into a subgroup were coded "1" and all others, "0." Black Protestant affiliation was entered in the same fashion. The religious activity score is a summary measure of several religious practices such as private prayer and Scripture reading.

were to their political decisions. The second inquired whether "organized religious groups of all kinds should stay out of politics" or if "it is important for organized religious groups to stand up for their beliefs in politics." The third asked whether "the government should take special steps to protect America's religious heritage," or if "there should be a strict separation of church and state." Finally, the survey asked whether the "influence of religion on American politics threatens to divide us as a country," or if "religious people must take political action to protect their rights." Those taking the "activist" options should be natural targets for contacting, especially by the Christian right, and in fact, each sentiment correlates positively with religious contacting (see Table 8.2).

Organizational and cognitive accessibility should also play a role in contacting. People who rely on religious media, identify with "pro-family" and Christian right groups, or actually belong to these groups should report more contacts. Similarly, partisans might be more frequent targets than independents, at least if the purpose of contact is to mobilize rather than convert. Reliance on religious media has the strongest correlation with contacting, while identification with and membership in Christian right groups have identical and fairly strong coefficients. Strong Republicans are more likely than strong Democrats to get contacts.

Some demographic traits might also be related to contacting. For example, residents in "religious" regions, such as the South and Midwest, should be contacted more, along with older people, who are more active in both religious and political networks. Other traits often linked to political participation, such as being male, educated, and wealthy, might have some effect. But only a few of these are related to contacting, and not very strongly. The educated and wealthy did receive more messages, but age and gender lacked even a modest relationship with religious communications. Southerners were approached slightly more often, but Midwesterners were not.

Many of the independent variables are interrelated, of course. Evangelicals, for example, attend church more frequently, think religion should influence politics, sometimes join Christian right groups, and often reside in the South. To sort out the independent effects of each variable, we used multiple regression (see Table 8.2). Religious media users, faithful religious practitioners, church attendees, small-group members, and Christian right activists are all more likely to be contacted. Evangelical traditionalists and, to a lesser extent, their Catholic counterparts, still have an advantage in contacting, even after these religious factors have been accounted for. Beyond this, only black Protestant affiliation increases contacts substantially above what other "religious" variables would predict.

In the main, then, people with similar religious practices and behaviors in each tradition are almost equally subject to contacting. The tendency for traditionalist Evangelicals and Catholics, as well as black Protestants, to receive more contacts is only partly accounted for by higher scores on these variables. And when everything is accounted for, both strong Republican and Democratic partisans are more likely to receive communications. Not surprising, better-educated and wealthier citizens also are contacted more often, but other demographic factors have no influence. All but one of the social theology items drops out of the equation once the other religious and political factors are in. Nevertheless, the model explains only a fifth of the variance, so we suspect that not all the target populations are reached and that some contacts are wasted on voters with unpromising religious and political profiles.[29]

These results confirm the conclusion we drew in 1996: most religious interest groups target committed believers, especially Evangelical traditionalists. And if we examine the "direction" of contacting, the source of messages again becomes clear. Using the same factors to predict the partisanship of cues shows that Evangelical traditionalists received a preponderance of contacts from Republicans, while black Protestants got the same from Democrats. Mainliners did not differ from the general public in either the content (slightly more Republican), or number (low overall) of contacts. Those who rely on religious media, belong to Christian right groups, and identify as strong Republicans also get more GOP-oriented messages (data not shown).

The Effect of Religious Contacting

Did all this religious activity influence the election? Assessing influence, especially in the electoral arena, has always been risky, intriguing and frustrating generations of political scientists. At the very least, success for the Christian right required an increase in Republican voting preferences, higher turnout among Republican religious constituencies, or both. The liberal counteroffensive sought to minimize Republican votes, especially among traditionalists and centrists, and to encourage Democratic votes among modernists and black Protestants.

As in 1996 Evangelicals were clearly the GOP's strongest constituency, with 74 percent choosing Bush and 73 percent voting Republican in the House of Representatives election. Mainliners were second (61 percent for Bush, 63 percent Republican in the House), then white Roman Catholics (56 percent for both races). The choice of candidates varied by subgroup, however, with more traditionalists than modernists voting Republican, especially among Evangelicals and Catholics. (Black Protestants, of course, voted overwhelmingly Democratic for president and the House.) Evangelicals were less likely to vote than Mainline Protestants, although they almost matched white Catholics. In each community, moreover, traditionalists were more likely to vote than either centrists or modernists. All this suggests that conservative religious groups that targeted traditionalists influenced both vote choice and turnout (Table 8.3).

Table 8.3. Bivariate Data: Electoral Impact
of Religious Contacts (in percent)

	Evangelical Bush House Voted			Mainline Bush House Voted			White Catholic Bush House Voted		
All	74	73	50	61	63	58	56	56	51
Theological subgroup									
Traditionalist	89*	89*	67*	76*	67	70*	79*	75*	64*
Centrist	58	56	38	60	65	53	55	55	53
Modernist	40	40	43	43	56	56	35	43	42
Religious contacts									
Church talk									
Yes	87*	83*	71*	70*	78*	77*	58	61	67*
No	64	65	41	58	58	53	55	55	49
Voter guides									
Yes	83*	80	59*	68	55	76*	51	50	59
No	71	71	48	60	64	56	56	57	50
Interest group									
Yes	91*	85*	69*	50	50	54	49	50	72*
No	71	71	48	61	64	58	57	57	49
Clergy action									
Yes	81*	78*	58*	63	61	63	56	64*	62*
No	69	69	45	60	64	57	55	49	45
Summary:									
Contacted	83*	80*	64*	66	63	65*	53	59	61*
Not contacted	52	56	32	57	63	53	60	51	41
$N =$	(382)	(330)	(780)	(267)	(240)	(478)	(241)	(198)	(479)

Source: Authors' data.

* Differences significant at $p < .10$.

Note: The data show the mean Republican vote for president, the House of Representatives, and the percentage turning out to the polls. Like other post-election surveys, ours is affected by the tendency of respondents to "over report" voting. We have corrected for this by using a formula to predict the likelihood of an actual vote.

But was more religious contact really the catalyst for Republican voting among Evangelical and other traditionalists? Yes. Evangelicals who talked with a friend in church gave Bush 87 percent of the vote, compared with only 64 percent of those who did not. The comparable figures for the House vote were 83 percent and 65 percent, respectively. Similarly, 71 percent of Evangelicals who talked to a friend in church voted, compared with only 41 percent of those who did not. Similar results come from having a voter guide in church, being contacted by a religious group, or hearing clergy discussion. Indeed, the summary measure at the bottom reveals large and statistically significant differences between Evangelicals who received at least one contact and those who did not, with the turnout gap especially wide.

In 1996 we found similar, though less impressive, tendencies for contacting to translate into GOP votes and higher turnout among Mainline Protestants and Catholics. But in 2000 patterns were mixed. Among Mainliners, political talk in church still led to more Republican choices—and higher turnout—but other types of contact had no influence on electoral choice; indeed, some coefficients suggest a slight Democratic edge. Although the summary measure shows that contacted Mainliners more often voted Republican, the coefficient is not statistically significant. Contacting did increase Mainline turnout, however. All this reflects the fact that Mainline Protestants received many fewer messages in 2000, with some emanating from liberal groups. Among Catholics, contacts clearly encouraged turnout (with a 20 percent margin to those contacted), but had few consistent partisan effects. Not only did competing Catholic voices seem to produce a stalemate, but Catholics also received many pro-Democratic cues from unions, environmental groups, and candidate organizations. This was true even for traditionalists, prime targets for the Republicans and their religious allies.

Despite the monolithic Democratic preferences of black Protestants, we can still detect some clear patterns. Parishioners who found voter guides in church were three times more likely to vote for Bush (but still gave him only 9 percent of the vote). The slight Republican bias of voter guides was more than cancelled out by the Democratic unanimity among parishioners whose pastors talked about the election: only 1 percent who heard such discussion voted for Bush. Most striking, however, pastoral action stimulated voting, increasing turnout from 39 percent to 61 percent. Only religious group contacts had a comparable effect, but for a much smaller audience. Thus although the usual pro-Republican impact of religious contacting was very weakly present even in the black church, clergy efforts reduced an already minuscule GOP contingent and produced a larger Democratic turnout.

Before we conclude that religious mobilization influenced the 2000 campaign, we must factor in variables related to the frequency of contacting and to electoral choices. As we have seen, theological subgroups matter, as traditionalists are more likely to be contacted and to vote—and to vote Republican. But these tendencies may stem from the connection between orthodox beliefs, conservative ideology, and Republican partisanship, not from contacting. Thus religious groups may be "preaching to the choir." Or perhaps the contacted people vote Republican because—as long was true of Mainline Protestants—they are disproportionately middle class, wealthy, and well educated. To examine these variables we used multivariate analysis, focusing on the influence of theological subgroup and contacting on electoral behavior, while holding party identification, ideology, gender, age, family income, and education constant (Table 8.4).[30] If under these stringent conditions we still find differences between those who were contacted and those who were not, we can say that religious groups had some influence.

Table 8.4. Multivariate Data: Electoral Impact of
Religious Contacts (in percent)

	Evangelical Bush House Voted			Mainline Bush House Voted			White Catholic Bush House Voted		
All	60	61	51	57	59	54	58	60	49
Theological subgroup									
Traditionalist	80*	79*	58*	67*	60	69*	62*	55	59*
Centrist	68	67	44	63	66	53	57	58	54
Modernist	62	61	42	47	62	57	45	52	47
Religious contacts									
Church talk									
Yes	76*	71*	60*	62	72*	72*	59*	57	61*
No	73	75	45	61	60	54	55	55	51
Voter guides									
Yes	79*	77	53	56	58*	70*	56	56	54
No	73	72	49	61	64	57	55	56	53
Interest group									
Yes	80*	75	55	57	54*	46	44	45*	62*
No	73	73	49	61	64	58	57	58	52
Clergy action									
Yes	75*	74	49	60	61	57	53	60*	56*
No	73	73	50	61	64	58	57	52	51
Summary:									
Contacted	81*	77*	58*	61	61	60*	52*	58	57*
Not contacted	66	63	40	61	66	56	60	52	48
$N =$	(382)	(330)	(780)	(267)	(240)	(478)	(241)	(198)	(479)

Source: Authors' data.

* Significant at $p < .10$

Note: The data show the mean Republican vote for president, the House of Representatives, and the percentage turning out to the polls, adjusted for effects of party identification, ideological identification, gender, age, income, and education. We used multiple classification analysis to hold constant the effects of partisanship, ideology, gender, age, income, and education. Like other post-election surveys, ours is affected by the tendency of respondents to "over report" voting. We have corrected for this by using a formula to predict the likelihood of an actual vote.

Even with controls religious communities still vary slightly in partisan choices. Thus their distinct voting profiles are not simply an artifact of party identification, ideology, and economic status—or even differential mobilization by religious groups. Still, the traditions are not nearly as distinct as in the bivariate data (see Table 8.3). Evangelicals vote Republican more often than Mainline Protestants or white Catholics do, but the margins are much smaller than in 1996, suggesting either that Evangelicals (and other traditionalists) have become more Republican or that contacting has been more effective. In all three religious traditions votes for

George W. Bush decline from traditionalists to modernists, but a comparable effect for the House appears only among Evangelicals. When everything is taken into account, Mainliners are still more likely to turn out than Evangelicals or Catholics, but in each community traditionalists vote most often. Evangelical and Catholic modernists have the lowest voting rates of the subgroups.

Effects of religious mobilization persist but are not as strong or pervasive as they were in 1996. Talking with friends in church had some effect, producing significantly larger turnout in all three traditions and more votes for Bush. Political discussion also produced significantly more GOP House votes among Mainliners, but seemingly more Democratic House votes among Evangelicals. On the other hand, voter guides seemed less effective. Although they swayed Evangelicals to vote for Bush (and produced a close-to-significant Republican House vote increase), their only other independent effect was increasing Mainline turnout, as well as apparently boosting the Democratic House vote. Voter guides made no significant difference among Catholics. Thus even the bivariate association of guides with higher Republican voting washes out with controls.

In 1996 direct religious interest group contact had the strongest effects among Evangelicals, adding 7 percent to the House GOP vote, 18 percent to Republican presidential nominee Robert J. Dole's tally, and 15 percent to turnout. The effects of contacts among Mainline and Catholic parishioners were mixed. In 2000, however, religious contacting was not only less extensive but less dominated by Christian conservatives. Group contacts increased Catholic turnout but seem to have discouraged Mainliners from voting. Clergy activity also presents a mix of results. When everything is taken into account most differences are statistically insignificant, but Evangelicals hearing clergy cues were more likely to choose Bush, whereas Catholics hearing similar admonitions were more likely to vote Republican for the U.S. House—and were more likely to vote period.[31]

Some of the "unexpected" findings here probably resulted from the extensive controls we imposed, especially given the small number of contacts in some subgroups. To provide a simpler assessment of the effect of contacting, we reran the analysis with the same attitudinal and demographic controls, but using a dichotomous "not contacted/contacted" variable (see bottom section of Table 8.4). Once again, contacting Evangelicals strikingly increased the Bush tally, the House Republican vote, and turnout. Among Mainline Protestants and Catholics, contacting solidly increased turnout, but vote choice was unaffected among Mainliners and inconsistent among Catholics, favoring Gore in the presidential race and Republicans in the congressional vote.

Overall, these findings suggest the mixed political efficacy of interest group activity. Clearly, religious contacting is often effective among the Christian right's primary constituency, Evangelicals, but the impact elsewhere is less clear. And the techniques also vary in effectiveness. As in

1996 informal influences from church discussion partners show considerable impact in all three traditions, especially in encouraging turnout, and to some extent increasing the GOP vote. Other interest group tactics, such as direct contact with voters, provision of voter guides, and pastoral action, had more modest and inconsistent effects, at least beyond Evangelical circles.

Among black Protestants, results are much simpler. Party identification, income, and other demographic factors mainly determined voting. But pastoral action remains in the equation: clergy discussions of registration, voting, and partisan choices are associated with significantly higher levels of voting and Democratic choice. Thus the highly visible Democratic strategy of educating and mobilizing black parishioners through their clergy was a massive success in 2000, thwarting much-touted Republican appeals to black voters and increasing Democratic vote totals.

Of course, the analysis here ignores long-run effects of religious activity. No doubt the growing Republican identification among Evangelicals stems in part from two decades of Christian right blandishments to vote for the GOP, conveyed through religious media, interest groups, and the conservative ministrations of Evangelical clergy. These long-term, "indirect" effects would be captured by the controls for party, not by the contacting items. In this vein religious contacts may serve not so much to convert skeptics but to create and reinforce basic partisanship.[32] And there is some evidence to support that assessment. For example, from our first contact with voters in the spring until our postelection survey, national party identification shifted slightly toward the Democrats. But Evangelicals contacted by a religious source tended to remain stable, whereas those not contacted often drifted toward the Democrats and thus were more likely to vote for Gore. Mainliners and Catholics saw no such effect.

Evangelicals were distinct in another way: they were the only group for which Republican contacts clearly swayed undecided or swing voters, not just confirmed partisans. Evangelical Republicans usually voted overwhelmingly Republican, with religious contacting adding only a few points to either turnout or GOP choice. But among Evangelical "independents"—both those leaning toward one of the parties and "pure" nonpartisans—contacting boosted the Republican vote. Again, no such pattern appeared among either Mainliners or Catholics.

A final note: candidates, parties, and other interest groups often mimicked religious contacting strategies. As a result their efforts often reinforced, but sometimes competed with, religious sources. Evangelical traditionalists not only received messages from Christian right groups, but also from Republican candidates and party committees hoping to activate this core GOP constituency. The same pattern holds for traditionalist and centrist Mainliners, who nevertheless got more pro-Republican contacts from the candidate and party groups than from religious sources. Roman Catholics on the other hand, even traditionalists, received many messages from Democratic sources, as well as from unions and environmental organizations. This no doubt explains some of the muted effects of religious contacting in that community. And modernists in all three white Christian traditions received more contacts from pro-Democratic sources than from conservative religious groups.[33]

Sorting out the impact of all these communications is a formidable task. But another multivariate analysis shows that religious contacting holds up well, even in the context of other campaign efforts. Among Evangelicals, religious contact increased the Bush vote from 66 percent to 77 percent, the GOP congressional vote from 62 to 78 percent, and turnout from 42 to 56 percent, controlling for "secular" contacts, as well as theological subgroup, party identification, ideology, and demographic variables. It would be difficult to imagine a more impressive demonstration of religious influence. For Mainliners, however, religious contacts (and other Republican cues) served only to increase turnout, with no net influence on vote choice. Finally, for Catholics, religious messages reduced the Bush tally, increased the House GOP vote, and bolstered turnout—once again after all the other factors were accounted for. Quite clearly, the success of religious contacting varies by tradition and subgroup, as well as with the cues from nonreligious sources.

Summary and Conclusions

What have we learned from this reconnaissance of religious interest group mobilization? First, religious contacting was fairly extensive in 2000, although the relative incidence of each technique changed somewhat from 1996. Second, Christian right messages did reach their primary target, traditionalist Evangelicals, and also found other listeners, such as traditionalist Mainliners and Catholics. We have also confirmed that the African-American church remains a central point for voter mobilization, although that role is still in clergy hands. Third, the countercampaign by liberal groups probably did reach some voters, especially religious modernists in the Mainline and Catholic traditions. Such activities did not match, but may have constrained, Christian right activities. Much of the increased liberal campaign occurred, moreover, among black Protestants and Mainline modernists, while other potential targets, such as Mainline centrists, experienced fewer contacts than in 1996. Thus religious contacting still favors Republicans, although perhaps by a smaller margin than in recent elections.

We have also observed the diversity of contacts, with religious groups subject to a potpourri of techniques. Only Evangelical traditionalists were truly "encompassed about with so great a cloud of [political] witnesses" (apologies to Hebrews 12:1 KJV) as to be sure of at least one contact, but many other religious people were reached as well. Finally, some interest group activity does get results. Generally—at least at the bivariate level—those contacted were more likely to turn out and vote Republican. And especially among Evangelicals, these effects survived very powerful controls for other prime electoral influences. Nevertheless, the overall impact of religious contacting, especially in the Mainline and Catholic traditions, was somewhat more muted than in 1996, with fewer consistent effects. Each technique used by religious interest groups was effective in some contexts, but not in others. This will no doubt encourage these organizations to reassess their strategies for future elections.

Notes

1. For a fine overview of electoral activity by interest groups, see Mark J. Rozell and Clyde Wilcox, *Interest Groups in American National Elections* (Washington, D.C.: CQ Press, 1998).
2. For our preliminary analysis of the religious divisions among voters in the 2000 election, see James L. Guth, Lyman A. Kellstedt, John C. Green, and Corwin E. Smidt, "America Fifty/Fifty," *First Things* 116 (October 2001): 19–26.
3. For an account of the formation of the Catholic Alliance by the former executive director of the Christian Coalition, see Ralph Reed, *Active Faith: How Christians Are Changing the Soul of American Politics* (New York: Free Press, 1996), 217–220. Soon after the 1996 election the Catholic Alliance severed ties with the Christian Coalition, in large part to quiet concerns among Catholic bishops that those ties undermined their authority.
4. Quoted in James L. Guth, "The Politics of the Christian Right," in *Interest Group Politics*, ed. Allan J. Cigler and Burdett A. Loomis (Washington, D.C.: CQ Press, 1983), 73.
5. For possible reasons for the failure of the "clergy-oriented" strategy among Evangelicals, see Ted G. Jelen, *The Political World of the Clergy* (Westport, Conn.: Praeger, 1993); also, James L. Guth, "The Bully Pulpit : Southern Baptist Clergy and Political Activism, 1980–92," in *Religion and the Culture Wars: Dispatches from the Front*, ed. John C. Green, James L. Guth, Corwin E. Smidt, and Lyman A. Kellstedt, (Lanham, Md.: Rowman and Littlefield, 1996), 146–147.
6. Reed, *Active Faith*, 121–124.
7. For a thorough but very critical overview of mobilization strategies used by the Christian right in 2000, see "Election Countdown: How the Religious Right Mobilizes Their Voters," *Right Wing Watch On Line*, November 1, 2000, http://www.pfaw.org/issues/right/rwwo/rwwo.001101.shtml, November 15, 2000.
8. For the origins of the Interfaith Alliance, see Richard L. Berke, "Mainline Religions Form Lobby for 'Alternate' View," *New York Times*, July 14, 1994, A11. For information on the Alliance's efforts in 2000, see http://www.interfaithalliance.org. Activities of People For the American Way are described in materials available at http://www.pfaw.org.
9. United States Conference of Catholic Bishops, *Faithful Citizenship: Civic Responsibility for a New Millennium* (Washington, D.C.: USCCB, 1999); United States Conference of Catholic Bishops, *Political Activity Guidelines for Catholic Organizations* (Washington, D.C.: USCCB, 2000). A critical analysis of individual bishops is Joseph L. Conn, "The Bishops' Biased Blessing," *Church and State* 53 (December 2000): 10–13. For a brief history of Priests for Life, see John Burger, "Priests for Life Fears Losing Father Pavone to Parish Life," *National Catholic Register* 77 (September 30–October 6, 2001): 1.
10. A good example is "An Open Letter to Candidates for Office from Roman Catholic Voters," *New York Times*, October 23, 2000, A7.

11. The survey of African-American clergy is reported in Associated Press, "Black Clergy Appear Divided in Politics," *New York Times*, April 20, 2001, A7. Yale Law Professor Stephen Carter's observations on the black clergy's role in the Democratic Party are found in "The Rights and Wrongs of Religion in Politics," *Center Conversations* (July 2001): 1–5.

12. This study surveyed a random sample of 4,004 adult Americans and an additional 1,000 white southerners between February and April 2000. Right after the 2000 election, 2,925 of the original respondents were interviewed again. The final data set was weighted to match the demographic characteristics of the U.S. adult population. The survey was conducted by the Survey Research Center at the University of Akron, sponsored by the Ethics and Public Policy Center, and funded by a grant from the Pew Charitable Trusts.

13. Although we focus on the largest American religious traditions, other religious groups were also involved in electoral mobilization. Many Jewish organizations sought to maintain their community's high turnout rates (and support for Democratic candidates). The presence of Senator Lieberman, an observant Jew, on the Democratic ticket may well have bolstered these efforts—although Lieberman's openly religious rhetoric caused much discomfort among some Jews. In addition, several American Muslim organizations endorsed George W. Bush, and some mosques helped mobilize voters. Other religious minorities, including Mormons, Hispanic Protestants, and Hispanic Catholics also reported receiving special religious appeals.

14. For the concept of religious tradition and size of these traditions, see David C. Leege and Lyman A. Kellstedt, eds., *Rediscovering the Religious Factor in American Politics* (Armonk, N.Y.: M. E. Sharpe, 1993), and John C. Green and others, *Religion and the Culture Wars*, ch. 10, 13–14. For the historic role of religious traditions in American party coalitions, see Mark Noll, ed., *Religion and American Politics: From the Colonial Period to the 1980s* (Oxford: Oxford University, 1990).

15. See Geoffrey C. Layman, *The Great Divide: Religious and Cultural Conflict in American Party Politics* (New York: Columbia University, 2001).

16. For the original statements of the "culture wars" thesis, see James D. Hunter's two works, *Culture Wars: The Struggle to Define America* (New York: Basic Books, 1991) and *Before the Shooting Starts: Searching for Democracy in America's Culture War* (New York: Free Press, 1994).

17. Our use of "theological subgroup" may be a bit misleading, suggesting a special emphasis on belief. Our classification includes affiliation and behavior as well, but both are strongly influenced by theological considerations within religious traditions. In this respect, it is also important to note that we do not include in these religious categories those who exhibit only nominal religious characteristics. Thus all those in the four traditions exhibit at least some religious commitment.

18. Remember, however, that the theological subgroup of respondents was determined by beliefs and practices central to their own tradition; comparisons of theological groups should be made primarily *within traditions*, while those across traditions should be made with caution. By any comparable measure, for example, Evangelical "modernists" are a good bit more orthodox and active in religious life than their Mainline or Catholic counterparts.

19. For the 1996 survey, see James L. Guth, Lyman A. Kellstedt, Corwin E. Smidt, and John C. Green, "Thunder on the Right? Religious Interest Group Mobilization in the 1996 Election," in *Interest Group Politics*, 5th ed., ed. Allan J. Cigler and Burdett A. Loomis (Washington, D.C.: CQ Press, 1998), 169–192. In analyzing the results for both years, we have counted respondents who didn't know, could not remember, or refused to say whether they had been contacted as "no contact."

20. For some observations on the differing impact of Protestant and Catholic congregations on parishioner politics, see Sidney Verba, Kay Schlozman, and Henry E.

Brady, *Voice and Equality: Civic Voluntarism in American Politics* (Cambridge, Mass.: Harvard University, 1995), 320–330. For a valuable correction and extension of these arguments, see Paul A. Djupe and J. Tobin Grant, "Religious Institutions and Political Participation in America," *Journal for the Scientific Study of Religion* 40 (June 2001): 303–314.

21. Elihu Katz and Paul F. Lazerfeld, *Personal Influence* (Glencoe, Ill.: Free Press, 1955). For informal political effects of congregational membership, see Kenneth D. Wald, Dennis E. Owen, and Samuel S. Hill Jr., "Churches as Political Communities," *American Political Science Review* 82 (June 1988): 531–548.

22. Verba, Schlozman, and Brady, *Voice and Equality*, 518–521.

23. For early experiments with voter guides, see Marjorie Hershey and Darrell M. West, "Single-Issue Politics: Prolife Groups and the 1980 Senate Campaign," in *Interest Group Politics*, ed. Allan J. Cigler and Burdett A. Loomis (Washington, D.C.: CQ Press, 1983), 31–59. A critical assessment of the Christian Coalition's voter guides is found in Larry J. Sabato and Glenn R. Simpson, *Dirty Little Secrets: The Persistence of Corruption in American Politics* (New York: Random House, 1996).

24. For the early efforts of the Christian Coalition with Catholics and black Protestants, see R. Scott Appleby, "Catholics and the Christian Right," and Allison Calhoun-Brown, "Still Seeing in Black and White: Racial Challenges for the Christian Right," in *Sojourners in the Wilderness: The Christian Right in Comparative Perspective*, ed. Corwin E. Smidt and James M. Penning (Lanham Md.: Rowman and Littlefield, 1997), 93–113, 115–137.

25. We have reviewed the political involvement of clergy in James L. Guth, John C. Green, Lyman A. Kellstedt, Corwin E. Smidt, and Margaret M. Poloma, *The Bully Pulpit: The Politics of Protestant Clergy* (Lawrence: University Press of Kansas, 1997).

26. For a provocative treatment of party and interest group mobilization in contemporary America, see Steven E. Schier, *By Invitation Only: The Rise of Exclusive Politics in the United States* (Pittsburgh.: University of Pittsburgh, 2000).

27. See Robert Wuthnow, *Sharing the Journey: Support Groups and America's New Quest for Community* (New York: Free Press, 1994), 333–338. Wuthnow suggests that small groups reinforce political messages from religious interest group leaders. We suspect they also facilitate transmission of these messages.

28. For a more detailed discussion of the "civic gospel," see Guth and others, *Bully Pulpit*, 63–72.

29. For a similar analysis using a different strategy, see Mark D. Regnerus, David Sikkink, and Christian Smith, "Voting With the Christian Right: Contextual and Individual Patterns of Electoral Influence," *Social Forces* 77 (June 1999): 1375–1140.

30. Party identification has long been the most potent way of explaining vote choice: Republicans vote Republican, Democrats vote Democratic. And that is the case here as well. Political ideology also helps explain voting, even when partisanship is accounted for, and indeed, it has a modest independent effect in our study, with liberals preferring Democratic candidates and conservatives preferring Republicans. In recent years, much has also been made of the "gender gap"—the preference of women for the Democratic ticket—and, again, in most religious traditions women were more Democratic than men were (especially among Mainliners, but much less among Evangelicals). On the other hand, age, income, and education had very different and often statistically insignificant effects on electoral choice, depending on the tradition, but substantially encouraged turnout in all four communities, as the scholarly literature would predict. For a comprehensive review of the factors influencing vote choice in recent national elections, see Warren E. Miller and J. Merrill Shanks, *The New American Voter* (Cambridge, Mass.: Harvard University, 1996). For the factors influencing turnout, consult Ruy A. Teixeira, *The Disappearing American Voter* (Washington, D.C.: Brookings, 1992).

31. For another analysis of the effect of two of these religious techniques over time, see Clyde Wilcox and Lee Sigelman, "Political Mobilization in the Pews: Contacting and Electoral Turnout," *Social Science Quarterly* 82 (September 2001): 524–535.

32. For more evidence supporting this conclusion, see John C. Green, Corwin E. Smidt, Lyman A. Kellstedt, and James L. Guth, "Bringing in the Sheaves: The Christian Right and White Protestants, 1976–1996," in Smidt and Penning, *Sojourners*, 75–91.

33. For comparable data from the 1996 American National Election Study, see Andrew Kohut, John C. Green, Scott Keeter, and Robert C. Toth, *The Diminishing Divide: Religion's Changing Role in American Politics* (Washington, D.C.: Brookings, 2000), especially chapter six.

9

Interests, Lobbying, and the U.S. Congress
Past as Prologue
Burdett A. Loomis

All too frequently interest group scholars claim that growth in the number of interest groups or the extent of grassroots lobbying is unprecedented. Although group politics do change over time, these claims can almost never be substantiated. Rather, the behavior of organized interests has a rich tradition in the United States, and scholars have documented group tactics and strategies for a century or more. Most notably, Arthur Bentley (1908) and Pendleton Herring (1928) laid out systematic analyses of the role of groups and interests in American politics.

In this chapter Burdett Loomis examines some continuities in how organized interests sought to influence government in the twentieth century. Building on a series of scholarly studies, the author illustrates the substantial continuities of lobbying in the 1920s, the 1950s, and the 1980s. As Christopher J. Bosso and Michael Thomas Collins argue in Chapter 5, the Internet may begin a new era in constituency representation for groups. But even high-tech paths to influence have been well trod by lobbyists who have provided information and made substantive arguments in much the same way that contemporary lobbyists do over the Internet today.

> I think the public ought to know the extraordinary exertions being made by the lobby in Washington to gain recognition for certain alterations of the tariff bill. Washington has seldom seen so numerous, so industrious, or so insidious a lobby. . . . It is of serious interest to the country that the people at large should have no lobby and be voiceless in these matters, while great bodies of astute men seek to create an artificial opinion and to overcome the interests of the public for their private profit.
>
> *President Woodrow Wilson, May 1913*

Organized interests and members of Congress have worked together from the early days of the U.S. government.[1] And the reaction to organized interests has been cautionary, if not alarmist, from the muckrakers in the early 1900s to Common Cause since 1970.

James Madison was prescient in drafting a Constitution that addressed the natural expression of economic interests in a republic, and his observations in *Federalist 10* are still relevant today. He argued, "[T]he most common and durable source of factions has been the various and unequal distributions of property. Those who hold and those who are without property have ever formed distinct interests in society."[2] Madison's constitutional design created a permeable Congress that encouraged participation from many interests without allowing any single faction to dominate. This balancing act—made more difficult by a proliferation of organized interests—has remained at the center of American legislative politics since the 1790s, and especially since the United States emerged as an industrial power in the late nineteenth century.

Congress and Organized Interests in Industrialized America

The post–Civil War era sets the stage for any consideration of Congress and interest groups over the past century. The growth of large industries, the construction of a coast-to-coast rail system, and the advent of instantaneous communication with the telegraph meant that the country needed more national direction, which would come from policymakers in Washington, D.C.

By 1912 Congress had evolved into its modern form, at least in size (96 Senators and 435 Representatives), and in 1916 the Seventeenth Amendment mandated the direct election of senators. With extended careers in Congress becoming more of a reality from 1900 to 1920, both legislators and interest groups understood that they could help each other in many ways—but especially by exchanging information and material benefits.[3] By the 1880s and 1890s some business interests had established a presence in the nation's capital. Even in the wake of the 1890 Sherman Anti-Trust Act, corporations exercised considerable influence in at least two ways. First, despite challenges from Progressives, Populists, and muckraking journalists, corporations consolidated their position as a favored interest in American society. Although the Standard Oil Trust was prosecuted successfully, U.S.

Steel was not. The company argued that even though it controlled half the country's steel production, it "had behaved well" and should not be penalized merely because of its size.[4] Second, as we see from the U.S. Steel example, corporations could live or die by how they presented themselves in Washington. Interest group scholar Grant McConnell concludes that the steel victory "established the pattern by which the corporation's leaders have necessarily been politicians."[5]

Still, corporations had some competition. Beginning in the late 1800s growing numbers and varieties of groups became active in national policymaking.

> [M]ore and more kinds of people—from feminists to labor leaders, and from prohibitionists to physicians—caught on to the scheme and enjoyed at least some measure of satisfaction . . . lobbyists could and sometimes did serve as facilitators and catalysts, loosing the system from inertia. Far from being disruptive, therefore . . . the lobbyists helped to focus, to rationalize, and, in the long run, to modernize late nineteenth-century congressional government.[6]

Such a conclusion meshes with the picture painted in 1908 by group theorist Arthur Bentley, who saw politics as a series of struggles among groups, with Congress as the venue.[7]

Despite substantial business investment in and influence over the legislative branch, John Judis argues, "the major legislation passed during the [Theodore] Roosevelt, Taft, and Wilson administrations represented a compromise between these [national] business groups and labor and the left. That reflected the relative power of the competing groups, but it was also the result of an entirely different kind of organization: the elite policy group."[8] Groups like the National Civic Federation, women's organizations, consumers' leagues, and new foundations (Russell Sage, Rockefeller, Carnegie) represented a host of societal interests and provided some vision of a national interest.

Access, Information, and Elections

For more than a century organized interests have sought to influence Congress; in turn, members of Congress have both relied on and attempted to shape the attitudes of organized interests. Indeed, it is hard to imagine Congress functioning today without interest groups, given legislators' insatiable need for information relevant to policymaking. How, then, to analyze the varied relationships between groups and Congress? At a basic level, both represent people and interests. Three overlapping lines of analysis show promise:

- The politics of *access*—interests frequently say that gaining access to legislators is a goal.

- The role of *information* in affecting policy outcomes.
- The importance of *elections* in establishing the legislative context for decision making.

In a thoughtful analysis of how legislators grant access and how organized interests gain it, John Mark Hansen argues that the "the close consultation with interest groups—granting access—is a congressional strategy for dealing with uncertainty."[9] Interest groups that have something to offer legislators can gain access to them. For example, organized interests can provide easy-to-use information that reduces legislators' costs of acting effectively under great time constraints. At the same time, organized interests seek to reduce uncertainty. For legislators, uncertainty arises over winning reelection; for interests, uncertainty relates to the effects of future policies and programs, especially those seen as potentially injurious. Groups have many legislators to choose from when seeking a few who are amenable to the groups' cause. At the same time, some key lawmakers, such as committee chairs, are especially valuable.

Exchanging information creates a strong bond between organized interests and legislators. Scarce and (apparently) reliable information is valuable, especially in an uncertain legislative environment. Although policy-based information is important, other types of intelligence can be equally, if not more, important. Interactions between interest groups and Congress foster a need for three kinds of information: policy, political (electoral), and procedural (internal to the legislative process).[10] Lobbyists and legislators continually attempt to reduce uncertainties by soliciting and exchanging information, often in the context of long-term relationships.

Whatever the era, the day-to-day lobbying context in Congress always relates back to the previous election and forward to the next one. And in a two-year electoral cycle, the next election is always around the corner. Although most legislators worry greatly about reelection, almost all of them win their reelection bids with relative ease.[11] Interest groups are almost always important elements of winning reelection, but the electoral relationships between interest groups and Congress vary according to chamber, partisan margin, the balance of power between parties and committees, the safety of incumbents, and the costs of campaigning. Thus in an era of few effective campaign regulations and a dominant Republican Party in Congress (the 1920s, for example), well-heeled interests could "invest" in a party and its incumbents, confident that these partisans would control the legislative process for at least the next two years. In the 1980s Rep. Tony Coelho, D-Calif., told business interests that they would have a Democratic Congress to deal with for some time, and corporate contributions shifted sharply away from Republicans over the decade.[12]

In eras of partisan parity, such as the mid-1950s and the late 1990s, the environment was both tempting and dangerous for organized interests. Interests could back one party or the other, hoping that their choice would win control of Congress. But if their party lost, interest groups faced the possibility of being shut out of the policy process—at least in access to majority party leaders. In the post-1994 era of narrow partisan majorities, congressional scholars are just beginning to address how such "partisan parity" affects policymaking in both chambers. Slim majorities mean that interest group "investments"—no matter how large—may have only modest payoffs, as narrow partisan divisions usually increase uncertainty surrounding legislative outcomes.

Congress and Organized Interests in the Twentieth Century

Although all legislative scholars would not agree on the length and defining qualities of congressional eras in the twentieth century, the general outlines of at least three major eras and two transition periods seem clear. The eras are the strong party era of 1890–1910, the "Textbook Congress" of 1937–1970, and the postreform era that began in about 1981 and continues today.[13] The first transition period begins after the procedural defeat of Speaker Joseph Cannon in 1910 and ends in 1937, when the Southern Democrats became a full-fledged bloc, allowing for the institutionalization of their Conservative Coalition alliance with congressional Republicans.[14] The second transition roughly spans the 1970s, when congressional Democrats engineered a host of reforms, mainly in the House, that changed the balance among committees, party leaders, the party caucus (or conference, for Republicans), and the individual legislator.[15]

Transitions differ from eras of institutional stability. Roughly speaking, the power relationships among the most important congressional components—parties, committees, and individuals—remain stable during an era, but become contested during a transition (Table 9.1). It is within the contexts of these eras and transitions that organized interests must find ways to approach Congress and respond to congressional initiatives.

The Strong Party Era, 1890–1910

Although the 1890s saw considerable turmoil in American politics, including a major partisan realignment, the strong partisan leadership of House speakers Thomas Reed, R-Maine, and Joseph Cannon, R-Ill., and Sens. Nelson Aldrich, R-R.I., and William Allison, R-Iowa, provided a stability that demonstrated clearly to legislators and lobbyists the location of power on Capitol Hill. Given the leadership's conservative, probusiness perspectives, corporate interests could prosper by offering quiet support to leaders.[16]

In the post–Civil War period before 1890, interest groups gained access when a wealthy candidate (or backer) bought a Senate seat, when state parties controlled selection in state legislatures, and when the groups financed the selection of an ally. Once in office, legislators frequently profited from

Table 9.1. Characteristics of Congressional Eras and Transitions, 1890–2000

Era or transition	Party leadership	Standing committees	Individual legislators	Other characteristics
Strong party era, 1890–1910	Very strong	Modest	House: weak; Senate: modest to strong	Strong speakers based on strong electoral parties; Senators Aldrich and Allison dominate Senate
Transition to Textbook Congress, 1910–1937	Declining	With seniority, committee chairs become stronger	House: weak; Senate: modest to strong	Party caucus gives way to stronger committees in House; era of some strong senators (Borah, LaFollete)
Textbook Congress era, 1937–1970	Weak with a few strong leaders	The Golden Age of Committee Government, especially in House	Gaining strength by acquiring staff and some individualism	Conservative Coalition dominates, but Rayburn and Johnson among greatest legislative leaders ever
Transition of democratizing reforms, 1970–1980	Weak but given tools in House to strengthen	Squeezed by leadership and subcommittees	Still gaining but often unable to legislate	Increasing floor amendments; subcommittee proliferation; backlash against strong executive branch; Senate is more individualistic
Postreform, 1981–2000	Moderately strong in early 1980s; strong in late 1990s	Regain some power, work with leadership	House: less powerful than 1970s; Senate: very strong	Two mini-eras in House: Democrats, 1981–1994; Gingrich and GOP, 1995–2000; small majorities, high party loyalty in both chambers

Source: Compiled from Joseph Cooper, "The Twentieth-Century Congress," in *Congress Reconsidered*, 7th ed., ed. Lawrence C. Dodd and Bruce I. Oppenheimer (Washington, D.C.: CQ Press, 2001); Eric Schickler, *Disjointed Pluralism* (Princeton: Princeton University, 2001); and author's information.

their positions. To address the needs of an industrializing nation, the Senate transformed its relations with organized interests. Senator Aldrich argued that "It is of the utmost importance to manufacturers *and* members of Congress . . . to have in existence some representative organization whose officers or agents can speak with authority on the various complex questions constantly arising."[17] In other words, lobbyists needed to be able to communicate neutral information rather than just enjoy extensive access to legislators.

The dominant Senate Republican leadership of Aldrich and Allison during 1890–1910 meant that interests could focus their relatively modest lobbying capacities in an era when the strong party majority could control both the congressional agenda and the legislative results. For many business interests, access came through grassroots contacts in the states, as interests helped fund partisan maneuvering in choosing supportive senators.[18] In fact, the strength of parties in the House and Senate defined the roles of organized interests, especially business interests. "The unity of Senate parties stood in direct contrast to the fragmented concerns of business enterprises. . . . Sugar growers battled sugar refiners, just as wool growers combated wool manufacturers. . . . Even monopolies within industries did not promote unity. They served to increase the size of the contestants."[19] By the late 1890s the House was increasingly dominated by highly disciplined party organizations. The realignment of the 1890s, culminating in the 1896 election, had "created two relatively unified congressional parties—one northern and industrial the other southern and agricultural."[20] With substantial electoral support and tight procedural control, Speaker Joseph Cannon, along with a small clique of fellow Republican leaders, served conservative business interests. But direct election of U.S. senators was on the horizon, and by 1913 organized interests would have to alter their tactics when parties could no longer usher chosen members into office.

Transition to the Textbook Congress, 1910–1937

In *Group Representation before Congress*, published in 1928, political scientist Pendleton Herring argued that Washington lobbying had changed considerably since the strong party era of Aldrich and Cannon. Indeed, Herring saw the rise of group politics as directly linked to the weakening of political parties, both within the electorate and on Capitol Hill.[21] Like other studies of politics in the 1920s, Herring conjures a modern vision of congressional lobbying, as he quotes one senator, "'I have seen the corridors leading up to the Finance Committee room so filled with [lobbyists] that it was almost impossible for an outside senator to get to the committee room, and barely possible to get in.'"[22] The focus on committees intensified in the wake of increased open hearings, which allowed organized interests to make presentations to a larger audience. Moreover, a major lobbying scandal in 1913 demonstrated to many groups that the days of buying access were over; gaining access remained important—crucial, even—but "the men with the power are [the] spokesmen of the organized groups."[23]

Herring offers the first comprehensive look at the Washington interest group universe, offering a baseline for later research efforts. For example, he notes that the number of trade associations (such as the Fertilizer Association) had grown from 800 in 1914 to 1,500 in 1923. Further, he estimates the number of Washington-based groups at 500 and contends that 60–100 of those are "consistently effective."[24] Even more valuable, Herring provides a coherent overview of the "new lobby," whose practices look a lot like those of organized interests at the end of the twentieth century.

For Herring, lobbies are more than the traditional groups that represent farmers, business, labor, and trade associations. He discusses women's groups and reformist organizations, as well as the growing power of professional societies such as the National Education Association.[25] Herring observed that lobbyists were easily on an intellectual par with legislators; in fact, many former members of Congress became lobbyists, joining the ranks of lawyers and ex-journalists. And lobbyists were well compensated, although Herring could only guess at their incomes (not unlike scholars in every era).

As for lobbying techniques, Herring observed remarkably modern activities. Lobbyists and their groups engaged in public relations work as they sought to frame issues for the public. Interest groups solicited grassroots responses by providing form letters for constituents to send to their legislators. Lobbyists sought out friends in the legislature, testified at hearings, tried to influence party agendas, and shared information with each other. Indeed, the lobbyists who made up the "Monday Lunch Club" of the 1920s were a clear precursor to similar gatherings, such as Grover Norquist's regular gatherings of conservative group representatives that began in the 1990s.

In the Congress of the 1920s, where party influence had waned, reliable sources of information had become increasingly important. The growing community of groups and lobbyists filled this void. Likewise, "The farm groups triumphed [in the 1920s] because the parties lacked not the power to contain them but the will to channel them. . . ."[26] In the end, lobbyists from agricultural and other groups needed to convince individual lawmakers that the groups could consistently provide useful information. Such a relationship formed the basis for the stable politics of access that characterized the Textbook Congress era.

Groups and the Textbook Congress: The Politics of Access, 1937–1970

Writing in the late 1980s, political scientist Kenneth Shepsle labeled the mid-century congressional era the "Textbook Congress."

With limited time and resources, legislators of the 1940s and 1950s concentrated on only a few activities. They simply did not have the staff or the money to involve themselves in a wide range of policy issues, manage a network of ombudsman activities back home, raise campaign finances, or intercede broadly in the executive branch's administration of programs. Rather, they picked their spots selectively and depended on jurisdictional decentralization and reciprocity among committees to divide the legislative labor.[27]

With some short-lived exceptions, the Textbook Congress era is defined by two complementary institutions: strong committees and the Conservative Coalition. Organized interests understood the implications of the coalition's existence. Democratic majorities needed to be very large if major labor, civil rights, or education bills were to pass the House.[28] The prospects for major change were not good, so interest groups focused heavily on committees, whose chairmen were disproportionately southern and conservative.

Political scientists took note of such tactics and developed the idea of the "iron triangle" (or whirlpool, or cozy triangle, or subgovernment), which linked groups, committees and subcommittees, and top personnel in specific bureaucratic agencies.[29] Although every interest in the legislative process wants to win, a secondary goal is to predict governmental actions with great accuracy. In the wake of the New Deal and World War II, the reach of government had grown substantially, and with Republicans' reticence to cut it back, a large and activist government was there to stay. This made predicting government actions crucial for any interest whose daily activities were affected by federal policies. If access had been important in the 1920s and 1930s, it became more so when governmental decisions touched growing numbers of interests and citizens.

In agricultural politics, groups' politics of access had changed noticeably by the 1950s, with the Farm Bureau declining in significance relative to commodity groups, whose aims were much more specific than those of the umbrella group. Hansen points out that among eighteen major commodity groups, four formed between 1865 and 1922; the remaining fourteen formed between 1932 and 1960.[30] If access were going to lead to an exchange of information—to benefit groups and legislators—the information had to be useful to the legislators and favorable to the groups.

Agricultural groups started to multiply earlier than other groups because federal farm policy was prominent in the 1940s and 1950s, in contrast to relatively modest intervention in areas such as education and the environment. Moreover, commodity interests were narrow enough to fit snugly into the highly specialized and static politics of the congressional committee system.[31] For commodity groups and other specific interests, such as military weapons manufacturers, a Congress of committee barons averse to change was perfectly acceptable. For many other interests, however, Congress was an obstacle. Indeed, advocates for social change did not rely on traditional organized interests, such as the NAACP, to make their case, despite that organization's long history and great legitimacy. Rather, activists developed new groups within a broad social mobilization context and pressured Congress from the outside, as with Martin Luther King Jr.'s 1963 march on Washington.

Still, access and information were crucial for racial, environmental, and social policy activists. Access came largely through the Democratic Party, although in the end many Republicans supported large chunks of Lyndon Johnson's Great Society legislation.[32] But the congressional landscape continued to be dominated by strong committee chairmen and the Conservative Coalition, despite an infusion of liberal and moderate Democrats, especially in the elections of 1958 and 1964. Although the winning Democratic candidates owed a lot to progressive groups, the landslides were more a result of voters' reactions to the Republican administration (1958) and the Goldwater presidential candidacy (1964).[33] These new Democrats would change Congress, but not until 1970 when their reforms began to be enacted.

Although organized interests did some grassroots lobbying (labor unions) and some public relations work (the nuclear industry) during the Textbook Congress, most groups used a traditional combination of direct and social lobbying.[34] That is, in both formal and informal settings, lobbyists made personal contact with members of Congress and top staffers. Despite attempts to regulate lobbying as part of the 1946 Legislative Reorganization Act,[35] no effective controls limited what lobbyists could provide to legislators. Becoming friendly with legislators—through honoraria, trips, expensive meals, and the like—increased access for many lobbyists, who could then provide and absorb relevant information as part of a long-term, trusting relationship.

From surveys of 114 lobbyists and 30 congressional members and staff during the late 1950s, perhaps the acme of the Textbook Congress, Lester Milbrath provides a rounded picture of a lobbyist's job. Milbrath finds that lobbyists and legislators focus on the information-provision elements of their relationships. Both lobbyists and congressional respondents (members and staff) rated the value of the "personal presentation of viewpoints" at more than 9 on a 10-point scale.[36] Milbrath's lobbyists approached a Congress that was ideally constructed to receive information based on trusting individual relationships between legislators and lobbyists. Party played little role in these bonds. And in the context of strong-committee government, lobbyists knew exactly whom they needed to approach. But these conditions would soon change.

By the mid-1960s the institutional arrangements that defined the Textbook Congress era were unraveling, as electoral politics reshaped the memberships of the House and Senate. Aside from the large numbers of young Democrats who came to Capitol Hill in 1958 and 1964, often from formerly GOP districts, the Supreme Court's "one person, one vote" decisions of the early 1960s and the passage of the Voting Rights Act of 1965 meant that the composition of Congress would change, especially in the South. The democratizing forces of reform on Capitol Hill were gaining ground, and the next decade would throw both Congress and interest group politics into disarray, as committees lost clout and individual legislators became more important elements in the decision making mix.

Transition through Reform: Fragmentation and Retail Politics, 1970–1980

Ever since Democrats had won control of Congress in 1955, growing numbers of legislators had become dissatisfied with the strong committee structure that allowed them little say in decision making. By the early 1970s the House Democratic Study Group—one of the first caucuses of members on Capitol Hill—had gathered enough strength to force the issue of redistributing power. Between 1970 and 1975 a series of reforms—enacted by the House as a whole and the Democratic majority—empowered subcommittees, individual members, the majority caucus, and, in the end, the majority party leadership.[37] At the same time, Congress reformed the budget process, which meant that a series of tough votes would be required each year on budget alternatives. In addition, the elections of 1974–1980 led to high congressional turnover; a flood of new members entered the House, and almost all expected to participate actively from day one. All of this meant that increasing amounts of congressional action took place in subcommittees and on the floor of the House. How did this affect lobbyists?

> These developments, taken collectively, spell both more opportunities for influence and more work for lobbyists: more policymakers with whom they must consult and to whom they must present their case; more legislative freshmen and issue amateurs requiring education; more meetings to attend; more hearings at which to testify and present technical information and policy rationales; more campaigns demanding contributions.[38]

Organized interests also had to address the implications of the federal government's extended reach, as expressed through both Great Society and Nixon presidency programs.[39] Interest groups had to contend with a Congress that was experimenting with how to make representative government effective in an era of societal complexity and executive branch dominance. Although the seeds of a new strong party era were sown in the mid-1970s, the parties needed to catch up to the reforms, which they did in the 1980s. But even with Democrat Jimmy Carter in the White House, the majority party found it difficult to govern. And groups could no longer turn to committee chairs; even those who remained strong had to worry about their status with committee members and the party caucus.

Thus beyond the growth of government and greater societal complexity, the fragmentation of congressional power made the work of organized groups increasingly difficult. Accelerated growth of the Washington lobby in the 1970s reflects the groups' need to be more attentive to more legislators through different tactical approaches.[40]

The Postreform Era: Strong Parties and Partisan Parity, 1981–2000

Between 1981 and 2000 Congress became more partisan—the effect of long-term changes in congressional electorates and the new tools of party leaders to strengthen their standing.[41] In the House, especially, the critical link between the electorate and party leaders has been the party caucus (for Democrats) or conference (for Republicans). The growing influence of conservative southern and mountain state legislators in the Republican Conference has moved the base of power for House leaders to the right; conversely, without large numbers of conservative southerners, the Democratic Caucus has grown more liberal. By the 2000 elections only about twenty-five congressional districts were competitive. The parties and their interest group allies concentrated much of their funding on this handful of seats. The average spending by a campaign in these races easily topped $2 million, and in one California race the candidates spent a combined total of more than $11 million.

Organized interests have funded these campaigns, spending hundreds of millions of dollars to affect just a few races in the House and Senate. In 1995 House Republicans rewarded their supporting interest groups with substantial access to party leaders, most visibly at weekly luncheons. Moreover, Majority Whip Tom DeLay, R-Texas, warned trade associations to avoid appointing former Democrats as chief executives or major lobbyists. Democrats had certainly favored certain groups and lobbyists, but the GOP's actions were widely viewed as limiting access in new ways.

Still, given the small margins in both chambers today, producing substantial change is difficult and unlikely even when parties are strong. Organized interests of all stripes have thus focused increasingly on constructing and conveying their messages through grassroots lobbying, advertising, and pubic relations campaigns. The highly partisan nature of Congress makes it worthwhile to participate actively in electoral politics. Thus social conservative groups won excellent access to majority Republicans after the 1994 elections. At the same time, such groups as Microsoft and pharmaceutical companies have spent tens of millions to influence how legislators and staff think about issues like market competition and drug pricing.

Although political scientists have begun to study congressional lobbying more systematically, there is little agreement about what tactics work in what circumstances. This is because interest groups use many different inside and outside tactics to influence how legislators vote, how hard they work to effect certain legislation, and how they think about issues. Many large-scale studies of groups and lobbyists have been conducted since 1980. Together they give a clear picture of the ever-growing lobbying community and its attentions to Congress.[42] The studies find that contemporary lobbyists and groups do a lot of what they did in the mid-1920s and 1950s.[43] Thus in the 1980s almost all Washington-based groups reported that they contact legislators (both formally and informally), testify at hearings, present research results, help draft legislation, and do some grassroots mobilization of legislators' influential constituents.[44] Even when interests pay more attention to framing national issues, as with prescription drug pricing or telecommunications policy, their actions mirror Herring's discussion of group-based "propaganda" in the 1920s. Still, the most pervasive activity of contemporary interest groups may be monitoring a wide range of governmental actions. Although we often think of Washington representatives as giving information to policymakers, the information flows consistently in the opposite direction—back to interest group leaders and corporate executives. Given the reach and complexity of government policy, many interests invest a great deal in obtaining the best information available.

Campaign Contributions and Congressional Caucuses

No analysis of the interactions between Congress and interest groups would be complete without mention of campaign costs and "informal caucuses" in Congress. Although congressional campaigns have always needed interest group funding, the cost of electioneering has grown substantially since 1975, even after accounting for inflation. The mid-1970s saw the rise of political action committees (PACs) in the wake of the 1974 Campaign Reform Act. In 1974, 608 PACs registered with the Federal Election Commission; ten years later there were 4,009.[45] PAC contributions to congressional campaigns rose from $34 million in 1978 to $225 million in 2000, with more funds being funneled through the parties' soft money accounts.

If groups fund electoral politics to determine who runs Congress, they also work inside the House and Senate to represent specific interests through dozens of caucuses, which organize around everything from clean air to automobile issues to the arts. As of 1970, 4 caucuses had been established; by 1980, 62; by 1990, 176; and by 1996, 252—although a few had disbanded over the years.[46] In many cases an organized interest's most powerful representation comes from elected officials who band together within Congress. Thus leaders of the steel and auto caucuses have enlightened many legislators to the existence of auto or steel interests in their constituencies. Moreover, no one is more effective in lobbying a legislator than another legislator. Even as the number of subcommittees fell dramatically in the postreform Congress, the growth of caucuses offset this trend. Capitol Hill remains a place where an organized interest can find a hearing and someone to plead its case.

The Politics of Uncertainty

Politicians and organized interests operate in a highly uncertain, highly contingent world. This was as true for Theodore Roosevelt (president of the Senate in 1901) or Joseph Cannon (speaker of the house in 1910) as it was for Speaker Tom Foley in 1994. With the shared goal of reducing this uncertainty as much as possible, legislators and lobbyists are often accomplices, sometimes adversaries. But the basic goal of gaining more certainty—whether on politics, policy, or process—shapes almost everything they do.

Thus both business and reformist interests have altered their strategies during the twentieth century, as have lawmakers. In 1900 senators might have been influenced by opportunities to profit from public service, a practice that continued, if secretly, well into the middle of the century.[47] But then groups began to rely more on access and information to make their points.[48] Access and information remained important over the last third of the century, a time defined by three broad trends in relations between interest groups and Congress. First, organized interests came to rely on tactics that blurred the line between inside and outside lobbying. That is, groups sought to convey information through Capitol Hill connections, district and state notables, and public relations campaigns, among other means. Moreover, interests could monitor individual legislators daily, to the point that even the most electorally secure representatives and senators understood that they were under scrutiny.

Second, the politics of influence became focused as much on agenda setting as on decision making. The insurance industry's successful lobbying on the Clinton health care package in 1993–1994 demonstrated the power of Schattschneider's idea of expanding the scope of conflict, as the debate shifted from program specifics to the broader issue of choice.[49] Third, especially in the 1990s, the distinction between lobbying and electioneering became unclear. Given partisan parity in both houses, organized groups have great incentives to "invest" in their favored party, with high hopes that the party will remain or become the majority. And lawmakers demand that interests help fund campaigns through some combination of PAC and soft money contributions. In this permanent campaign context, every issue and every vote can have electoral consequences. Thus electoral uncertainties are added to the usual legislative uncertainties. And the stakes are high: shifting a few votes can dictate which party controls one or both chambers.

Ironically, such conditions may produce a kind of stasis that comes from an inability to govern effectively. Legislators will raise money and win reelection; lobbyists will block the legislation that they most oppose. And the public will become more cynical toward legislators and interest groups— not unlike the early 1900s, when Progressives, Populists, and muckrakers developed broad social movements to put reform on the agenda.

Notes

1. Grant McConnell, *Private Power and American Democracy* (New York: Vintage, 1966), 14; James Sterling Young, *The Washington Community 1800–1828* (New York: Harcourt Brace, 1966).
2. James Madison, "Federalist 10," in *The Federalist Papers*, ed. Clinton Rossiter (New York: Mentor Books, 1999), 31.
3. Peter Swenson, "The Influence of Recruitment on the Structure of Power in the U.S. House of Representatives, 1870–1940," *Legislative Studies Quarterly* 7 (February 1982): 7–36.
4. McConnell, *Private Power and American Democracy*, 56.
5. Ibid., 56.
6. Margaret S. Thompson, *The 'Spider Web': Congress and Lobbying in the Age of Grant* (Ithaca, N.Y.: Cornell, 1985), 272–273.
7. Arthur Bentley, *The Process of Government* (Chicago: University of Chicago, 1908); David B. Truman, *The Governmental Process* (New York: Knopf, 1951). See also Chapter 15 in this volume for further development of Bentley's ideas.
8. John Judis, *The Paradox of American Democracy* (New York: Pantheon, 2000), 38–39.
9. John Mark Hansen, *Gaining Access* (Chicago: University of Chicago, 1991), 12.
10. See John R. Wright, *Interest Groups and Congress* (Boston: Allyn and Bacon, 1996), 88; David Whiteman, *Communication in Congress* (Lawrence, Kans.: University Press of Congress, 1996), 40; Darrell West and Burdett Loomis, *The Sound of Money* (New York: Norton, 1998), 30–33.
11. The literature here is voluminous, but two 1978 books give a nice sense of this dualism: Thomas Mann, *Unsafe at Any Margin* (Washington: American Enterprise Institute, 1978); Richard F. Fenno Jr., *Home Style* (Boston: Little, Brown, 1978).
12. Brooks Jackson, *Honest Graft* (New York: Alfred A. Knopf, 1988).
13. Joseph Cooper, "The Twentieth Century Congress," in *Congress Reconsidered*, 3d ed., ed. Lawrence Dodd and Bruce I. Oppenheimer (Washington, D.C.: CQ Press, 2001), 335–366; Roger Davidson, ed., *The Postreform Congress* (New York: St. Martin's Press, 1992); Kenneth Shepsle, "The Changing Textbook Congress," in *Can the Government Govern?* ed. John E. Chubb and Paul Peterson (Washington, D.C.: Brookings, 1989).
14. In *The Permanent Majority* (Tuscaloosa, Ala.: University of Alabama, 1983), Mack Shelly III begins many of his examinations of the coalition in 1933, but others see 1937 as the point at which the alliance was formalized. See Eric Schickler, *Disjointed Pluralism* (Princeton: Princeton University, 2001), 137; James T. Patterson, *Congressional Conservatism and the New Deal* (Lexington, Ky.: University of Kentucky, 1967).
15. Davidson, *The Postreform Congress;* Ronald Peters, *The Atomistic Congress* (New York: Sharpe, 1992); Shepsle, "The Textbook Congress."
16. In many ways this era resembled the1950s—another period of stability—during which the business ethos dominated to the point that corporate interests felt only a modest need to lobby actively in Washington.
17. Quoted in David J. Rothman, *Politics and Power* (New York: Atheneum, 1969), 207.
18. Ibid., 165.
19. Ibid., 219.
20. David W. Brady, *Critical Elections and Congressional Policymaking* (Stanford: Stanford University, 1988).
21. Pendleton Herring, *Group Representation before Congress* (Washington, D.C.: Brookings, 1928), 46.
22. Ibid., 21; see also Louise Overacker, *Money in Elections* (New York: Macmillan, 1932).
23. Herring, *Group Representation before Congress*, 41.
24. Ibid., 19, 245.

25. Ibid., ch.10, 11, 12. The National Education Association would be considered a union in later years, but was more accurately placed as a professional society in the 1920s.
26. Hansen, *Gaining Access*, 61.
27. Shepsle, "The Changing Textbook Congress," 238.
28. David Mayhew, *Party Loyalty among Congressmen* (New Haven: Yale, 1966).
29. See J. Lieper Freeman, *The Political Process* (New York: Random House, 1965); Douglass Cater, *Power in Washington* (New York: Vintage, 1964), among others.
30. Hansen, *Gaining Access*, 164ff.
31. Barbara Hinckley, *The Seniority System in Congress* (Bloomington, Ind.: Indiana University, 1966).
32. James Sundquist, *Politics and Policy* (Washington, D.C.: Brookings, 1968) remains an excellent overview of the policy initiatives of 1953–1968.
33. Jeff Fishel, *Party and Opposition* (New York: David McKay, 1973).
34. George B. Galloway, *History of the House of Representatives* (New York: Crowell, 1961), 166. Galloway distinguishes between old-style direct lobbying and so-called new-style lobbying, which includes advertising, grassroots efforts, and public relations. New-style techniques are far more prevalent in the postreform period. For a somewhat different view, with more examples of grassroots lobbying and public relations work, see James Deakins, *The Lobbyists* (Washington, D.C.: Public Affairs, 1966).
35. Roger Davidson and Walter Oleszek, *Congress and Its Members*, 7th ed. (Washington, D.C.: CQ Press, 2001).
36. Milbrath, *Washington Lobbyists*, 213.
37. See Norman Ornstein, ed., *Congress in Change* (New York: Praeger, 1975); Burdett Loomis, *The New American Politician* (New York: Basic, 1998); Shepsle, "The Changing Textbook Congress."
38. John Tierney, "Congress and Organized Interests," in *Congressional Politics*, ed. Christopher Deering (Chicago: Dorsey, 1988), 203.
39. James Sundquist, *The Decline and Resurgence of Congress* (Washington, D.C.: Brookings, 1981).
40. Although Kay Schlozman and John Tierney's study uses 1983 data, it provides an excellent snapshot of Washington interest groups. See *Organized Interests and American Democracy* (New York: Harper and Row, 1986).
41. Among many others, see David Rohde, *Party and Leaders in the Postreform House* (Chicago: University of Chicago, 1991); John Aldrich, *Why Parties* (Chicago: University of Chicago, 1995); Barbara Sinclair, *Legislators, Leaders, and Lawmaking in the U.S. House of Representatives* (Baltimore, Md.: Johns Hopkins University, 1995); John Bond and Richard Fleischer, eds., *Polarized Parties* (Washington, D.C.: CQ Press, 2000).
42. Much of what follows relies on Frank R. Baumgartner and Beth L. Leech, *Basic Interests: The Importance of Groups in Politics and in Political Science* (Princeton: Princeton University, 1998).
43. The studies considered here include Schlozman and Tierney, *Organized Interests and American Democracy;* Jack Walker, *Mobilizing Interest Groups in America* (Ann Arbor: University of Michigan, 1991); and John P. Heinz, Edward O. Laumann, Robert L. Nelson, and Robert H. Salisbury, *The Hollow Core: Private Interests in National Policymaking* (Cambridge: Harvard University, 1993).
44. Baumgartner and Leech, *Basic Interests*, 152.
45. Norman Ornstein, Thomas Mann, and Michael Malbin, *Vital Statistics on Congress 1999–2000* (Washington, D.C.: American Enterprise Institute, 2000), 102.
46. Susan Webb Hammond, *Congressional Caucuses in National Policymaking* (Baltimore, Md.: Johns Hopkins University, 1998), 42.
47. See Robert Caro's description of Lyndon Johnson's relationships with Texas oil and construction firms in *Years of Lyndon Johnson: The Path to Power* (New York: Vintage, 1990).

48. Milbrath, *Washington Lobbyists;* Raymond Bauer, Ithiel de Sola Pool, and Louis Dexter, *American Business and Public Policy* (Chicago: Aldine, 1963); Truman, *The Governmental Process.*

49. See, among others, Theda Skocpol, *Boomerang* (New York: Norton, 1996); West and Loomis, *The Sound of Money;* and David Broder and Haynes Johnson, *The System* (Boston: Little, Brown, 1997).

III. GROUPS IN THE POLICYMAKING PROCESS

10

What Corporations Really Want from Government
The Public Provision of Private Goods
R. Kenneth Godwin and Barry J. Seldon

Scholars who study lobbying and how lobbyists influence politics typically focus on high-profile political issues that affect large numbers of citizens, issues that are almost always controversial and draw to the fray many well-known interest groups. Attention has usually focused on legislative votes and the factors that allegedly influence them, such as political action committee contributions and coalition building among organized interests.

But do such studies accurately reflect the lobbying that goes on in Washington? In this chapter R. Kenneth Godwin and Barry J. Seldon assert that situations where corporate lobbyists seek private goods—government-provided benefits that help a single firm, such as a regulatory waiver for a single manufacturing plant—are more common. This kind of lobbying may involve direct contact, often behind the scenes, between an individual corporation's lobbyists and key legislators, such as those on particular committees or subcommittees or those from a firm's home district.

The authors test their assertions by examining corporate lobbying in three industries with differing levels of government regulation. The authors find that heavily regulated firms spend more on lobbying than do lightly regulated firms. And lobbyists in regulated industries concentrate on goods that are private to the firm and largely forgo cooperative efforts with other firms. Godwin and Seldon suggest that because past interest group research has neglected the study of private goods, "research has underestimated the effects of corporate lobbying and has overestimated the amount of coalition behavior by corporate lobbyists."

The authors wish to thank professors John Green and Nancy Kucinski for their assistance in preparing this chapter.

A lobbyist from a major defense contractor speaking to a class on interest groups was asked, "What was the most important vote you influenced?" The lobbyist responded, "Do you mean the most important vote, or the most important thing I did for [the firm]?" She went on to explain that her most significant achievement was obtaining a 25 percent increase in the price of her firm's missile. But a recorded vote never took place. The price increase occurred during committee markup of an omnibus defense bill. Although this outcome boosted the firm's profits by $50 million over five years, no legislator voted directly on the price increase.

The Public Provision of Private Goods

Lobbying situations like the missile price increase are not rare, but they are rarely studied. Instead political scientists generally analyze highly visible issues that affect numerous firms, citizen action groups, trade associations, or individuals. Political scientists then use these analyses to develop models and generalizations about what interest groups want, how they get what they want, and how public officials respond to lobbying efforts and campaign contributions. In this chapter we show that research that neglects lobbying situations like the missile price increase also neglects issues on which the largest category of lobbyists (those working for individual corporations) spend most of their time. In many ways, researchers studying interest groups are like the guy who lost his keys in the dark alley but looks for them under the streetlamp because the light is better there. It is unsurprising that interest group researchers may not find the keys to understanding lobbying behavior by studying highly visible issues that involve substantial conflict.

In this chapter we examine the hypothesis that a corporate lobbyist is less likely to ask legislators for votes on bills than for help in obtaining government contracts, regulatory waivers, and government subsidies for the lobbyist's corporation. We refer to government-provided benefits that help a single firm as *private goods*. Some examples of private goods are:

- A government contract to build a new tank for the army.
- A decision by the Environmental Protection Agency to allow a chemical company to phase out its organic-phosphate pesticide over a longer period than allowed by the original regulation.
- A decision by the U.S. Patent Office to give a pharmaceutical company a ten-year extension on a drug patent.

Collective Goods versus Private Goods

The opposite of private goods is collective goods. Collective goods are benefits that the government provides to many groups, firms, or individuals, such as a reduction in the corporate income tax rate, a change in the minimum wage, and legislation that requires all firms to provide health insurance to their workers. You can think of government benefits as lying on a continuum. At one end are purely private goods like the missile price increase, a government contract, and a regulatory waiver to a single plant. At the other end are purely collective goods such as a reduction in income taxes on all corporations or an increase in Medicare benefits to older Americans. In between are benefits with different levels of "collectiveness," such as regulations or tax changes that affect a single industry, tariffs on a single product such as computer chips, subsidies for a particular crop, and loan guarantees for first-time home buyers.

An analogy might help clarify this idea. Assume that you are a student at a state university who receives financial assistance; some of this assistance comes from working for the university. You would like the government to reduce your cost of attending college. One way to do this is for the university to give you a scholarship. This would be a private good—only you would receive the scholarship. Alternatively, the government could lower the tuition for all students at all state universities. This would be a collective good. In between these two extremes are goods that affect some, but not all, students. Your university might decide to pay higher wages to student employees who receive financial assistance, or the legislature might choose to reduce the tuition of in-state students. Figure 10.1 shows the private-collective continuum and some goods along it.

A strategy for obtaining these benefits would be closely related to where the benefit falls on the private-collective continuum. In the case of the scholarship, you might ask two or three professors to write letters of recommendations for you. And you would give the financial aid office information that justifies giving you the scholarship. Notice that only a few people are involved in this decision: the professors and the financial aid officer. On the other hand, lowering tuition for all university students requires action by many public officials. The members of the state board of higher education must propose a tuition cut, a majority of members of the legislature must approve the board's recommendation, and the governor must sign the bill. To gain this benefit you probably would work through the student government organization at your university, which would form a coalition with the student government organizations of other state universities. This coalition would lobby the state board of education, the legislature, and the governor.

Between these two extremes is, for example, the decision to grant student workers a wage increase. This issue might involve the university's vice president for financial affairs and the managers of campus businesses that must pay the increased wage costs. To obtain this benefit you presumably would organize the student workers on your campus, who would appeal to the university's vice president and business managers.

The number of officials needed to supply a desired benefit and the lobbying resources needed to influence those officials increase as you move from the private to the collective end of the continuum. For

Figure 10.1. A Continuum of Publicly Provided Goods

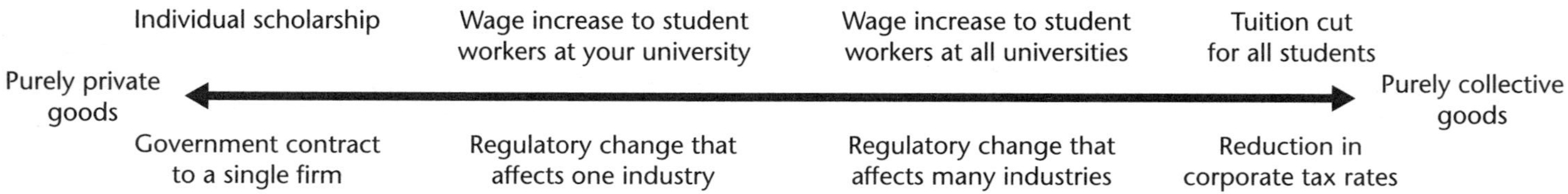

Purely private goods

Individual scholarship

Government contract to a single firm

Wage increase to student workers at your university

Regulatory change that affects one industry

Wage increase to student workers at all universities

Regulatory change that affects many industries

Tuition cut for all students

Reduction in corporate tax rates

Purely collective goods

Source: Authors' example.

example, getting a regulatory waiver for a single plant could be accomplished by a single congressperson who calls an agency official and encourages him or her to grant the waiver. But reducing the corporate tax rate requires support from the Republican Party, action by several congressional committees, votes by the entire House and Senate, and the cooperation of the White House.

What difference does it make in our understanding of lobbying if political scientists concentrate on how interest groups pursue highly collective goods while corporate lobbyists pursue private goods? We would be overlooking a major portion of lobbying activity and its consequences. Collective goods such as changes in the minimum wage and a decision to allow oil exploration in Arctic wilderness areas are highly visible because they involve conflicts between organized interests. And they are sources of ideological clashes between the political parties. In these conflicts both sides are organized and have extensive political resources. Because no single interest is likely to dominate collective goods issues, focusing on them alone might lead us to conclude that the American political system is so diverse and competitive that almost everyone gets represented.

But private goods are different. They involve little conflict, and often only one side (the one with a lobbyist) gets represented. Under these conditions a single interest can dominate a policy decision. In the example of the missile price increase the firm was a clear winner and the taxpayers were clear losers, but only the firm's voice was heard in committee markup. Not surprising, the side that was heard defeated the side that was not. To the extent that students of politics overlook such situations, we are likely to underestimate the impact of organized interests on public policy.

A less obvious consequence of concentrating on collective goods is that we underestimate the influence of corporate campaign contributions on policy outcomes. Congressional campaigns often cost more than $1 million, and political action committees rarely donate more than $5,000 to a particular candidate. As many disparate interests contribute to the winning candidate, it is unlikely that a single contribution will influence a legislator's decision on a collective good. If, however, most corporate lobbyists are interested in private goods, then even a $1,000 contribution may give the lobbyist the necessary access to a legislator to obtain the desired private good. When we add up the costs and benefits of all the private goods that governments supply, the total impact of these goods may be greater than the total impact of the collective goods that governments provide.

How Important Are Private Goods?

Presumably corporations don't care whether profits obtained from government actions come from a private good or a collective good. The question the firm asks is, "Where is the most efficient place on the private-collective continuum to spend lobbying resources?" If lobbying for private goods has a higher return, then corporate lobbyists will expend more resources pursuing private goods than pursuing collective goods. But if collective goods have a higher return, lobbyists will spend their time and money seeking them instead.

In the classic exchange model of lobbying and political campaigns, interests provide campaign contributions, votes, and other resources that legislators need to gain reelection. In return, legislators provide goods to the interests. Lobbyists attempt to maximize their firm's profits for the lobbying resources allotted, and legislators try to maximize their chances of reelection. We can imagine lobbyists' decision process as follows: First they identify the governmentally supplied goods that will affect their firm's profits. Then they estimate the resources needed to lobby for each good and the probability of success. The decision calculus involves weighing expected benefits against the costs involved in lobbying. The lobbyist would pursue issues where expected benefits are greater than expected costs:

$$P \times B > C$$

where P is the probability of success in obtaining the benefit, B is the value of the benefit to the firm, and C is the cost of lobbying for the good. The lobbyist would refrain from lobbying if $P \times B < C$.

Thus if the expected benefit (the value of the benefit multiplied by the probability of success) is greater than the cost of the lobbying resources, then the lobbyist will pursue the good. The lobbyist will expend resources for all goods where the expected profit return for an additional dollar spent lobbying is greater than the profit the corporation could obtain by investing that dollar in other activities such as hiring more salespeople or improving technology.

Legislators also make calculations. Legislators' actions have political benefits and costs. Legislators use the following calculation to decide which goods they will provide:

$$E = V/R$$

where E is efficiency of effort, V is the net votes gained from supplying the good, and R is the resources the legislator must expend to provide the good.

Legislators estimate the net vote gain from providing a particular good and the amount of resources needed to provide the good. By dividing the net vote gain by the required effort, legislators can determine their efficiency. Legislators then provide those goods that have the greatest efficiency. Legislators' resources include their time, influence, and expertise and the time, influence, and expertise of their staff.

An important aspect of the legislator's decision calculus is that voters will approve of some actions, be indifferent to others, and disapprove of others. If a lobbyist asks a legislator to do something that will likely cost him or her votes in the next election, then the interest must provide the legislator with enough resources to offset the lost votes and provide a net gain in votes. Thus a legislator's "price" for producing goods that constituents dislike will be higher than the price for goods that constituents are indifferent to. The legislator will charge the lowest price for goods that constituents support.

Policy researchers, such as James Wilson and Theodore Lowi, have long maintained that public officials prefer to deal with policies that have low visibility to the public, involve little conflict among competing interests, and are narrow in scope.[1] Why? Because the winners know they received the policy benefits, but the losers rarely know they have paid the costs. For example, if the senator who chairs the Environment and Public Works Committee calls the Environmental Protection Agency and encourages it to grant a regulatory waiver to a firm in the senator's district, the firm will know of this effort and will reward the senator. In contrast, those who live near the polluting firm are unlikely to be aware of the senator's effort; thus they will be unable to punish him or her.

The example of the missile price increase was a decision that had a high benefit-cost ratio for legislators. The firm knew it was $50 million richer and rewarded the legislators with electoral support. The taxpayers, who knew nothing of the action, did not punish the legislators. Even if some taxpayers had been aware of the budget change, they could not have identified the legislators responsible for the price increase because there was no recorded vote.

Compare the missile price increase with a vote on the highly publicized issue of allowing electricity producers to use more high sulfur coal. Although companies that own the coal will reward a legislator for a favorable vote, environmental groups will know of the vote and exact punishment. These groups may contribute funds and campaign workers to the legislator's opponent in the next election, and they may urge environmentally aware citizens to vote against the legislator.

So, it's safe to assume that legislators prefer policies that encourage rewards from winners and avoid retribution from losers. Those low-visibility and low-conflict policies are likely to be at the private goods end of the continuum.

Legislators also prefer policies that benefit their constituents. It is much safer politically for legislators to work on behalf of firms in their district than on behalf of firms outside their district. For example, if a legislator from North Carolina receives a large campaign contribution from a tobacco firm in the state and urges other legislators or regulatory agencies to help the tobacco firm, the public will probably deem this legitimate. The legislator simply is representing a constituent. But if a legislator from New York City receives a large contribution from a North Carolina tobacco company and lobbies on behalf of that company's interests, then the public tends to believe that the legislator has been bought.

William Browne's research on agriculture policy shows this pattern. Brown interviewed lobbyists from 130 organizations and legislators and staff from 112 congressional offices. He discovered that firms almost always approached a legislator from their home district. And 98 percent of the issues that firms named as important affected only their organization. Browne concluded that the agricultural policy process brings together legislators who need constituent support and constituents who want private goods.[2]

Legislators have good reason to prefer supplying private goods rather than collective goods—do firms also favor private goods? Yes. If the benefits a lobbyist seeks are purely private to his or her firm, then the decision to expend resources is straightforward. As the benefits move toward the collective goods end of the continuum, the lobbyist must estimate how other organizations will contribute to the lobbying effort. Mancur Olson's *The Logic of Collective Action* shows that there are substantial transaction and decision costs in the pursuit of collective goods. Olson demonstrates that firms may prefer to "free ride" on the efforts of others rather than pay a share of the lobbying costs. (Free riders are firms that reap the benefit of a collective good while paying little or none of the cost of obtaining it.) In addition, as the number of organizations pursuing a collective good grows, the difficulties involved in mobilizing for collective action increase.[3] (Think how much more difficult it would be for you to organize student workers at your university than to apply for a scholarship.)

Another reason that corporate lobbyists may prefer lobbying for private goods is that fewer public officials are needed to provide them. Sometimes a phone call from a staff member in a senator's office is enough to speed up the granting of a license or a regulatory waiver. Even in cases where large government contracts are involved, the private good can be decided by a vote in subcommittee. Decisions on highly collective goods usually involve many more decisionmakers. This greatly increases a firm's lobbying costs.

Finally, firms seek private goods because the likelihood of opposition from other firms or interest groups is low. Legislators know that when requests for goods lead to conflict between organized interests, the losers will know of their losses and may attempt to punish the legislators.[4]

In summary, the higher expected rewards to firms and legislators from private goods, the difficulties involved in collective action, and the threat of opposition from other firms and interest groups indicate that firms will concentrate on lobbying for private goods. Despite this, most political science research on lobbying and political action committee contributions investigates highly visible issues such as the confirmation of a Supreme Court nominee. But if the expected return to corporate lobbying is greater for private goods than for collective goods, then political science research is overlooking an important part of the policy process.

A Test of the Private Goods Hypothesis

If firms have an easier time obtaining private goods and public officials prefer to provide private goods, then we should be able to predict which firms will spend more on lobbying and which legislators those firms will lobby. The corporations most likely to have large lobbying expenditures are those that rely on government action to provide private goods. These will be firms that depend heavily on government contracts and firms that are heavily regulated. In contrast, firms that are not heavily regulated or whose profits do not depend on government contracts should spend little on lobbying. This will be true despite the fact that many collective goods, such as corporate income taxes, worker safety regulations, and minimum wage legislation, substantially affect all corporations.

A firm will lobby legislators who are most efficient at producing the private goods it wants. These will be legislators who sit on the committees and subcommittees that deal with the contracts or regulatory agencies critical to the firm. The legislators who will charge the lowest price for providing such goods are legislators from the firm's home district. Therefore, corporate lobbyists should concentrate on these two sets of legislators.

In addition, we predict that corporate lobbyists are more likely to lobby alone than as members of coalitions with other firms. We derive this hypothesis from Olson's arguments on the difficulties of collective action. This hypothesis is contrary to the conventional wisdom in the interest group literature. Most writers on lobbying maintain that it is better to lobby as a member of a coalition than to go it alone.[5] We believe, however, that although coalitions are appropriate for seeking some collective goods, they are inappropriate when lobbying for private goods. (Remember the different strategies involved in reducing tuition for all students and in getting a scholarship for yourself.)

To test our hypotheses we studied corporations in three industries with differing levels of government regulation: passenger airlines, rubber-resin manufacturers, and publishing.[6] We limited our analysis to firms with total assets greater than $2 billion (past research indicates that large corporations are much more likely to have lobbying offices in Washington than are smaller corporations). Five passenger airlines, seven rubber-resin companies, and seven publishing firms met our criteria for the study. Because of the small number of industries, firms, and respondents, we tested our hypotheses using a qualitative approach that maximizes the number of opportunities to falsify predictions, rather than on tests of statistical significance. Fortunately, our expectations of which firms will lobby, whom they will lobby, and the likelihood of a coalition forming generate many specific and potentially falsifiable predictions.

The Industries

Despite "deregulation," passenger airlines remain heavily regulated, and government actions strongly affect their profits. The Federal Aviation Administration (FAA) regulates airplane and airport safety and noise, allocates international routes, and decides the amount of time pilots and flight attendants may be on duty. A decision by the Treasury Department to expand customs facilities in Chicago rather than Minneapolis benefits United Airlines and harms Northwest Airlines. Fuel taxes, landing fees, and ticket excise taxes influence the production costs of all airlines. In short, numerous decisions by multiple government agencies affect an airline's profits and competitive position. Because the industry is highly regulated, we expect its firms to expend substantial resources lobbying, to direct most of their efforts toward obtaining private goods, to concentrate on home-district representatives and members of relevant committees, and to lobby alone rather than in coalitions.

Government regulation also significantly affects profits in the rubber-resin industry. But much of the regulation is at the state level because state agencies have the primary responsibility for enforcing the Resource Conservation and Recovery Act, the national legislation that contains the most important regulations affecting the industry. Therefore, we expect rubber-resin firms to divide their lobbying efforts between Washington and the state capitals. We anticipate that the lobbying patterns of rubber-resin firms will be similar to those of the airlines, but expenditures at the federal level will be smaller.[7]

Our third industry is print publishing, which we chose because its profits are relatively independent of government activity. Government regulations on newspapers, magazines, and books are minimal, and, except for postal rates and government documents, government subsidies to the industry are unimportant. Thus, of the three industries, publishing firms should expend the fewest lobbying resources.

The Lobbyists

To discover the relative importance the firms place on private and collective goods, we asked each firm's Washington lobbyists for the following information:

- Which public officials they contact regularly and how frequently they contact them.
- How much time (percentage) they spend on issues that affect only their company or their company and a competitor.[8]
- Their most important issues over the past three years.
- Their major accomplishments.
- How much time (percentage) they devoted to each issue they named during the interview and to issues we had identified before the interview.

We also collected data on which firms had a political action committee (PAC) and to whom the PAC contributed. An interviewer questioned all PAC directors from the firms in our sample, asking how they decided whom to contribute to and how much to contribute.[9] Before the interviews we gathered data on actual contributions so the interviewer could ask about contributions that didn't seem to fit the decision process.

Results

As we hypothesized, airlines spent the most resources lobbying the national government and print publishing firms spent the least. Four of five airlines had multiple lobbyists in Washington and all five had PACs. Three of the seven rubber-resin firms had a lobbyist who maintained an office in Washington, and the same number had a PAC. At the time of our interviews, only two publishing firms whose sales came mainly from publishing printed material had Washington lobbying offices. Only one had a PAC.

On Whom Do Lobbyists Expend Resources?

All airline lobbyists reported speaking almost daily with the staff of House members from districts where their airline had hubs. Each lobbying office contacts every representative from hub districts weekly and hub senators monthly. Airline lobbyists also reported that staff members of home-district legislators frequently contact them to see if the legislator could assist the firm. Subcommittees receive even greater attention from airline lobbyists. The lobbyists reported contacting members of aviation subcommittees at least weekly and subcommittee staff almost daily. Airline lobbyists rarely contact legislators not from their hub areas and not from relevant subcommittees. We also discovered that airline lobbyists spend more time with regulatory personnel than with legislators and their staff. Each airline lobbyist reported speaking daily with FAA officials.

Whereas the airlines have more than one lobbyist in each of their offices, each rubber-resin office had only one professional lobbyist. In addition, because the implementation of the Resource Conservation and Recovery Act is a state concern, the rubber-resin lobbyists reported spending a significant portion of their time in state capitals rather than in Washington. During periods of peak activity in Washington, rubber-resin lobbyists reported speaking to home district representatives and key subcommittee members about once a week and contacting the legislators' staff members three or four times a week. Rubber-resin lobbyists reported spending little time contacting federal regulatory agencies, but indicated that they spent substantial time with state regulatory officials.

The two lobbyists from the publishing firms reported less frequent contacts with legislators than did lobbyists from the other two industries. When publishing lobbyists did contact legislators, they were more likely to speak with members of relevant subcommittees than with representatives from their home district. The lobbyists reported contacting subcommittee staff members and federal agency personnel at least weekly. Though airline and rubber-resin lobbyists reported few interactions with the White House, publishing lobbyists reported working extensively with the White House staff on General Agreement on Tariffs and Trade and North American Free Trade Agreement negotiations dealing with copyright issues.

Allocating Resources between Collective and Private Goods

If we are correct about the importance of private goods, firms in highly regulated industries allocate resources to public officials based on their ability and willingness to supply those goods. Airline lobbyists reported spending 75–95 percent of their time on issues affecting only their firm or their firm and one other. Only seven of the twenty-seven priority issues listed by airline lobbyists dealt with collective goods. Among the private goods airlines sought, only three required floor votes. Every airline lobbyist we interviewed reported winning a private good as his or her most important success. Several such successes were worth hundreds of millions of dollars. For example, Southwest Airlines received a noise regulation waiver from the FAA for its entire fleet of airplanes.

The Wright Amendment is one of the best examples of how a private good can affect unorganized consumers. The amendment, which prohibited commercial airlines from flying out of Love Field in Dallas (a hub of Southwest Airlines) to any state not contiguous with Texas, was added to an aviation bill when the Dallas-Ft. Worth Airport (DFW) was built. The amendment prevented flights from Love Field from competing with flights from DFW (the home hub of American Airlines and a major hub of Delta Airlines). A Department of Transportation analysis found that the Wright Amendment caused flights from DFW to have the highest ticket costs of any major city in the United States, raising the cost of travel out of the Dallas metropolitan area by $200 million a year.[10] The Wright Amendment enormously boosts the profits of American Airlines and Delta Airlines. While Jim Wright and Newt Gingrich were Speakers of the House (Wright from 1987 to 1989, Gingrich from 1995 to 1999), they used their influence to protect American and Delta's privileged profit margins. After Wright and Gingrich resigned, Sen. Phil Gramm, R-Texas, and Rep. Dick Armey, R-Texas, have worked to preserve Love Field restrictions.

These legislators have not been alone in assisting airlines with hubs in a legislator's state or district. All airline lobbyists reported routinely seeking assistance from members of Congress. For example, when Southwest Airlines requested the noise waiver for its airplanes, more than fifty representatives wrote the FAA on Southwest's behalf. Not all the legislators were from districts where Southwest had a major hub—the chairperson and members of a key subcommittee that oversees the FAA also wrote. All airline lobbyists reported asking senators from their hub states to contact both the FAA and the White House to help their airline win international routes. The legislators then pressured the White House and the FAA for policy decisions that gave their airline an advantage over a competitor.

Private goods also dominated the agenda of the rubber-resin lobbyists. They reported spending at least 75 percent of their time on issues that dealt only with their firm, they listed private goods as priority goals twice as frequently as collective goods, and all lobbyists listed a private good as their major lobbying achievement. For example, one lobbyist listed a major military contract as her major achievement; another succeeded in obtaining a regulatory waiver for a recycling plant. As with airline lobbyists, the rubber-resin lobbyists expected their home-district legislators to provide private goods to their firms. The rubber-resin lobbyists asked their representatives to help them not only with federal regulatory agencies, but also with state legislators and state regulatory officials.

Consistent with our expectations of coalition forming, corporate lobbyists in the airline and rubber-resin industries reported little cooperative lobbying to achieve collective goods. For example, a major issue for the rubber-resin industry was the cost of disposing of scrap tires. Although this issue affected all firms in the industry, its major impact was on Goodyear. Instead of forming a coalition, the other tire firms expected Goodyear to do almost all of the lobbying.

This pattern repeated itself every time one firm had a much greater stake than other firms in a collective good.[11] For example, Delta and American airlines both benefit from the Wright Amendment. But American paid almost the entire cost of keeping these restrictions in place. When our interviewer asked a Delta lobbyist how much time he spent on the issue, he responded that the Wright Amendment was "Mr. Crandall's concern." (Robert Crandall was the chief executive officer of AMR, American Airlines' parent company.) American's full-time lobbyists made the Wright Amendment a top priority and paid several attorneys in Washington and Dallas to work on the issue. Delta's lobbyists merely alerted friends in Congress that Delta supported American's position.

Although the reports of lobbyists from the airline and rubber-resin firms supported our hypothesis that private goods dominate corporate lobbying efforts, the activities of the two publishing lobbyists did not. Both lobbyists listed a private good as their major lobbying accomplishment, but 70 percent of the priority issues they worked on concerned such collective goods as copyright provisions in foreign trade agreements and postal rates for printed materials. The publishing lobbyists did not lobby cooperatively on the collective goods issues, but divided them. Each lobbyist specialized on the collective goods that had the greatest impact on her firm. This arrangement was efficient because each issue required specialized knowledge and regular contacts with specific public officials.

In summary, the resource allocations of the lobbyists we interviewed support the hypotheses that heavily regulated firms spend more on lobbying than lightly regulated firms, that lobbyists in regulated industries concentrate on goods that are private to their firm, and that cooperative efforts by corporate lobbyists are less frequent than researchers generally suppose. The activities of the two publishing lobbyists, however, suggest that collective goods can be more important than private goods for industries that are not heavily regulated.

How Political Action Committees Allocate Their Funds

To discover if PAC contributions follow patterns similar to lobbying expenditures, we asked PAC directors to rank twenty possible reasons for giving to a candidate (Table 10.1). Responses were on a scale from one (not important) to four (very important). PAC directors give priority to:

- Legislators who sit on key committees and subcommittees (particularly the committee and subcommittee chairs).
- Legislators who have supported the firm in the past.
- Home-district legislators.

Federal Election Commission (FEC) data on these PACs verify the reported patterns. On average, the PACs studied gave more than three times as much to home district representatives and members of relevant committees as they gave to other legislators.

When we look at PACs within particular industries, we find that airlines contribute almost exactly as our private goods hypotheses posit. For all but one airline, PAC directors indicated that past help in obtaining a private good was the most important influence on contribution decisions.[12] For airline PACs, neither ideology nor political party was important in contribution decisions. For rubber-resin PACs, being a member of the committee with primary responsibility for the Resource Conservation and Recovery Act, past assistance to the firm in obtaining a private good, and assistance in lobbying state and federal agencies were equally important factors. The directors of rubber-resin PACs also indicated that they supported challengers against proenvironment incumbents in close races.

A factor we expected to influence the probability of a contribution was whether the PAC director expected a candidate to win. Although past research has shown that firms and trade associations give to candidates who are likely to win, PAC directors ranked this item nineteenth out of twenty possible reasons for giving. However, our analysis of FEC data showed that with the exception of rubber-resin PACs backing challengers to proenvironment incumbents in close races, the PACs we studied did not give to challengers. This was the only case where the verbal responses from our interviewees differed substantially from their observed behavior.

Table 10.1.   Why Political Action Committees
Gave to Candidates

Candidate characteristic	Average score
Sits on a committee that is important to our interests	4.00
Has been very supportive of issues important to our corporation	3.86
Is from a district or state where we have facilities	3.71
Has helped us with the executive and regulatory agencies	3.71
Leadership position places the candidate in a position of influence on issues that affect us	3.57
Has been helpful to our industry as a whole	3.43
Has a great personal interest in issues that concern us	3.43
Has helped us with other members of Congress	3.43
The opponent is definitely a threat to us	2.71
Is involved in a close race	2.71
We like his or her ideology	2.00
May be helpful to us in the future	1.43
Is a popular candidate among our contributors	1.43
A contribution would help obtain access to him or to his staff	1.43
We dislike the opponent's ideology	1.43
Has helped us with state and local governments	1.43
Was in a position to hurt us if we didn't contribute	1.43
We were asked to contribute and saw no reason not to	1.43
Was likely to win the election	1.28
Belongs to the political party most favorable to our interests	1.28

Source: Authors' data.

4 = Very important   3 = Important   2 = Somewhat important   1 = Not important

How Corporations Obtain Collective Goods

Given the emphasis corporate lobbyists place on private goods, an obvious question is, "How do firms pursue collective goods?" A logical strategy would be to have the industry trade association lobby on issues that affect the entire industry.[13] To determine if the trade associations played a key role in lobbying for collective goods, we asked the corporate lobbyists to describe how they worked with the trade association lobbyists and how successfully the trade association lobbied on issues important to the industry. We also attempted to interview the trade association lobbyists for each of our three industries. Our interviewer successfully completed interviews with the chief lobbyists of the Air Transport Association (ATA) and the Rubber Manufacturers Association (RMA). Our interviewers were unable to interview the lobbyist for the publishing trade association, who instead provided a list of the issues on which he spent either "considerable" or a "great deal of time" (but only on the condition that we not identify him or his trade association in any published material).

We asked the trade association lobbyists to list the issues they saw as most important to their industry and the time and other resources they devoted to each issue. Before the interviews we prepared a list of key issues affecting the three industries. If the trade association lobbyist did not mention an issue on our list, the interviewer asked if he or she had lobbied on the issue and, if so, how extensively. Table 10.2 lists the issues the trade association lobbyists identified as most important to their industries.

Our interviews with the corporate and trade association lobbyists uncovered several differences among the three industries in how the

Table 10.2.   Priority Issues for Trade Associations

Airlines	Rubber-resin	Publishing
Excise taxes on tickets	Scrap tire disposal and and taxation	North American Free Trade Agreement and General Agreement on Tariffs and Trade
Modernization of air traffic control	State storm water regulations	Copyright renewal act
National fuel taxes	Superfund issues	High-performance computing act
State fuel taxes	Transportation of hazardous waste	Digital audio home recording
Noise abatement at local airports	Resource Conservation and Recovery Act reauthorization	Library of Congress fees
Trust-fund spending by Federal Aviation Authority on airports	Regulation of baby bottle nipples	Freedom of Information Act amendments
	North American Free Trade Agreement provisions for rubber-resin	Government Printing Office electronic information
	Federal funding for basic research	Postal service mailing rates
		Mail order use tax
		National film preservation
		Publisher liability for pornography and news stories

Source: Authors' data.

lobbyists pursued collective goods. The airline lobbyists delegated almost all responsibility to the ATA. For example, a major collective good for the airline industry is modernization of air traffic control. The ATA lobbyist developed the lobbying strategy on this issue, prepared technical information for policymakers, and coordinated the lobbying efforts. The airlines participated by contacting legislators and regulatory officials with whom they had particularly close relationships, but not until the ATA lobbyist determined the appropriate time. The airline lobbyists were uniformly supportive of the ATA's efforts.

The lobbying pattern of the rubber-resin industry was somewhat different. Each rubber-resin corporate lobbyist included a collective good as a top-three priority. Thus the corporate lobbyists were less willing to follow the RMA's lead in lobbying on the collective good issue critical to their firm. The greater independence of lobbying efforts by rubber-resin firms reflected the greater diversity of interests among RMA members. Although all the airlines produce similar services, there is substantial product diversity within the RMA. RMA members focus on such goods as tires, bushings, castings, sealants, and baby bottle nipples.

Equally important, a number of RMA members, such as Bridgestone-Firestone, are foreign corporations. This often leads to conflicts of interest among members over such issues as U.S.–regulated pollution control. Despite their different interests, our corporate respondents indicated that they generally were pleased with the RMA's lobbying efforts and left the lobbying for most collective goods to the trade association.

Because we were unable to interview the publishing trade association (the lobbyist sent in the form instead), we relied on information from the two corporate lobbyists on how their firms worked with the trade association lobbyist. The corporate lobbyists indicated that there was little cooperation or coordination between them and the trade association lobbyist. In fact, both corporate lobbyists said they devoted so much time to collective goods because their trade association was not doing enough on the collective goods issues important to their firms.

Despite the differences among the trade associations in the three industries, one lobbying pattern was clear: trade associations rarely lobbied on any issue that did not affect directly (and almost exclusively) their members. In other words, trade associations seldom lobbied for goods that were collective beyond their industry. For example, the ATA listed only airline issues, and the lobbyist for the publishing trade association listed only publishing issues as receiving lobbying attention.[14] Coupled with our information on the lobbying patterns of the corporations, this finding suggests that lobbyists concentrate their resources on goods that are at the same level of collectiveness as the lobbyist's employer. Corporate lobbyists spend their resources pursuing goods that are private to their company, and trade association lobbyists seek goods that are private to their industry.

Discussion

Although the number of industries, firms, and lobbyists interviewed for this study is small, our interviews confirm the importance of private goods to corporations in heavily regulated industries. Measures of the time lobbyists devoted to particular issues, the goods that the lobbyists named as most important to their firms, and the lobbyists' most important accomplishments showed that private goods had a higher priority than collective goods for lobbyists in the airline and rubber-resin industries. The preference of lobbyists for private goods reflects the incentive structures facing those who demand and those who supply publicly provided goods. Lobbying costs are lower for private goods because it takes fewer public officials to supply them and because lobbyists' requests for private goods often are unopposed by other organized interests.

Our interviews with the PAC directors indicated that they are influenced more by a candidate's past assistance to their firm in obtaining a private good and less by the candidate's ideology or voting record. This suggests that past researchers who concluded that corporate contributions have little influence on legislators' behavior were wrong. Although there may be little relationship between corporate PAC contributions and legislators' roll call votes, roll call votes are not the primary objectives of corporate lobbyists. To determine if an interest's contributions affect the behavior of a legislator, it is first necessary to know what the corporation wants the legislator to do.

A third aspect of corporate lobbying is the relatively small amount of coalition activity. When corporate lobbyists did participate in coalitions they were highly unequal, with the smaller stakeholders in the collective good forcing the largest stakeholder to shoulder a disproportionate share of the lobbying effort. Past interest group research detected lots of coalition activity, and the literature suggests that lobbyists almost always try to form coalitions with potential allies.[15] We believe this discrepancy in findings is the result of different methods for identifying lobbying issues.

For example, an excellent study of coalition activity by Marie Hojnacki found that two-thirds of the business group lobbying she examined took place in coalitions.[16] But Hojnacki analyzed lobbying activity by studying five highly visible collective goods issues.[17] Given that the likelihood of coalition forming is highly correlated with the level of conflict surrounding an issue and the number and strength of opposition groups, Hojnacki's issue selection made it inevitable that she would find extensive coalition behavior.[18] To see how different research methods affect findings, take the example of the family and medical leave bill, an issue Hojnacki studied. The bill affected the operating costs of all the firms in our study and was decided during the period covered by our interviews. But none of our interviewees mentioned the medical leave issue, perhaps because they viewed lobbying on the bill as an inefficient use of their resources and chose to be free riders on the efforts of others instead.

In contrast to Hojnacki's approach, our study asked two questions: "What types of publicly supplied goods attract the greatest lobbying activity by firms?" and "How do firms pursue those goods?" To answer these questions we identified industries expected to expend differing levels of resources on lobbying. We then interviewed corporate and trade association lobbyists in those industries and asked them to list the most important issues to their firm or association and the amount of time and other resources they spent on each issue. Our approach is likely to uncover lobbying on low visibility issues on which there is less conflict, but it will miss lobbying activities that require little time or effort by the lobbyist.

Conclusion

The broad implications of our research are two. First, the goods corporations seek from government and the tactics they use depend not only on the importance of the good but also on where the good lies on the private-collective continuum. If political scientists are to understand patterns of interest group influence, they must first identify where the desired benefit lies on that continuum. Only then can the political scientists identify which organizations and lobbying strategies are most appropriate to the pursuit of that benefit. Second, because past interest group research generally has neglected private goods, that research has underestimated the effects of corporate lobbying and has overestimated the amount of coalition behavior by corporate lobbyists.

Notes

1. Theodore J. Lowi, *The End of Liberalism*, 2d ed. (New York: Norton, 1979); James Q. Wilson, *Political Organizations* (New York: Basic Books, 1973).
2. William P. Browne, "Organized Interests and Their Issue Niches: A Search for Pluralism in a Policy Domain," *Journal of Politics* 52 (May 1990): 477–509; William P. Browne, Cultivating Congress (Lawrence: University of Kansas, 1995).
3. Mancur Olson Jr., *The Logic of Collective Action* (Cambridge: Harvard University, 1965).
4. We offer a formal proof of our expectations for why lobbyists will prefer private goods in Barry J. Seldon and Kenneth Godwin, "Firms' Investment in Lobbying for Collective and Private Goods: Results from a Game-Theoretic Model" (paper presented at the meetings of the American Political Science Association, Washington, D.C., September 4, 1998).
5. See Marie Hojnacki, "Interest Groups' Decisions to Join Alliances or Work Alone," *American Journal of Political Science* 41 (January 1997): 61–87.
6. Using past case studies of regulation, we chose several industries as potential candidates. We then interviewed stock analysts of those industries to estimate the degree to which firms' profits depend on federal regulation and to identify public policy issues important to the industry. When dealing with conglomerates, we

included a corporation only if 50 percent or more of its total sales came from the product under consideration.

7. We completed our research before the Bridgestone/Firestone tire problem on sport utility vehicles became public.

8. A private good often includes two firms because it gives one a competitive advantage over the other. For example, if one airline wins a new international route, another airline that wanted the route did not receive it.

9. To ensure that we did not inadvertently encourage lobbyists to give answers that would confirm our hypotheses, we did not share our hypotheses with the interviewer.

10. *Dallas Business Journal,* July 29, 1996. An independent economic analysis of the Wright Amendment found that it increases the average ticket price out of the Dallas-Ft. Worth Airport by between 17 percent and 20 percent. Recently the Department of Transportation reinterpreted the Wright Amendment to allow direct flights from Love Field to all states so long as the planes carry fifty-six or fewer passengers.

11. Readers familiar with *The Logic of Collective Action* will note that this pattern fits exactly Olson's expectation that in these situations smaller stakeholders will exploit larger ones.

12. The PAC directors were asked why a legislator received money. If the response was that the legislator had helped the airline achieve its goals, the interviewer asked the directors what particular goal, if any, had been most important to the decision.

13. Trade associations are institutional arrangements that firms use to reduce the cost of pursuing collective goods. If firms pursued the collective good independently there could be duplication of effort. In addition, trade associations eliminate the free rider problem that can occur when an industry pursues a collective good. Trade associations overcome the free rider problem by using funds collected from all the firms in their lobbying effort.

14. The Rubber Manufacturer's Association listed federal funding for basic research as an issue where the benefits of its lobbying might seem to extend beyond the rubber-resin industry. But the lobbyists' efforts were devoted to directing research dollars toward rubber-resin research and away from alternative industries.

15. For a review of past research on coalition forming, see Hojnacki, "Interest Groups' Decisions."

16. Ibid.

17. The issues involved Energy Tax proposals, striker replacement legislation, campaign finance reform, a job training program, and family and medical leave legislation.

18. Hojnacki, "Interest Groups' Decisions," 70–73.

11

Corporate Lobbyists as Political Actors
A View from the Field
Rogan Kersh

Political scientists have regularly struggled to assess the importance of lobbying; many analyses have been simplistic, even useless. Much of the difficulty comes from a lack of understanding of what lobbyists actually do. How do you quantify "schmoozing" or assess the implicit bargains that transpire between lobbyists and legislators over an obscure bit of tax law? Moreover, neither legislators nor lobbyists want to fully acknowledge their reliance on each other, even when such reliance is central to decision making in a complex democratic society.

Although journalists and the occasional academic have offered glimpses of corporate lobbying, none present the detailed information that Rogan Kersh provides in this chapter. Kersh closely observed the work of a handful of corporate lobbyists who gave him remarkable access to their daily activities. Beyond the interesting stories, Kersh demonstrates that corporate lobbyists (and by implication, most lobbyists) enjoy considerable latitude in representing clients. Indeed, lobbyists frequently try to further their own interests along with their clients'. Only by close observation can Kersh arrive at such a conclusion, and his scholarship offers numerous insights into the work of an important set of actors in Washington politics.

A Tale of Two Hearings

To the chance observer happening upon a U.S. House of Representatives subcommittee hearing in mid-July 1999, the scene might have merited no more than a glance. A small room seating some seventy-five spectators was packed to overflowing with well-dressed men and women in roughly equal numbers. Facing them were several members of Congress, behind whom a stream of staffers wandered in and out, perching on chairs and consulting the legislators or the audience. A row of witnesses was at the room's center, including one mother and her young son, fidgeting as he waited to testify. A politically aware visitor might have noted the hearing's topic—the privacy of medical records and other health information—absorbed a few minutes of testimony from witnesses or legislators, and moved on. A visitor who learned that the audience was almost all lobbyists might have wondered how they could justify sitting—or, for several at the back of the room, standing—all day, with so little to merit their high-priced attention.

All too familiar to any C-SPAN viewer, this bland scene disguised a charged political contest: a "hearing within a hearing." Medical privacy was a prominent, if extremely complicated, topic during the 106th Congress (1999–2000) and a lightning rod for more general concerns about the U.S. health care system. A self-imposed deadline loomed over the hearing: if Congress did not pass a comprehensive privacy act by mid-August, the Clinton administration would be empowered to issue regulations. Nearly all concerned interest groups favored congressional action, from groups supporting a sweeping legislative affirmation of privacy rights to (mostly corporate) interests fearing the restrictive effect of such regulations. Why the broad support? Because the administration had not yet issued a clear position and was seen as more impervious than Congress to influence by either side. This July hearing marked the best, and perhaps final, opportunity to develop compromise legislation. Despite such urgency, the issue's complexity relegated the hearing to relative isolation: there were no television cameras and only a handful of print reporters.

Most of the lobbyists in the audience were keenly aware of the proceedings' import. And what might appear to visitors as random motion—a staffer leaving the room followed immediately by a lobbyist; a line of questioning pursued by a subcommittee member; a small collection of legislators, staffers, and lobbyists huddled in conversation after the hearing, then vanishing together down the hall—was for lobbyists the center of the day's action. Such subtle actions imparted information, confirmed legislator and interest group positions, enhanced or diminished allegiances, and reshaped legislative strategies. Scripted witness testimony and legislators' prefatory comments drew comparatively little audience attention. Only one witness, a law professor and public interest lobbyist, departed from her prepared statement—and to potent effect. She pressed her case for stronger privacy guidelines so passionately that she was granted more than twice as much time to speak and fielded four times as many questions as her fellow witnesses.

At hearing's end four legislators (two from each party) and several staffers surrounded the public interest witness and a young corporate lobbyist who had been especially active behind the scenes during the hearing; they all talked animatedly about the proposed legislation. This group then repaired to a senior legislator's office and spent two hours privately debating the bill; much of the discussion pitted the two lobbyists against one another. Afterward the participants scattered: Members of Congress headed home or to a colleague's fundraiser, and staffers returned to their offices (one high-ranking subcommittee aide typed eleven pages of notes on the hearing, then began redrafting the bill for the committee's markup session). The two lobbyists returned to work to summarize the experience for clients and colleagues. Both reported that their side was making headway and set out a detailed strategy for upcoming deliberations.

Each lobbyist had devoted considerable time to preparing for the hearing. The public interest lobbyist worked up her statement, talked to reporters, and sought coalition partners in support of expansive health privacy rights. The corporate lobbyist, though not a witness, had been instrumental at every other step: she was heavily involved in drafting the bill, helping sign up congressional cosponsors, organizing the hearing and strategizing with staff about its timing and composition (she identified several witnesses and wrote testimony for two of them), and meeting with staffers during the hearing to clarify points and scribble questions for legislators to ask witnesses: all this even though the medical privacy issue was only a distant concern to the corporation she represents.

What might a social scientist make of this sequence—especially the seamless integration of lobbyists into the regular work of public policy and the tenuous connection of the corporate lobbyist's extensive efforts to her client's interests? Very little, most likely. Methodologically, such anecdotes are all but useless as data, evidence, or otherwise legitimate bases for creating and testing hypotheses.[1] And even if this account could be defended as typical of lobbyists' policy involvement, its theoretical value is limited in today's scholarly market. Interest group studies concentrate overwhelmingly on other elements: political action committee spending as a source of political influence, models of lobbyist-legislator interactions, and organizational resources as determinants of success in affecting policy outcomes.

But I contend that such an example, abstracted and extended over hundreds of like observations, is vital to understanding interest groups and their lobbyists. Based on more than two years of firsthand analysis of Washington lobbyists in their natural habitats, this essay chronicles their labors in detail. In addition to the activities noted in the opening sketch, lobbyists develop and promulgate new policy ideas; communicate political information and strategies among staff of congressional committees, between members of Congress, and across government branches; brief executive and agency officials; alert clients to issues—often ones far removed from a client's "interest"; and determine client strategy thereafter.

Many lobbyists also devote substantial time to impressing clients, though this may have little relation to policy outcomes. Though most of these activities are acknowledged in the burgeoning academic literature on interest groups, vexing questions remain about how and why lobbyists perform their work, and about the role of lobbyists in the U.S. political system.[2] Understanding lobbyists through their own eyes could help researchers learn more about these pressing concerns.

This chapter sketches a general portrait of lobbyists' professional practice, then concentrates on two important aspects: lobbyists' relations with their clients and lobbyists' relations with the policy officials they seek to influence. I propose that lobbyists are best understood as autonomous actors rather than as agents of clients or public officials. By *autonomy* I mean something closer to discretion than independence: lobbyists' activity is constrained in certain ways, but these boundaries are much looser than is generally acknowledged, permitting lobbyists to pursue their professional interests within a wide sphere of self-determination. Such an understanding of lobbyists both complicates and illuminates accounts of interest group activities in the U.S. policy system.

Overview and Method

Remarkably little is known about how lobbyists—particularly those representing private interests—affect policymaking, and less still about how important lobbyists' influence is, how often their efforts succeed, or even how they (or their clients or objective observers) measure success. This opacity owes to researchers' difficulty in obtaining relevant data and the consequent inclination to focus on the measurable, especially political action committee funding and internal group resources, as proxies for influence. Such approaches have left many puzzles unanswered. For example, a recent review of the vast public-choice literature on interest groups, which portrays lobbyists as rational actors seeking to "bribe" politicians, ruefully concludes that the literature's few findings "do not amount to an impressive figure, despite the great number of studies."[3] This study attempts to unveil lobbyists' professional activity to better comprehend organized interests' role in policymaking.

It does so in uncommon fashion: by focusing directly on lobbyists. In most scholarly accounts of policymaking, individual lobbyists are an afterthought. They appear as a means for registering the preferences of others, either as agents for clients' or corporations' principals, or as a member of congressional "legislative enterprises."[4] A common model is:

Client interest → Public official "target" → Policy outcome

This model portrays lobbyists as vehicles for clients' (or, sometimes, public officials') interests, striving to influence decisionmakers. Social science studies usually look past lobbyists to focus on public officials and the interests that compete to translate their desires into public policy.

But in practice, lobbyists do not act in faithful obedience to their clients. Instead lobbyists advance their own interests, including retaining clients, signing up new ones, bolstering their reputation in the Washington policy community, and promoting what they see as worthy public policy outcomes. These goals cannot always be achieved by faithfully striving to match client preferences to officials' policy positions. To understand what lobbyists do and why, we need to know more than what interests they represent and which public officials they want to influence.

Of course, lobbyists do not actively oppose their clients' preferences, nor do lobbyists dominate the public officials they lobby. But there is ample space for autonomy and discretion, so much so that lobbyists must be taken seriously as political actors in their own right. This is an accepted view among national political actors, who are as likely to ask, "Where does lobbyist Smith stand on this issue?" as they are to ask, "Where does Big Insurance Company stand?" Both judgments are relevant; their relative importance depends on many factors, from a legislator's constituency concerns to where an issue stands in the policy process. But the key point here is that decisionmakers often assess "interests" (like insurance companies) separately from individual lobbyists.

In reality, client interests are often extremely vague. Many lobbyists shape their clients' preferences; they even create interests where none existed before. When clients do have strong preferences, lobbyists often work as hard to alter those as they do the views of their political targets. Policymakers' hold over lobbyists is diminished by the mutual benefit character of most exchanges between lobbyists and public officials, and also by the fact that much of what lobbyists seek from officials is not terribly costly to obtain. Many lobbyists are better described as independent trustees than as mere delegates of their sponsoring firm, trade association, individual client, or a member of Congress.

"To really understand lobbying," one longtime Washington decisionmaker told me a few years ago, "you'll have to get in the trenches and watch these folks at work." I took that advice seriously and developed an unusual approach to studying lobbyists: sustained, direct observation.[5] During the two years of the 106th Congress, I followed a group of eleven Washington, D.C., health care lobbyists as they worked. I supplemented these observations with open-ended interviews with some of the clients these lobbyists represent and with hundreds of other lobbyists, thirty members of Congress and several dozen staffers, twenty executive branch officials, and a few journalists who cover interest groups. But the heart of this study is observation of the eleven lobbyists.

This type of research involved sitting in lobbyists' offices as they re-searched an issue or talked on the phone; observing lobbyist discussions with their clients; attending more than 150 meetings with target legisla-tors, congressional staff, and executive branch officials; and attending nearly one hundred interest group coalition meetings, some sixty con-gressional hearings, more than fifty fund-raisers for legislators or charita-ble causes, private dinner parties (still an important locus for Washington policymaking), and several dozen staff strategy meetings, including those where a firm allocates its political action committee contributions among members of Congress. I also traveled with lobbyists on their business trips outside Washington, attending trade associations' annual conven-tions and joining tours that took congressional staff around lobbyists' home firms. Additionally, all eleven lobbyists granted me access to the records of their trade: incoming and outgoing phone calls and emails, strategy memos, materials used in preparing lobbying documents, and the documents themselves—by the hundreds.

In addition to collecting telling anecdotes, I coded all lobbyists' ac-tions along such dimensions as purpose, importance, context, target(s), and so forth. I accompanied each lobbyist for more than fifty hours of "active" working time.[6] I sought to observe a typical range of activities for each lobbyist, including work during calm periods and such high-profile times as when important bills were on the House or Senate floor. I based this range on detailed reconstruction of the lobbyists' daily cal-endars and spaced visits so that I followed each lobbyist on a roughly regular schedule.

My observations are concentrated in a single field—health care—although most of the lobbyists I followed also work in other areas. My choice was one of scope: health care, featuring an immense range of issues, is sufficiently broad to provide analytic variety but contained enough to permit comparisons of different lobbyists' work. Another qualifier: nine of the eleven lobbyists primarily represent private (usu-ally corporate) interests. I structured the group thus because corporate lobbyists are by far the least studied interest group actors compared with lobbyists for consumer groups, unions, state and local govern-ments, and other membership organizations.[7] Within those boundaries, the group of eleven lobbyists is diverse in age, gender, experience, pol-icy expertise, and type of clients (Table 11.1). A condition of my study was anonymity; I therefore refer to lobbyists by number ("Lobbyist 1," and so on).[8]

Lobbyists in Action

How do these Washington lobbyists spend their time? The best in-depth summary of lobbyists' professional activity is fifteen years old and derived from survey data.[9] It seems useful to supplement this and other

Table 11.1. Characteristics of Lobbyist Sample ($N = 11$)

Category	Number of lobbyists
Professional affiliation[a]	
Single firm	4
Trade association	3
Independent	4
Gender	
Women	5
Men	6
Age	
Thirties	3
Forties	5
Fifties	2
Sixties	1
Party affiliation	
Democratic	6 (2 highly partisan)
Republican	5 (2 highly partisan)
Background	
Capitol Hill	8 (2 former members of Congress)
Administration	2
Legal	1 (no government experience)

Source: Author's data.

[a] An example of a single firm is Drugs 'R Us Corp. An example of a trade association is the National Association of Hospitals. An example of an independent is John Doe, Esq., lobbyist (works for range of clients on a retainer basis).

survey-based accounts with direct observations. Between January 1999, when the 106th Congress convened, and mid-December 2000, when it finally concluded in the wake of the protracted presidential election, I witnessed several hundred hours of lobbyist activity across a wide range of contexts. I noted every significant action the eleven lobbyists took, in five-minute increments. Figure 11.1 presents a broad overview of the results, sorted into five major categories:

- Client interaction.
- Legislative activity, such as providing information to staffers and legislators, writing legislation, or researching and analyzing current and upcoming bills.
- Implementation activity, such as commenting on proposed regulations or preparing amicus briefs.

- Electoral activities, mostly concerning campaign contributions.
- Other professional activities, including informal meetings with officials or fellow lobbyists, general research and analysis, business development, generic media commentary, and administrative office work.

The eleven lobbyists spent most of their time on activities in the legislative and "other professional" categories. Client interaction was the third most active category, followed by electoral activity and "implementation-

Figure 11.1.   How Lobbyists Spend Their Time

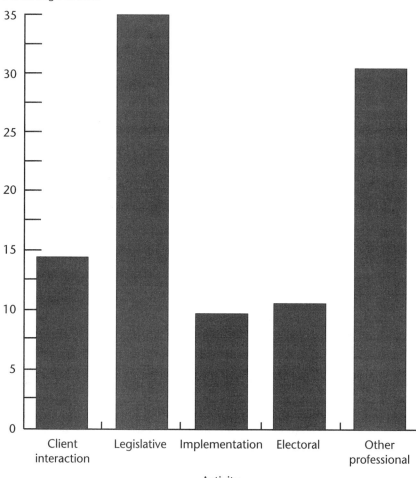

Percentage of time

Source: Author's data.

stage" work (that concerning the executive branch or courts). There is some overlap among these categories: legislative activity was sometimes meant for client consumption, but other times it targeted legislators and staffers directly. And some client interactions took place on Capitol Hill, as when lobbyists sat with clients as they testified before House and Senate committees.

A few conclusions are apparent from this overview. The lobbyists spent much more time targeting legislators than they spent targeting officials in the executive branch or courts (implementation category). This is no surprise given the greater permeability of the legislative branch to interest groups. Even the two lobbyists in my sample who had an agency or executive-branch background dedicated more working hours to legislative activities. Perhaps more striking is the comparatively small amount of time devoted to interactions with clients and electoral activities. If anything, my observations overemphasized these categories, as I specifically asked to watch lobbyists' interactions with clients and to attend fund-raisers and intrafirm discussions of political action committee allocations.

Looking more closely at the different categories of lobbyist activity provides further insight into lobbyists' work. The next section provides an account of lobbyists' relations with their clients, followed by a study of lobbyists' interactions with legislators.

Lobbyists and Clients: Representation, Impressions, and Autonomy

Although the relationship with clients is among the most important in any lobbyist's professional network, the dominant assumption of perfect correspondence between lobbyist and client interest is inaccurate. As mentioned, most lobbyists represent multiple clients. Even "in-house" lobbyists bill their firm for multiple projects, which in turn are supervised by several different corporate officials, often with widely varying interests, purposes, and expectations. One single-firm lobbyist I followed answers regularly to eleven senior officials in five locations worldwide. The lobbyist said that the officials "aren't normally on the same page about . . . what I ought to be doing in Washington on any given day or week or month."[10]

Lobbyists' actions are often explicable not in conventional influence-seeking terms—as attempts to change decisionmakers' preferences or otherwise affect public policy—but as efforts intended for a client audience, aimed at impressing, placating, or otherwise influencing current and potential clients. And though clients' concerns help explain many lobbyists' actions, lobbyists have compelling reasons (and often the ability) to exercise professional autonomy independent of client interests. To illuminate these seemingly contradictory points, we turn to the interplay of lobbyists and clients.

Representation—or Favorable Impressions?

Most lobbyists have clients in mind most of the time. But frequently lobbyists' purpose has little to do with influencing public officials or otherwise "representing" client interests, but rather with creating favorable impressions for clients. Many lobbyist actions—including contact with members of Congress or other high-ranking officials—are designed for client consumption.

During my first few months of observations I followed one lobbyist, a representative for a medium-size corporation, for five days of intensive legislative lobbying. "Hill week," the lobbyist grinned on Monday morning. "Like 'Hell week.'" A major bill of interest to his firm was under consideration on the Senate floor, and another was scheduled for markup in a House committee. This lobbyist had little chance of influencing the outcome of the vote or the markup: "I'm not up here to twist arms and change somebody's vote," he said on Tuesday, as we stood in a Senate anteroom with dozens of other lobbyists. "And neither are most of them," pointing to his fellow lobbyists. "We're pretty much all here so we have something to report home this afternoon." Most of the lobbyist's work that week involved waiting, gossiping, and rumor-trading; the high point came when he obtained a copy of the "chairman's mark," which is used to guide committee deliberations in the House markup session. "The amount of time we [lobbyists] spend running after pieces of paper—most of them not worth the ink printed on 'em—is crazy," he groused during one long break in the action. "We're no different from dogs chasing a stick, except at least they get to chew on it a little."

Nothing the lobbyist did that week could remotely have been construed as "wielding influence," as he predicted on Monday. Yet at the end of each day, back in the lobbyist's office, the picture he painted to clients on the telephone put him squarely in the action. "We're gettin' close," he told a client on Thursday, with a conspiratorial wink to me as I scribbled notes. "Gonna talk to Senators [A and B] this evening, and [a committee staffer], and then we'll get this piece [a provision of the bill] passed." A long string of "insider" revelations followed, as was the case in other late-afternoon conversations with the client—virtually none of which came from public officials but rather from fellow hall-dwelling lobbyists. A few of his claims proved accurate, most did not.

That lobbyists are skilled at claiming credit is no surprise. But to this observer, expecting to code the lobbyist's work in established scholarly terms—*influence legislation, build legislative coalitions, counteractive lobbying,* and so forth—the distance between the lobbyist's high-priced but low-impact labors and the ongoing legislative turmoil was surprising. "Look," he told me during a postmortem on Friday evening. "I told you this [week] wasn't about fighting and winning legislative battles for [his firm]. I needed some good stories from the front, and I got them. And [his client] will write them up, and they'll go in a report somewhere, and he and the big bosses will be happy with their Washington intelligence. And that's what it's all about."

To be sure, some lobbyists do play vital roles in crafting public policy, especially before bills reach the markup or floor stage. But far more often, acting primarily or solely to provide fodder for reports to clients is what occupies many lobbyists. The point is not to belittle lobbyists for wasting time or stretching the truth, but to note that the audience—and indeed the purpose of lobbyists' actions—is often their clients, rather than the policymakers (or public and media) lobbyists ostensibly labor to impress.[11]

Among my sample of eleven is a former member of Congress who is now a well-connected lobbyist. I accompanied him to lunch one day with his former colleagues. Twenty minutes into the meal, the lobbyist received a cell phone call from a persistent client. Amid much ribbing from the senator and staffers at the table, the lobbyist excused himself, took the call, and spent nearly half an hour placating the client. As the conversation concluded, he half-apologized "for being so hard to reach, but I'm here with Senators ____ and ____ in the Senate dining room." "Well," the client broke in jocularly, "you tell 'em you're workin' for *me* now." Watching the lobbyist intently, I saw his face darken for a moment, then relax into a (false) chuckle. "You bet . . . and I'll be carrying your water this afternoon" (on a particular bill).[12]

Lobbyists' attention to client impressions helps explain many of their actions, including seeking (and sometimes interrupting, for a client's urgent call) high-level meetings with legislators and agency administrators or devoting hours to arranging events that have no evident legislative goal. This finding calls into question researchers' long-standing assumption that lobbyists' work orbits around influencing policymakers. Such an observation may also have normative import. If lobbyists swarming over Capitol Hill (or executive branch agencies, state offices, and so forth) are merely seeking a tidbit to keep clients satisfied, perhaps the extent of their influence, or their "demosclerotic" effect on policymaking, is less extreme than routinely advertised.[13]

Though the argument about lobbyists' inclination to do things that register well with clients may depart from standard accounts of interest group activity, it appears to fit existing assumptions about lobbyist-client relations. Lobbyists acting in their clients' name look a lot like agents of client principals. But as the next section details, lobbyists enjoy great autonomy despite the important lobbyist-client relationship.

Creating Space for Autonomy

In the landmark study, *The Hollow Core*, four social scientists contend that most lobbyists (those "serving large corporate actors") generally "lack the autonomy from clients that is a necessary condition of the mediator role." ("Mediators" are independent lobbyists, or "hired guns" in Washington terms; the *Hollow Core* authors find that few of them exist in contemporary Washington.[14]) According to the authors' analysis, "the fact that most client organizations are directly involved in representation through their own officers implies that the organizations exercise close control over the objectives and strategies involved in representation . . . [by] monitoring of employee behavior." Therefore client directives severely curtail most lobbyists' freedom: "Few Washington representatives have a substantial degree of autonomy."[15]

The authors base this claim on an extensive set of interviews and surveys of individual lobbyists. The authors examine such variables as how long these lobbyists worked for their employing organization, other professional characteristics, and lobbyists' expressed sense of freedom at work. What the authors cannot determine, however, is how lobbyists carry out their orders—whether lobbyist efforts closely match client interests and directives, or whether lobbyists regularly act independently (working on issues unrelated to client concerns, cutting deals with policymakers that benefit the client less than might have been possible, brokering "show horse" meetings on Capitol Hill that impress clients without advancing their interests in any specific way, and so on).

I investigated relations between clients and their lobbyists by observing numerous encounters between the two, most of which occurred by telephone or email, and by privately interviewing clients about their expectations of the firm's (or trade association's) Washington lobbyists. During these interviews I also attempted to determine the extent of clients' substantive knowledge about policies important to them, including their organization's specific positions, and about what their lobbyists did on a daily basis to promote the firm's goals.

My observations strongly suggest that lobbyists are able to establish considerable autonomy from their clients, whether they work for a single company, a trade association, or are independent hired guns. This space for discretion exists for two reasons. First, most clients know little of Washington activity and decisions, even those directly affecting their interests, in part because of the ambiguous and complex nature of the policy process. Second, countervailing pressures draw lobbyists away from acting as faithful stewards of their clients. These pressures include lobbyists' constant need to attract additional clients, lobbyists' natural inclination to appeal to their Washington peer community, and public policy interests or ideologies that lobbyists may hold independent of (and which may supersede) client preferences.[16]

Together these claims upset a foundational assumption of much contemporary interest group research: that client and lobbyist interests correspond one-to-one.[17] Given Washington lobbyists' multiple competing motivations, this view too often seems untenable. Figures 11.2 and 11.3 provide systematic accounting of this point. Figure 11.2 is based on the percentage of time each of the eleven lobbyists spent on client-related activities, with totals drawn from more than 200 hours of client-lobbyist observations, including face-to-face discussions and speakerphone discussions.[18] Each five-minute action was sorted into one of six categories:

- Receive directions (client instructing lobbyist to pursue a course of action).
- Discuss issues, plan strategically (substantive exchange, with both client and lobbyist expressing ideas and opinions).
- Explain issues (the lobbyists do almost all the talking, educating and instructing clients and often introducing preferences and interests along the way).
- Solicit business (seeking new clients or, more often, persuading existing clients to pay attention to a hitherto overlooked issue, with help from the lobbyist).
- Prepare client (before a client's testimony or meeting with public officials in Washington, lobbyists typically brief the client at length on the phone and in person).
- Broker meetings (lobbyist arranges or attends meetings between client and public official, or client's testimony before Congress).

I did not code what would have amounted to a substantial additional category, which might be termed *trivial pursuits:* joke-telling, personal gossip, the odd philosophical rumination ("Ever wondered whether computers will replace people ... and how we'll reproduce then?" a client once mused for no apparent reason, leading the embarrassed lobbyist to remind him he was on a speakerphone), even flirtations.

Lobbyists spent minimal time receiving directions from clients about professional duties (5 percent of 135 hours), even though most research presumes—usually implicitly—that direction-taking is the heart of lobbyist-client exchanges. (Worth noting is that my coding erred on the side of including anything resembling a directive.[19]) Lobbyists spent far more time, nearly 30 percent of the total, explaining issues to their clients, conversations that typically involved much *creating* of preferences and interests. Lobbyists spent another 13 percent preparing clients for Washington meetings, exchanges that usually featured lobbyists in command. And the proportion (23 percent) devoted to mutual discussion of an issue was relatively short on strategy and planning for lobbying campaigns, on and off Capitol Hill. Lobbyists do strategize in detail, I found, but most of that work occurs independently of the client. As Lobbyist 1 noted: "Usually I won't waste [my client's] time laying out my action plan; I do the work, and let them know how it's going or how it turned out."

Also noteworthy is the amount of time (14 percent) lobbyists spent soliciting business. As one might expect, corporate lobbyists far outpaced

Figure 11.2.   How Clients and Lobbyists Interact

Percentage of lobbyists' time

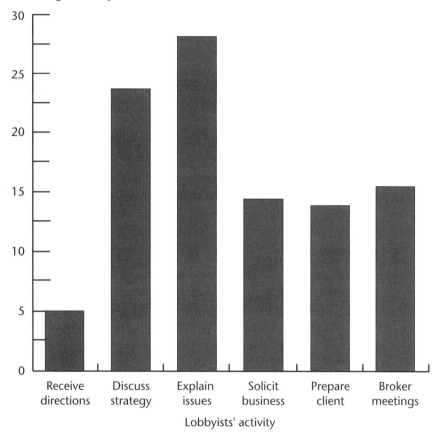

Lobbyists' activity

Source: Author's data.

their public interest counterparts in seeking new clients or additional business. But lobbying or law firm representatives, whose income depends on signing up their own clients, were not notably more active in this area than were trade association or single-firm lobbyists.

Figure 11.3 returns to the division of lobbyists' labor displayed in Figure 11.1. Taking "legislative-based" and "implementation-based" work together, Figure 11.3 displays how often lobbyists' significant actions were performed primarily on behalf of clients' policy interests, lobbyists' personal interests, or some combination of the two.[20]

Although the results are mixed—it was often hard to isolate the purpose behind an action, so the "combination" category is by far the largest (54 percent of observed actions)—clearly lobbyists are as often acting in their own interest (22 percent) as in their client's interest (23 percent).

Figure 11.3.   Lobbyist Action: In Whose Interest?

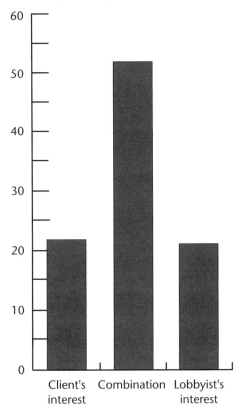

Percentage of lobbyists' time

Source: Author's data.

The variance among different types of lobbyists (single firm, trade association, independents) was slight, as in Table 11.1. A comparison of this result with the preceding discussion of lobbyist activities highlights a thought-provoking distinction between lobbyists' efforts at impressing versus representing clients.

Lobbyists are best described along the lines of Michael Lipsky's "street-level bureaucrats," whose discretion to take consequential actions is only loosely constrained by their superiors. As Lipsky details, agency administrators, despite having sharply limited control over bureaucrats in the field, receive genuine benefits from the arrangement.[21] Space precludes a full discussion of how clients gain from lobbyists' autonomy, but two benefits deserve brief mention here. First, in the complex and uncertain realm of federal policymaking, lobbyists provide clients with personal security. Many of the clients I interviewed described their lobbyists' work in such terms: "I sleep better at night knowing that [Lobbyist 2] is looking out for my needs in Washington," one hospital executive told me. More than half of the clients I interviewed were aware that lobbyists might not always be carrying out their commands, implied or otherwise. As an insurance company vice president put it: "I figure that half of the money I spend on lobbying is wasted. Trouble is," he added with a laugh, "I don't know which half!"

Second, reputation is an essential part of any client's success. Clients with high-profile lobbyists can enhance their reputation in the Washington community, affirmed by the rounds of back slapping and hearty exchanges with public officials that accompany most clients' trips to the national capital—usually thanks to arduous advance work by their lobbyists.

If lobbyists are not always engaged in fulfilling clients' desires, perhaps this is because their efforts are devoted to furthering public officials' interests. A long line of research dating to the 1950s and 1960s suggests that lobbyists exist in close symbiosis with, and are even servants to, legislators and executive administrators. The following section explores the nature of the connection between lobbyists and public officials. As in the preceding account of lobbyist-client relations, it turns out that a prevailing feature is lobbyist autonomy.

Lobbyists and Legislators: Autonomy through Mutual Benefits and Low Costs

Robert Salisbury's influential study of the "paradox of interest groups in Washington" holds that lobbyists enjoy extensive access to decisionmakers but little ability to advance client interests. Salisbury concludes that policymakers are therefore exploiting interest groups. More recently, Scott Ainsworth theorized that lobbyists should be recognized as part of legislators' "legislative enterprises." "Long before votes become an issue," writes Ainsworth, "legislators structure their environment to channel interest group influence and facilitate access for particular interests."[22] Together, these and similar studies suggest that lobbyists are best understood as agents of policymakers.

Based on my observations, lobbyists depend heavily on legislators and other public officials for information and, at times, favorable actions and decisions.[23] But lobbyists are nonetheless able to act with substantial independence from policymaker demands. This is true in part because legislators depend on lobbyists, thus creating a relationship of mutual benefit. Also, the information and access that lobbyists seek from legislators are not especially costly for lobbyists to secure or for legislators to provide. Before detailing these points further, let's look at an overview of lobbyists' work in the legislative realm (Figure 11.4).

Figure 11.4.   Lobbyists' Legislative Activities

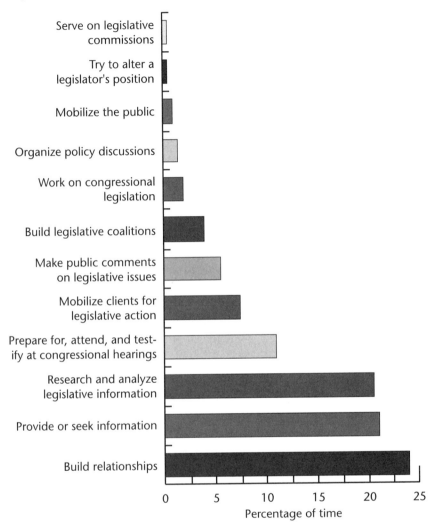

Source: Author's data.

Managing Information and Building Relationships
Are All in a Day's Work

More than two-fifths of these lobbyists' legislative-related time is occupied with managing information, half of which is spent on research and analysis. Lobbyists devote several hours on most days to absorbing, discussing with colleagues, and analyzing in written memos both substantive and political aspects of the issues on their agenda. Lobbyists' research sources include daily briefings that summarize relevant legislation—*National Journal*, Congressional Quarterly, *Hotline*, and the Bureau of National Affairs are common providers—as well as daily newspapers, twice-weekly journals covering Capitol Hill, and congressional or executive branch reports. Lobbyists also peruse their peers' written summaries of issues, which are often based on private analysis. One five-page study on the Medicare prescription drug benefit, prepared by Lobbyist 8, had circulated within a few days of its "publication" (delivery to clients and congressional and committee offices) among all but two of the lobbyists I followed. Rarely do lobbyists consult academic studies in their policy analyses, unless these have been summarized or otherwise restated in quickly digestible form.

Beyond efforts to secure, comprehend, and provide information, lobbyists devote on average another quarter of their legislative-related activities to building relationships with members of Congress and staffers. Due to more restrictive rules passed by Congress in 1995, these informal contacts occur less frequently over expensive dinners and lunches, though those still take place (meals with a "friend" of a legislator or staffer are generally exempt from the ban). Telephone and email contact is most common: one lobbyist keeps a list of every important staffer on the four House and three Senate committees most germane to her work, and tries to contact each staffer at least once every six weeks.

The eleven lobbyists spent a nominal amount of time (1 percent) mobilizing public support for their preferred policies. This is somewhat surprising given the prominence of public lobbying in recent journalistic and scholarly accounts of interest group activity. It is possible that much of the time I coded as "public commentary" (5.5 percent of the total) was also designed to influence public opinion, as William Browne has persuasively suggested.[24] It is also the case that Washington-based lobbyists are less likely than others within a firm or trade association to design and pursue grassroots advocacy campaigns. Lobbyists also rarely engaged in explicit attempts to "convert" or otherwise alter legislators' preferences on an issue (0.5 percent); I looked hard for such activity, given its prominence in academic literature.[25]

Another intriguing finding arises from an omission in the figure. I originally included as a separate category, "Identify and pursue specific legislator and staff lobbying targets," but my lobbyists devoted so little time to this activity that I folded it into "research/analysis" or "otherwise influence legislation." This runs directly contrary to most social-science models of lobbying, which assume that lobbyists select specific targets on Capitol Hill. Figuratively speaking, lobbyists do not aim a rifle carefully at a certain legislator or staffer; rather, they typically work with a shotgun and a large quantity of grapeshot. They "hit" whomever they can, usually shooting on the run.[26]

Commodities and Credit Secure
Lobbyist Autonomy

If lobbyists' legislative work reflects policymakers' preferences, then presumably lobbyists act on legislators' (or staffers') requests—either direct or implicit. For all legislative actions that lobbyists judged of high or medium importance, I sought—again, usually in consultation with the lobbyist—to find out both the inspiration for the action and its intended beneficiary.[27] Figures 11.5 and 11.6 display the results, revealing that lobbyists are not in thrall to legislators, nor are lobbyists faithful members of legislative enterprises. Rather, lobbyists usually act on their own initiative. And legislators are the primary beneficiaries no more often than are clients, other parties, or lobbyists themselves.

How do lobbyists surmount their dependence on public officials to pursue their own initiatives and goals? I found two answers. First, lobbyists have valuable commodities—campaign contributions, legislative information, support for legislators taking unpopular political stands, endorsements, and so forth—that make the lobbyist-legislator relationship one of symbiotic exchange rather than policymaker dominance. Second,

Figure 11.5.   Inspiration for Lobbyists' Legislative Actions

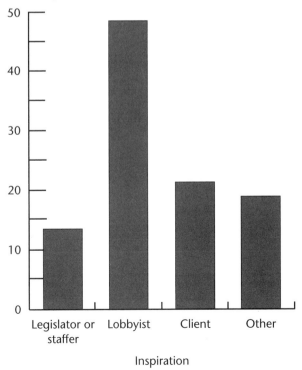

Percentage of time spent on legislative activities

Source: Author's data.

Figure 11.6.   Intended Beneficiary of Lobbyists'
Legislative Activities

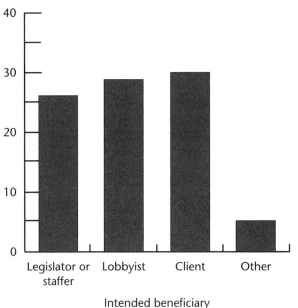

Percentage of time spent on legislative activities

Source: Author's data.

most lobbyists ask legislators not to switch a vote or introduce a provision but to provide basic information or even mere "face time." Again, because lobbyists often act to impress clients, even a brief and insubstantial conversation between a lobbyist and a public official can go a long way.

Lobbyists are most vulnerable to legislator demands when payment from a client depends on a particular legislative outcome. But this happens only rarely given most lobbyists' ability to influence client expectations and, perhaps more important, to account for ostensibly negative results in positive terms. Let us go back to the medical privacy hearing introduced at the beginning of this essay. Recall that a small group of legislators and staffers invited two lobbyists to a private discussion after the hearing. This was the first of five such meetings in the subcommittee chair's office. The two lobbyists, each leading figures in their respective medical privacy camps, had faced off before in person and in the trade press. Each was frequently able to declare success (privately to clients and in public); moreover, they both mentioned to me in passing that they had "never lost a major legislative battle." Given that the two were in direct opposition on many issues, the claim seemed absurd (on one side, at least). Yet each could persuasively explain how an apparent setback was actually a victory. And in later interviews, clients of each lobbyist made similar judgments.

Such political credit-claiming is familiar among other political actors, especially legislators, thanks to David Mayhew's 1974 taxonomy.[28] Lobbyists' ability to claim credit mimics, and in some ways may outpace, that of legislators. House and Senate committee and roll call votes are highly malleable: multiple votes on the same topic provide cover for legislators on different sides of an issue.[29] This institutional mechanism conveniently aids lobbyists in much the same way. If a bill a lobbyist supports is defeated, it is usually possible—and not necessarily disingenuous—to claim victory in terms of limiting damages or helping shield a client from the bill's potential harms.

Moreover, unlike legislators, lobbyists are not required to vote or otherwise stand and be counted on particular provisions. Clients or researchers trying to conclude whether a lobbyist lost on a given issue—in other words, to hold the lobbyist accountable—are attempting an often unrewarding task. Thus the sway politicians might hold over lobbyists desperate for clear-cut victories is considerably lessened, opening space for lobbyist autonomy.[30]

Autonomous Actors in the Public Sphere

What can we learn about interest groups and lobbying from closely observing lobbyists at work? That lobbyists should be recognized (with qualifications) as autonomous actors in the policy sphere, with compelling interests of their own and room to pursue those. A portrait of U.S. policymaking that accounts for interests and legislator preferences without recognizing the vital and frequently independent role of lobbyists is incomplete. Definitively demonstrating that lobbyists are *consequential* as well as autonomous is beyond my scope here; suffice to say that their power is neither so great as accounts of "special interest dominance" suggest, nor as irrelevant as many scholars imply.

The claim about lobbyist autonomy has implications for the study of interest groups. Rational-choice theorists and other formal modelers could profitably expand their account of "interests," recognizing that lobbyists have powerful incentives (and few costs) to pursue their own preferences. Students of policy subsystems or issue networks should view lobbyists as significant and at least partly independent actors in the system and not assume that groups and public officials complete the picture.[31] And as historical-institutional accounts of interest group politics emerge, lobbyists should be prime objects of scrutiny alongside groups and policymakers as agents of change.[32]

Interest groups are undeniably central to the American political process. Lobbyists, as the connective tissue relating groups to policymakers, act with a degree of autonomy from both. Their resultant influence, and the ways in which it deviates from the expected, deserve sustained analysis in the study of interest group politics.

Notes

1. John P. Heinz and his coauthors begin their book, *The Hollow Core: Private Interests in National Policy Making*, with a short anecdote about an oil lobbyist; they then dismiss such "stories" as insufficiently "systematic and empirical." John P. Heinz, Edward O. Laumann, Robert H. Salisbury, and Robert L. Nelson, *The Hollow Core: Private Interests in National Policy Making* (Cambridge: Harvard University, 1993), 4–7, 408. See also Richard A. Smith, "Interest Group Influence in the U.S. Congress," *Legislative Studies Quarterly* 20 (1): 120–122 (1995); Frank R. Baumgartner and Beth L. Leech, *Basic Interests: The Importance of Groups in Politics and in Political Science* (Princeton: Princeton University, 1998), 120–146, 165–167 (on limitations of interest group case studies).

2. As the best comprehensive review of interest group scholarship to date notes of existing research: "what else are [lobbyists] doing, and how would we know it?" Baumgartner and Leech, *Basic Interests*, 154.

3. Frans Van Winden, "On the Economic Theory of Interest Groups: Towards a Group Frame of Reference in Political Economics," *Public Choice* 100 (1): 21 (1999).

4. Scott H. Ainsworth, "The Role of Legislators in the Determination of Interest Group Influence," *Legislative Studies Quarterly* 22 (4): 518 (1997). For a succinct statement of principal-agent theory as applied to clients and lobbyists, see Heinz and others, *The Hollow Core*, 373–374. Robert Salisbury describes the "classic model of lobbying" in similar terms: "A group sends its representative to Washington to press its case for or against some policy option, or it hires one of the many would-be agents already located in the nation's capital. . . . The presumption in this model is that the group knows what its policy interest is." In contrast, Salisbury emphasizes lobbyists' "need and dependence" on government officials. Robert Salisbury, "The Paradox of Interest Groups in Washington—More Groups and Less Clout," in *The New American Political System*, 2d. ed., ed. Anthony King (Washington, D.C.: American Enterprise Institute, 1990), 224, 229.

5. The best defense of participant observation in political science is Richard Fenno's *Watching Politicians: Essays on Participant Observation* (Lanham, Md.: University Press of America, 1992). The following publications include some direct observation of political actors: Andrew McFarland, *Common Cause: Lobbying in the Public Interest* (Chatham, N.J.: Chatham House, 1984); Burdett A. Loomis, *A Legislative Year: Time, Politics, and Policies* (Lawrence: University Press of Kansas, 1988); and William P. Browne, *Cultivating Congress: Constituents, Issues and Interests in Agricultural Policymaking* (Lawrence: University Press of Kansas, 1995). Legislators rather than interest group lobbyists are the primary focus of the last two.

6. "Active" time is lobbyist work that I was able to code as a specific action, accounting for somewhat less than half the total hours I spent with each representative. (The remainder included actions too brief to record, travel and other "down time," hours lobbyists spent answering questions from me, and so forth.)

7. Allan J. Cigler laments the "lack of comprehensive, in-depth studies of individual organized interests," terming this "a major weakness of the literature in light of evidence that membership groups are a relatively small and declining proportion of the organized interest universe." Allan J. Cigler, "Research Gaps in the Study of Interest Group Representation," in *Representing Interests and Interest Group Representation*, ed. William Crotty, Mildred A. Schwartz, and John C. Green (Lanham, Md.: University Press of America, 1994), 30. On health care as a field featuring numerous "divisive" issues (compared with defense and agriculture, for example), see Frank R. Baumgartner and Beth L. Leech, "Lobbying Alone or in a Crowd: The Distribution of Lobbying in a Sample of Issues" (paper presented at the Midwest Political Science Association, Chicago, Ill., April 2000), 3 (quote); and Heinz and others, *Hollow Core*, 48–51, 210–213.

8. I also sometimes switch gender pronouns in this chapter to better ensure lobbyists' anonymity.

9. Kay Lehman Schlozman and John T. Tierney, *Organized Interests and American Democracy* (New York: Harper Collins, 1986), 149–157. Baumgartner and Leech review this and other surveys of lobbyist tactics in *Basic Interests*, 147–157. See also Ken Kollman, *Outside Lobbying: Public Opinion and Interest Group Strategies* (Princeton: Princeton University, 1998), 35; and on corporate lobbying tactics, Graham K. Wilson, "Corporate Political Strategies," *British Journal of Political Science* 20 (3): 282–285 (1990).

10. Quote marks throughout indicate comments I recorded in writing within thirty minutes of their being spoken. I did not use a tape recorder, as my access to sometimes highly confidential proceedings would have been seriously compromised. Thanks to Mitch Duneier for recommending this explanatory note.

11. Further details, including measures of the frequency with which lobbyists take client-based versus more substantive actions, appear in Rogan Kersh, "Washington Lobbyists and Their Clients" (paper presented at the Midwest Political Science Association annual meeting, Chicago, Ill., April 2001).

12. Only one of the two senators he named was actually at the lobbyist's table, but both were in the room. I heard only the lobbyist's end of this conversation, though the client was loud enough to be semiaudible on a cell phone. The lobbyist related the client's comment immediately afterward, along with his own irritated editorial comments.

13. See, for example, Jonathan Rauch, *Demosclerosis* (New York: Times Books, 1994). Rauch defines demosclerosis as "government's progressive loss of the ability to adapt," largely due to lobbyists blocking government action.

14. Most of the independent lobbyists I followed or interviewed dislike the "hired gun" moniker, but the term is common in both policy and academic parlance; on the latter, see Salisbury, "Paradox of Interest Groups," 207.

15. Heinz and others, *Hollow Core*, quotes at 61 (my emphasis), 67, 188. See generally 59–79, 184–189, 373–374, 411.

16. Most federal lobbyists—whether they work independently or for a single client—are part of the Washington policy community. Typically they move from Capitol Hill or an agency into private (or public interest) practice; their professional peers are predominantly fellow policy wonks and politicos, not the corporate or otherwise D.C.–extrinsic clients they represent.

17. For more detail on the claims, see Kersh, "Washington Lobbyists and Their Clients."

18. As in Figure 11.1, percentages are of aggregated actions coded in five-minute increments. This excludes brief meetings or telephone calls (unless several occurred in close proximity, totaling at least five minutes).

19. For example, Lobbyist 8 reports to a vice president at his pharmaceutical company's home offices. After a long discussion about a series of negative media reports on an issue important to the company—which I coded primarily as "discussing issues/strategy" and partly as "explaining issue"—the vice president said, "I'll sign off on that. We're leaving this [planned meetings with congressional staffers to blunt the damage] in your hands; I figure once you line the rest of them up [collaborate with friendly lobbyists] we'll have no trouble getting our message across. Go get 'em up there [on Capitol Hill]!" As with most such instances, however, the lobbyist developed the strategy.

20. Here, as elsewhere in this study, I coded all actions based on whether the lobbyist (or I) judged them of high, medium, or low importance. Figure 11.3 features the "high" and "medium" importance items, leaving aside those judged of low importance.

21. Michael Lipsky, *Street-Level Bureaucracy* (New York: Russell Sage Foundation, 1980); an updated discussion appears in Steven Rathgeb Smith and Michael Lipsky, *Nonprofits for Hire: The Welfare State in the Age of Contracting* (Cambridge.:

Harvard University, 1993), 115–119. Thanks to Burdett Loomis for suggesting this analogy between lobbyists and Lipsky's bureaucrats.

22. Salisbury, "Paradox of Interest Groups," 213-214; Ainsworth, "The Role of Legislators," 517.

23. For reasons of space, I deal only with legislators here; but lobbyists' exchanges with executive branch and other officials are not significantly different with respect to lobbyist autonomy.

24. William Browne, "Lobbying the Public: All-Directional Advocacy," in *Interest Group Politics*, 5th ed., ed. Allan J. Cigler and Burdett A. Loomis (Washington, D.C.: CQ Press, 1998), 348–349. On public lobbying, see also Schlozman and Tierney, *Organized Interests*, 172–182.

25. See David Austen-Smith and John Wright, "Theory and Evidence for Counteractive Lobbying," *American Journal of Political Science* 38 (1): 25–44 (1996). I coded lobbyists' legislative actions based on whether the lobbyists' intent was to change member preferences, shore up already-existing preferences, or frame (or reframe) member preferences on an issue relatively unfamiliar to them. Results will appear in a separate study. Thanks to Marie Hojnacki for helpful discussions of this topic.

26. A fuller account of this targeting point appears in Rogan Kersh, "Washington Lobbyists as (Semi-) Autonomous Actors" (paper presented at the Midwest Political Science Association annual meeting, Chicago, Ill., April 2000).

27. I coded each five-minute action segment as "high," "medium," or "low" importance, in consultation with the lobbyists. I observed 14,990 minutes of "high" and "medium" legislative-related activity.

28. David R. Mayhew, *Congress: The Electoral Connection* (New Haven: Yale University, 1974).

29. Walter Oleszek, *Congressional Procedures and the Policy Process*, 5th ed. (Washington, D.C.: CQ Press, 2001), 161–162, 171–172, 220–227.

30. Lobbyists may better be able to satisfy specific client demands in fields other than health care. Tax policy, for example, features far more "rifle-shot" provisions directly benefiting a client (for example, "extend Section 127 benefits to employees of mid-sized firms in Indianapolis").

31. Thus, for example, Jeffrey Berry's complex diagram of the telecommunications issue network would separately list the principal lobbyists active in that realm, both from private and public sectors. Jeffrey Berry, *The Interest Group Society*, 3d. ed. (New York: Harper Collins, 1997), 212.

32. David Hart's chapter in this volume, emphasizing both contingency and structural patterns of change, is exemplary in its attention to effective (and ineffective) chief executive officer lobbyists in the high-tech industry.

12

Lobbying the Press
"Talk to the People Who Talk to America"
Clyde Brown and Herbert Waltzer

Lobbying activities by organized interests take many forms. A major avenue for political influence is creating a favorable public image and policy environment. As a consequence, the public often becomes the target of lobbying efforts. For example, oil companies have tried to overcome their negative environmental image by advertising on the nightly news. And advertising efforts by many companies and trade associations after the September 11, 2001, terrorist attacks on New York and Washington, D.C., were designed not to sell products or services but to persuade the public of the organizations' patriotism. Such messages are called *advertorials,* sponsored messages placed in the media by organized interests to create a favorable environment to pursue their goals.

In this chapter Clyde Brown and Herbert Waltzer examine a relatively new form of advertorial lobbying, which focuses not on the public at large but on the press and the setting of society's policy agenda. The authors suggest that "organized interests have every motive to work with and through journalists to get their positions disseminated to the public." Looking at advertorials placed in two major publications read widely by journalists, Brown and Waltzer find that such advertising has created "opportunities for organizations to make themselves available as authoritative sources for stories relating to their interests." Advertorials that offer journalists awards and fellowships and seminars in policy areas relevant to the organized interest are among the most blatant evidence that interests do lobby the press. The authors conclude that because economic interests sponsor three-fourths of all advertorials, this form of lobbying extends the advantage of business and corporate interests in influencing public policy.

The authors wish to thank Gayle K. Brown, Miriam B. Waltzer, and Susan Brater.

249

"Talk to the people who talk to America" is the challenge to organized interests from *The American Journalism Review* (*AJR*) in advertisements on its own pages, urging organized interests to sponsor advertisements that communicate their policy views to journalists. The periodical touts itself as the preeminent "national media magazine" read closely by media executives and "thousands of working reporters, editors, producers, columnists and commentators across the country." Similarly, *The Columbia Journalism Review* (*CJR*) claims that: "An advertisement in *CJR* is like calling a press conference and being certain that the news media will take note."[1]

We see and hear advertisements from organized interests every day, whether on the Op-Ed and other pages of the *New York Times*, *Washington Post*, and other major newspapers; in news, public affairs, and cultural magazines; or on television and radio. The advertisements are noncommercial—they are intended not to directly sell a product or service but to create a favorable public opinion and policy environment for the interest. Although the style and format of these advertisements differ, they often look like editorials and thus are called *advertorials*.

Advertorials are growing in number and sophistication. More—and more diverse—interest organizations are investing in them. A broader range of media outlets are printing and airing them. Why? Because interest organizations expect advertorials to influence the sociopolitical views and behaviors of their audience.[2] Advertorials in journalism periodicals in particular aim not to directly influence public opinion but to reach an intermediate audience—the journalists who write and produce news, analysis, commentary, and editorials. Advertorials in journalism reviews announce award competitions, advertise fellowships for journalists, and offer the organization's expertise as an authoritative source for journalists.

Outside Lobbying and Advertorials

Interest group scholar Ken Kollman distinguishes between "inside lobbying," which is direct access to and contact with those who make and implement public policy, and "outside lobbying," which involves efforts to bring constituent and public opinion pressures to bear on decisionmakers.[3] As a technique of outside lobbying, advertorials join such practices as protests, letter writing campaigns, and mobilization of group members and the public. Outside lobbying campaigns often include efforts to influence what appears in the news. For that to work an organization and its spokespersons must be known and accessible to journalists, who can then approach the organization for reliable and responsive information, for pithy quotes and "sound bites" that expand and enliven stories, and for eye-catching visuals.

In this essay we examine advertorials placed by interest organizations in *CJR* and *AJR* from 1985 to 2000. We ask four questions: What types of advertorials were run and with what frequency? What interest organizations sponsored them? What policy areas were addressed? What are the trends in advertorial use and sponsorship? We focus on the unique types of advertorials in journalism periodicals, namely those placed by organized interests to assert their authority on an issue and to announce awards and fellowships for journalists in relevant policy areas.

First, some vocabulary. *Organized interests* or *interest organizations* are nonparty organizations that seek to influence government policy and its implementation. We use the terms to include "not only associations such as trade associations, unions, professional associations, and environmental groups that have individuals or organizations as members, but also politically active organizations such as universities, hospitals, public law firms, and, especially, corporations that have no members in the ordinary sense."[4] We also distinguish between *commercial advertisements*, which promote goods and services to create or enlarge markets, and *institutional advertisements* or *advertorials*, which are paid, sponsored messages placed in the media by organized interests to create a favorable environment to pursue their goals. We categorize advertorials into three groups, with subtypes within each group (Box 12.1):

- *Image* advertorials, which attempt to create a favorable climate of public opinion.
- *Advocacy* advertorials, which explicate the interest's goals and views on controversial public issues.
- *Journalism* advertorials, which target the press.

Organized Interests and Advertorial Campaigns

The literature on lobbying by organized interests contains little systematic study of advertorial campaigns.[5] Influential political scientist V. O. Key Jr. doubted the influence of outside lobbying activities, describing the function of "propagandizing campaigns" as "difficult to divine" even though they are "rituals in obeisance to the doctrine that public opinion governs" and are "on the order of the dance of rainmakers. . . . Sometimes these campaigns have their effects—just as rain sometimes follows the rainmaker's dance."[6] Key concluded that such efforts influence neither public opinion nor the decisions of policymakers, and most studies conclude that outside lobbying has marginal effects when compared with pressure from colleagues, constituents, the executive branch, and party leaders.[7]

Then how do we explain the increasing number, sophistication, and cost of advertorial campaigns? Kollman states that "interest group leaders consider outside lobbying effective and . . . policymakers sometimes consider it influential."[8] Kollman sees outside lobbying enhancing inside lobbying, as outside lobbying "signals" the interests and views of

---

Box 12.1. Types of Advertorials

Five types of image advertorials aim to create a favorable climate of opinion.
- *Identification:* bringing the interest's name and logo to public attention.
- *Goodwill:* identifying the interest with popular values, causes, or personalities.
- *Responsible public citizen:* extolling the interest's "good works."
- *Public service:* providing information or advice on the interest's area of expertise, encouraging political or community participation.
- *Miscellaneous.*

Six types of advocacy advertorials aim to win support for the interest's stance on controversial issues of public values or policy.
- *Ideological:* promoting the basic values, principles, norms, or institutions that the interest supports; criticizing contrary or challenging views.
- *Defensive:* explaining and defending the interest's practices, positions, or finances.
- *Right to reply:* responding to reports about the interest that the interest finds incomplete, inaccurate, unfair, or biased.
- *Position-taking and agenda-building:* seeking to place an issue of concern on the active policy agenda; expressing and advocating the interest's position on a policy issue.
- *Ally recruitment:* asking the audience to support the interest's agenda-building or policy position with action.
- *Miscellaneous.*

Three types of journalism advertorials target the press.
- *Source-only:* announcing and volunteering the interest as an authoritative resource on specific topics.
- *Award:* announcing competitions for excellence in journalism on specific topics.
- *Fellowship:* announcing fellowships, grants, and seminars on specific topics.

Source: Authors' information.

---

the organization's members and supporters to policymakers and influences the public.[9] Furthermore, journalists describe and decry the undue influence of "special interests," as do many politicians, who nevertheless accept campaign contributions from organized interests and grant lobbyists access.[10]

The principal targets of advertorials in the elite press are policymakers, opinion leaders, and citizens who are attentive to and active in civic affairs. In the mass, regional, and local media, advertorials primarily target the general public. Advertorials in press periodicals aim to grab journalists' attention, to be a "definer" of stories in the news media, and thereby to influence the stories' audience. Whatever the target, the goal is to protect and promote the organization's interests.

Literature is also sparse on interests' efforts to win access and influence by offering expertise and opinions to journalists and news organizations. News coverage affects the political fortunes of organized interests because the media are important shapers of public opinion. Daily competition for the attention of the major news media is fierce, and interest organizations want to affect decisions on what is printed and aired. The news media are major players in "agenda setting," giving prominence to some issues rather than others, thereby increasing their perceived importance.[11] Every day is full of "newsworthy" events ("stories") that never make it to print or broadcast. The agenda setting process is "an ongoing competition among issue protagonists to gain the attention of the media professionals, the public, and policy elites."[12]

Similarly, "framing"—putting a particular spin on issues and events—by the news media brings attention to certain elements of political reality over others by providing alternative definitions, constructions, or depictions of a policy problem or event.[13] Finally, the news media play a major role in "priming"—focusing on an issue or event in a way that leads people to attach special insight or importance to it when making political judgments about the performance of government institutions and officeholders, especially the president and political candidates and organizations.[14]

Organized interests, therefore, care whether stories affecting them make the news and about the specifics and prominence of coverage. Interests care about what picture of reality is presented, how problems are defined, how they and other interests are labeled ("good guys" or "bad guys"), and what policy alternatives are presented and how they are evaluated. In sum, organized interests must take the news media seriously and have an effective strategy for linking to the press. Because news items have a legitimacy that advertising does not, interest organizations want to be used by reporters as a "reliable source" and to make sure that the resulting news item is as close as possible to the organization's position.

Benjamin Page, Robert Shapiro, and Glenn Demsey examined the impact on citizens' policy preferences of statements in the news media by political actors, including organized interests.[15] The authors stress that most people have little incentive to research policy information when they can rely on the news media as an accessible, low-cost source. But who are the "trusted agents" in the news media to whom citizens delegate the tasks of information gathering, analysis, and political evaluation?[16] And whom do journalists rely on for their stories? How credible are these sources and what influence do they have with the public?

The authors found that the most trusted agents, those perceived as relatively neutral, are anchorpersons and field reporters and the experts they use for their stories. Farther down the credibility scale are popular presidents, and then, even farther, other political actors. Although interest organizations have low credibility and zero or even negative influence on public opinion, the authors express concern that the "unobtrusive indirect efforts by special interests—through influences on experts and commentators, for example—may be more dangerous than would be a direct clash of interests in full public view."[17]

Journalists and Their Sources

Journalists rarely have the training, time, or expertise to do intensive research. They usually rely on a narrow range of sources, especially government officials, for their information and analysis.[18] *News sources* are the governmental institutions and personnel, interest organizations and their spokespersons, and individuals (academics, former government officials), upon whom journalists rely for expertise-based information, analysis, and commentary.[19] Journalists and news sources have a symbiotic relationship: journalists receive information and offer publicity to sources who, in effect, subsidize the costs to reporters and news organizations of news gathering. The return on investment to the interest organization is increased when the story is published as desired and the source's interest is unreported or masked.[20]

In news production, therefore, the relationship between source and reporter is crucial. It is "a dance, for sources seek access to journalists and journalists seek access to sources . . . either . . . can lead, but more often than not, sources do the leading."[21] Interest organizations and their spokespersons want to be well-thumbed cards in journalists' Rolodexes, especially journalists who are highly visible and well respected. Because all organized interests do not have equal resources, the playing field is not level in the competition to gain media attention, ink, and airtime.

Advertorials in press periodicals raise the issue of journalism ethics. The code of ethics of the Society of Professional Journalists states that journalists are obligated to "provide a fair and comprehensive account of events and issues." Journalists in "straight news stories" are expected to be accurate, complete, objective, fair, impartial, and balanced. They are admonished to "Test the accuracy of information from all sources. . . . Identify sources whenever feasible. . . . The public is entitled to as much information as possible on sources' reliability. Distinguish between advocacy and news reporting."[22] Therefore, although sources are a reporter's "bread and butter . . . dependence on them creates some genuine complexities."[23] Put indelicately by a fictional journalist, "When sources began praising your work, you knew it was turning to shit." [24]

American Journalism Review and *Columbia Journalism Review*

The news media are increasingly recognized as a political institution.[25] As such, they are an important news subject for journalists. *AJR* and *CJR* are the major reviews of journalism criticism.[26] *CJR* is published six times a year by The Graduate School of Journalism at Columbia University. The founding editorial in 1961 stated the mission: "to assess the performance of journalism in all of its forms, to call attention to its shortcomings and its strengths, and to help define—and redefine—the standards of honest, responsible service."[27] It markets itself to advertisers as "the nation's oldest, most respected, and most widely read monitor of print, broadcast, and online news for media professionals."[28]

The average paid circulation per issue of *CJR* for the second half of 2000 was 21,116, with an estimated 2.2 readers per copy. A 1997 marketing survey reported that 62 percent of subscribers were media professionals. Four-fifths of *CJR*'s media professionals were "involved in determining the types of news stories and topics that are reported," and 44 percent of these were "very involved."[29]

The Philip Merrill College of Journalism at The University of Maryland owns *AJR*. The magazine began in 1977 as *The Washington Journalism Review* but changed its name in 1993 to signal a broader perspective and audience. Published monthly from its inception through 1986, *AJR* now is published ten times a year. Its average per issue circulation for the second half of 2000 was 26,427, with an estimated 1.9 readers per copy. A December 1990 profile reported that 68.7 percent of its circulation was among journalists and media executives.[30] According to one analyst, *AJR* stands for "ethical journalism and the primacy of news."[31]

CJR's 2001 rate for a full-page black and white advertisement was $6,380, sliding down to $1,490 for one-sixth of a page. The cost of a black and white full-page advertisement in *AJR* was $6,399; one-sixth of a page cost $1,369. Both journals offer reduced rates for multiple placements; color advertisements and those placed on the covers were more expensive.

From 1985 to 1991 *AJR* offered organized interests the opportunity to purchase "source listings" in special sections. "Sources" pages are small, boxed listings of interest organizations, their addresses, contact persons, and telephone numbers. The lead on the page stated that it "represented paid listings of industry experts interested in answering your questions. If you are a journalist or government official, we hope you will find these listings useful. If you represent an organization that should be included please contact [*AJR*]."[32] From 1985 to 1996 the journal contained a "Directory of Selected Sources." Published in the July-August issue and organized by policy area, the directory included interest organizations' names, addresses, and telephone numbers of contact persons, a brief description of the organization, and the types of information available there. At the list's peak in 1996 it contained more than 600 associations, corporations, and unions. News organizations were invited to purchase multiple copies for staff members.

Since 1989 *AJR* has published an annual paid listing of awards, grants, and scholarships offered to journalists by interest organizations. In 1991 the journal began including special advertising sections on specific policy issues. Each section has an essay on a subject commissioned by the journal's advertising department and includes advertorials and a source listing. The sections are intended to assist journalists covering such issues as the environment, health care, and child abuse.

The two journals are hospitable environments for interest organizations to make themselves and their policy views known to journalists. *AJR*, for example, claims a readership of editors and publishers of every daily newspaper and 1,500 of the largest weeklies in the United States; every radio, television, and cable station manager and news director in major markets; corporate heads of the communications industry; thousands of reporters, columnists, and anchors; and more than 1,500 government officials (including a spot in every congressional office).[33] In sum, the journals offer the attention of those who make and report the news.

A Brief History of Advertorials

A twentieth century phenomenon, advertorials were overwhelmingly dominated by corporations from the start. In 1908, for example, the American Telephone and Telegraph Company (AT&T) conducted a print media campaign to "sell" to the American public and government a monopolistic national telephone system. The objective was to counter the perceived public fear that AT&T would follow a "public be damned for profits" policy. Other utility companies joined AT&T in using advertorials to promote a climate conducive to private, monopolistic services.[34] In the Progressive Era, in response to the revelations and attacks of the muckrakers, the railroad, steel, and meatpacking industries supplemented their inside lobbying with advertorials.[35]

During the Great Depression business interests conducted extensive public relations campaigns defending free enterprise and business practices. The classic example is Warner and Swasey Company, a Cleveland manufacturer. Starting in 1936 Warner and Swasey published more than 1,000 advertorials offering lessons in economics, advocating free enterprise, and praising hard work, thrift, and patriotism.[36]

Business was not alone in conducting advertorial campaigns. Since the 1930s unions have used them in the struggle to win collective bargaining rights, to improve wages and working conditions, and to exclude

cheap foreign-made goods. During World War II the Advertising Federation of America, at the urging of the federal government, drew up a code
of ethics for advertisers to aid the war effort. Advertisements were to promote "intelligent patriotism," "glorify service with our fighting forces,"
"arouse enthusiasm of workers for productive achievement," and wage a
war against absenteeism, malingering, and accidents by workers in war
production industries.[37]

Advertorials became a lobbying tool in the 1970s in campaigns by
business firms and their associations. Confronted with what they perceived
as a biased press that knew little of economics, an adversary culture led by
emerging antagonistic consumer and public interest organizations, and a
sustained decline in public trust, business leaders initiated public relations
efforts to promote their political perspectives and favorable corporate and
industry images.[38] The industries that felt the most beleaguered—petro-
leum, energy, and chemical—led the pack. Highly regulated businesses
such as transportation and utilities used advertorials to oppose stricter regulation and to propose deregulation. Businesses that depended heavily
on federal government contracts, like aerospace and defense, initiated
campaigns to establish the businesses' corporate identities and publicize
their contributions to national security and scientific and technological
progress. The 1970s also saw anti-Vietnam War advertorials, including the
famous picture of a battered and bandaged Uncle Sam with the heading "I
WANT OUT."

The *New York Times* (the *Times*) presented a prime opportunity for organized interests to share their views when it opened the lower right
quadrant of its newly launched Op-Ed page to advertorials in 1970. Mobil
Oil (now ExxonMobil) was the first to take advantage of this on October
19, 1970, and has been placing advertorials on the Op-Ed page of the
Times every Thursday since. The new Op-Ed page quickly became popular with readers and remains second only to the front page as the most
read page of the *Times*. Interest organizations of all stripes have increasingly used the Op-Ed page to express their views.[39]

Advertorial campaigns are an everyday occurrence now. They were
prominent in the debates over health care policy, the environment, and
international affairs during the Clinton presidency,[40] and they continue
to be important in the Bush administration. Recent examples include
Philip Morris countering antitobacco legislation and litigation, Microsoft
and the Bill and Melinda Gates Foundation parrying the adverse effects
of prosecution and court decisions condemning the corporation as a
"predatory monopoly," and Ford Motor and Bridgestone/Firestone defending themselves in a conflict over product liability. After the terrorist attacks on the World Trade Center and the Pentagon on September
11, 2001, the print and electronic press were filled with advertorials by
organized interests expressing patriotism and sympathy for victims and
their families.

The Objectives of Advertorial Campaigns

The objectives of an advertorial campaign depend on the sociopolitical circumstances an organized interest seeks to address. Objectives may include:

- Making the public aware of the organization's identity, interests, and activities.
- Building and sustaining good will.
- Publicizing the "good works" of the organization.
- Counteracting public mistrust and hostility.
- Counterbalancing allegedly misleading or simplistic information and comment by critics and the press.
- Redressing inadequate access to and the alleged bias of the media, whether it is in news or entertainment (such as unflattering portrayals of ethnic or racial groups on television or in film).
- Satisfying constituencies that want active defense and promotion of their interests.
- Maximizing control over communicated messages.
- Setting an agenda and framing issues.
- Expanding the scope of conflict on a policy issue by "getting the audience involved in the fight."[41]

In sum, the goal of an advertorial campaign is to influence the opinions and behavior of the public and officials and thereby to create a favorable environment of public opinion and policy in which the interest organization can pursue its goals. Reaching and influencing the news media is a central element of such a campaign.

Organized Interest Advertorials in *AJR* and *CJR*

Our research explored the frequency with which organized interests placed advertorials, which interests placed the most advertorials and what type was used, and what these advertorials addressed. To answer these questions we collected, coded, and analyzed the organized interest advertorials that appeared in *AJR* and *CJR* from 1985 to 2000.[42]

We catalogued 2,510 advertorials sponsored by 368 unique interest organizations. Each organized interest was classified into one of twenty-one organizational types.[43] Our classification system added slightly to the typology developed in Kay Schlozman and John Tierney's *Organized Interests and American Democracy*.[44] Corporations were identified by economic "type" (the product or service they sell) on the basis of a shortened version of the categories in the 1999 *Fortune 500* list. Other "economic" interest organizations (trade associations, professional associations, labor unions and employee organizations, farm groups, and peak business associations that represent the general interests of business and industry on broad policy concerns) were similarly coded.[45] Each advertorial was classified into *either* one of five image categories, one of six advocacy categories, or one of three journalism categories. Last, the policy content of each advertorial was coded using the table of contents organization in the 1999 *Congressional Quarterly Almanac* (categories include agriculture, international affairs, health, and so on).[46]

Timing of Advertorials

How often do organized interests place advertorials? With occasional reversals, there is a decreasing trend in the number of advertorials from 345 in 1985 to 79 in 2000; the low point is 58 in 1999 (Figure 12.1). The first eight years (1985–1992) had an annual average of 239, compared with an annual average of 75 for the second eight years (1993–2000) of the time series. From 1985 to 1992 image advertorials averaged 53 a year, advocacy advertorials 33, and journalism advertorials 153. The corresponding annual averages for 1993–2000 were image 17, advocacy 8, and

Figure 12.1.   Number of Advertorials by Category, 1985–2000

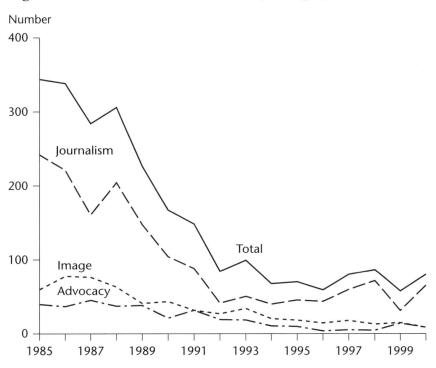

Source: Authors' data.

journalism 50. The number of annual sponsors also declined, from 79 in 1985 to 25 in 1999. The annual average dropped from 70 in the first eight years to 37 in the second eight.

What explains the decline? Surely organized interests have not lost interest in influencing the press, public opinion, and policy. Are organized interests shifting resources to other avenues and means of communication? We address this question later.

Types of Organized Interests

What kinds of organized interests use advertorials? Although business interests, especially corporations, place advertorials with greater frequency than do other economic interest organizations, cause groups (organizations that care intensely about one or a few issues), and institutions (universities, nonprofit organizations, hospitals), the difference is not as large as it used to be (Figure 12.2). For the sixteen years studied, corporations sponsored 46.3 percent of the advertorials. Adding in other economic interests raises the total by 29.2 percent to 75.5 percent of all advertorials. For the first four years (1985–1988) corporate advertorials averaged 53.3 percent of the total, for the next four years 37.5 percent, for the next 31.3 percent, and for the last four 25.6 percent. Corporations as a single category sponsored the most advertorials from 1985 to 1996, when institutions took the lead.

Institutions sponsored an increasing proportion of advertorials in the 1990s. Institutions' share grew dramatically from 5.3 percent in 1990 to 51.7 percent in 1998 and ended at 49.4 percent in 2000. Yet this entire time institutions were third in frequency, sponsoring only 10 percent of the total, following corporations and trade associations (16.4 percent) and ahead of cause groups (9.5 percent). Cause groups placed 2.6 percent of advertorials in 1985, peaked at 20.7 percent in 1991, and ended at 20.4 percent in 2000. They exceeded double-digits in nine of the sixteen years.

A couple of points are not evident in Figure 12.2. First, broadening the definition of cause groups to include citizen and public interest groups, social welfare organizations, civil rights groups, religious groups, identification and social associations, and public law firms marginally increases the category by 1.4 percent to 10.9 percent. Second, trade associations were the largest component of other economic interests (16.4 percent of total advertorials), followed by professional associations (7.5 percent), labor groups (4.6 percent), peak business (0.4 percent), and farm groups (0.3 percent). Corporations out-advertised labor ten to one, and few like-minded interests pooled resources to jointly sponsor advertorials (44, 1.8 percent).

Types of Advertorials

Organized interests must decide whether to sponsor image advertorials that affect what the public thinks about them, advocacy advertorials that take stands on policy issues, or, in the case of *AJR* and *CJR*, journalism

Figure 12.2.   Advertorial Sponsorship by Organized
Interest Type, 1985–2000

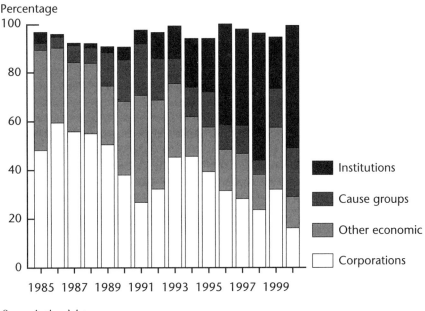

Source: Authors' data.

Note: Totals do not add to 100 percent because miscellaneous groups are not included.

advertorials that assist and recognize the efforts of the press. The study showed journalism advertorials as the largest category with 64.7 percent (1,624) of total advertorials, followed by image advertorials (554, 22.1 percent) and advocacy advertorials (332, 13.2 percent; Table 12.1). *AJR* is the numerically larger of the two journals with 71.3 percent of all advertorials and 76.4 percent of journalism advertorials.

"Source-only" journalism advertorials dominate (47.5 percent of all advertorials). These advertorials are devoid of image or advocacy content; they simply offer the organized interest's personnel as an authoritative source to journalists. Almost 11 percent of the advertorials were the award type (journalistic competitions on specific topics), and slightly more than 6 percent offered fellowships (opportunities for journalists to advance their knowledge and skills on specific policy issues). If numbers count, then journalism advertorials are significant, especially source-only advertorials.

Among image advertorials, advertorials that identify the organization and what it does were the most numerous, amounting to almost 10 percent of the total. Responsible public citizen advertorials—where an organized interest publicizes its good deeds—ran a close second with 9.1 percent. There were few goodwill and public service advertorials.

Table 12.1.   Frequency in Placing Different
Types of Advertorials, 1985–2000

Type of advertorial	Number placed (%)
Image	
Identification	236 (9.4)
Responsible public citizen	229 (9.1)
Goodwill	48 (1.9)
Public service	37 (1.5)
Miscellaneous	4 (0.2)
	544 (22.1)
Advocacy	
Position-taking and agenda-building	285 (11.4)
Ally recruitment	35 (1.4)
Ideological	6 (0.2)
Defensive	4 (0.2)
Right to reply	1 (0.0)
Miscellaneous	1 (0.0)
	332 (13.2)
Journalism	
Source-only	1,193 (47.5)
Award	273 (10.9)
Fellowship	158 (6.3)
	1,624 (64.7)
Total	2,510 (100.0)

Source: Authors' data.

Position-taking and agenda-building was the largest category of advocacy advertorials with 11.4 percent of the total. Ally recruitment advertorials are position-taking and agenda-building advertorials that also encourage political action. Given the target audience of journalists, it is not surprising that very few advertorials (1.4 percent) ask for explicit, active political support. Position-taking and agenda-building and ally recruitment advertorials decreased in number during the sixteen years. For the first eight years position-taking and agenda-building advertorials averaged 13 percent, ally recruitment 2.4 percent. For the second eight years position-taking and agenda-building averaged 8.6 percent, and ally recruitment averaged 0.3 percent. The other four categories—ideological, defensive, right to reply, and miscellaneous—averaged only .4 percent over all sixteen years.

Types of Economic Interests

Among corporations, insurance services placed the most advertorials, 205, which amounted to 8.2 percent of all advertorials and 17.6 percent of all those sponsored by corporations (Table 12.2). Insurance services include such industry giants as State Farm Insurance, ITT Life Insurance, and BlueCross BlueShield. Energy was the second largest category (156 advertorials) with Phillips 66 running more than one-third of the total. Media and entertainment, motor vehicles, and telecommunications round out the top five corporate sectors.

Table 12.2. Top Ten Corporate and Noncorporate Economic Types, 1985–2000

Corporate	Number of advertorials placed (%)
Insurance services	205 (8.2)
Energy	156 (6.2)
Media and entertainment	142 (5.7)
Motor vehicles	96 (3.8)
Telecommunications	94 (3.7)
Defense and aerospace	65 (2.7)
Miscellaneous	58 (2.3)
Pharmaceuticals	57 (2.3)
Chemicals	51 (2.0)
Tobacco	50 (1.0)
Other	188 (7.5)
Total	1,162 (37.9)

Noncorporate	Number of advertorials placed (%)
Insurance services	205 (8.2)
Labor	116 (4.5)
Miscellaneous	63 (2.5)
Health	61 (2.4)
Transportation (nonauto)	49 (2.0)
Banking services	41 (1.6)
Energy	37 (1.5)
Media	34 (1.4)
Mail, package, and freight	33 (1.3)
Chemicals	26 (1.0)
Other	68 (2.7)
Total	733 (26.4)

Source: Authors' data.

Note: Percentages are share of total advertorials placed (2,510). Noncorporate economic types include peak business associations, trade associations, professional associations, labor unions, and farm groups.

There were about 1.5 times as many corporate advertorials (1,162) as noncorporate (733). Among noncorporate advertorials, those sponsored by labor unions and other employee organizations (116) are about one-seventh of the total. The largest noncorporate category was insurance services with 205 advertorials placed primarily by professional associations of insurance agents. Health and medical equipment (61) came in fourth behind labor and miscellaneous and ahead of transportation-nonauto, mostly advertorials by a railroad trade association.

Top Advertorial Sponsors

State Farm Insurance sponsored more advertorials than any other interest organization, but its 97 advertorials are only 3.9 percent of all advertorials (Table 12.3). Prominent in the top ten sponsors are the American Council of Life Insurance, National Association of Life Underwriters, and Health Insurance Association of America. Combined with advertorials sponsored by BlueCross BlueShield, American Insurance Association, and other insurance-centered organizations, insurance was the most active interest in the two journals. Insurance had three of the top four advertisers. Also well represented were Phillips 66 and Mobil Oil from the energy sector, and diverse transportation interests such as Ford Motor and Association of American Railroads (American Trucking Association and Aircraft and Pilots Association just missed the list). One institution, Kaiser Family Foundation, which runs primarily fellowship advertorials, broke into the top ten.

There is no dominant sponsor among the top ten. This is not the case in advertorials that appeared on the Op-Ed page of the *Times*, where Mobil ranked first each year from 1985 to 1998 with advertorials every Thursday, making up more than 25 percent (719) of all advertorials (2,805).[47] The second place finisher in the *Times* study was Northrop (157 advertorials, 5.6 percent); Phillips 66 was third (93 advertorials 3.3 percent). The relative shares of State Farm (3.9 percent), American Council of Life Insurance (2.4 percent), National Association of Life Underwriters (2.4 percent), and the others on the pages of *AJR* and *CJR* are more in tune with Northrop and Phillips 66 of the *Times*' Op-Ed page than with Mobil.

Journalism Advertorials

The major purpose of this study was to investigate the relationship between organized interests and working journalists as revealed by advertorials on the pages of two major professional publications. Organized interests have every motive to work with and through journalists to get their positions disseminated to the public. What organizations were most active in offering assistance to journalists (Table 12.4)? Advertorials that include an extension of assistance, regardless of advertorial type, are called "source offers." Sixty-two percent (1,555) of all advertorials in the data set included a source offer. Many advertisements, including directory advertorials, were

Table 12.3.   Top Ten Advertorial Sponsors, 1985–2000

Organized interest	Number of advertorials placed (%)
State Farm	97 (3.9)
Phillips 66	61 (2.4)
American Council of Life Insurance	60 (2.4)
National Association of Life Underwriters	59 (2.4)
Kaiser Family Foundation	55 (2.2)
Ford Motor	51 (2.0)
Philip Morris	49 (2.0)
Association of American Railroads	48 (1.9)
Mobil Oil	45 (1.8)
Health Insurance Association of America	43 (1.7)
Total	568 (22.7)

Source: Authors' data.

Note: Percentages are share of total advertorials placed (2,510).

classified as source-only advertorials (1,193) because they lacked image or advocacy content. Rounding out the source offers were 145 image, 203 advocacy, and 14 other journalism advertorials.

There is substantial overlap in the top ten sponsors lists for source offers and all advertorials. State Farm, American Council of Life Insurance, National Association of Life Underwriters, and Phillips 66 head the list of source offer sponsors and occupy the top four positions on the overall list. The Association of American Railroads and the Health Insurance Association of America are also on both lists. Other interests often refrain from offering aid to the press (for example, only fifteen of Ford's fifty-one advertorials contained a source offer, and only twenty of Philip Morris's forty-nine did).

The number of award (273) and fellowship (158) advertorials is small in relation to the source-only advertorials (1,193). Although the source-only list is populated exclusively by economic concerns, the award and fellowship lists contain mostly institutions and professional associations.

Source-only advertorials range in style from small and simple advertisements, with only the name of the interest organization and contact information for spokespersons, to larger advertisements that try to catch journalists' attention. For example, Chevron sponsored an advertorial with the headline, "HALF THE STORY ISN'T BETTER THAN NONE," appearing with just the top half of each letter to emphasize the point. The text read:

> Sometimes sources give you only a one-sided version of an issue. Their side. Just half of the story. And that can be no story at all. It makes your job more difficult. We do our best to offer complete

Table 12.4.   Top Ten Sponsors of Source Offers and Source-Only, Award, and Fellowship Advertorials, 1985–2000

Source offers (1,555)	Number (%)	Source-only (1,193)	Number (%)
State Farm	90 (5.8)	State Farm	86 (7.2)
American Council of Life Insurance	60 (3.9)	National Association of Life Underwriters	59 (4.9)
National Association of Life Underwriters	59 (3.8)	American Council of Life Insurance	57 (4.8)
Phillips 66	56 (3.6)	Hong Kong Economic Affairs Office	41 (3.4)
Association of American Railroads	44 (2.8)	Health Insurance Association of America	39 (3.3)
Health Insurance Association of America	42 (2.7)	Phillips 66	38 (3.2)
Hong Kong Economic Affairs Office	41 (2.6)	Lillian Vernon	37 (3.1)
Lillian Vernon	37 (2.4)	American Trucking Associations	32 (2.7)
Lederle	35 (2.2)	American Insurance Association	27 (2.3)
American Trucking Associations	32 (2.1)	Lederle	27 (2.3)
		McKesson Envirosystems	27 (2.3)

Award (273)	Number (%)	Fellowship (158)	Number (%)
Aircraft Owners & Pilots	23 (8.4)	Kaiser Family Foundation	43 (27.2)
ICI	18 (6.6)	National Press Foundation	13 (8.2)
American Chiropractic Association	16 (5.9)	International Center for Journalists	11 (7.0)
American Speech- Language- Hearing Association	15 (5.5)	Alicia Patterson Foundation	8 (5.1)
California Teachers Association	11 (4.0)	Kaiser Center for Specialized Journalism	8 (5.1)
Kaiser Family Foundation	10 (3.7)	Columbia University	5 (3.2)
RFK Journalism Award	10 (3.7)	Education Writers Association	5 (3.2)
Gerald R. Ford Foundation	9 (3.3)	Fund for Investigative Reporting	5 (3.2)
John Hancock Insurance	9 (3.3)	Knight Fellowship (Yale)	4 (2.5)
American Association for Advancement of Science	7 (2.6)	Casey Journalism Center	3 (1.9)
International Association of Firefighters	7 (2.6)	Center for Foreign Journalists	3 (1.9)
		Massachusetts Institute of Technology	3 (1.9)
		Social Science Research Council	3 (1.9)

Source: Authors' data.

Note: Percentages are the share of advertorial type.

information on issues that involve us. Not just political answers but in-depth background. On us. Like solutions to environmental problems. America's dependence on foreign oil. Perspectives on the complex world of energy. We welcome your questions. And you can be sure you'll get the full story in return.[48]

State Farm Insurance and Allstate Insurance, frequent sponsors of source-only advertorials, offered prepackaged video and audio spots, as well as press kits and responses to queries on fire safety, frozen water pipes, tornadoes, earthquakes, and personal insurance. The American Plastics Council promised "answers to your questions about plastics and the environment," the International Rescue Committee wanted to be consulted on "refugee crises," and the Kaiser Family Foundation requested calls on questions about "health reform."[49] Dow Chemical urged reporters on deadline to call them: "Dow's Information Line is available for media questions any hour of the day or night. When you call us, you'll get an answer immediately or we'll put you in touch with the appropriate expert. And you'll always get someone who understands deadlines."[50]

Organized interests increasingly sponsor awards (many monetary) for excellence in journalism on policy issues in which the interest has a stake. Awards are offered annually by such diverse interests as Bristol-Myers Squibb (cholesterol and high blood pressure), John Hancock Financial Services (business and finance), Aircraft Owners and Private Pilots Association (general aviation), Playboy Foundation (First Amendment), Death Penalty Information Center (capital punishment), American College of Radiology (imaging and radiation to diagnose and treat diseases), California Teachers Association (public education), and Gerald R. Ford Foundation (presidency and national defense).

We observed a similar trend in interest organizations placing advertorials offering fellowships, seminars, and workshops to enhance journalists' expertise in specific policy areas. Sponsoring groups include the Kaiser Family Foundation (health), Institute of Current World Affairs (refugees), and Foundation for American Communication (economics). Often, organized interests cosponsored seminars and workshops with universities and press clubs.

Policy Content of Advertorials

What policy concerns do sponsors address when they design advertorials? Do image, advocacy, and journalism advertorials lend themselves to different policy emphases? Table 12.5 documents the policy content of all advertorials, as well as image, advocacy, and journalism advertorials separately. To simplify the presentation, only issue areas greater than 5 percent of an advertorial category are listed.

Almost a quarter of the image advertorials (130, 23.5 percent) dealt with arts and culture. Most of these were from corporations portraying

Table 12.5.   Top Policy Content Areas by Advertorial
Category, 1985–2000

Area	Image Number (%)	Advocacy Number (%)	Journalism Number (%)	All Number (%)
Banking, finance, and insurance	25 (4.5)	10 (3.0)	356 (21.9)	391 (15.6)
Health	51 (9.2)	53 (16.0)	191 (11.8)	295 (11.8)
Technology and communication	90 (16.2)	15 (4.5)	114 (7.0)	218 (8.7)
Transportation	48 (8.7)	42 (12.7)	101 (6.2)	191 (7.6)
Miscellaneous	32 (5.8)	3 (0.9)	139 (8.6)	174 (6.9)
Energy	25 (4.5)	39 (11.7)	95 (5.8)	159 (6.3)
Environment	37 (6.7)	22 (6.6)	94 (5.8)	153 (6.1)
Arts and culture	130 (23.5)	0 (0.0)	22 (1.4)	152 (6.1)
Law and judiciary	9 (1.6)	33 (9.9)	25 (1.5)	67 (2.7)
Total	554	332	1,624	2,510

Source: Authors' data.

Note: Only content areas greater than 5 percent in at least one advertorial category are included. Percentages are the share of advertorial type.

themselves as responsible public citizens for sponsoring cultural events, such as PBS programming, art exhibits, and public affairs television. Image advertorials also touted corporations' contributions to technological advances and national defense, and to addressing health and environmental concerns. Few image advertorials related to banking, finance, and insurance, but many journalism advertorials did (21.9 percent). Given that insurance companies and associations were the top advertorial sponsors, it is not surprising that they were active in the policy area most relevant to them. But that these interests used source offers almost exclusively is intriguing. Other policy areas that stand out in terms of journalism advertorials are health, technology and communication, transportation, energy, and the environment.

Advocacy advertorials did not appear as often. The 332 advocacy advertorials were only 13.2 percent of total advertisements. In contrast, we classified 49.3 percent of advertorials on the *Times* Op-Ed page as advocacy advertorials.[51] Advertorial sponsors in *AJR* and *CJR* were more interested in convincing journalists to include sponsors' side of the story in the news than in directly winning converts. Among the relatively few advocacy advertorials, the policy areas that received the most attention were transportation, health, energy, law and the judiciary, and the environment.

The Case of the Vanishing Advertorials

Some comment should be made about the decline in the number of advertorials in these journals and *AJR*'s decision to terminate its "Sources" pages and "Directory of Selected Sources." Some people felt these elements became out of date almost on publication: with the blizzard of mergers, acquisitions, and new firms, the business sector is constantly changing.[52] Likewise, organized interests continually enter and leave the political arena and change addresses and personnel—and sometimes policy interests.

To explain this decline we distinguish between "old" and "new" media. The old or traditional media—print and broadcast—remain important places for interest organizations to reach government officials, the public, and the press. But newspapers and magazines face competition from newsletters in specific policy areas. And cable and low-frequency broadcasting challenge the "old" radio and television stations and networks.

Likewise, *AJR* and *CJR* face competition from other media reviews that provide alternative outlets for source offer advertisements. Organized interests can replace (or supplement) their source advertorials in professional journalism periodicals with purchased space in such annual publications as the *Yearbook of Experts, Authorities and Spokespersons*, and the *National Directory of Corporate Public Affairs*. Interest organizations are listed without fee in Leadership Directories' *Yellow Books* on government affairs, corporations, associations, law firms, financial institutions, the non-profit sector, and foreign representatives in the United States. And in CQ Press's *Public Interest Profiles, Washington Information Directory, International Information Directory*, and *State Information Directory*. The desks and shelves of newsrooms are piled with these and kindred volumes.

In a similar vein, interest organizations can fill their Rolodexes of media outlets and journalists from such annual publications as *News Media Yellow Book, Hudson's News Media Contact Directory, Power Media Selects*, and *Talk Show Selects*. These and other listings of potential placements for stories and statements are within arms' reach of press and government affairs staffers in the offices of organized interests.

More significant are the "new media" opportunities for organized interests. Interests can fax and email "news alerts" for simultaneous dissemination to news organizations, individual journalists, and policymakers. Organized interests use the World Wide Web to reach and respond to people with customized messages, whether the audience is government officials, journalists, members, supporters, opponents, or anyone interested in the interest organization's views on public policy.

Among the advertorials studied, the first email address of a sponsor appeared in the November 1995 issue of *CJR*, and the first website address appeared in the January 1996 issue of *AJR*. Organized interests now routinely include their email and website addresses in advertorials: a search of three organizational directories identified 58.4 percent of the 368 advertorial sponsors as having websites.[53] We hypothesize that "press rooms" and "news media centers" on organized interest websites have caused the decline in print media journalism advertorials.

Organized Interest Lobbying on the Internet

Websites can lower the costs of news making for interest organizations and news gathering for journalists. To be sure, journalists must be lured to the websites, and the websites must be inviting and useful. Accordingly, organized interests design journalist-friendly websites with "news centers" that offer online access to organizational histories, biographical sketches of key personnel, reports, advertorials and other publications, transcripts of speeches and press briefings, press kits, news releases, audiovisual clips, contact information for organizational spokespersons and experts, and links to other friendly sites. The websites can store vast amounts of material and be easily navigated with topical archiving and indexing and fast search engines. Furthermore, many are interactive, allowing journalists to ask questions and receive answers in "real time"—in essence, to hold a virtual press conference.

Opportunities for gathering news on the Web raise ethical issues for journalists. Should the website be cited as a source? Should the story report that an interview was conducted online? How can the reliability of a Web source be evaluated and reported, especially when such sources often have unclear identities and dubious track records for reliability?

The Internet also allows organized interests to bypass the traditional news media gatekeepers and directly reach their targets. The organization can engage site visitors in direct dialogue, sample opinions, and collect information.

Deep pockets are not needed to mount and maintain a website. Indeed, some argue that the Web's affordable cost helps to democratize policy debates, reducing the control of the media and government. Websites "are a means by which any organization—no matter how financially limited—can sustain its message over time and reach the world."[54] The new communication technology does change the lobbying game, but it has not created parity among the players: Web use is not ubiquitous. One question is whether public access to and use of the Internet will expand to make Web users more representative of the American public. Even more important, however, is whether the same political actors—in this instance the business interests that dominate the traditional media—will adapt and extend their dominance to the Web.[55] The Web has not leveled the playing field; it has taken a few degrees off the tilt, but it is unlikely to achieve parity.

Conclusion

The advertorials in *AJR* and *CJR* add an important dimension to advertorials as a tool of political influence. Journalism advertorials account for almost two-thirds of the sponsored messages in these publications. Advertorials that offer awards and fellowships and seminars in policy areas relevant to the organized interest are evidence that interests do lobby the press. More significant is the finding that almost half of all advertorials were source-only—opportunities for organizations to make themselves available as authoritative sources for stories relating to their interests. Source advertorials jumped to almost two-thirds of the total when we included other advertorials offering information to journalists. This indirect route to reach ultimate target audiences, a route that often masks the sources of information and views in the story, raises fundamental questions about the character and balance of news and the policy debate. Recall that economic interests sponsored three-fourths of all advertorials, with corporations accounting for almost half.

Many social scientists contend that politics in America is biased in favor of big business and worry that this undermines the democratic process.[56] These analysts point not just to the number and kinds of organizations and lobbyists but also to specific documented activities such as campaign contributions, spending on issue advocacy campaigns, and lobbying expenditures. "The sector of American society that is best represented by interest groups is big business," writes interest group specialist Jeffrey M. Berry in the conclusion of his popular textbook, *The Interest Group Society.* He says that business has an advantage "in being able to purchase multiple forms of representation."[57] Our study of organized interest advertorials contributes more fuel to that fire by documenting another form of political influence—lobbying the press—that corporations and other business interests have historically and disproportionately used to their advantage.

The relationship between organized interests and the press is a two-way street. Journalism advertorials, especially source offers, are an outside lobbying technique used by organized interests to reach the press and, if successful, to shape the news. Journalists often accept these invitations to tap the expertise and views of organized interests. We should all stay attentive to the public's access to alternative viewpoints, journalists' responsibility to fully disclose their sources in news reporting, and the consequences of advertorial campaigns on the configuration of political influence in the United States. In old and new media, "Talk[ing] to the people who talk to America" is and will remain a basic feature of organized interest politics.

Notes

1. *Columbia Journalism Review* media kit, n.d.
2. Clyde Brown, Herbert Waltzer, and Miriam B. Waltzer, "Daring to Be Heard: Advertorials by Organized Interests on the Op-Ed Page of the *New York Times*, 1985–1998," *Political Communication* 18 (January–March 2001): 23–50.
3. Ken Kollman, *Outside Lobbying: Public Opinion and Interest Group Strategies* (Princeton: Princeton University, 1998).
4. Kay Lehman Schlozman and John T. Tierney, *Organized Interests and American Democracy* (New York: HarperCollins, 1986), 10.
5. Exceptions are Burdett A. Loomis and Eric Sexton, "Choosing to Advertise: How Interests Decide," in *Interest Group Politics*, 4th ed., ed. Allan J. Cigler and Burdett A. Loomis (Washington, D.C.: CQ Press, 1995), 193–214; Herbert Waltzer, "Corporate Advocacy: Advertising and Political Influence," *Public Relations Review* 14 (spring 1988): 41–55; Brown, Waltzer, and Waltzer, "Daring to Be Heard."
6. Kollman, *Outside Lobbying*, 4; and V. O. Key Jr., *Public Opinion and American Democracy* (New York: Alfred Knopf, 1961), 528.
7. John Kingdon, *Congressmen's Voting Decisions*, 3d ed. (Ann Arbor: University of Michigan, 1989).
8. Kollman, *Outside Lobbying*, 5.
9. Ibid., 8.
10. For a journalist's analysis, see Jonathan Rauch, *Government's End: Why Washington Stopped Working* (New York: PublicAffairs, 1999).
11. Maxwell E. McCombs and Donald L. Shaw; "The Agenda-Setting Function of the Mass Media," *Public Opinion Quarterly* 36 (spring 1972): 176–187; Maxwell E. McCombs, "The Agenda-Setting Approach," in *Handbook of Political Communication*, ed. Dan D. Nimmo and Keith R. Sanders (Beverly Hills, Calif.: Sage, 1981), 121–140; Shanto Iyengar and Donald R. Kinder, *News That Matters: Television and American Opinion* (Chicago: University of Chicago, 1987).
12. James W. Dearing and Everett M. Rogers, *Agenda-Setting* (Thousand Oaks, Calif.: Sage, 1996), 27.
13. William A. Gamson, *Talking Politics* (New York: Cambridge University, 1992).
14. Shanto Iyengar, Donald R. Kinder, Mark D. Peters, and Jon A. Krosnick, "The Evening News and Presidential Evaluations," *Journal of Personality and Social Psychology* 46 (April 1984): 778–787; and Vincent Price and David Tewksbury, "News Values and Public Opinion: A Theoretical Account of Media Printing and Framing," in *Progress in the Communication Sciences*, ed. George A. Barnett and Franklin J. Boster (Greenwich, Conn.: Ablex, 1997), 173–212.
15. Benjamin I. Page, Robert Y. Shapiro, and Glenn R. Demsey, "What Moves Public Opinion?" *American Political Science Review* 81 (March 1987): 23–43.
16. Anthony Downs, *An Economic Theory of Democracy* (New York: Harper and Row, 1957).
17. Page, Shapiro, and Demsey, "What Moves Public Opinion?" 40.
18. Dan Berkowitz, "TV News Sources and News Channels: A Study in Agenda-Building," *Journalism Quarterly* 64 (summer–fall 1987): 508–513.
19. Jay G. Blumler and Michael Gurevitch, "Journalists' Orientations to Political Institutions: The Case of Parliamentary Broadcasting," in *Communicating Politics: Mass Communication and the Political Process*, ed. Peter Golding, Graham Murdock, and Philip Schlesinger (New York: Holmes and Meier, 1986), 67–92.
20. Oscar H. Gandy, *Beyond Agenda Setting: Information Subsidies and Public Policy* (Norwood, N.J.: Ablex, 1982), 14.
21. Herbert J. Gans, *Deciding What's News: A Study of CBS Evening News, NBC Nightly News, Newsweek and Time* (New York: Pantheon, 1979), 116.

22. See *Quill* 88 (April 2000): 24.
23. Clifford G. Christians, Mark Fackler, and Kim B. Rotzoll, *Media Ethics: Cases and Moral Reasoning* (White Plains, N.Y.: Longmann, 1995), 75.
24. Jim DeBrosse, *The Serpentine Wall* (New York: St. Martin's Press, 1988), 92.
25. Timothy E. Cook, *Governing with the News: The News Media as a Political Institution* (Chicago: University of Chicago, 1998).
26. James Boylan, "The Media Critics," *Columbia Journalism Review* 38 (March–April 2000): 34–35.
27. Ben Yagoda, "Columbia Journalism Review," *Columbia Journalism Review* 38 (March-April 2000): 38–39.
28. *Columbia Journalism Review* media kit, n.d.
29. Ibid.
30. *American Journalism Review* media kit. n.d.
31. David Hall, "American Journalism Review," *Columbia Journalism Review* 38 (March-April 2000): 36–37.
32. *Washington Journalism Review* 8 (May 1986): 51.
33. *American Journalism Review* media kit, n.d.
34. Quentin J. Schultze, "Advertising and Public Utilities, 1900–1917," *Journal of Advertising* 10 (4): 41–44, 48 (1981).
35. Roland Marchand, "The Fitful Career of Advocacy Advertising: Political Protection, Client Cultivation, and Corporate Morale," *California Management Review* 29 (winter 1987): 128–156.
36. Randall Poe, "Masters of the Advertorial," *Across the Board* 17 (September 1980): 25.
37. Richard Tansey and Michael R. Hyman, "Ethical Codes and the Advocacy Advertisements of World War II," *International Journal of Advertising* 12 (4): 351–366 (1993).
38. Peter L. Banks, "New Attack on the Legitimacy of Business," *Harvard Business Review* 59 (September–October 1981): 82–89.
39. Brown, Waltzer, and Waltzer, "Daring to Be Heard," 32–34.
40. Ibid, 38–42.
41. E.E. Schattschneider, *The Semi-Sovereign People* (New York: Hold, Rinehart and Winston, 1960), 4.
42. The data set does not include advertorials that appeared in *AJR*'s "Director(ies) of Selected Sources" or "Special Advertising Sections." Coded information included the publication, publication date, principal sponsor of each advertorial, organized interest type of the sponsor, economic interests of corporations and noncorporate "economic" organizations when they were the sponsor, and type of advertorial. Advertorials with multiple sponsors were noted. Advertisements containing an offer to be a source of information to the press were designated as "source" advertorials.
43. The types are corporations; peak business associations; trade associations; professional associations; labor unions and employee organizations; farm groups; citizens and public interest groups; cause groups; social welfare and advocacy groups; civil rights groups; religious groups; identity and other social groups; public interest law firms; institutions; individuals; American federal executive branch institutions; American state and local government institutions; American intergovernment associations; foreign governments; international and world regional organizations; and miscellaneous organizations/groups.
44. Schlozman and Tierney, *Organized Interests and American Democracy*, ch. 3, 38–57.
45. The economic types are alcoholic beverages; chemicals; commercial banking services; commercial Insurance services; computers, computer parts, and data services; construction and construction materials; defense and aerospace; diversified outsourcing services; electronic and electronic equipment; energy production and

distribution; food and food services; forest products; furniture; health care and medical equipment; labor; mail, packages, and freight delivery; media and entertainment; merchandising and wholesaling; mining, metals, and metal production; motor vehicles and parts; pharmaceuticals; public utility service; rubber and plastics; scientific, photo, and control instruments; telecommunications; textiles and apparel; tobacco and tobacco products; transportation-nonauto; and miscellaneous.

46. The policy categories are abortion and family planning; agriculture; appropriations; arts and culture; banking, finance, and insurance; budget; congressional affairs; defense; education; employment and labor; energy; environment; executive branch; government and government operations; health; industry and regulation; international affairs; international economic development and trade; law and judiciary; politics and elections; science; social policy; taxes; technology and communication; transportation; U.S. economy; and miscellaneous.

47. Brown, Waltzer, and Waltzer, "Daring to Be Heard," 37–38.

48. *Washington Journalism Review* 10 (July 1988): 14.

49. *Columbia Journalism Review* 33 (November–December 1994): 9; *Columbia Journalism Review* 33 (September–October 1994): 8; and *Columbia Journalism Review* 33 (May–June 1994): 8.

50. *Columbia Journalism Review* 25 (September–October 1986): 15.

51. Brown, Waltzer, and Waltzer, "Daring to Be Heard."

52. Ernest M. Durso, Vice President for Advertising, *Columbia Journalism Review*, telephone interviews by Herbert Waltzer, July 19, 2000 and May 3, 2001.

53. *Associations Yellow Book* (New York: Monitor Publishing, 2001); *Washington Information Directory* (Washington, D.C.: CQ Press, 2000); and *National Trade and Professional Associations of the United States* (Washington, D.C.: Columbia Books, 2000).

54. Robert L. Heath, "New Communication Technologies: An Issues Management Point of View," *Public Relations Review* 24 (fall 1998): 275.

55. Richard Davis, *The Web of Politics: The Internet's Impact on the American Political System* (New York: Oxford University, 1999), 3–39.

56. For an introduction to this literature, see Michael T. Hayes, *Incrementalism and Public Policy* (New York: Longmann, 1992), 44–79.

57. Jeffrey M. Berry, *The Interest Group Society* (New York: Longmann, 1997), 218 and 222.

13

Organized Interests and Issue Definition in Policy Debates

Beth L. Leech, Frank R. Baumgartner, Jeffrey M. Berry,
Marie Hojnacki, and David C. Kimball

The public often conceives of lobbying as taking place in hushed conversations in Capitol Hill hallways, backrooms, restaurants, and offices. This is true to an extent; private meetings and unwritten agreements can sometimes determine the outcome of legislation. But more often lobbying happens in full view and seldom relates to a particular provision of a bill. Rather, much lobbying revolves around how issues are defined. For example, opponents of the Clinton health care reform package of 1993–1994 took the issue of universal health care and redefined it as a matter of patient choice, arguing that government bureaucracies would be picking health care providers and driving up taxes. In attempting to define (or redefine) issues, organized interests embark on public relations campaigns, advertising binges, and grassroots efforts that complement traditional face-to-face lobbying.

In this chapter Beth L. Leech and her colleagues argue that we should examine issue redefinition systematically to understand how and when it occurs. For example, interests may sponsor research projects whose findings could change how the public sees an issue. Many groups use this strategy, often investing considerable resources. And not all are successful. The authors note that there is both substantial competition in issue definition as well as considerable resistance to changing how issues are perceived. Still, agendas do matter, and it is no wonder groups devote so much attention and resources to moving their issues to the top of the list.

Research was supported through National Science Foundation grant SBR-9905195 from August 1, 1999, to December 31, 2000. National Science Foundation grant SES-0111224 supported research from July 1, 2001, to June 30, 2003, with significant support from Penn State University. Interviewing has benefited from Marie Hojnacki's Robert Wood Johnson Fellowship as well. Interviews were conducted from February 1999 to August 2000. Renewed interviewing began in July 2001 and will continue until at least December 2003. The authors would like to thank the following Penn State students for working on various aspects of this project: Christine Mahoney, Matt Levendusky, Nick Semanko, Michelle O'Connell, Roberto Santoni, Sara Hlibka, Lauren Cerminaro, John Riley, Andy Semanko, Jennifer Teters, Jen Schoonmaker, Darrin Gray, and Susanne Pena. The authors would also like to thank Patrick Hennes at Carbondale, Erin Desmarais at Tufts, and Tim La Pira at Rutgers.

When consumers buy products over the Internet, they pay no sales tax unless the retailer also has a bricks-and-mortar store in the consumer's home state. Sales taxes are state and local taxes, and the Web is, after all, worldwide. And so in the spring of 2000 the U.S. House of Representatives voted to extend a federal ban on sales taxes on Internet sales for another five years. Promoting "e-freedom" seemed like the right thing to do. Keeping the Internet free would encourage innovation, proponents argued, and innovation was what the Internet was all about. Internet taxes were portrayed as an additional burden on taxpayers that would stifle growth.

By August, however, the bill was languishing in the Senate. Traditional retailers and state and local governments had begun a strong lobbying campaign to change the way legislators and others thought about the issue. Retailers and governments argued that the debate was not about freedom but about fairness. Bricks-and-mortar retailers had to charge sales taxes, and it was unfair to give Internet retailers an advantage. In addition, a shift away from state-based retailers who collect sales taxes robbed local governmental budgets, threatened local governmental services, and constituted improper federal meddling in local governmental affairs.

A lobbyist siding with the retail industry explained, "The initial impulse among just about everyone on [Capitol] Hill is to extend the moratorium on Internet taxes. Our main challenge is to educate legislators about the existing inequity in sales tax collection and get them to understand the problems with a blanket extension of the Internet tax moratorium. . . . We've seen a sea change in the last few months in the way Congress looks at this issue." A lobbyist for an antitax group lamented that "the other side has succeeded in reframing the debate away from taxpayer rights to government revenue and fairness issues."

A similar change occurred during former president Bill Clinton's efforts to enact a health care reform package in 1993. Clinton proposed the package to address Americans' concerns about health care coverage, but the definition of the issue almost immediately began to spiral away from Clinton's vision. Rather than focus on the needs of the uninsured, discussion turned to the possibility of giant government bureaucracies rationing health care, limiting options, and driving up taxes. Though most Americans would say they were in favor of better health care coverage (the way Clinton hoped his package would be viewed), most Americans would also say they were opposed to governmental restrictions on the type of care they could receive (the definition of the health care proposal that seemed to take hold).

The ways legislators and the public think about an issue can be a powerful force in determining how they will act. Thinking about a different aspect of a complex issue can lead people to change their minds—altering their support or stopping it altogether. This is true not just in politics but in other types of decision making. Think about buying a new car and imagine the salesperson asking you to decide whether you would like the tan or the white exterior. Have you made your decision? Now imagine that tan is a custom color that would cost an additional $1,200. Does your decision change as a result of focusing on the cost rather than simply the aesthetics?

Dueling definitions are common in politics. A politician's decision about whether to provide a service to constituents may be different if the focus is on the benefit the constituents will receive rather than the additional taxes they must pay. Abortion rights advocates and opponents of abortion know that focusing on different aspects of this emotionally charged issue is crucial to winning converts. While one side focuses on the rights of the woman and the specter of injuries and death from back-alley procedures, the other side focuses on the life of the unborn child and the gruesome aspects of the clinical procedure. For one side the issue is about individual rights, for the other it is about the sanctity of life.

So the way people understand an issue can be integral to its political outcome. Interest groups, lobbyists, and other policy advocates shape perceptions of policies by focusing attention on the justifications for their goals. But what gives these arguments their power? Is it easy to redefine how people see an issue? If not, under what circumstances can interest groups and other policy advocates change the way legislators and others think about an issue? How common are such changes and how difficult are they to achieve? This chapter addresses these questions using information gathered during a multiyear, multi-investigator project that explores the process of government advocacy in Washington.

The Advocacy and Public Policymaking project is a large academic study of policymaking and the role of interest groups in Washington, D.C. The project examines a random sample of 120 policy issues through interviews with hundreds of lobbyists and government officials and through a vast array of information from governmental records, media reports, and interest group publications. When this chapter was written we had gathered information on more than seventy of the policy issues and had completed two years of a planned four years of data collection. Even at this point in the research, however, it is clear that large-scale redefinitions in the way issues are thought about at the national level are rare in the short term. We use several cases from our research to help illustrate how policy advocates try to affect issue definitions and why the task is usually so difficult.

But first a word about the terms in this chapter. Political scientists use *issue definitions, issue frames,* and *changes in focus* to refer to the phenomenon we discuss in this chapter. We prefer the term *issue definition* to describe the way people conceptualize a policy issue, but readers should be aware that political scientists who write about the different "frames" for thinking about an issue are often talking about the same phenomenon. When we discuss changes in focus we are describing the process of shifting between two or more existing issue definitions.[1]

Overview of the Project

Many previous studies of lobbying and interest group activity have focused on a handful of well-known policy debates selected from media descriptions of Washington. Although these studies have taught us how interest group activity unfolds in the public eye, they do not explain what day-to-day life is like in Washington, how much time lobbyists spend on such large-scale issues, and how often quieter, less well-known issues come into play. By taking a random sample of issues, we are able to portray the full spectrum of interest group activity in Washington and how interest group influence varies depending on the scale of the issue involved.

Of course, a chronic problem for researchers is that there is no such thing as a list of all the issues in which interest groups are involved. We could sample from the bills introduced in Congress, but this would leave out issues that never make it to the congressional agenda. And this method would give too much weight to issues that are never really acted upon by anyone but the member of Congress who introduced the bill.

A common solution is to make up a list of issues based on mentions in newspapers or in specialty political publications such as the *CQ Weekly*. This list might include some items not on the formal congressional agenda, but it would include only those issues with enough prominence to be mentioned in the media. We know from studies of individual agencies and individual interest groups that sometimes interest groups have the most power when they are least observed. The interest group that is able to get a line item inserted into a larger bill may never be written about in the news and thus may never have another interest group directly oppose it.

We took an innovative approach to selecting interest group issues. First we chose a random sample of interest groups from among those registered under the federal Lobbying Disclosure Act of 1995. In our list interest groups that were more active in politics had a greater chance of being chosen, because their names would appear once for every issue on which they lobbied. We arranged an interview with a lobbyist from each of the selected groups and asked the lobbyist to describe the group's activities on the most recent federal policy issue on which it had been active. The result is a random sample of policy issues that ranges from well-known issues like patients' rights and normalized trade with China to issues so narrow that we must describe them vaguely ("a line item in the defense appropriations bill") to avoid identifying the people we interviewed.

We then conducted a certain number of follow-up interviews depending on the issue's complexity and the number of different perspectives involved (in some cases as many as fifteen interviews). Interviews focused on lobbying activities, coalitions on all sides of the issue, arguments and evidence, the venues of government decision making, and other questions. We collected additional information on each issue from all published news stories; all congressional bills, hearings, testimony, and committee action; political action committee information from the Federal Election Commission; lobbying expenditures recorded by the Office of the Clerk of the House of Representatives; and all publicly available interest group websites on the topic. Eventually, quantitative analysis of how lobbying varies across these issues and of the factors that contribute to interest group success will be possible. Summaries of all our cases; primary documents, including news releases, congressional bills, interest group statements, and news stories; and a wealth of other information is available at our website: http://lobby.la.psu.edu.

What Causes Issue Redefinition?

Changes in the way an issue is thought about sometimes follow a change in the outside world. Attacks on the World Trade Center and the Pentagon on September 11, 2001, steered the debate on many issues—immigration, Internet privacy, public health expenditures—toward concerns about national security. Before September 11 policy proposals that involved significant government spending or revenue loss were discussed in the context of a dwindling budget surplus. After September 11 these proposals were examined for their potential to stimulate the economy and protect the nation, with the budget almost an afterthought.

As another example, in the 1950s policy questions about tobacco were primarily restricted to economic concerns: Was everything okay for the tobacco farmer? But by 1964 when the surgeon general issued his report on the dangers of smoking, the issue definition surrounding tobacco had begun to shift, and concerns about the health implications of tobacco battled for attention alongside concerns about its implications for economic growth.[2]

But there can be widely varying lag times between supposed trigger events and changes in issue definitions. The first major study linking smoking with health problems was published in 1939; the first study presenting clear evidence that smoking causes lung cancer was published in 1954.[3] Yet the policy focus for years continued to emphasize economic aspects of tobacco over health aspects. In addition, many issue definitions change without an obvious change in the outside world. Internet retailing was not substantially different in August 2000 than it was in April 2000, and yet the definition of the issue shifted.

The way issue definitions change and the reasons why these definitions are powerful are connected to the way the human brain operates. Although analogies between the mind and a computer are common, we know that the brain works much differently from the way a computer works. Our attention is limited—we cannot attend to an infinite number of factors at once; instead we focus on what we think is most relevant. In terms of issue definition, relevance depends on what we have done in the past, what has most recently been suggested to us, and what fits our previous conceptions about the issue. Political scientist Bryan Jones has suggested that issue redefinitions come from "bottlenecks of attention" that result from this inability to consider all possible relevant information at once.[4] Because all policy issues are potentially multidimensional (virtually all have an economic aspect as well as a social aspect, for example), not all aspects of an issue can be considered at once. Rapid shifts in a decision about an issue can occur, even without any change in a person's underlying preferences and beliefs, just by changing the focus to another part of the issue.

Political scientist Richard Smith found such shifts in attention in Congress as it considered changes in education policy.[5] Likewise, political scientist Gary McKissick has argued that much of lobbying consists of attempting to redefine an issue or to get legislators to focus on a different aspect of a complex issue.[6] Because most legislators remain with one political party throughout their careers, represent the same constituents, and retain the same views about the role of government in daily life, they tend to have well-entrenched policy preferences. So it is unlikely that a lobbyist could change a legislator's political beliefs simply by talking with the legislator, supplying information, or donating campaign funds. But lobbyists do not have to change the legislator's underlying belief structure, they need only to focus the legislator's attention on what is most advantageous to the lobbyist's cause.

The work of these and other scholars—as well as our own research—suggests that completely new definitions of issues are rare. New definitions tend to be limited to cases where there has been some new discovery, scientific or otherwise, as we saw with tobacco policy. More common are multiple definitions of an issue that coexist over a long time. What varies is the amount of attention and credence given to any one of those issue definitions.

In this sense the study of issue redefinition is closely linked to the study of agenda setting. Whereas the study of agenda setting investigates which *issues* receive attention and action by the government and the public, the study of issue redefinition investigates which *aspects* of those issues receive attention and what considerations are deemed important. Our research has shown that even shifting attention to some preexisting aspect of an issue is not as simple as it seems. In the next sections we will discuss how interest groups and their lobbyists go about trying to affect issue definitions and why it can be so difficult.

Changing Issue Definitions

There is no obvious route, no surefire method for changing or reinforcing the conventional definition of a political issue. And given the resources necessary to do so, developing a cogent strategy is crucial.

Sometimes an issue is so critical to the future of the interest group's members that the group must take action even when the chances of success are small.

A strategy is a plan that identifies targets and maps out tactics and resources to reach the targets. Interest groups must consider how they will allocate resources among all the issues on the horizon at the beginning of the year or the beginning of a new Congress. Groups must also be flexible and able to respond to what emerges concerning their priority issues. When changing or reinforcing a prevailing issue definition is necessary, a key strategic decision is whether to mobilize the membership or broader public.

Grassroots Support

This may seem like an obvious choice. Legislators and administrators care far more about what citizens think than they care about what lobbyists think. A primary job of all lobbyists is to bring the voice of the people to Washington. Yet it doesn't always make sense to focus on grassroots mobilization. When United Airlines announced plans to buy out another large carrier, U.S. Airways, United realized that an impediment to approval from the Antitrust Division of the Justice Department was a concern that this merger would lead to others. Instead of six major carriers, there could be just three major carriers in a matter of a year or two.

United wanted to steer debate away from the effects of reduced competition on airline prices to the advantages the merger would bring to travelers. As one spokesman argued, "With this merger you can go from Bangor, Maine, to Tokyo with one stop in Boston. Seamless travel. You put your luggage on in Bangor and you pick it up in Tokyo." The problem for United was that the number of people in Bangor who wanted improved service to Tokyo was small. More broadly, this just isn't the type of issue that the traveling public is going to get excited about. Although United made a modest effort to convince a few mayors of cities that would get improved service to contact their legislators, the airline focused on private meetings with legislators and Justice Department officials, emphasizing the legal arguments as to why the merger was justifiable under antitrust law.

When grassroots mobilization is possible, it can be a powerful force. When the Clinton administration issued a draft of proposed ergonomic regulations, the business community quickly sprang into action. Its strategy was to move debate from workplace safety, which was the focus of the Occupational Safety and Health Administration (OSHA), to excessive costs on business. Lobbyists for corporations and trade associations in Washington formed a coalition and worked strenuously to get the word out to other business organizations. The lobbyists told business trade groups that OSHA's cost projection of $4.5 billion a year to companies was woefully understated and the yearly tab would be in the tens of billions of dollars.

The goal of these lobbyists was to scare companies that would be subject to the regulations. One lobbyist said he loved to go to a meeting of a soft drink association and say, "Do you know that you'll have to have a second person on delivery trucks because there are only so many lifts [of cases of bottles] they'll be allowed to do?" OSHA's regulations were ambiguous and lobbyists interpreted them liberally to create the most dire scenarios. And it worked. Business executives began contacting their legislators. Said one lobbyist, "When a legislator gets a call from someone whose UPS facility has 40,000 employees in their district, that makes a difference." As debate shifted more to cost and away from safety it began to favor business. After George W. Bush took office in 2001, Congress passed a bill invalidating the regulations, and Bush signed it.

Research

Another common strategy for changing issue definitions is research. A rigorous study that yields counterintuitive findings can change the way people see a problem. These findings are newsworthy, and thus media coverage can fuel a reconsideration of an issue. "City Slickers," a report issued by the Environmental Working Group, elicited a gusher of publicity around the country. The report statistically analyzed where agriculture subsidies are distributed, and the press could not resist reporting that $1.2 million a year was going to people who had addresses in zip code 90210 (Beverly Hills, California). Farm subsidies are traditionally defended on the grounds that they preserve family farms. The report helped many Americans understand that the issue isn't family farms, but government subsidies of corporate farm interests, which was exactly the goal of the Environmental Working Group.[7]

Yet for every report like "City Slickers" there are scores that never receive any publicity. It is one thing to produce research but quite another to get anyone in the press to pay the slightest attention to it. Washington is awash in interest groups competing for media coverage. Most research produced by interest groups is intended for a smaller audience—key policymakers who have authority over the issue at hand. Getting these policymakers to read a research report is as big a hurdle as trying to get the *Washington Post* or *New York Times* to cover your press conference. The best that most lobbies can hope for is 15 minutes with a legislative or agency staffer, who probably will only read the one- or two-page summary that accompanies the larger study.

Another problem with research is that not all groups have sufficient credibility to give their reports scientific authenticity. Corporations are especially suspect and will often fund work at think tanks because something published under their own name has limited credibility. Liberal citizen lobbies, such as environmental groups, have been the most successful in attracting attention for their research.[8] Yet issues are not so malleable that a single study, even one as compelling as "City Slickers," can decisively reorient a prevailing definition. Thus interest groups must broaden their arsenal with other advocacy tactics.

Paid Media

A related tactic is paid media—the purchase of print advertising or, rarely, television commercials. Rather than spend money producing research that might attract little attention, why not spend money communicating directly with citizens through advertising? Because buying enough advertising to stand a realistic chance of influencing public opinion is extremely expensive.[9] Still, some wealthy interests use it as part of their larger lobbying strategy. The nuclear industry, for example, has used paid media and public relations to contend with a public that is highly skeptical of nuclear power plant safety. It is not clear whether this approach has had much impact.

Long-term Commitment

The most important strategic decision in redefining issues is long-term commitment. Lobbies are competing for limited space on the agenda of Congress or an agency. Oftentimes the first step is to make key policymakers understand that a problem exists—what John Kingdon calls the "softening up" period.[10] Getting people to pay attention and then do something about the problem can take years, even decades—and it may never happen if policymakers prefer the status quo.

Take the reimbursement rate for Pap smears, a routine medical procedure that screens women for cervical cancer. Pathologists and lab owners have been upset for some time by what they see as an inadequate rate for Medicare reimbursement. The initial tactic in a plan to get Congress to pressure the Health Care Financing Agency to change the rate was an invitation from a pathologist to his representative, Neil Abercrombie, D-Hawaii, to accompany the pathologist to a lab to see how the tests are done and to reinforce how vitally important they are. Abercrombie and thirty-six cosponsors then agreed to introduce legislation in the 105th Congress (1997–1999) to change the reimbursement rate. The legislation was reintroduced in the 106th Congress (1999–2001) with 103 cosponsors. The lobbies believed that continuous work on the issue would eventually bring enough legislators on board, and that these legislators would force a change in the fee structure. And indeed, the Pap smear coalition was making progress in showing legislators that if labs were losing money on Pap smears, the labs would cut back or eliminate the screening they performed for this test, one of the most effective cancer screening tools available.

Converting Resources

Interest groups have a variety of resources and must decide how to convert them into political influence.[11] Money is the most obvious resource and can be used to hire lobbyists and other people to fill skilled positions at the organization. Membership is another important resource, and lobbies with many members or professionals with skills conducive to political activity are believed to have an advantage in the political process.[12] Status is another resource—the esteem in which people hold the organization. And a related resource is credibility, an organization's reputation for producing high quality research and reports and the degree to which its lobbyists are trusted. To maximize credibility some organizations have invested heavily in employing Ph.D.s and other policy wonks to build a reputation for technical expertise.

A group's resources and the way they are used to make the lobby politically effective constitute the group's organizational capacity. The greater an organization's capacity the better chance it has of redefining an issue or preventing other groups from redefining it. Our case studies demonstrate over and over that advocacy related to issue definition is a long-term process. In 2000 the U.S. Forest Service issued a set of regulations banning additional road building in many national parks. This was an enormous victory for environmental groups, which had been working for years to convince Washington that the central issue was not harvesting trees to supply the nation's need for lumber, but the environmental degradation caused by constructing roads to get the timber out.

It's hard to know when the redefinition effort began, but it goes back at least as far as the Carter administration (1977–1981). Environmental groups worked hard to influence the administration's key planning documents (RARE I and RARE II) on the forests. Over the years environmental groups like the Sierra Club, the Wilderness Society, and the Natural Resources Defense Council kept working on the issue of road-building in the national forests, and their expertise gave them access to the Forest Service when sympathetic administrators took over after the election of Bill Clinton. The environmental groups have continued work on the issue since the Bush administration revoked the Clinton rules and said it would modify them.

There is no special secret to redefining issues. Most issues change only incrementally and a commitment of resources over the long term is critical. The lobbying we observed on long-term issues shows stability and a firm commitment by the lobbies to their ongoing priorities. For all the technological change in America, the strategy and tactics of lobbying on issue definition has changed little. Expertise, the ability to mobilize members at key junctures, and the allocation of lobbyists' and researchers' time remain crucial. But opportunities for more rapid action may arise when elections bring change or when unexpected events transpire. Lobbies most capable of grabbing these opportunities will be the lobbies that have been working in the trenches, using their resources to continually strengthen their organizational capacity.

Impediments to Change

Even unlimited resources to mobilize supporters, publish issue advertisements, and contact members of Congress would not make it easy to change the definition of an issue. We identified a series of interrelated factors that make redefinitions difficult, including preexisting coalitions with preexisting arguments about an issue, the use of "budget scoring" and procedural controls, and the limited nature of agenda space and how important expectations become in light of that limitation.

Old Dogs, Old Tricks

Washington is full of staff, advocates, and policy experts familiar with the ins and outs of government programs. There are few novel arguments to those in the know. Thus redefinition occurs when groups not previously aware of a program, or not as familiar with it, begin to take interest. This means, as political scientist E.E. Schattschneider made plain, that agenda setting and raising awareness of issues to new constituencies are fundamental to issue definition.[13] But attracting the attention of new groups of policymakers is difficult and well beyond the lobbying capacities of many groups.

One reason the same lineup of policy advocates tends to interact over and over is that almost all lobbying concerns the expansion, restriction, or modification of an existing government program. Coalitions line up almost automatically based on their support or opposition to the program in question, and these coalitions are rarely new. Rather, previous supporters of the program argue for its expansion, and opponents continue their opposition (most of the cases we have studied involve the expansion or contraction of an existing program). This is the trench warfare of lobbying, and it is not the stuff of high rhetorical flourish. Rather, it involves long-term and repetitive efforts to establish a case. Over several decades many of these issues may be redefined dramatically, but in any given Congress most of the coalitions of support and opposition are simple recreations of the coalitions that existed last time.

Focusing the Debate

Government leaders with control over procedural issues can squelch efforts to redefine issues. The president and the leaders of the House and Senate are often able to structure legislative debates in ways that avoid certain arguments or make these arguments more difficult for their opponents to make credibly. Take the China trade disputes in the summer of 2000.

Congress was set to vote on whether to grant China permanent normalized trade relations (PNTR). Such trade status would make China a favored partner in U.S. trade and would relieve China of having to reapply each year to receive that status, as had been the case previously. Environmental groups and unions tried to defeat the measure by pointing to China's poor human rights records and to the possible damage to the environment of more rapid industrialization in China.

But supporters of the trade status, including the Clinton administration and much of the congressional leadership, had structured the vote in such a way that a vote against PNTR would primarily harm the U.S. economy, not the Chinese. China was already widely expected to gain entry into the World Trade Organization (WTO), which would allow it to trade freely with the United States, because the United States is a WTO member. But if the United States did not approve the permanent normalized trade status with China it would not receive the same benefits that China received under WTO rules.

Much of the value of the administration's arguments in support of PNTR came from proper timing. The administration first worked in international institutions and multilateral trade organizations concerning Chinese trade, and only after that was accomplished did the legislative battle begin. By controlling the timing of the debates, supporters of PNTR were able to make the debate seem superfluous.

In addition, Washington policy debates are dominated by budget scoring done by the Congressional Budget Office, the Joint Committee on Taxation, or others, in which the impact of a proposed change is assessed in terms of its impact on the federal budget. When a policy idea is presented, members of Congress immediately begin to talk about the costs, and many will react to the issue based solely on this dimension. Costs are narrowly construed to include only costs to the federal budget, and often only to the part of the federal budget under the jurisdiction of a given committee. Costs to the private sector, to the states and localities, to individuals, or even to other federal programs may not become part of the debate; similarly, benefits or savings to those groups may not be discussed. Overcoming the hurdle of cost can be a daunting legislative task.

Agendas Matter

If a proponent of change can draw enough attention to an issue and push it outside the confines of the usual decisionmakers in the area, then many of the previously mentioned constraints may not apply. New participants may be unfamiliar with old arguments; attention may not focus just on a particular program, but on the issue more generally; and budget issues may be overshadowed by attention to social problems.

But getting to the top of the political agenda is easier said than done. Many of our cases involve situations where poorly organized or organizationally weak professional communities would likely prevail if their issue were suddenly catapulted to the headlines of the nation's newspapers. But this process is neither easily controlled nor inexpensive to manipulate. Further, it does not guarantee success. Sometimes increased attention sparks a countermobilization by opponents that could do more harm than good.

In addition, because just a few issues will make it to the top of the agenda in any given Congress, policymakers and lobbyists prefer to spend time on issues where their involvement might make a difference. Therefore, any widely held perception that an issue is "not going to move" can be a self-fulfilling prophecy. Organizations must be prepared to lay the groundwork for change over the years, but they must also understand that important allies with many issues to work on will choose or be forced to work on the issues that are "moving."

If all Washington policymakers are basing their behavior on the expected behavior of others, then two outcomes are possible. For most issues there will be no reason for anyone but the usual suspects to get involved, and the issue will be stable. By the same token, some issues will be perceived as "moving," and a rapid succession of new participants may suddenly get involved. This cascade of new involvement can be of two types: one of enthusiasm for change that will sweep away an established way of thinking, or one of countermobilization of defenders of the status quo who recognize that their definition of the issue is under serious attack. When both occur, the result is usually to reinforce stability. But occasionally dramatic change can happen.

What Makes Change Easier

It's hard to change an issue definition, but it's not impossible. Every one of the issues we have studied is multidimensional. In no case in our sample, and probably none in government, is there only one way to portray an issue. This means that issues will constantly be the object of serious debate and that, occasionally at least, new pieces of evidence, changing social mores, journalistic investigations, political campaigns, or even old fashioned political leadership may lead to dramatic shifts in how we justify our policies—and therefore which policies are justified. Occasionally, the political landscape changes to create a window of opportunity for interests seeking to redefine an issue and change public policy. Electoral change, governmental champions, and external events can provide such a window.

Changing the Cast

A change in presidential administration creates opportunities to push public policy in a new direction. A new president may favor the same changes to a law that the previous president threatened to veto. Equally important is the "bully pulpit"—an unrivaled ability to shape debate and public opinion—that the White House provides for its occupant. The shift from Bill Clinton to George W. Bush has created many opportunities. Several issues of interest to business groups (income tax cuts, bankruptcy reform, moving class action lawsuits to federal courts) stalled during the Clinton presidency. President Clinton was in a position to veto legislation on these issues, but he also moved debate into territory that put business interests on the defensive. For example, Clinton repeatedly argued against income tax cuts in which most of the benefits would go to the wealthiest Americans. As a candidate and as president, George W. Bush doggedly argued that Americans deserved a tax cut as a reward for budget surpluses, and that such a cut would stimulate economic growth. After only a few months in office President Bush passed the largest income tax cuts in twenty years.

Change in party control of Congress also creates opportunities for issue definition, as committee chairs rotate and a different set of policy preferences come to the fore. The abortion issue is a good example. In the early 1990s a Democratically controlled Congress passed a law increasing the penalties for abortion protesters arrested for blocking access to clinics. This focused the abortion debate on the behavior of some of abortion's most extreme opponents, often putting antiabortion rights forces on the defensive. After Republicans won control of Congress in 1994, GOP leaders and antiabortion rights groups moved quickly to draft legislation banning late-term "partial-birth" abortions. Although Congress failed to override President Clinton's veto of the legislation, thirty states passed laws banning partial-birth abortions (although most have been voided by courts). More important, antiabortion rights groups shifted debate away from the tactics of abortion protesters to the unpleasant details of late-term abortion procedures. An advocate for the abortion rights side conceded that "the other side initially won the media war on this issue by getting the issue defined as 'partial-birth abortion.' " It is important to note that both issue definitions existed long before the partisan shift, but the partisan shift allowed one definition to take precedence over the other.

Finding a Champion

Short of dramatic electoral change, sometimes finding a well-placed advocate in Congress helps a group define an issue and gain support for its position. In the late 1990s union leaders were seeking legislation that would protect health care workers from bloodborne diseases like AIDS and hepatitis by requiring hospitals and medical offices to use safer needles. But the unions knew that if the issue were defined as a way of protecting union members, the Republicans who controlled the congressional committees with jurisdiction over the issue would want nothing to do with it. But defining the issue as a public health problem made Republicans more receptive. The Republicans and the unions never became allies, but the chairman of the House Education and the Workforce Committee, Rep. Cass Ballenger, R-N.C., introduced a version of the legislation and shepherded it through the legislative process. In November 2000 President Clinton signed the legislation into law.

This case points to another side of the procedural controls problem we discussed earlier. Although these controls can limit definitional change, they can also instigate it when prominent government officials are part of the coalition pushing for change. Close connections between lobbyists and the leaders of major congressional committees, the leadership of the House and Senate, and within the executive branch are important resources in any lobbying campaign.

But relying heavily on a single champion in Congress can be risky. If the legislator leaves Congress the momentum behind an issue may die. In the 106th Congress the American Medical Association worked with Rep. Tom Campbell, R-Calif., to push legislation that would change antitrust laws to allow doctors to bargain collectively when negotiating fees and treatment coverage with health insurers (such as HMOs). Currently, antitrust laws prevent doctors from banding together when negotiating terms of coverage with insurers. Campbell's status as a respected legislator, a free-market conservative, and a legal scholar of antitrust law made him a compelling advocate. Despite strong opposition from business and insurance groups and Republican leaders in the House, Campbell and the American Medical Association convinced many representatives that the legislation was needed to level the playing field between doctors and insurance companies. Campbell's legislation passed the House by a two-to-one margin only to stall in the Senate. With Campbell no longer in Congress (he ran unsuccessfully for the U.S. Senate in 2000), the doctors' antitrust legislation has not been reintroduced in the 107th Congress (2001–2003).

The safe needle and doctors' antitrust campaigns reveal to lobbyists the importance of having close connections with government officials. Although lobbyists have little ability to set the agenda and no ability to affect the procedural rules of Congress or the executive branch, lobbyists can use alliances with government leaders to build powerful coalitions. Studies of interest groups cannot overlook these coalitions.

Reality Intrudes

Although outside events such as elections and social change do not always immediately lead to an issue redefinition, interest groups and other policy advocates can use these events to help their cause. For example, when gas prices spiked and electrical blackouts interrupted business in California in early 2001, it became possible to define the state of energy policy in the United States as an "energy crisis." This definition of crisis allowed oil companies and the new president, George W. Bush, to move their proposal for expanding drilling in previously protected areas of Alaska into the foreground. Even more recently, the attacks on the World Trade Center and the Pentagon shifted the focus of energy policy toward questions of national security and reducing American dependence on foreign oil.

Budgetary shifts are an important type of outside triggering event in terms of their effects on the policy process. A change in the federal budget outlook can affect the opportunity to define an issue. One example is the 3 percent tax assessed on all telecommunications bills—traditional phones, cell phones, and computer access fees. For years telephone companies have wanted to repeal this federal excise tax, which was passed in 1898 to fund the Spanish-American War. In times of budget deficits, as during most of the 1980s and 1990s, the tax repeal failed to gain support because it would mean a loss of federal revenue. But when the federal budget produced record surpluses in the late 1990s, budgetary arguments against the repeal weakened. The House and Senate each passed a repeal of the excise tax in 2000, but President Clinton vetoed the Treasury-Postal Appropriations bill that included the final version of the legislation. With the federal budget moving back in the direction of deficits, the window of opportunity for repealing the tax appeared to have closed. But the recession at the end of 2001 offered the repeal effort new hope, as lawmakers considered measures to stimulate the economy.

Issue Definition and Democracy

Although issue definition is interesting and important to our understanding of everyday politics, its larger significance should not be overlooked. The way lobbying affects our conception of political problems goes to the heart of the debate over the role of interest groups in a democracy. Interest groups try to alter the definition of an issue to fulfill their own interests. In doing so they may blind us to the implications of alternate choices for solving a public policy problem. Is that compatible with democratic politics?

As we think about this question we see three separate issues. The first is the nature of political power. Only the most naive observer of American politics could assume that all interest group sectors have the same capacity to influence issue definition. Among competing groups, how large is the differential in key resources (such as access to policymakers)? This question leads naturally to a second: what is the mix of lobbies working to change or reinforce issue definitions? Issue definition would be less biased if all relevant interests were actively engaged in trying to influence policymakers and the public. If opponents are challenging prevailing conceptions and new issue frames are competing against others, then a policymaking process that has interest groups at its center is much more justifiable.

Third, differences among groups in resources and participation raise concerns about the manipulation or reinforcement of beliefs, symbols, myths, and language. Ideally, policy decisions would be reached after an objective evaluation of valid evidence supporting each policy alternative. In reality some alternatives are never considered because of the advocacy of certain groups that oppose them. As political scientists have long argued, prevailing conceptions of what is an appropriate policy alternative can be so strong that certain problems or approaches are kept off the political agenda entirely.[14] For example, if income redistribution is labeled "socialistic"—a loaded term that conjures images of foreign, un-American approaches—advocating for income redistribution policies becomes more difficult. And certain populations can be stigmatized by prevailing issue frames. If poor people are repeatedly labeled as lazy and uninterested in working, then welfare proposals are likely to be punitive.[15]

Some social scientists argue that biases in issue definition reflect broad patterns of interest group influence. These groups manifest the preferences of the upper class and big business and, over time, manipulate issue definitions to suit their long-term interests. To test the veracity of this charge, the study of issue definition must look beyond a single issue. Research should pursue many cases and search for patterns. Do those patterns suggest recurring biases in the way issue definition emerges? If so, must we conclude that policymaking in America is undemocratic?

In short, we judge the politics of issue definition by examining the distribution of resources, the diversity of lobbies incorporated into the policymaking process, and patterns in the way alternative definitions are included or excluded. We emphasize these questions because issue definition is not a neutral, technical process. Moreover, we believe that democratic politics is not compatible with monopolization of resources, that it is not compatible with closed policymaking systems that inhibit participation of all relevant interests, and that it is not compatible with biased definitions that preclude consideration of valid alternatives. Studying the politics of issue definition is a window on how our voices are heard (or not heard) by those who govern us.

Conclusion

Debates on issue definitions are time worn and rarely subject to dramatic change. In any given Congress only a few, if any, issues will change dramatically; most lobbying efforts do not lead to new legislation or new issue definitions. But over the long term Washington's understanding of various policies will change, and continued efforts by those involved to gather support, to generate statistics, and to build a coalition for their way of thinking can have significant consequences. We hope in this project to demonstrate the limits and possibilities of lobbying and persuasion. We need to understand what keeps some policy issues stable and what causes others to be redefined. Although the rare but fundamental process of issue redefinition should not be our exclusive focus—redefinition is, after all, atypical—a complete understanding of lobbying and advocacy must explain both the typical and the mundane aspects of lobbying.

Notes

1. See Bryan D. Jones, *Reconceiving Democratic Decisionmaking* (Chicago: University of Chicago, 1994).
2. For a more detailed discussion of this issue, see Frank R. Baumgartner and Bryan D. Jones, *Agendas and Instability in American Politics* (Chicago: University of Chicago, 1993).
3. Lee A. Fritschler, *Smoking and Politics*, 2d ed. (Englewood Cliffs, N.J.: Prentice-Hall, 1983).
4. Jones, *Reconceiving Decisionmaking.* The phrase *bottleneck of attention* comes from Herbert A. Simon, "Human Nature in Politics: The Dialogue of Psychology with Political Science," *American Political Science Review* 79 (June 1985): 302.
5. Richard A. Smith, "Advocacy, Interpretation, and Influence in the U.S. Congress,"*American Political Science Review* 78: (March 1984): 44–63.
6. Gary McKissick, "Issue Manipulation: Interest Group Lobbying and the Framing of Policy Alternatives" (Ph.D. diss., University of Michigan, 1997).
7. Jeffrey M. Berry, *The Interest Group Society*, 3d ed. (New York: Longmann, 1997), 235–236.
8. Jeffrey M. Berry, *The New Liberalism: The Rising Power of Citizen Groups* (Washington, D.C.: Brookings Institution), 133–137.
9. See Darrell M. West, Diane J. Heith, and Chris Goodwin, "Harry and Louise Go to Washington: Political Advertising and Health Care Reform," *Journal of Health Policy, Politics, and Law* 21 (spring 1996): 35–68.
10. John W. Kingdon, *Agendas, Alternatives, and Public Policies*, 2d ed. (New York: HarperCollins, 1995), 127–131.
11. James Q. Wilson, "Democracy and the Corporation," in *Does Big Business Rule America?* ed. Ronald Hessen, (Washington, D.C.: Ethics and Public Policy Center, 1981), 37.
12. V. O. Key Jr., *Public Opinion and American Democracy* (New York: Alfred A. Knopf, 1961), 503–504.
13. E.E. Schattschneider, *The Semi-Sovereign People* (New York: Holt, Rinehart and Winston, 1960).
14. Peter Bachrach and Morton S. Baratz, "Two Faces of Power," *American Political Science Review* 56 (December 1962): 947–952; John Gaventa, *Power and Powerlessness* (Urbana: University of Illinois, 1980).
15. Anne Schneider and Helen Ingram, "Social Constructions of Target Populations: Implications for Politics and Policy," *American Political Science Review* 87 (June 1993): 334–347.

14

High-Tech Learns to Play the Washington Game
The Political Education of Bill Gates and Other Nerds
David M. Hart

The image of the high-tech industry in the United States has been one of tremendous technological sophistication and equally profound political naivete. After all, what was Microsoft's Bill Gates if not the quintessential nerd? Although corporate giant IBM has interacted with the government for decades, other high-tech firms took longer to enter the political fray. Not until rapid growth of the computer-driven technology industry in the 1980s demanded greater political sophistication from technology firms did their executives, who were not much oriented toward politics, start looking toward Washington.

In this chapter David Hart examines the three-step organization and politicization of the American high-tech industry, broadly defined. Focusing on the attitudes of the larger-than-life chief executives of firms such as IBM, America Online, and Microsoft, Hart depicts an industry that has not yet developed stable relationships with government institutions. With the rapid rise and decline of corporations, the differing goals of corporate chieftains, and the instability of the high-tech business world, it's no wonder that the "high-tech industry in Washington today is a sprawling array of corporate offices, trade associations, coalitions, lobbying firms, and other entities." Such disarray surely hampers the industry's influence, but it also reflects the underlying energy of an industry just entering adolescence. With great financial resources and an understanding of the importance of information, the high-tech industry will continue to evolve as a political force, even as it strives to exercise influence in the short term.

Two Ways of Seeing Interest Group Politics

On March 3, 1998, William H. Gates III, founder and chief executive officer (CEO) of Microsoft, testified for the first time before a congressional committee. Gates's appearance garnered much media attention, including front page coverage in the national press. Sens. Slade Gorton, R-Wash., and Patty Murray, D-Wash., "struggled to keep up with the Microsoft chief as camera crews and a crowd of onlookers followed him out of the Hart Building."[1] Inside the hearing room Gates sparred with Senate Judiciary Chairman Orrin Hatch, R-Utah, about whether Microsoft had violated the Sherman Antitrust Act. Two of Gates's fiercest rivals and most ardent critics, Scott McNealy, CEO of Sun Microsystems, and James Barksdale, CEO of Netscape Communications, were next to him at the witness table and joined in Hatch's attack. Though undoubtedly good theater, the hearing (like many on Capitol Hill) yielded no new legislation. Nonetheless, it served an important political purpose. It provided Joel Klein, the assistant attorney general in charge of the Justice Department's Antitrust Division, with (as he put it) "a real sense of comfort" in his dogged pursuit of Microsoft, which culminated in the filing of a major lawsuit against the firm two months later.[2]

This brief episode, like many political events, can be understood in two seemingly contradictory ways. From one vantage point—the one that dominated press coverage—Gates's testimony was the result of personal ambitions and rivalries (verging on a crusade on the part of Microsoft's enemies in the eyes of some), tactical maneuvering, and matters of chance. Hatch just happened to represent a state in which two of Microsoft's lesser-known rivals, Novell and WordPerfect, were headquartered. In addition, Hatch was soon to declare his abortive candidacy for the 2000 Republican presidential nomination and was seeking headlines to advance that quest. Gates, for his part, was a computer nerd whose lack of political savvy was the flip side of his technical virtuosity and single-minded dedication to his firm. The world's richest man had once stood aloof from the messy business of politics, but well-connected competitors forced him to get his hands dirty.

From another vantage point, the one favored by most social scientists, Gates's testimony epitomized the inevitable encounter between the high-technology industry and the federal government. Gates personified Microsoft, one of the best-known and fastest-growing firms in an industry that was transforming American society. High-tech products, especially Microsoft's market leading Windows operating system and Office productivity suite for personal computers (PCs), permeated everyday life so deeply that they were bound to make some people and organizations uneasy about a Microsoft-led information revolution. These people and organizations, in turn, were bound to petition their government to take action against the perceived malefactors. And some elements of the government (in this case the Senate Judiciary Committee and the Antitrust Division) were bound to be responsive to these petitions.

The apparent contradiction between the two perspectives lies in the way they relate particular events to larger processes of policymaking and political development. An extreme version of the first perspective would claim that if things hadn't happened just the way they did, everything would be different. That is, if the chairman of the Senate Judiciary Committee were from a different state, the Microsoft suit would never have been filed, and high-tech's most powerful firm would not have evolved into a Washington powerhouse. An equally extreme version of the second perspective would say that this hearing didn't matter, and that the collision between government and the high-tech industry was inevitable.

Less extreme and more measured versions of the two perspectives can be reconciled. It *was* inevitable that the high-tech industry and its leading firm would become important players in policymaking and politics at some point. But the particularities of the testimony placed their stamp on the outcome, too. Gates's combative attitude toward the threat of government action set in motion processes not easily stopped and catalyzed alignments not easily undone. The events of March 3, 1998, will shape the still-unfolding experience of the high-tech industry on the Washington scene.

This chapter tells the story of the high-tech industry's entry into interest group politics over the past three decades through a series of historical episodes. Each episode illustrates broad social processes that were bound in some way to shape that entry. Each episode also illustrates how unpredictable and seemingly trivial matters of personality and timing had significant long-term consequences.

Red and White and (Big) Blue All Over: How IBM Came to Washington

The computer was invented just after World War II to perform esoteric tasks such as designing nuclear weapons. The International Business Machines Corporation (IBM) was largely responsible for popularizing its commercial applications over the next thirty years, much to the surprise of IBM's founder, Thomas Watson Sr., who famously said in 1943 that five computers would be adequate to meet world demand. The firm's dominance became so complete that insiders described the nascent high-tech industry as "IBM and the Seven Dwarves."

By the end of the 1960s IBM had become one of the world's largest and most profitable corporations. As such it was a natural target for the left-leaning movements so important in American politics during that turbulent decade. But the movements' criticism was less intense and less damaging than IBM executives anticipated. Nonetheless, the threat motivated the firm to get involved in Washington in new ways. IBM (and the high-tech industry as a whole) was able to reap the benefits of this involvement without suffering the full wrath of social critics and the regulatory burdens they imposed.

Social science theory suggests that opportunities and threats alike can motivate corporations to begin to lobby policymakers, make campaign contributions, and otherwise behave like interest groups. In practice, threat seems to be the more powerful motive. Threat seizes the attention of executives more readily than opportunity, and they find it more acceptable, ideologically and socially, to take political action to fend off regulation than to claim their share of the pork barrel. Pork still gets distributed—there is no shortage of claimants—but much of American politics is a cascade of threats and responses, a continual "expansion of the scope of conflict."[3] The less powerful in society are threatened by the more powerful. The less powerful take their case to the government, seeking to elicit a counterthreat. And the more powerful follow suit. Because corporations, especially big corporations, tend to be powerful social actors, they are often following suit in politics.

Political opportunity beckoned "Big Blue" (IBM's nickname, thanks to its logo and employees' ubiquitous blue suits) at the height of its power. Both the welfare state and the warfare state, from the Social Security Administration to the Atomic Energy Commission, used computers heavily. Yet IBM's share of the federal market was always far less than its share of the big business market. IBM rarely tried to exert political influence to sell more computers to the government, despite the close relationships between top IBM executives and policymakers.

But IBM did react aggressively to threats from Washington, especially threats supported by social movements. In 1969 the Antitrust Division of the Department of Justice rocked IBM by filing a massive lawsuit against it. Antitrust policymakers acted on behalf of what they perceived to be the public interest in curbing corporate power in market transactions, an idea originated by social movements decades earlier. IBM generated some 50,000 tons of documents in its defense.[4] A few years later, the labor movement flexed its still-substantial muscle by pushing a bill to impose heavy taxes on multinational corporations. The proposal "touched a nerve" at IBM, which generated about half its revenues and profits outside the United States.[5]

Most immediately the social movements of the 1960s, which coalesced into interest groups in the 1970s, went after IBM for its military contracts, its hiring policies, and its presence in South Africa. These threats did not strike at Big Blue's core business the way the antitrust suit and labor union tax bill did. But the new consumer movement championed by Ralph Nader was more dangerous. IBM's top leadership worried that Nader might fan public concern about the massive databases that IBM was building for its customers. In the worst-case scenario the computers could be regulated the way that autos, Nader's first and most famous target, had been.[6]

IBM responded to this array of threats by creating a new corporate function to deal with public policy, which it located in Washington in 1975. This response put IBM in step with its peers—the Fortune 500 descended on the capital in droves during this era to cope with the newly expanded scope of conflict.[7] The high-tech industry was no longer an esoteric preserve of scientists in white lab coats; it was big business. Although the opening of IBM's Washington office was predictable, its style of operation was a little unusual. The distinguishing features owed something to the personalities involved and something to the Nader threat that never materialized.

One key personality, even though he had retired before the office opened, was IBM's Thomas Watson Jr. A lonely liberal Democrat in a sea of Republican CEOs, he proclaimed that public service was a corporate responsibility on par with service to employees, customers, and shareholders. He disliked the way most businesses operated in Washington, telling his successor, Frank Cary, "that probably the worst way [to achieve policy goals] is to have a Washington office staffed with professional lobbyists."[8] Although Cary chose to open a Washington office anyway, he saw that long-time IBM employees, rather than professional lobbyists, worked there. These employees helped pioneer an "issue management" system, which focused on developing expertise rather than the backslapping bonhomie that Watson found objectionable. IBM's corporate policy positions were conventional—free trade, less regulation, lower taxes—but it did a better job than other firms of articulating them. And IBM was more pragmatic, refusing to "fight Vietnams" on minor issues involving ideological principles or special deals for the firm.[9]

The issue management approach fit well with IBM's self-conception and public image as a rational organization. Nonetheless, the IBM Washington office might have stayed relatively small had it not been for the ability of its first director, Charles McKittrick, to cultivate a powerful constituency within the firm. All corporate public policy offices are vulnerable to internal politics, because these offices produce no revenue and their achievements are often arcane, even hidden.[10] McKittrick had impeccable Big Blue credentials and a familiarity with the firm's byzantine internal politics. He insisted on reporting directly to the CEO but carefully maintained his horizontal network of contacts at IBM's Armonk, New York, headquarters. These contacts, combined with his issue managers' Washington policy networks, helped McKittrick identify opportunities for his office to help "clients" within the firm (such as particular product divisions). The reward for this spadework was sustained, steady growth; some one hundred professionals worked for IBM's governmental programs office at its peak in the late 1980s, making it one of the largest corporate offices in the capital.

IBM's immense policy capacity allowed it to cover more issues in greater depth than most of its peers could.[11] Some of the firm's main competitors simply crossed their fingers and let IBM do the talking for the whole high-tech industry.[12] Firms with policy capacity comparable to IBM were typically in industries that faced more serious threats. AT&T, for example, had to cope with perpetual regulatory scrutiny, both before and after it was broken up in 1984. "Big Oil" worried about price controls, energy crises, and Middle East turmoil. Chemical and auto firms bore the brunt of environmental regulation. These firms confronted more skeptical audiences and had less freedom of action in Washington than IBM had.

The experience of other firms weighed on the minds of IBM managers when they decided to enhance their firm's policy capacity. Conditions in the late 1960s and early 1970s were ripe for an attack on IBM comparable to that on General Motors or Dow Chemical. IBM was making it possible for government agencies and large corporations to collect unheard-of amounts of information about ordinary Americans. This information might be used, critics contended, to manipulate and control the public. A large movement built around this issue might well have produced an entirely different, if equally large, IBM public policy organization—one that was much more defensive and constrained than what actually emerged. Ralph Nader, however, never threw himself into this cause, and no other comparable movement leader emerged. Privacy never reached the top of the public agenda in this period. Only a few studies and minor changes in federal law as it pertains to the private sector mark the public record on the issue in the 1960s and 1970s.[13]

IBM, then, emerged as an interest organization in a political environment surprisingly free of rancor. The firm could and did pursue an unusually wide range of policy issues. It built a reputation as an organization of relatively unbiased policy experts. It forged alliances that transcended the ideological and partisan divides that limit many firms and interest groups. This outcome wasn't merely the product of impersonal social forces. People who had real alternatives and could have made different choices were an important factor. IBM's choices in the 1960s and 1970s had long-term consequences not only for IBM but for the high-tech industry as a whole.

The "Fairchildren" Grow Up:
High-Tech Supply Chain Politics

Although IBM still dominated the high-tech industry in the late 1970s and early 1980s, things were starting to change dramatically. The PC revolution was underway and IBM was scrambling to catch up. Despite the perception of some in Washington that *IBM* and *high-tech* were synonymous, the industry had always been more than Big Blue—indeed, the popular history of California's Silicon Valley neglects IBM altogether. The founding fathers in this tale are the "traitorous eight," a group of scientists who left Shockley Semiconductor to found Fairchild Semiconductor in 1957. Fairchild then spawned an array of successful start-ups (known as the "Fairchildren"), including Intel.[14] By the time the PC exploded onto the market the Fairchildren and firms like them were beginning to develop distinctive policy interests. Collectively, they stepped out from IBM's shadow, inventing an unusual style of engagement with Washington. Yet in doing so they built on the foundation laid by IBM.

Like that of IBM, the political mobilization of American semiconductor manufacturing firms was motivated primarily by threat. The threat to semiconductor firms came from Japan rather than from domestic critics. Japanese electronics firms, under the guidance of the powerful Ministry of International Trade and Industry, were rapidly overtaking their American competitors, particularly in the market for dynamic random access memory chips (DRAMs). Unlike the consumer movement, Japanese competition did not threaten the high-tech industry uniformly. In fact, firms that bought DRAMs, such as PC manufacturers, benefited from competition between Japanese and American DRAM producers, at least in the short run. But the American producers, especially merchant producers like Fairchild and Intel, were driven near bankruptcy. ("Merchant" producers sell their products on the open market; "captive" producers, to be discussed later, are fully owned subsidiaries that supply their sister divisions within a vertically integrated electronics company.) Merchant producers supplied most of the energy and resources that made the Semiconductor Industry Association (SIA) into a force to be reckoned with in policymaking within a decade of its founding in 1977.

Social scientists would see this political mobilization as unsurprising, and not merely because threat played a crucial role. The growth and increasing complexity of the high-tech industry made it inevitable that an increasingly diverse set of interest organizations would represent the industry.[15] Specialized suppliers of high-tech components, for instance, were bound to have different preferences on some issues than firms that assembled those components into computers. Vertically integrated firms that encompassed the entire high-tech "food chain"—from captive chip manufacturing to computer assembly facilities—would have yet another set of views. Once any one of these groups became large enough or felt intensely enough about something, it would seek to voice its own positions. From this perspective the rise of Japanese competition simply triggered a predetermined process.

Seeking representation, of course, does not automatically mean finding it. Any "latent" interest group in society must overcome the "collective action problem," as Mancur Olson argued in 1965.[16] Social science researchers inspired by Olson explain that semiconductor manufacturers were able to organize because of the small number of elite firms, their close proximity to one another in Silicon Valley, and the shared technical background of their leadership.[17] Their counterparts in the PC manufacturing business had more trouble. These firms were scattered around the country, and many of their CEOs had never met one another. It was not until a new trade policy advocated by SIA went into effect in 1986 and chip prices rose significantly that PC makers managed to put together the Computer Systems Policy Project to serve as a counterweight to SIA in Washington.[18]

SIA's effectiveness, however, was not just a result of its intrinsic advantages. It benefited from good timing, too. By the time SIA hit its stride, Japanese competition had already swept through major sectors of American industry, such as autos and steel, setting off fierce political debates. The demise of these "sunset" industries could be understood as the natural working of the free market, moving labor-intensive production to places where labor was cheap. But this logic did not work for capital-intensive high-tech products. Even Ronald Reagan could rationalize government intervention in the semiconductor case. Beyond the merits of the case, Reagan's administration was motivated by partisan competition. The "Atari Democrats" were trying to use the semiconductor trade issue and others like it to undermine the Republican hold on the business community (Atari was a pioneering manufacturer of video games). The high-tech industry was a particularly promising target for these Democrats, because (unlike autos and steel) it symbolized the future and was unattached to any partisan camp.[19]

SIA's tactical choices were as important as its timing. One decision was to build a coalition with vertically integrated electronics firms, including IBM, Digital Equipment, and Hewlett-Packard, temporarily denying a similar coalition to semiconductor buyers one step down the food chain. The vertically integrated firms had ambiguous interests in the semiconductor trade issue. As producers of chips they feared Japanese control of chipmaking equipment, a vital input one step further up the food chain. As buyers of chips they welcomed the quality improvements and price cuts Japanese suppliers made. Aggressive outreach by SIA helped to persuade these firms not merely to become members and to bring their corporate positions in line with SIA, but to head off any opposition that might emerge from broader high-tech industry groups in which PC makers were represented. The coalition "deprived us of a forum," according to the Washington representative of Compaq, a rapidly growing PC maker based in Houston, Texas.[20]

Another of SIA's tactical decisions was to locate its headquarters in Silicon Valley and not in Washington. This decision helped perpetuate the perception among policymakers that high-tech was not a Washington "special interest." Policymakers, especially in recent times, have perceived outsiders to be less self-interested and therefore more likely to be aligned with the national interest. Although perhaps not entirely disinterested, high-tech (as represented by SIA) seemed to stand for the national interest in the face of the Japanese economic threat, just as General Motors had seemed to stand for the national interest in the face of the Soviet threat during the cold war.[21] That is not to say that SIA was out of touch with or unable to affect goings-on in the capital. SIA made heavy use of the well-connected and highly skilled Washington law firm of Dewey Ballantine to keep its members informed.[22] If SIA's decision to locate 3,000 miles west of Washington exacted a cost, it was outweighed not only by the enhancement of high-tech's symbolic association with the national interest but also by the ease with which the association could mobilize and deploy its most vital assets, the CEOs of its member firms.

Direct participation by senior executives was SIA's signature tactic. CEOs founded the group and stayed involved.[23] As IBM's Watson Jr. had contended, high-tech CEOs were often extremely effective lobbyists, able to get the support of policymakers who might brush off other professional lobbyists. The CEOs' commitment symbolized the importance of the policy issue at hand. Moreover, SIA's most effective lobbyists were not merely top managers, they were entrepreneurs who had built exceptional firms.

Intel cofounder Robert Noyce was the leading example. Hardly a typical nerd, Noyce was socially graceful and technically brilliant. He commanded attention. Intel hired its first dedicated public policy staff person in 1983, largely to ensure that Intel and SIA realized Noyce's value in Washington. According to David Yoffie of the Harvard Business School, "Noyce spent 20 percent of his time during the early 1980s on political action." In 1988, with Intel's blessing, he became the first CEO of Sematech, a government-subsidized semiconductor research and development consortium that SIA advocated to complement the U.S.–Japan Semiconductor Trade Arrangement.[24]

In trade and technology policy, then, SIA won big victories in the 1980s. It did so by making shrewd decisions that made the most of the tight-knit Silicon Valley community. SIA exploited and maintained high-tech's reputation as a public-spirited industry unbeholden to an ideology or political party. Yet in so doing, SIA also contributed to the fragmentation of high-tech representation in Washington. This fragmentation was predestined; barriers to collective action among like-minded segments of the industry were bound to fall as long as the available resources continued to grow. But SIA's specific tactics were important too, providing a model of representation that could be imitated and motivating firms that disagreed with SIA's positions to take action. The Computer Systems Policy Project, a CEO forum created by PC makers, illustrates the sincerest form of flattery at work in high-tech interest group politics.

Resistance Is Futile:
Microsoft Adapts to Washington

At the beginning of the 1990s high-tech was a discernible presence in American interest group politics. IBM's public policy office had a staff that could handle almost any issue, and a growing array of high-tech firms like Apple and Oracle had opened their own smaller Washington shops. The list of high-tech trade associations was growing, but many in the high-tech policy community doubted that the industry's representation was keeping pace with its growing importance in the economy. The late Eben Tisdale, who ran Hewlett-Packard's Washington office, famously quipped that the industry had "deep pockets and short arms."[25]

Microsoft, for example, did not open a Washington office until 1995 despite surpassing its rivals in the PC software business and joining the ranks of the Fortune 500 in 1988. Even then Microsoft's interest in Washington lagged far behind Washington's interest in Microsoft. Not until about the time of Bill Gates's appearance before Orrin Hatch, some seven years after Gates learned that antitrust prosecutors were investigating his firm, did Microsoft become serious, perhaps too serious, about making its mark in the capital. The lag between the external threat to the firm and its exaggerated reaction reflects the barriers to political involvement that face any entrepreneurial firm but also the particularities of Gates and the firm he built.

The most common barrier to a typical start-up's involvement in Washington is the collective action problem. Any small, young firm has little chance of determining a policy debate or an election, so the firm has little incentive to take political action on its own.[26] Not surprising, Microsoft's initial forays into public policy, like those of the Fairchildren, came through trade associations that mustered industrywide campaigns on vital issues. In 1988, for example, just thirteen years after Microsoft was established and only two years after its initial public offering (IPO) of stock, Microsoft helped to found the Business Software Association (BSA) to combat software piracy, a problem that hit its bottom line directly.

Another barrier confronting start-ups thinking about entering the political marketplace is the fixed cost of Washington representation. A firm that wants a representative independent of trade associations must hire and support professional staff or cover the retainer for an outside lobbying firm. Although a modest $100,000 government affairs budget might plant a firm's flag in the capital and lie unnoticed on the firm's balance sheet, such an investment is unlikely to yield benefits beyond keeping corporate leadership apprised of current events. A million-dollar Washington office, on the other hand, would produce much greater visibility within the Beltway, but at the same time might be perceived at headquarters as a significant cost for a firm with sales of $100 million a year in a highly competitive industry. Microsoft surpassed $100 million in sales before its 1986 IPO and reached $1 billion by 1990. Cost alone seems unlikely to have stood in the way had the firm wanted independent representation in Washington before the late 1990s.

A bigger obstacle for Microsoft might have been a lack of executive attention to politics and policy. Entrepreneurs may fail to engage in public policy debates not because they think the costs of such engagement exceed the benefits, but because they are busy tending their businesses. Gates's single-minded focus on building Microsoft is legendary. *Star Trek* fans among his adversaries portray Microsoft as the Borg, assimilating everything in its path. Washington was for a long while just one of many potential distractions that Gates ignored while he laid waste to his corporate competition. At the time that his firm first came under antitrust investigation in 1991, for example, Gates viewed Apple's lawsuit alleging that Windows infringed on the Mac OS copyright as a much more serious external threat.[27] Microsoft won that case, relegated Apple to the margins of the high-tech industry, and continued its extraordinary growth in the following decade, surpassing $5 billion in sales in 1995 on the way to more than $20 billion in 2000.

To say that Gates ignored public policy for many years is not to say that he was ignorant of it. His parents were involved in public causes, and Gates served as a U.S. Senate page as a teenager. As policy issues increasingly intruded on Gates's growing business during the 1990s, he displayed a willingness to lend his name and his firm's name to efforts to address them. Gates and Microsoft took an interest in government control of encryption software as early as 1991, for example, and in the privatization of the Internet two years later. He made personal contacts at the highest levels of the federal government during the Clinton administration, including the president himself, Vice President Al Gore, and Speaker of the House Newt Gingrich.[28]

Yet like IBM's Tom Watson Jr. before him, Gates chose not to build much of an organizational structure to manage government affairs for Microsoft. As late as October 1997, *Roll Call*, the Capitol Hill newspaper, reported that "Gates still remains virtually invisible in Washington."[29] With only a tiny office in the capital to focus and amplify Gates's modest personal involvement in the policy process—and to attend to the myriad details below Gates's job description—Microsoft remained a "Washington wimp."[30] The decision to minimize Microsoft's Washington involvement (which Gates referred to as "some overhead" in a 1995 interview) was based at least in part on his interpretation of IBM's experience under Watson's successors.[31] In Gates's view IBM had paid too much attention to Washington and not enough to the fast-moving business it was in. The effort that made the "Incredible Bunch of Morons" (as Microsoftees nicknamed IBM) successful in Washington, Gates thought, contributed to its demise as the high-tech industry's dominant business.[32]

To many policymakers, though, Microsoft's aloofness implied that the firm "held Washington in disdain."[33] Microsoft's competitors worked hard to deepen this perception. Fear and loathing of Microsoft and Gates convinced high-tech entrepreneurs like Sun's Scott McNealy and Oracle's Larry Ellison of the wisdom of investing in a Washington presence. They hired high-profile figures not previously associated with the high-tech industry, such as Supreme Court nominee Robert Bork and former Senate minority leader Robert Dole, to spread their message. Oracle even hired an investigator to go through the trash of Microsoft-friendly groups in 1999.[34]

This campaign made it more likely that powerful decisionmakers would endorse Assistant Attorney General Joel Klein's professional judgment about prosecuting Microsoft. From the perspective of Microsoft's critics and competitors, government investigations and filings in the early and mid-1990s had produced meager results. The suit lodged in May 1998 represented a major expansion of the scope and objectives of the federal case, alleging a pattern of illegal practices aimed at maintaining and extending Microsoft's monopoly in PC operating systems.

In late 1997 and early 1998, with the threat of another antitrust case looming, Gates joined the political arms race with his competitors in earnest. Microsoft separated its public policy office from its Washington sales office in March 1998 and increased its professional staff from two in 1997 to at least ten by early 1999. The firm dramatically expanded its list of consultants, thereby building its connections to both parties and most of the major presidential candidates. Reported lobbying expenditures rose from $2 million in 1997 to nearly $4 million in 1998 and $5 million in 1999. Contributions to candidates by Microsoft's political action committee quadrupled between 1995 and 1998 and then again in 1999–2000. Soft money contributions from company funds zoomed from $80,000 to $800,000 to more than $900,000.[35] Microsoft pushed its policy proposals with advertising, supported existing interest groups and helped create new ones, conducted polls, made politically significant charitable contributions, and otherwise deployed the full panoply of instruments available to the sophisticated and well-funded Washington corporate player.[36]

The return that Microsoft received on this investment remains hotly debated. Some of the firm's most heavy-handed moves backfired. The firm lobbied to cut the Antitrust Division's appropriation and reaped criticism even from its allies. "'That might have been the dumbest political move of the year,' said a senior [congressional] leadership aide."[37] Members of prominent Republican Ralph Reed's political consulting firm lobbied Republican presidential candidate George W. Bush on Microsoft's behalf, forcing Reed, who consulted for Bush as well as Microsoft, to make a highly public statement of regret about the apparent conflict of interest. Blasted for arrogance when it had appeared to ignore Washington, Microsoft went so far in the other direction that it was blasted again. Among candidates and consultants, the firm was said to be something of a cash cow that heedlessly dumped money into the capital.[38]

Slowly, though, the tenor of the discussion began to change. In April 2000 the *New York Times* reported that Gates was "treated . . . as a national treasure" in his meetings with the leadership of both parties in Congress and the president.[39] Microsoft was increasingly viewed as an upstanding corporate citizen taking its rightful place in policy discussions relevant to the high-tech industry, such as education and the digital divide. The election in 2000 of a new administration not wedded to the 1998 antitrust case raised the prospect that Microsoft might receive the biggest payoff of all: settlement of the case on lenient terms and without a breakup of the firm.[40] Such an outcome would not be a result of Microsoft "assimilating" Washington as it had its adversaries in the business world. The reverse was closer to the truth: Bill Gates and his crew had adapted to Washington.

Instant Interest Groups: The New Economy Converges with Old Politics

By the time *United States v. Microsoft* reached its climax, some tech-savvy pundits were arguing that the case was already irrelevant. The Windows-dependent PC was being supplanted, they claimed, by a multitude of Internet access devices. Even if Microsoft had merited government scrutiny for exercising monopoly power in the 1990s, at the end of the millennium technological tides were sweeping that power away. These claims are far from proven; the irrelevance of Microsoft's business behavior to the twenty-first century economy remains speculative. The firm's political experience, along with that of IBM and the semiconductor industry before it, however, is undoubtedly highly relevant to twenty-first century politics. The "New Economy" of the Internet era has been joining the high-tech chorus in Washington at warp speed.[41] Some leaders of the New Economy have drawn on the legacies and lessons of the past, while others have reenacted the learning processes of their forerunners, including Bill Gates.

These nascent experiences demonstrate once more the parallel importance of social science principles and quirks of personality and chance in understanding interest group politics. Two experiences in particular, those of the Technology Network (known as TechNet) and America Online (AOL), will stand in here for the sprawling and still unfinished story of "Washington Meets the New Economy." Both feature high-tech business celebrities, John Doerr and Steve Case, whose choices shaped organizations and events. Both also illustrate broader processes beyond individual control.

Threats figure centrally in the story. William Lerach, a San Diego trial lawyer made rich by suits against firms with volatile stock prices, was the threat that mobilized TechNet. In 1996 Lerach pressed a California ballot initiative (Proposition 211) that would have made such suits easier to win. John Doerr, a venture capitalist specializing in Internet start-ups, convened Silicon Valley's opponents of Proposition 211, who quickly raised some $40 million for an advertising blitz that defeated the measure.[42]

AOL also faced a potential legal threat in 1996. New federal legislation made Internet service providers like AOL liable for offensive content, such as pornography, that passed through their networks. AOL CEO

Steve Case believed that this rule would thwart AOL's growth, and his firm joined the fight that eventually nullified the legislation in the Supreme Court in 1997.

Two different processes figured prominently in the next parts of this story. The law of supply and demand affected TechNet, and money was the commodity in question. Modern political campaigns demanded more and more of it, and the Proposition 211 campaign suggested that Silicon Valley coffers engorged by the Internet boom might supply it. Thus in 1997 TechNet, as the Silicon Valley opponents of Proposition 211 renamed themselves, adopted as its primary function brokering donations from wealthy New Economy executives to candidates, along the way raising candidates' awareness of issues important to the executives. Building on the industry's tradition, TechNet hosted members of both political parties. No longer seriously threatened by trial lawyers, TechNet, like IBM in its heyday, was free to pursue many opportunities. The Achilles heel of this strategy, though, was TechNet's lack of clarity about which opportunities deserved the highest priority and what it wanted to do about them. Like Microsoft, TechNet seems to have acquired a reputation as a fountain of cash that required few commitments from the recipients.[43]

AOL's political development reflects the inevitable influence of government regulation. The core of its business was not the silicon, code, or computer systems of previous generations of high-tech firms; it was communication. The communications industry, including the postal system, telephony, broadcasting, and some forms of publishing—all of which paralleled activities facilitated electronically by AOL—is regulated by the government (or owned by the government in the case of the U.S. Postal Service). Regulated industries tend to be heavily represented in the policy process because their profits depend on government decisions.[44]

Even though the regulations that would apply to Internet service providers were unclear as AOL came to dominate the business in the late 1990s, AOL understood that it would confront in some fashion the Federal Communications Commission and the politically powerful industries that AOL's services threatened to supplant. By the time AOL reached *Fortune*'s list of the 1,000 largest firms in the United States in 1996, it had already opened a Washington office with at least four professional staff, with leadership drawn from the communications industry.[45] Within a couple of years AOL had moved from defense to offense, pushing initiatives across the country to force politically powerful local telephone and cable television monopolies to offer AOL's services through their networks at high speed. Cognates to AOL's "open access" campaign appeared in regulated industries from financial services to retailing, as Internet start-ups attempted to crack the legal protections that benefited entrenched incumbents throughout the economy.[46]

AOL and TechNet responded to forces that social science theory highlights, such as the law of supply and demand for campaign finance and the political importance of regulation, but some aspects of their development were quite unpredictable, stemming largely from leadership. Doerr was essential to the formation and growth of TechNet. As the financial midwife to a string of successful high-tech start-ups, punctuated by the record-shattering IPO of Netscape in 1995, Doerr had unparalleled clout and an awesome reputation in Silicon Valley. His commitment to TechNet helped make political involvement fashionable among Internet entrepreneurs, and that drew politicians from former vice president Gore on down to TechNet like bees to honey.

Yet Doerr, like Bill Gates, did not want to adapt to Washington. He talked about radically reinventing politics and basked in the media limelight ("Gore-Doerr 2004" buttons were seen at some TechNet events), but his organization had little capacity to enact policy changes and was reluctant to share credit with organizations that did. Journalist Sara Miles characterized TechNet's political strategy as "both wildly overambitious and strangely shapeless."[47] In catalyzing Silicon Valley's money and prestige, Doerr filled a major gap in the high-tech industry's Washington portfolio. Yet TechNet also added a new dimension to the industry's political fragmentation.

Although Steve Case is as prominent in the New Economy as John Doerr and Bill Gates, his political style (and that of his firm) is very different. Case evinces little interest in ignoring, refashioning, or conquering Washington. He plays an "inside strategy," leaving AOL (in the estimation of Rep. Billy Tauzin, R-La.) ahead of the "Silicon Valley boys."[48] Although a video game enthusiast in his youth, Case never imbibed the ingrown culture of the computer nerd. He received a degree in political science and worked for consumer giants Procter and Gamble and Pizza Hut before joining AOL's precursor in 1983. His firm is headquartered just outside Washington, D.C. All of these factors seem to make him more sensitive to political threat and opportunity than his West Coast colleagues.

The same factors also make him less of an idealist (or zealot, depending on one's point of view) than many in the high-tech industry. Or to put it another way, he is a very pragmatic businessman. Take AOL's acquisition of Time Warner in 2000. Time Warner operated many of the local cable television monopolies that AOL had been attacking in its open access campaign. The acquisition gave AOL the opportunity to be the sole Internet service provider on Time Warner's cable systems or to bargain with other large cable operators to exchange access and shut out all other competitors. Open access was no longer a business necessity. Although AOL denied media reports that it changed its position on open access in the wake of the acquisition, the firm's critics claimed that it dramatically scaled back support for the campaign it had once spearheaded.[49] As a condition for approving the merger, the Federal Communications Commission and the Federal Trade Commission required AOL Time Warner to open its cable systems to competing Internet service providers. But it is very difficult for regulators to ensure that AOL Time Warner is actually treating its competitors identically to AOL. And there are many ways, both technological and financial, that the firm can subtly thwart the intent of this requirement.

AOL and TechNet point to diverging paths forward for the New Economy in Washington. AOL bought into the old politics of the Washington interest group system as soon as it could, far ahead of the rest of the New Economy. As AOL Time Warner it has gone even further, leaving the New Economy behind and becoming a giant in the old politics. AOL Time Warner is an immense multimedia entertainment conglomerate. Along with Time Warner's cable systems, AOL acquired television networks, movie studios, magazines, and much more, including the fleets of lawyers and lobbyists that make such a firm tick.

By contrast, TechNet remains committed rhetorically to its motto, "new politics for a new economy." CEOs of Silicon Valley start-ups still figure significantly on its membership list, and it still emphasizes personal outreach by its members to both Democrats and Republicans. In practice, though, the old politics is creeping in. TechNet named former congressman Rick White (whose old district included Microsoft's headquarters in Redmond, Washington) as its fourth CEO in January 2001 and its first from outside the high-tech industry. The organization also beefed up its capacity to influence Congress by starting new chapters in high-tech hotspots around the country and by hiring a larger staff of policy experts.

Critical Path: The Future of High-Tech Industry Politics

The high-tech industry in Washington today is a sprawling array of corporate offices, trade associations, coalitions, lobbying firms, and other entities. This representation reflects the continual expansion of the underlying industry. The industry's "arms" may still be a bit short, but they are "growing," as Hewlett-Packard's Tisdale put it in 1997.[50] The enduring image of the industry as a collection of politically naive nerds, which still crops up regularly in the press, is largely obsolete. In IBM's case the image is decades out of date. A series of threats catalyzed the high-tech industry's involvement in national politics, and since then the industry's Washington representatives have found new opportunities to stay involved. Indeed, some members of the high-tech interest group community are as sophisticated as any in the capital.

But the fragmentation of this community also reflects the underlying industry. High technology is an extremely complicated and highly turbulent business; its policy interests are diverse and sometimes transient. Threats have more often divided than united the industry. The lack of a common enemy has been a blessing, freeing the industry from inflexible alliances, but also a curse, permitting organizations to multiply in abundance.

A clever social scientist might have predicted these broad outlines of high-tech's political profile, but the particulars are highly contingent and very important. For every Steve Case willing to work the political system for all it is worth, there is a Bill Gates who wishes it would go away and then has to make up for lost time. Such differences in the behavior of key decisionmakers contribute to variation in the level and quality of representation across the industry and over time. Similar differences also perpetuate the diversity of the high-tech association scene. Members of the high-tech interest group community disagree not only about policy issues but about tactics, such as the value of TechNet's fund-raising prowess. High-tech association start-ups have been common, and exits, whether by merger or disbandment, have been few.

The high-tech industry has had the good fortune of coming to political maturity in an era in which the Democratic Party sought a business constituency. Lacking unions and perceived as environmentally friendly, the high-tech industry was a prime candidate. It has effectively exploited partisan competition for its affections, which became especially ardent in the Internet boom years of the late 1990s, when the industry brought not only conventional political resources to its allies but a special magic. The image of the politically naive nerd found an equally exaggerated counterpart in this period: high-tech as "belle of the ball" or even "the new conquerers."[51]

The boom of the 1990s is over, but its reverberations continue. The high-tech industry's interest groups may well go through a shakeout, with the identity of the surviving organizations and the personalities of the key decisionmakers within them shaping the industry's political development over the longer term. But predicting these consequences is impossible. Social science is not going to put journalists out of business in this realm. One can say for certain only that the growth and diversification of the industry will continue despite occasional setbacks, and these changes will be reflected, after a lag, in Washington. The industry's dynamism will provoke threats that both unite and divide it. This dynamism will also provide opportunities for policy entrepreneurs to create new interest organizations and new issue domains and for partisans to construct new alignments of support. The disruptive force of the high-tech industry has only begun to be felt in interest group politics.

Notes

1. Juliana Gruenwald, "Microsoft Hearing Explores Whether Antitrust Laws Need Upgrade," *Congressional Quarterly Weekly Report*, March 7, 1998, 558–559.
2. John Heilemann, "The Truth, the Whole Truth, and Nothing But the Truth: The Untold Story of the Microsoft Case," *Wired*, November 2000, 260–311, quote from 278.
3. E.E. Schattschneider, *The Semi-Sovereign People* (New York: Holt, Rinehart and Winston, 1960).

4. John Opel, speech to Outside Attorneys Dinner, March 23, 1982, John Opel papers, IBM Archives.
5. Leslie D. Simon, interview by the author, May 14, 1999.
6. Frank Cary, speech, March 11, 1970, Frank Cary papers, IBM Archives.
7. David Vogel, *Fluctuating Fortunes* (New York: Basic, 1989); Mark A. Smith, *American Business and Political Power: Public Opinion, Elections, and Democracy* (Chicago: University of Chicago, 2000).
8. Transcript, IBM Annual Meeting, April 27, 1970, IBM archives, 10; Thomas J. Watson Jr. and Peter Petre, *Father, Son, and Company* (New York: Bantam, 1990), 427.
9. Quote from Charles E. McKittrick Jr., interview by the author, February 10, 1999.
10. Rogan T. Kersh, "Corporate Lobbyists and Their Clients: Beyond Principal-Agent Theory" (paper presented at the annual meeting of the Midwest Political Science Association, Chicago, Ill., April 2001).
11. This term originates with Cathie Jo Martin, "Mandating Social Change: The Business Struggle over National Health Reform," *Governance* 10 (4): 397–428 (1997).
12. Bruce Holbein, interview by the author, April 21, 1999.
13. Whitfield Diffie and Susan Landau, *Privacy on the Line: The Politics of Wiretapping and Encryption* (Cambridge: MIT, 1998), 125–137.
14. Gordon Moore (with Kevin Davis), "Learning the Silicon Valley Way," Center for Research on Employment and Economic Growth, Stanford University, July 28, 2000.
15. The classic source of this "pluralist" perspective is David Truman, *The Governmental Process: Political Interests and Public Opinion* (New York: Knopf, 1951).
16. Mancur Olson, *The Logic of Collective Action* (Cambridge: Harvard University, 1965).
17. Philip A. Mundo, *Interest Groups: Cases and Characteristics* (Chicago: Nelson-Hall, 1992), 41–66; Mark L. Busch and Eric Reinhardt, "Geography, Trade, and Political Mobilization in U.S. Industries," *American Journal of Political Science* 44 (4): 703–719 (2000).
18. Whether the policy shift caused the price rise is still a touchy subject. The issue is examined at length in Kenneth Flamm, *Mismanaged Trade?: Strategic Policy and the Semiconductor Industry* (Washington, D.C.: Brookings, 1996).
19. James E. Shoch, *Trading Blows: Party Competition and U.S. Trade Policy in a Globalizing Era* (Chapel Hill: University of North Carolina, 2001).
20. David B. Yoffie, "How an Industry Builds Political Advantage," *Harvard Business Review* 66 (May–June 1988): 82–89; Douglas A. Irwin, "Trade Politics and the Semiconductor Industry," in *The Political Economy of American Trade Policy*, ed. Anne O. Krueger (Chicago: University of Chicago, 1996), 11–72; Joe Tasker, interview by the author, December 1, 1999.
21. "What's good for the country is good for General Motors and vice-versa," General Motors CEO Charles Wilson during a congressional hearing considering his appointment as secretary of defense in 1953.
22. Andrew Procassini, *Competitors in Alliance* (Westport, Conn.: Quorum, 1995), 189.
23. In the case of captive producers, the head of the semiconductor division substituted for the CEO.
24. Yoffie, *How an Industry Builds*, 88; George Scalise, interview by the author, July 14, 1998; Michael Maibach, interview by the author, June 15, 2000.
25. Eben Tisdale, interview by the author, July 14, 1998. Tisdale had been using this line for years before this interview.
26. Olson, *Collective Action;* Kevin W. Hula, *Lobbying Together: Interest Group Coalitions and Legislative Politics* (Washington, D.C.: Georgetown University, 1999); John de Figueiredo and Emerson H. Tiller, "Organizing and Engaging in Nonmarket Activity: A Transactional Analysis of Corporate Lobbying at the FCC" (paper presented at the annual Meeting of the American Political Science Association, Washington, D.C., September 1999).

27. Ken Auletta, *World War 3.0: Microsoft and Its Enemies* (New York: Random House, 2001), 150–151.

28. See, for instance, Ruth Marcus, "Clintons Vacate Capital for Martha's Vineyard II; President Jogs 4 Miles, Golfs 18 Holes," *Washington Post*, August 28, 1994, A14.

29. Juliet Eilperin, "High-Tech Lobbying: Microsoft Steps Up Effort," *Roll Call*, October 27, 1997.

30. W. John Moore, "Ganging Up on Microsoft," *National Journal*, February 7, 1998, 301.

31. "Mind Behind the Microsoft Miracle," *Washington Post*, December 3, 1995, H1.

32. Heilemann, "The Truth", 273–274.

33. Ben Wildavsky and Neil Munro, "Culture Clash," *National Journal*, May 16, 1998, 1104. Senate Commerce Committee policy director Mark Buse is the source of the quote.

34. John Markoff and Matt Richtel, "Oracle Hired a Detective Agency to Investigate Microsoft's Allies," *New York Times*, June 28, 2000, A1. The details of Microsoft's opposition's campaign can be found in Heilemann, "The Truth"; and Wendy Goldman Rohm, *The Microsoft File: The Secret Case Against Bill Gates* (New York: Times Books, 1998).

35. These figures are drawn from the Center for Responsive Politics' database compiled from Federal Election Committee reports. The center reports that Microsoft and its employees contributed about $4.3 million in soft money, PAC, and individual contributions in 1999–2000 (*Capital Eye*, winter 2001, 5). My figures exclude individual contributions, because these may or may not be coordinated with the corporate strategy. Bill Gates has made very modest individual contributions.

36. Front page stories in major newspapers that cover many of these points include Rajiv Chandrasekaran and John Mintz, "Microsoft's Window of Influence: Intensive Lobbying Aims to Neutralize Antitrust Efforts," *Washington Post*, May 7, 1999, A1; James V. Grimaldi, "Microsoft Mounting a Well-Funded Lobby Effort," *Washington Post*, May 17, 2000, A1; and John M. Broder, "Microsoft Tries Another Court: Public Opinion," *New York Times*, June 12, 2000, A1.

37. Jim Vandehei, "Microsoft Plans to Boost Lobbying Presence on Hill," *Roll Call*, November 11, 1999.

38. Hanna Rosin, "Mining Microsoft," *New Republic*, June 8, 1998, 12–13.

39. Marc Lacey and Eric Schmitt, "Gates Keeps Washington Dates," *New York Times*, April 6, 2000, D1.

40. I do not mean to imply that the facts and law of the case have no bearing on its outcome, only that political considerations are likely to play some role.

41. In this essay *New Economy* encompasses any good or service sold over or provided through the Internet and firms founded to do business in this fashion.

42. Chris Watts, "Proposition 211," Stanford University, Graduate School of Business case S-P-23, October 1997.

43. Jeffrey H. Birnbaum, *The Money Men* (New York: Crown, 2000), 217.

44. George Stigler and Claire Friedland, "What Can Regulators Regulate? The Case of Electricity," *Journal of Law and Economics* 5 (1): 1–16 (1962).

45. Graeme Browning, "Bill Burrington: Pushing Team Spirit in Cyberspace," *National Journal*, November 25, 1995, 2933.

46. Robert D. Atkinson, "Revenge of the Disintermediated: How the Middleman is Fighting E-Commerce and Hurting Consumers," Progressive Policy Institute, Washington, D.C., January 26, 2001.

47. Sara Miles, *How To Hack a Party Line: The Democrats and Silicon Valley* (New York: Farrar, Straus, & Giroux, 2001), 70.

48. Neil Munro, "Building a Case," *National Journal*, July 31, 1999, 2218–2225.

49. Alec Klein, "Access Issue Isn't Open-and-Shut Case," *Washington Post*, September 20, 2000, G5.
50. W. John Moore, "A Hard Drive in Washington," *National Journal*, September 27, 1997, 1906.
51. Lizette Alvarez, "High-Tech Industry, Long Shy of Politics, Is Now the Belle of Ball," *New York Times*, December 26, 1999, A1; Neil Munro, "The New Conquerors," *National Journal*, October 2, 1999, 2796–2799.

15

Exchange Theory and the Institutional Impetus for Interest Group Formation

William P. Browne

Sometimes we can learn more by looking to the past than by trying to parse out the future. In this chapter William Browne goes back to Arthur Bentley, the academic "father" of interest group scholarship, to explore how groups emerge from a complex set of political and economic conditions. For Bentley and other scholars, such as Robert Salisbury, the concept of "exchange" among groups (and between groups and the government) is central to understanding how and why groups form and why they lobby Congress. Moreover, Bentley's formulations link politics directly to group actions, in contrast to economist Mancur Olson's focus on individual self-interest.

Browne spins a tale of two groups—the slightly fictionalized Dumpers Defense League and the Forest Users Defense League—that form in response to U.S. Forest Service rules that upset the status quo (or "equilibrium") in access to water supplies. Browne demonstrates that the decision to engage in group politics depends on the actions of the government and other political interests. Interest groups define themselves, pool resources, frame issues, seek to influence decisions, and more, all while assessing whether their actions are worth the time and money invested.

At the heart of all these decisions and activity, Browne argues, lies a series of exchanges, all framed by contingencies and imperfect information about costs and benefits. In short, interest group politics reflect a human process in which exchanges involving individuals, groups, corporations, and government agencies create relationships that both produce outcomes and provide the context for change.

This chapter is for Robert H. Salisbury for all the obvious reasons: theorist, teacher, and friend.

Where do interest groups come from? Or, put differently, how do they form? In this chapter we'll explore these questions through a fictionalized but procedurally accurate tale about how an environmental issue—dumping toxic waste in national forests—prompted businesses to form an interest group to fend off government action. But surely business organizations are a bit of a bore, so we'll pretend that a second, citizen-supported, interest group also formed to help government defend its extensive forestlands. The give and take between the two organizations suggests two important points in how scholars view interest group formation. First, interest group members want to influence government decisions. Second, government and its policies are the catalysts for interest group formation. Our tale then, relative to our central question of how interest groups form, suggests that big government may lead to the creation of many interest groups—and not the other way around.[1]

Prologue: The Bumpy Road of Interest Group Studies

The study of interest groups winds a tortuous path through the scholarly wilderness, to the point that its origins have remained murky. Arthur F. Bentley, a multidisciplinary scholar and apple farmer, is generally regarded as the field's founding father.[2] Bentley's groundbreaking, but oft-ignored, 1908 book, *The Process of Government*, was a critique of government scholars—scholars whose work was once described as "bloodless and boring."[3] Well into the 1950s political science largely emphasized "legalistic descriptions of formal rules."[4] Bentley had become frustrated with endless institutional descriptions of laws and regulations, the tying together of such rules into public policies, and the resulting structure of government organizations. In a sense, Bentley asked: Where was the politics, those actions that really provided for the laws, regulations, policies, and organizations? Bentley wanted to know why decisions were made the way they were. So he proposed a methodology to determine the reasons behind the decisions.

Bentley's methods emphasized discovering the process of government and politics.[5] For him, a process was the collection of all the separate actions that led to a unique public decision or a policy outcome. He proposed that students of process look for those actions and, most important, who participated in them. These participants were actors in what Bentley called an *interest*. He also labeled them collectively as a *group*, which meant the same thing as an interest. By using this terminology Bentley became, somewhat by accident, the founder of modern interest group scholarship.

But Bentley was not writing about what we now know as interest groups. To him an interest (or group) included actors in the public (or institutional) and private sectors trying to influence government, as well as those who pay close attention to these attempts (the attentive public).

His "interest" included those in favor and those opposed to the decision, or everyone who was interested and took action accordingly. Bentley's message was straightforward: pay attention to the group's actions, ascertain motives, explain what happened politically—all within the overall process. And do not just examine the end product, be it law, policy, or governmental agency.

Bentley had little scholarly impact in his day, and most academics continued to approach politics from an institutional framework. In 1951 political scientist David Truman published *The Governmental Process*, an explicit reference to Bentley's work.[6] Truman aimed to explain the components of the "process of government" as they were influenced by some elements of Bentley's interests. Truman observed that identifiable interest groups from the private sector formed to lobby the government. These interest groups, which shared common characteristics or values, consciously banded together to obtain a specific governmental decision. In other words, they engaged in collective action. And each occupied a place in the governing process, which Truman, like Bentley, argued should be the most central subject of inquiry. Earlier academics, who seldom knew of Bentley, had written of Truman's interest groups as little more than questionable, even illegitimate, political actors. These unholy "pressure groups" were ordinarily portrayed as little more than aberrant collectives that, from outside the government, pursued their own selfish policy preferences.[7]

Truman placed lobbying and other actions of interest groups within a piece of Bentley's comprehensive concept of process. But Truman did not portray government personnel as part of Bentley's interest, or his group. From the perspective of making government work, Truman's interest groups were no longer regarded as obscene interlopers—his biggest contribution. Moreover, to his everlasting credit, Truman tried to explain how interest groups formed. Ironically, this effort led scholars away from Bentley's focus on exchanges among all actors and thus away from the encompassing process of decision making. For Truman, interest groups formed as a result of instability in politics, often expressed through a sudden disequilibrium (the Great Depression or the onset of the Korean War).[8] Truman began by arguing that political conditions were ordinarily stable, or in a state of equilibrium. Everyone inside and outside of government was relatively content, or at least placid. Still, Truman noted that new interest groups were continually forming, often in waves; the political equilibrium needed continual rebalancing. For example, a more complex economy and more leisure time might stimulate the growth of interest groups representing specialized values. Thus interest groups could form around concerns about conservation and the environment: the Sierra Club attracted wilderness lovers; the Audubon Society sought bird watchers; Ducks Unlimited served duck hunters and habitat protectors; and Trout Unlimited organized around stream protection that would enhance fishing.

Truman also noted that during crises or major events that disrupted political equilibrium, those who had lost from the event formed interest groups to restore political influence; winners also formed interest groups to protect what they had won. Thus although environmental interest groups helped win passage of the 1970 Clean Air Act, they grew considerably more numerous in its aftermath.[9] Labor organizations became active lobbies after government became more professional, bureaucratic, and institutionally protective of workers' rights. And labor lobby activity broadened beyond earlier reliance on protest and violence.[10]

One problem with Truman's shifting equilibrium explanation for interest group formation is that it never addressed his concern with explaining process, specifically the give and take with public officials. What actions led to joining? And what motivations led prospective members to join? People did not simply wake up with newfound intentions of joining an interest group. So why and how did people join?

This process problem provided the basis for the second theory of interest group formation. Two observations proved central. First, economist Mancur Olson demonstrated that it was illogical for any single person or social institution to join a large interest group.[11] An interest group's success or failure in lobbying was hardly affected by a single person's decision to join. Free riders to lobbying gains were the norm; all Los Angeles County residents breathed cleaner air when smog was reduced, not just members of environmental interest groups. Political scientist Robert Salisbury elaborated by concluding that people decided to join interest groups because someone asked them and because they were offered tangible and highly selective benefits.[12] Interest groups have offered such personal benefits as social and political status, a chance to publicly and perhaps prominently express political views, an opportunity to attend informational conferences and educational seminars, free research and information gathering, low-cost group insurance programs, a low-interest credit card, and travel to attractive tourist sites to attend conferences and socialize with fellow interest group members. Moreover, only members gained these goodies. There were no free riders. Lobbying, it seemed, was offered as a secondary or even unimportant reason for joining. And, besides, everybody who shared the commonly held values won what members won from public policy.

Thus interest groups marketed membership largely on personal, or selective, reasons for joining. Members, this theory suggested, wanted expressive, solidary (social), or material benefits before they were willing to pursue a political value. This logic provides the procedural explanation for how new interest groups form. An entrepreneur comes forward with an interest-based cause. The entrepreneur identifies people with a common characteristic or common value who might share the interest. The entrepreneur then markets the interest group to prospective members, emphasizing tangible benefits rather than the lobbying side of the cause.

New members pay dues or otherwise contribute money, time, or effort to the interest group. Established interest groups, the logic went, use the same procedural techniques to expand their memberships. For example, an angler might join Trout Unlimited to buy a new Orvis fly-fishing reel at a $100 discount.

The problem with this process explanation is that it is incomplete; it takes the interest out of joining interest groups. Where was the politics, the responsiveness to government, the social wants? The idea of process was torn asunder. This separation of interest from interest group suggests that another look at interest group targeting, marketing, organization, and representation is warranted. By examining the effects of governing institutions, we will see how some interest groups formed. As Salisbury once suggested, Bentley's "interests" are "generated as government grows."[13] But are interest groups?

Exchange Theory, Transactions, and the Costs of Governance: An Interest Group Tale

The theory of interest group formation just discussed is called *exchange theory*. Entrepreneurs exchanged tangible benefits for members' money. Although exchange theory followed equilibrium theory in origin, the exchange framework was neither new to political analysis nor unique to the study of interest groups. In fact, Bentley wrote about the exchange concept in his original critique of institutional political science. Four decades later, he and John Dewey picked it up again. Bentley and Dewey called exchange theory, "transactional analysis," which meant that some process of observable exchange held individuals together within Bentley's encompassing idea of a politically consequential interest.[14] Given Bentley's immersion in psychology and sociology, he argued that the exchanges—or more accurately the transactions—rewarded in wide and varied ways, including emotionally, those who shared an interest. The rewards to each party to the exchange were *transaction benefits*, such as the social and political status obtained in joining some interest groups. *Transaction costs*, on the other hand, were the costs of joining an interest group. These included membership dues or the trouble of determining whether an interest group represented one's personal values.

Now to our story. (The actual events have been altered to ensure anonymity and to make the story more interesting.)[15] The activities, which took place over nearly four years in the 1990s, began with a single House member, Representative Cook, who was always worried about the next election. (Hence we have an institutional beginning, mired in both the organized Congress and the organized electorate.) Complaints from a few constituents suggested that small and medium-size manufacturing firms were using inexpensive waste management disposers who illegally deposited their loads in national forests. Representative Cook served on the House Agriculture Committee and on its subcommittee overseeing national forests, a responsibility of the U.S. Department of Agriculture and its agency, the Forest Service.

Representative Cook sent his staff to investigate. Upon finding some validating evidence, Cook immediately called a press conference to charge that wastes, even toxic wastes, were being dumped in national forests. At the same time Cook demanded that the Forest Service issue regulations to eliminate this potentially dangerous practice. Cook benefited by appearing effective and increasing his reelection chances; those were his transaction benefits, especially as he redefined the issue to include toxic waste disposal. This redefinition also gained Cook greater media attention in return for a more explosive story for the press. But Cook's most direct exchange came with the Forest Service.

Even though the dumping was already illegal, the Forest Service wrote additional antidumping regulations, implemented a sophisticated policy of tracking down firms whose waste had been dumped, and established stiff penalties for toxic waste manufacturers and their disposal firms—all punishments already permitted by law. As a result some Forest Service personnel appeared responsive to Cook. Their agency's responsiveness enhanced the congressman's image back home and, for Forest Service benefit, gave these particular bureaucrats a strong friend on an important committee in Congress. Agency appropriations, agency assignments, and perhaps the careers of the individual bureaucrats stood to be enhanced. Thus the shared interests of the two institutional parties to the exchange produced transaction benefits while new government rules were made, perhaps unnecessarily. So far the transaction costs to legislators, the press, constituents, and the Forest Service were very low.

Business Is Threatened; an Interest Group Is Born

Now we come to the consequences of Representative Cook's actions. The creation of new governing rules or institutions has also been subjected to exchange theory analysis. Two economists recently won Nobel Prizes for their work on exchanges and transactions and their effect on the costs of institutional governance. Both economists long ago gave up the belief that governing institutions brought social and economic efficiency.[16] For the private sector the economists demonstrated that governing institutions increased the costs of goods and services produced and exchanged in the economy.

Indeed, private sector prices rose as the government-imposed transaction costs increased the cost of production. Small and medium-size manufacturers had to use safer—and more costly—means of disposal or risk being fined. Moreover, all manufacturing firms of this size had to investigate where and how their disposal contractors were dumping—even unwitting disposal of waste in national forests could be penalized and exact added costs in negative publicity. Firms also wanted to know whether the new Forest Service regulations were an isolated institutional response or whether they suggested an increased governmentwide reaction to toxic waste disposal or even general manufacturing waste dumping. In other words, businesspeople wanted to know what prompted the Forest Service's response.

Firms reacted by lobbying—a new transaction with institutional (governmental) representatives. Lobbying, the firms hoped, would convince Congress to change the policy and thus lower economic transaction costs. Any capital costs and personnel time and energy that could be reduced by modified regulations would be a transaction benefit of lobbying.[17] For example, some firms hoped to get the Forest Service to cover—or subsidize—the financial costs of adjusting to the new rules. Thus the firms were prepared to lobby up to, and perhaps beyond, the point that the transaction costs of lobbying equaled the economic transaction costs lost because of the new regulations.

But lobbying by individual firms presented problems. First, obtaining information about how government operated would have high transaction costs. Not only would firm officials be operating in an unfamiliar work environment, they would lack information about how to reach the appropriate regulators and what to say to them. Second, the transaction costs of negotiating with institutional representatives would be high. Negotiating takes time and would divert firm personnel away from their regular business. Hiring a successful independent lobbyist for each firm would have been a financial burden and would have consumed the time and energy of firm executives to educate the lobbyists about relevant business issues.

Because of these high potential costs, firms found collective action appealing. Modifying the regulations would produce material benefits; the transaction costs of lobbying were lower than the transaction costs of complying with the new regulations. Thus another political exchange took place. When an attorney suggested that the firms form an interest group, many executives jumped at the idea. The transaction costs of each firm lobbying on its own were too high, especially when the firms shared an interest in the same institutional rules. So, the attorney organized the interest group, identified likely members, contacted them, set fees for membership, hired and informed another skilled lobbyist, and also agreed to provide information to member firms about how, in the least costly ways, they could adjust and prepare for these and future institutional rules. The entrepreneurial attorney became the Dumpers Defense League's executive director and primary lobbyist.

More than 120 small and medium-size firms throughout the United States joined the Dumpers Defense League, and membership grew to more than 300 in three years. All members recognized that the group existed because government regulations imposed high economic transaction costs, and because the transaction costs of individual firms negotiating with unfamiliar government representatives were also high. The transaction benefits of joining were at least somewhat clear: each firm could determine and measure the costs of existing governmental regulations. The benefits of not cooperating with government rules could be estimated— and so could the consequences. This encouraged members to help plan lobbying demands, strategy, and tactics.

Members gained the additional transaction benefit of being involved to the advantage of their firm. For example, the interest group executive asked members whether she should demand subsidies to cooperate with government or, alternatively, a new right to dump biodegradable but nontoxic waste in national forests. Members' excitement at the prospect of winning such material benefits outweighed their concern that nonmember firms might also benefit from altered government rules. Free ridership appeared to be a nonissue, even though members bore high lobbying costs of up to several thousand dollars per year. Members merely asked the executive director to recruit additional members to share the costs. One selectively available and very material transaction benefit of joining the interest group was the opportunity to gather information and receive operational intelligence relevant to long-term firm management. This newly available knowledge about governing institutions could be useful in future firm decisions about manufacturing materials and handling the wastes from these materials. Even this selective, tangible benefit was directly related to public policy concerns. Process was first and foremost the reason to join.

What have we seen so far in this example? First, an extended process at work: the initiation of political exchanges within government, the flow of transaction benefits among institutional representatives, the effects of economic transaction costs on the private sector, the desire of firms to resist those transaction costs, and the willingness of large numbers of firms to pay the transaction costs of joining a new interest group. Similar rationales probably explain a common finding of all scholars who have studied why members join their interest groups: Members value the selective and collective benefits of lobbying.[18]

Environmentalists Respond

The new manufacturing interest group did not go unnoticed by prominent environmental advocates. They found the Dumpers Defense League disheartening because conflict between the Forest Service and producer interest groups had not previously involved the direct interests of small and medium-size manufacturers, nor for that matter large industrial corporations. Antagonists of the Forest Service had mostly come from interest groups representing water users. The groups included organizations of farmers and ranchers and of local governments. Although business interest groups had sometimes testified before Congress that local governments needed greater access to less expensive water supplies, their lobbying went no further. This had clearly not been business's battle, or battleground (despite business's interest).

What environmentalists feared was a disruption in this political equilibrium. They believed that environmental interest groups were winning most national forest conflicts with water user interest groups. Institutions were slowly coming to see this issue from the environmental perspective. A new manufacturing interest group involved in national forest issues might change that distribution of power, especially if manufacturers formed a coalition with agricultural producers and the producers of local government services. That appeared likely because many federal officials had been considering increasing the uses of nationally owned public lands, such as forests. Environmental interest groups hoped to limit uses, not multiply them to allow such things as more manufacturing noise and air pollution, more hunting, more snowmobiling, more tourists, more fishing and excursion boats, more cattle grazing, more mining, and more oil drilling.[19]

Environmental advocates talked among themselves about the need for a new type of environmental interest group, one composed of national forest users who could be at least symbolically important in politics. Such an interest group, they hoped, would restore whatever influence environmentalists might lose to a producer coalition. The policy that would unify the new interest group would limit the use and degradation of public lands. One activist, a Democratic party staff assistant to a western state legislator, proposed that an interest group be formed from the ranks of hikers and cross country skiers who quietly passed through national forests with minimal exploitation. These foot-powered forest users might be convinced to join a group if its articulated purpose was to prevent the negative health effects of exposure to toxic manufacturing waste.

Representatives of several environmental interest groups that monitored public lands use—such as Greenpeace USA, the Sierra Club, the National Audubon Society, and the National Wildlife Federation—agreed to be patrons for a new organization if that legislative staffer quit his job and became the group's entrepreneurial organizer.[20] The established interest groups would pay the start-up costs of a new interest group if it spoke on behalf of issues identified by established patrons. The established groups also agreed to help by providing lists of possible members, creating and printing mass mailings, designing and writing the first few newsletters, arranging for several entertainment and sports celebrities to endorse the new organization, and introducing the new interest group and its lobbyists to the Department of Agriculture, Forest Service, and congressional and executive branch personnel.

To assist the new group, named the Forest Users Defense League, each patron group spent less than $25,000 and contributed the part-time services of one staff person. This modest assistance lowered the new interest group's transaction costs of organizing and lobbying. There was no need to invest, raise, or borrow start-up financial capital.[21] In exchange for those transaction benefits, the new interest group pledged loyalty to the causes of other environmental interest groups and, with its new niche, lent increased prominence and breadth of interest to the environmental lobby.

The established interest group representatives who had worked with Forest Service regulators favored by Representative Cook introduced the regulators to the new organization's lobbyist entrepreneur. The lobbyist promised to protect existing institutional rules and, indirectly, the career stake these regulators had in those rules. That commitment, or transaction benefit, was favorably received. As part of this public sector–private sector exchange, Forest Service personnel promised to provide information and data useful in lobbying and in acquiring public and media attention. The new interest group executive was also introduced to Representative Cook as one of his new allies. The interest group vowed to be active in Cook's congressional district and bring him favorable publicity. Cook said he would speak for the interest group and its goals of protecting "his" regulations whenever possible. Moreover, Cook could help the interest group raise operating revenue from his constituents. And the congressman also joined the group, which further blurred the distinction between private and public sector interests.

All that remained was to develop a marketable plan for contacting and enticing dues-paying members to the Forest Users Defense League. The interest group entrepreneur targeted potential members by using lists of members of patron interest groups and extracting the names of people living near large national forests. Then he contacted the American Hiking Society, a group that maintained lists of nearly all local hiking clubs. From those clubs he solicited names of members. He also purchased a list of clients who had skied at commercial cross country ski clubs within the past two years. As a result he had the names of people who probably saw themselves as stakeholders in the health issue of manufacturers' dumping. As an interest, the stakeholders were self-styled environmentalists who lived nearest to the threats, hikers who had previously joined organizations, and the most active, prosperous cross country skiers. After two mailings 10,000 new members contributed an average of nearly $25 each. Several local hiking and skiing clubs raised and contributed an additional $100,000, with promises of future local fund-raisers with donations going to the national organization.

How did the interest group appeal to its potential members? Its primary message was protecting newly threatened environmental regulations on national forest use, with an emphasis on how hard fought and how rare these victories had been. The advertised threats included all of the cliches: manufacturing greed, a wealthy special interest, damage to politically vulnerable public servants of the Forest Service, disregard for public health, and the specter of Representative Cook's imaginary toxic waste disposal. The interest group presented data on toxic waste production and disease-related toxic effects. We see here the creation of an expressive interest group, one prompted by rage and one in which tangible transaction benefits to the members were largely ones of good feelings about expressing political beliefs.[22] Local Forest Users Defense League members organized rallies nationwide. Local newspaper coverage was extensive. The national staff of four full-time workers prepared and distributed materials on organizing local rallies, appropriate speech content, rally slogans, poster preparation and content, and gaining press attention before and after the protests. This was the political grassroots at work, albeit prompted by a national organization.

The transaction costs for starting the interest group were low. Besides the help from patron interest groups and a committed and politically experienced entrepreneur willing to take a low salary and travel extensively, group messages were inexpensive. No new information was generated, because existing governmental and interest group data supported the core messages of the group, which also recycled Representative Cook's charges. Producing information would have been costly; borrowing information and repeating the troublesome claims of others were practically free.[23] But for the postage, marketing the opportunity for contributing members to express themselves was free as well. Fears about government performance in the face of greedy businesses were sufficient to evoke people's outrage.

Weaknesses in Exchange Theory Interpretation

Exchange theorists once commented on the high and nearly insurmountable transaction costs of organizing interest groups when members are separated by extensive social and geographic distance.[24] But times and technology have changed, and those distances have decreased dramatically. This "death of distance" has made it possible to reach out quickly and inexpensively to many.[25] Thus the transaction costs of recruitment for the Forest Users Defense League were low in terms of the amount expended for each individual reached and the amount of information dispersed. Unlike Mancur Olson contended, it was not just the relatively small business interest group that was organized easily at a low rate of exchange.[26] A large collection of diverse stakeholders was organized swiftly and efficiently, too. The only selective benefit needed to attract people to the Forest Users Defense League was an expressive one triggered by existing emotions about government. In contrast, it was a high-transaction-cost feat to identify, reach, and set common goals for hundreds of businesses across the nation, which previously had no reason to be familiar with one another or their common values.

Why did members enter into an exchange or transactional relationship with the Forest Users Defense League entrepreneur? The transaction costs of membership were incredibly low, even at the amount of the average contribution. Many joined for $5. Individuals felt compelled to belong to an interest group that was fighting a dangerous foe on behalf of governing institutions that protected policies the contributors valued. Many people who shared an interest, therefore, joined the interest group without thinking very much about the costs. Perceptions of government's worth alone then accounted for membership; joiners understood themselves to be part of a desirable structured process. There were no measures, estimates, or even guesses as to what government could do to impose increased transaction costs (of, say, attentive vigilance) on members. Accordingly, this interest group operated at a distinctly lower (more imperfect) level of providing member information than did the business lobby. When members didn't pay much, they never expected much.

Our new environmental interest group was a political one, organized around nothing but political ends. It won over its supporters for the purely political reasons of general (or public)—not personal or social—value, all because of peoples' institutional faith in government and their willingness to be angry if government lost. Without doubt this new organization, as well as the business group, demonstrated the watchfulness that interest groups bring to society by encouraging increased political attention by interested parties. Certainly what took place in this tale highlights how exchange theory, transaction benefits, transaction costs, and the concept of process in explaining political events are helpful in overseeing existing—and transactional—institutions of government.

Our example also illustrates the weaknesses of earlier uses of exchange theory. First, earlier scholars saw all collective benefits and interests in them as equally weighted, or of equal value, in gaining the attention of potential interest group members. That is hardly true. Creating a new public sector organization was harder than creating a public policy; both were harder than passing a law. In addition, one law did not have the same value to one interested citizen as a second law did to a second interested citizen. Therefore, one of the two citizens was most easily recruited by political persuasion, or by interest group marketing. Either that or one of the two laws was most marketable.

Second, earlier scholars forgot that perceptions of interest group benefits determined their importance. Measurement of benefits was seldom possible or necessarily worth the transaction costs.[27] Thus potential members were likely to never consider being free riders or, probably, never to think of the transaction costs of joining.

Third, earlier scholars assumed far too much in believing that potential members were perfectly informed: about politics and their interests in it, about the selective benefits of interest group membership, and, therefore, about why they joined organized interests. As Bentley may have indicated with his transactional analysis, different individuals—as a group—appeared to have a common interest. Still, their interests in that group were highly variable, both in substance and intensity. In summary, it made sense for business firms to join the Dumpers Defense League and, contrary to exchange theory beliefs, for rank-and-file citizens to join the closely related Forest Users Defense Fund. And government personnel, through the new interest groups, obtained some tangible benefits in exchange for members collectively participating in the joint decision process of public institutions and private interests.

Conclusion

In our example of waste management, governing institutions were a logical part of interest group formation. The need for indirect and direct contact with institutional representatives was central to generating entrepreneurial and member momentum. Someone from the interest group had to talk to someone in government. When unfamiliar institutional (governmental) representatives were there to negotiate with, individuals sharing private sector values realized that collective action would lower the transaction costs of lobbying. But such resources as lobbying expertise and political experience in dealing with governmental institutions were absent without collective interest group action, because the costs of effective lobbying would be prohibitive if not spread among several joiners. Thus everyone valued a knowledgeable interest group leader who could serve as an agent before government.

In addition, when institutional representatives were present, an interest group lobbyist could enter into a transactional agreement with them to exchange benefits. Government is intended to be responsive. The interest group benefits of greater issue knowledge and official recognition by public officials made it likely that the emerging organized interest would be prominent and informed as a collective action organization, especially with an impressive spokesperson.

Therefore, potential joiners who would affiliate for political reasons that were associated with their own ideas of "good (personally valued) public policy" were more likely to contribute to the group when existing institutions of government were in place. Potential joiners had only partial knowledge on issues and likely believed that seemingly expert and rhetorically impressive interest group leaders would compensate for this weakness—and the leaders did. The lobbyist was the members' agent before government, offering sound advice to members much as an insurance agent or investment broker would. This meant that those who practiced exchange theory were incorrect: well-informed measures of transaction costs and benefits did not determine membership.[28] Rather, perceptions of the likely value and likely availability of transactional exchanges mattered far more; and many of those perceptions were not based on accurate knowledge. People guessed that collective action paid off, and they were willing to lobby on the cheap as part of an interest group, but only as long as it had that impressive and experienced spokesperson.

Thus we should call this *leadership advantage exchange (sub)theory*. American history gave us a prize example in the founding and political entrance of the Grange movement. Its organizing entrepreneur recruited six cofounders; all but one of these seven early leaders came from governing institutions of interest to farmers. The movement began five years after the establishment of the U.S. Department of Agriculture. By hiring people with institutional experience, the Grange became the single most prominent American interest group of the agrarian nineteenth century.[29]

The existence of governing institutions was important for a second and closely related reason. Let's call this *likely interest group success exchange (sub)theory*. As noted above, benefits matter. Institutions made it appear that desirable legal and public policy goals were likely to be met, albeit imprecisely. Any desired change in governance was only incremental with institutions already in place. Without governing institutions to attack or support, however, the alternative for an interest group was to create new ones. Transaction costs of doing so were surely perceived to be unreasonably high, even by the politically ill informed. Incremental accomplishments, such as the reform of existing institutions, were far more plausible. This meant that interest group entrepreneurs could hold out real examples of incompetent public officials, inappropriate laws and regulations, and misguided public policy results—all of which needed reform. These examples provided collective goods incentives for politically concerned potential members to join. The incentives were even more attractive because the interest group promised to reform governing rules specifically to the members' collective satisfaction. This was never thought to be publicly intended social reform, but merely a modification on behalf of the members' interest. In contrast, enacting new laws or regulations unrelated to anything else was but a hypothetical dream. The same was true for a new public policy or governmental agency. Likely joiners of an interest group that sought to create completely new policy often were highly skeptical of victory. So they were less likely to affiliate than those wanting incremental institutional change.

It was in this second context that the declining Grange was supplanted in influence by the other most historically prominent U.S. farm interest group, the American Farm Bureau Federation (AFBF). The AFBF grew from an attempt in 1911 by the Department of Agriculture to organize farmers locally in cooperation with agricultural officials. Local farm bureaus were to use peer influence to motivate other farmers to modernize their practices. But those locals soon turned to politics. By 1920 the AFBF was lobbying for the locals in Washington, D.C., and pioneering the use of modern constituent feedback and electoral threats from back home to members of Congress. AFBF prospered from its well-understood insider political status, the resulting advice of agricultural policy professionals who spoke regularly to farmers, and the widespread understanding of its members that the organization was intended to reform rather than reinvent farm policy. Unlike any other part of American government, agriculture was resplendent with governments' farm service institutions. During the Great Depression of the 1920s and 1930s, farm bureaus attracted primarily larger and more commercial landowning farmers who wanted to enhance government assistance rather than redirect it to the rural poor.[30]

AFBF's rival interest group, the National Farmers Union, failed to gather large memberships in support of its simultaneous and earlier efforts on behalf of impoverished tenant farmers.[31] Poor farm renters and sharecroppers simply didn't believe that the political process could be reversed to their advantage, even with the backing of the secretary of agriculture. Despite the secretary's enthusiasm, governing institutions had long operated with a large-farm bias that did not go unnoticed by small-scale farmers. Thus Bentley's process failed small-scale farmers as they elected not to be politically grouped. Large-scale farmers made no such political mistake. They knew their interest and followed it through that process.

The Forest Users Defense League avoided making the same mistake. In an era of reduced social distance, the organization came to fruition more easily than the Dumpers Defense League did. And the process of politics according to Bentley continued apace, with organized groups forming within the context of allied broad interests and competing governing institutions.

Notes

1. For a comprehensive view of scholarly work that supports my argument, see Virginia Gray and David Lowery, *The Population Ecology of Interest Representation: Lobbying Communities in the American States* (Ann Arbor: University of Michigan, 1996), 17–20. See also Burdett A. Loomis and Allan J. Cigler, "Introduction: the Changing Nature of Interest Group Politics," in *Interest Group Politics*, 5th ed., ed. Allan J. Cigler and Burdett A. Loomis (Washington, D.C.: CQ Press, 1998), 11–17. My analysis differs from these authors' analyses in that I see American government's influence as being far more than a post-1930s phenomenon.
2. Arthur F. Bentley, *The Process of Government* (Chicago: University Press of Chicago, 1908).
3. Robert H. Salisbury, ed., *Interests and Institutions: Substance and Structure in American Politics* (Pittsburgh: University of Pittsburgh, 1992), x.
4. Ibid.
5. Paul F. Kress, *Social Science and the Idea of Process: The Ambiguous Legacy of Arthur F. Bentley* (Urbana: University of Illinois, 1970), 22–26, 246–249.
6. David B. Truman, *The Governmental Process: Political Interests and Public Opinion* (New York: Alfred A. Knopf, 1951), 33–34.
7. This article is not about the lobbying of socioeconomic and governing institutions as they operate on their own. The article recognizes, however, that most organized lobbying interests are these individual institutions. Robert H. Salisbury, "Interest Representation: The Dominance of Institutions," *American Political Science Review*

78 (March 1984): 65–66; David Lowery and Virginia Gray, "The Dominance of Institutions in Interest Representation: A Test of Seven Explanations," *American Journal of Political Science* 42 (1): 231–255 (1998). Including socioeconomic institutions in this piece would have added too much. However, institutions use the same processes as interest groups when they organize to lobby.

8. Truman, *The Governmental Process*, 28–30.

9. The examples on environmental policy are from a superb volume by Richard E. Cohen, *Washington at Work: Back Rooms and Clean Air* (New York: Allyn and Bacon, 1995). This work is almost what Arthur F. Bentley probably suggested political research should be about.

10. Doug McAdam, Sidney Tarrow, and Charles Tilly, "To Map Contentious Politics," *Mobilization* 1 (March 1996): 27.

11. Mancur Olson Jr., *The Logic of Collective Action* (Cambridge: Harvard University, 1965), 5–52.

12. Robert H. Salisbury, "An Exchange Theory of Interest Groups," *Midwest Political Science Review* 13 (February 1969): 1–32; David Plotke, "The Political Mobilization of Business," in *The Politics of Interests*, ed. Mark P. Petracca (Boulder, Colo.: Westview, 1992), 175–198. These analyses were derived from George Caspar Homans, *Social Behavior: Its Elementary Forms* (New York: Harcourt, Brace, and World, 1961) and Peter M. Blau, *Exchange and Power in Social Life* (New York: Wiley, 1964).

13. Robert H. Salisbury, "Interest Advocacy and Interest Representation," in Salisbury, *Interests and Institutions*, 86.

14. John Dewey and Arthur F. Bentley, *Knowing and the Known* (Boston: Beacon, 1949). See also Myron Q. Hale, "The Cosmology of Arthur Bentley," *American Political Science Review* 54 (1960): 957.

15. I first heard this story from a public interest lobbyist who put me in contact with the other characters in the tale. All of them were frank and they delighted in the tale's telling. All were also promised anonymity in case the story ever bore retelling in an academic or political setting. The original tale was embarrassing to the congressperson, the businesses, the lobbyist who represented them, and several of the public interest group representatives. It was a tale of cynicism, entrepreneurial greed, misrepresentation, love of politics, information gone crazy, and misguided government. It also involved a far more minor and boring set of details than that described here. It did not involve the Forest Service.

16. Ronald H. Coase, "The Nature of the Firm," *Economica* 4 (November 1937): 386–405; Ronald H. Coase, "The Problem of Social Cost," *Journal of Law and Economics* 3 (October 1960): 1–44; Douglass C. North, *Structure and Change in Economic History* (New York: Norton, 1981); Douglass C. North, *Institutions, Institutional Change, and Economic Performance* (Cambridge, England: Cambridge University, 1990).

17. Coase, "The Problem of Social Cost."

18. The earliest examples were William P. Browne, "Benefits and Membership: A Reappraisal of Interest Group Activity," *Western Political Quarterly* 29 (1976): 258–273; Terry M. Moe, *The Organization of Interests: Incentives and the Internal Dynamics of Political Interest Groups* (Chicago: University of Chicago, 1980).

19. Jacqueline Vaughn Switzer, "Influencing Environmental Policy in Rural Communities: The Environmental Opposition at Work," *Policy Studies Journal* 29 (2001): 128–138.

20. Patronage of interest groups was first noted in the academic literature by Jeffrey M. Berry, *Lobbying for the People: The Political Behavior of Interest Groups* (Princeton: Princeton University, 1977), 45–55.

21. In this case the patron groups provided instant resources that would have been otherwise unavailable. For organizational resources, see Truman, *The Governmental Process*, 111–210; Berry, *Lobbying for the People*, 45–78.

22. They were labeled expressive interest groups by Ronald T. Libby, *Eco-Wars: Political Campaigns and Social Movements* (New York: Columbia University, 1998), 1–26, 207–216.

23. J. B. Stevens, *The Economics of Collective Choice* (Boulder, Colo.: Westview, 1993).

24. Mancur Olson Jr., "Space, Agriculture, and Organization," *American Journal of Agricultural Economics* 67 (December 1985): 928–937.

25. Frances Cairncross, *The Death of Distance: How the Communications Revolution Will Change Our Lives* (Boston: Harvard Business School, 1997).

26. Olson maintained that "a large or latent group will *not* organize for coordinated action merely because, as a group, they have a reason for doing so, although this could be true of a smaller group." *The Logic of Collective Action*, 65.

27. This measurement consideration tends to be the focus of institutional economists who use exchange theory. See North, *Institutions, Institutional Change and Economic Performance*. Bentley did not focus on measuring costs and benefits and was reluctant even to specify what these often-emotional benefits would be. He never mentioned transaction costs in his transactional analysis; *The Process of Government*, 231–283.

28. Solon J. Buck, *The Granger Movement: A Study of Agricultural Organization and Its Political, Economic, and Social Manifestations, 1870–1880* (Lincoln: University of Nebraska, 1963), 41–43, 52–59, 109; Lowell K. Dyson, *Farmers' Organizations* (Westport, Conn.: Greenwood, 1986), 233–252.

29. John Mark Hansen, *Gaining Access: Congress and the Farm Lobby, 1919–1981* (Chicago: University of Chicago, 1991); David E. Hamilton, *From New Day to New Deal: American Farm Policy from Hoover to Roosevelt, 1928–1933* (Chapel Hill: University of North Carolina, 1991); Jess Gilbert, "Eastern Urban Liberals and Midwestern Agrarian Intellectuals: Two Group Portraits of Progressives in the New Deal Department of Agriculture," *Agricultural History* 74 (spring 2000): 162–180.

30. Ibid.

31. Grant McConnell, *Private Power and American Democracy* (New York: Knopf, 1966).

IV. ASSESSMENTS

16

Interest Groups and Gridlock
Jeffrey M. Berry

Over the past twenty years scholars and journalists have written a good deal about the notion of gridlock in American politics. Two questions have dominated their discussions: First, does gridlock actually exist? And second, what political institutions are responsible for government's inability to act decisively? Although the focus has usually been on divided government and relations between the president and Congress, interest groups may contribute to policy gridlock. In this chapter Jeffrey Berry asks whether more interest groups lead to more gridlock, less gridlock, or whether they cancel each other out, leaving policymaking to other forces in the political system.

Berry, a leading interest group scholar, develops a data set to test these alternatives. Using information from three Congresses across a twenty-eight-year period, he concludes that growth in the number and type of interest groups has not contributed to legislative stalemate. That is, a highly representative interest group universe does not inordinately delay or derail policymaking. Berry emphasizes the "sheer complexity" of the legislative process, with organized interests just one influence on legislative outcomes.

It is almost part of our national character to complain that our political system has broken down. We are sure not only that the current system is failing, but that there was an earlier, simpler time when government worked the way it is supposed to. One complaint about modern government is "gridlock": the inability of Congress and the president to enact important legislation. Public cynicism feeds this complaint, and many political scientists, journalists—even politicians—feel the same way. Though richly evocative, the traffic jam metaphor is hardly precise. Critics who charge that Congress has become less capable of addressing national concerns have in mind a range of problems. When pundits, kibitzers, and scholars talk about gridlock, they usually ascribe the decline of government to at least one of the following problems.

First, the government may do less because demand for its services outstrips capacity. Samuel Huntington has argued that as more and more sectors of society ask government for help, Congress becomes overloaded with competing demands.[1] Just as a business can attract more customers than it can handle, so too can government attract too many clients. But unlike a corporation, which can quickly attract capital to expand if product demand is strong, Congress cannot easily increase its capacity. Its membership of legislators is fixed and in recent years budget pressures have forced Congress to reduce its staff after increasing it for many years. Moreover, hiring more staff may increase demand rather than satisfy it. To return to our traffic metaphor, every time master planner Robert Moses built a new bridge into Manhattan to alleviate traffic congestion, he made it more attractive for people to move to the suburbs and drive into the city.[2] The solution makes the problem worse. So in this view congressional gridlock results from institutional infrastructure that cannot bear the weight of increasing demands, and more capacity may be a step in the wrong direction.

Second, there may not be too many demands but just the opposite: Congress has been too good at doling out favors. Mancur Olson argued that the increasing number of subsidies, tax breaks, and trade restrictions—all passed at the behest of some lobby during a period of activist government—restricts what Congress can do to solve current problems.[3] Eliminating these inefficiencies means taking away benefits from many well-represented business sectors.[4] The U.S government excels at awarding benefits but is not so good at taking them back. Times have changed and new policies are needed for the United States to compete effectively in the world marketplace. Yet Congress is unable to act, entangled in its own web of outmoded policies. Jonathan Rauch, the most impassioned of the gridlock critics, says simply, "The federal government is rotting."[5]

Third, gridlock is said to result from the growth of interest groups; it's what interest groups are doing today rather than what they did in the past that is wrecking our system. Interest group scholars have documented the rise of group politics but have not linked that growth to legislative gridlock.[6] Experienced and well-respected Washington journalists have showed no such hesitation in connecting the dots. According to Kevin Phillips, "Washington is malfunctioning" because of "the enormous buildup and entrenchment of the largest interest group concentration the world has ever seen."[7] Unlike our first explanation, the logic here is not that group demands are overwhelming Congress's institutional capacity, but that many powerful interest groups with contradictory policy preferences put Congress in a deadly crossfire. Understandably, legislators would rather duck than fight.

A fourth explanation of gridlock is party decline. When political parties were strong congressional leaders could exert some discipline over rank-and-file members. As instruments of majoritarian democracy, the parties in Congress were an effective counterweight to lobbying groups. Former Republican congressman Vin Weber notes, "We have always had special interest groups." The reason we have gridlock now, however, is "that in the past we had political parties that filtered their claims on the government and organized popular opinion and political power to come to some sort of compromise on those conflicting claims and produce a governing agenda."[8]

Finally, government's weakening capacity to resolve serious challenges is said to reflect an increasing atomization of American politics. With a larger number of lobbies that sometimes duel and other times join forces, interest group sectors are increasingly fragmented. This makes it difficult for the policymaking system to get beyond niche politics. Anthony King concludes that "American politicians continue to try to create *majorities;* they have no option. But they are no longer . . . in the business of building *coalitions.* . . . Building coalitions in the United States today is like trying to build coalitions out of sand. It cannot be done."[9] Thus large-scale change has become increasingly difficult. There are lots of separate kingdoms but few grand alliances.

Divided Government

These five explanations of gridlock place interest groups at the center of the problem. Lobbying is believed to have made it more difficult for legislators and the president, for Republicans and Democrats, to enact the laws we need to solve our most pressing problems. Interest groups overload, undermine, or simply make it too dangerous to take action.

Political scientists have yet to document gridlock in any consistent fashion. Indeed there is no consensus in the discipline that American government is in gridlock at all. The research here will contribute to this debate by focusing on the relationship between interest group lobbying and the passage of legislation. Using data amassed from 205 case studies of legislation considered by three different sessions of Congress, we will see if the amount or type of lobbying affects legislative outcomes.

Given the centrality of interest groups to the explanations outlined above, it is a little surprising that the research on gridlock has largely ignored lobbying organizations. Most of the literature on gridlock has focused instead on divided government. As Americans continue to put one party in control of the White House and the other party in charge of at least one house of Congress, divided government is logically linked to reduced performance of the political system.

A premise of the literature on divided government is that party decline has led to gridlock. As voters became increasingly independent, they split their tickets more frequently. Partisan identification is less influential as voters pick and choose among candidates, selecting leaders on their personal appeal or the issues they promote. Members of Congress, who have an independent financial base to fund their campaigns, are not beholden to their national parties when they arrive in Washington. Thus they are less subject to party discipline, and this lack of loyalty makes it difficult for party leaders to broker deals to move legislation forward. Conceivably, the rise in party unity in recent years may be a harbinger of stronger congressional capacity in the future, but at the same time there is ample reason to doubt claims of party renewal.

Although party decline has led to divided government, researchers have not focused on the root causes of gridlock. Instead, the emphasis has been on developing measures of how gridlock is manifested. If Congress has not been mired in gridlock, there is little reason to trace the complex link between party decline and the internal congressional conflicts that lead to stalemate. In this vein David Mayhew's *Divided We Govern* tests the basic premise that split control of government leads to a less productive Congress.[10] Contrary to the expectation that Congress is gridlocked when government is divided, Mayhew finds that just as much important legislation is passed when control of government is split as when it is unified.

Some scholars have taken issue with Mayhew's methodology. George Edwards and his colleagues extend Mayhew's approach to include important bills that Congress doesn't pass. They find that "the odds of important legislation failing to pass are considerably greater under divided government."[11] Narrowing Mayhew's conception of important legislation, Sean Kelly shows that when a more restrictive definition is used, periods of divided government are less productive than unified periods.[12]

Of course there are other ways of assessing the impact of divided government than determining how many important bills pass. Gary Cox and Mathew McCubbins demonstrate that unified control under the Democrats results in higher tax receipts. Bryan Jones, James True, and Frank Baumgartner find that budgeting is more volatile under divided governments. David Brady and Craig Volden, as well as Keith Krehbiel, show how institutional constraints, like the filibuster and the veto, are more important than divided or unified government in leading to gridlock. Sarah Binder finds that conflict between the House and Senate "may be as important to explaining policy deadlock as the usual sus-pect, conflict between the branches."[13]

Nevertheless, looking broadly at all the relevant literature, Morris Fiorina concludes that Mayhew's basic finding holds. Fiorina determines there is

> little empirical support for the strong claims that have been made about the negative effects of divided control. Whether one looked closely at deficits, at legislative productivity, at inter-branch conflict, at presidents' ability to conduct foreign affairs or staff their administra-tions, there was little in the empirical record that pointed to significant differences between years of unified government and years of split control.[14]

But so far analyses on gridlock have excluded lobbying as a possible influence.[15] Scholars do not usually explain why interest groups have been ignored, so we must rely largely on inferences. The most obvious explana-tion for disregarding lobbies is that parties, not interest groups, control Congress. There may be tens of thousands of lobbyists in Washington, but none of them work for organizations stronger than either of the political parties. A related but less stringent view is that interest groups are actively involved in all important legislative battles and have some impact, but the interplay between Congress and the president and the conflict between the two parties dominate the outcome. A third explanation is that interest groups cancel each other out—there are likely to be groups on all sides of any issue. Legislators know that some groups will support them (possibly with campaign contributions) no matter what side the legislators choose. Brady and Volden take a position like this, arguing that interest groups' preferences are subsumed in election results, and therefore the authors don't have to factor the preferences directly into their analysis.[16]

Although these explanations appear reasonable, on closer analysis they are problematic. Party or institutional perspectives cannot rule out an interest group role in legislative outcomes. Lobbying organizations are part of policymaking and can constrain or facilitate passage of any piece of legislation. The reason interest groups are ignored in this literature is not so much theoretical as pragmatic. Trying to model all possible influences on legislative outcomes is so complex that it will sooner lead to academic chopped liver than to a coherent explanation of gridlock. In studies from Mayhew's elegantly simple empirical test to Brady and Volden's formal model, the strategy is just the opposite: to reduce the number of explana-tory variables. And no readily available databases can provide information on the relationship between lobbying and legislative outcomes. To add data collection on interest group activity to the kind of research done so far is to vastly expand the scope of work.

Yet there is ample reason to look beyond party control to interest groups and other potential influences on legislative output. For one, most theoretical explanations of gridlock focus on interest groups rather than on divided government. Conceivably, divided and unified control have no bearing on legislative output because the system is overloaded with demands or caught between conflicting interest groups. Output may vary little because interest groups generate a constant and high level of conflict. Could we explain the failure of the Clinton health care plan solely on the basis of party politics, while ignoring the hundreds of groups that lobbied on the bill? Is Congress's decades-long reluctance to take on the tobacco industry strictly a function of partisan division? Whether any one piece of legislation on health or tobacco is worthy of passage is beside the point. Legislators do not choose inaction in a vacuum; there is a political context that extends beyond partisan differences.

A second reason is that the growth of interest group politics has made policymaking more complex, and increased complexity makes lawmaking more difficult. The health care sector alone has more than 700 lobbies in Washington.[17] The explosive growth in interest groups has altered the relationship between groups and government. "Bargaining becomes more complex, control and coordination by key actors becomes more difficult, boundaries become harder to define, and the likelihood of conflict between competing coalitions increases."[18]

Third, interest groups are interconnected with political parties. Political scientists have too readily accepted that interest groups don't care who controls Congress because political action committees (PACs) disproportionately favor incumbents and, thus, lobbies have access to whomever chairs the committees. Even though most interest groups work to maintain access to legislators of both parties, many groups do have preferences about which party controls Congress. Some groups provide soft money contributions to the national parties, volunteer labor in campaigns, and sponsor fund-raisers. PAC contributions to open seat candidates show a sharply partisan pattern.

Contributing to Gridlock or Facilitating Passage?

In turning from the literature on gridlock and divided government to the literature on interest groups, determining whether lobbies contribute to gridlock becomes a little more complicated. The argument so far is that more and more interest groups are jumping into the legislative process and might be a significant obstacle to passing important legislation. Yet some work on interest groups suggests they may make it easier to get legislation through Congress. A third hypothesis is equally compelling: so many competing interest groups may cancel each other out and reduce their impact on the likelihood of passage.

For each of these three hypotheses, let us be clear as to what the causal path is presumed to be. The hypothesis that interest groups contribute to gridlock is, more precisely, a supposition that the growth of interest group politics has made it more difficult to pass legislation. The logic is that some change in the interest group community has altered the legislative process. Although we have had interest groups as long as we have had Congress, the charges of gridlock are relatively recent. Because the involvement of interest groups per se is a constant, the relevant variables could be the *number* of groups lobbying, the *type* of groups involved, or the *power* of key groups on each issue. This last idea, that certain groups may have become more powerful in recent years and thus more capable of either impeding or facilitating passage, cannot be directly tested here.

Recent research, however, throws doubt on the idea that individual groups have become increasingly powerful within their policy domains. Heinz and his colleagues demonstrated that issue networks are characterized by a "hollow core."[19] That is, within networks no centrally located interest groups act as either a communications hub or coordinator of long-term advocacy. The most plausible course of influence along these lines is that the most generous PACs have a disproportionate amount of influence. Yet the research on PACs and legislative voting has not shown any consistent pattern of influence in the legislative process.

Because we know the number of interest groups lobbying on each of the 205 issues in this study, testing whether more interest groups make it more difficult to pass legislation is relatively straightforward. (These data are derived from research that will be described more fully below.) The number of interest groups involved in a session of Congress varies, so if interest group density affects legislative output it should be easy to detect. In terms of the type of interest groups involved, each advocacy organization was coded based on the constituency it represents. We will look at all the major categories, but a primary focus will be citizen groups. Citizen groups are lobbies that organize members or donors around interests other than their vocation or profession, such as environmental or consumer issues. This is where the rate of growth in the lobbying population has been sharpest.[20]

Moreover, many scholars have suggested that citizen groups get most of the credit for destabilizing the legislative process. The expansion and broadening of the interest group system has meant that "The national debate over all aspects of public policy became more balanced, but also more conflictual, heated, and ideological."[21] Agriculture is a good example. Where farm groups once had the United States Department of Agriculture and the agriculture committees in Congress to themselves, they now face fierce competition from environmental and consumer groups.[22]

Citizen groups are often described as hostile participants in the legislative process. Thomas Mann finds that ideological activists press "extreme, nonnegotiable demands, making the search for accommodation elusive and daunting efforts to build a coalition from the center out."[23] These groups' strategies make sense, says John Gilmour, because "The language of moderation and compromise does not appear to generate many memberships." [24] Citizen groups are different from other lobbies in the way they claim the high ground of principle and in their willingness to publicly disagree with their legislative friends and enemies. Probably more significant, however, is that citizen groups' success in gaining legislative allies upset traditional policy subsystems, making negotiations more complex by increasing the number of participants with distinct points of view who need to be satisfied. Citizen groups have been surprisingly successful in pushing their issues onto the congressional agenda and putting business interests on the defensive. [25]

The hypothesis that interest groups have raised legislative productivity is also tied to the growth in the number of lobbying organizations. With more lobbies, interest group communities become more fragmented. Robert Salisbury calls this the "paradox of more interest groups and lobbyists wielding less influence over policy results." [26] But why might more lobbying facilitate passage of legislation rather than simply reducing interest groups influence to a point where they don't affect the process one way or the other? It may be that large, resourceful trade groups and leading corporations, facing stiffer competition from emerging lobbies, are no longer strong enough to block legislation; legislators are thus able to take advantage of these groups' weakness to resolve major policy problems. AT&T was once powerful enough to stop anything it didn't like. When Congress takes up telecommunications policy today, AT&T is just one of hundreds of lobbies with an interest in the legislation.

Second, having more interest groups might facilitate legislative agreements because a change in the political environment—in this case an expanding and diverse interest group population—can stimulate Congress to adapt to meet new demands or expectations. A study of international trade negotiations and regulatory standards found that the growth of citizen group advocacy pushed trade negotiators to find solutions to complex, multisided regulatory problems. [27] The expanded set of competing lobbies and the conflicting regulatory standards in the United States and the European Union contributed to negotiators' sense that they needed to work together to devise solutions that pleased many different countries, manufacturers, and citizen lobbies. In recent years Congress has developed many alternative routes for resolving complicated legislative issues. [28]

The hypothesis that the number or type of interest groups is unrelated to legislative outcomes is cogent as well. Over time and across policy issues interest group influence on congressional output may vary considerably and, consequently, fail to show any consistent positive or negative influence. Anything can happen on any piece of legislation, and the likelihood that a statistical relationship will emerge across many issues may be small. Legislating on important problems is a complex process that sometimes takes years. Interest group advocacy is just one of many relevant variables, including public opinion, the partisan and ideological division of Congress, the priority the White House places on the legislation, and unusual or salient events that may galvanize attention and pressure Congress to act. Another explanation is that interest groups may grow in number but inevitably coalesce into a few factions. If legislators typically contend with coalitions representing two or three sides on an issue, does it matter if each side encompasses three groups or thirty? Or as Brady and Volden see it, interest group positions could be reflected in the aggregate by those elected in the preceding congressional election.[29] Whatever influence groups have has already been fixed before the lobbying begins, so lobbying does not significantly affect legislative output.

Measuring Gridlock

Before each of these hypotheses can be tested some means of measuring gridlock must be established. Most scholars would define gridlock as Congress's tendency toward inaction on significant policy problems. It's a simple idea, but deceptively so. Congress was designed by the framers to be a slow and deliberative body. How can we distinguish inaction from thoughtful deliberation? After all, policymaking is incremental. What seems gridlocked in one session of Congress may be dealt with in a responsible and bipartisan manner in the next.

In *Divided We Govern* Mayhew identifies important legislation between 1946 and 1990 by comparing the number of important acts passed in each Congress.[30] The greatest problem with this approach is that some filter must be used to distinguish important from unimportant (or at least less important) legislation, and the choice of filter will influence the outcome. As noted already, both Kelly and Edwards and his colleagues found more evidence of gridlock when they modified Mayhew's method of selecting issues to be included.

To complicate matters further, some analysts argue that the central question is not what bills pass, but what happens to legislation on the way to passage. Divided government can yield more compromise and, hence, more diluted policy approaches.[31] Presidents and their legislative allies and opponents continually make calculations as to how much leverage they have. That leverage—their strength in bargaining—is surely affected by partisan strength and partisan control of Congress.

A related way of viewing gridlock is to ask what problems Congress resolves. According to Jonathan Rauch, the "question is not 'Why does nothing get done in Washington?' Things always get done in Washington, today no less than ever. . . . The crucial question, rather, is this: Why is it that what Washington does is less and less effective at solving problems."[32] This is the bottom line: when Congress acts, what difference does it make? Even when legislators disagree about how to solve a problem, they usually want to pass something—even something superficial—

to show voters that they are working on a pressing issue. When House Republicans defeated a broad health care bill in the 105th Congress, GOP legislators immediately introduced a narrower patient bill of rights.

Although these alternatives to Mayhew's basic strategy are appealing and could provide powerful evidence on gridlock, they are difficult to test. Even if valid scales could be developed, gathering the appropriate evidence for each issue would be a labor intensive endeavor. Data sets on more than a handful of issues would be difficult to assemble.

Acknowledging the pragmatism of the basic approach used by Mayhew and some of his critics is not to damn them with faint praise. Calculating how many bills passed different sessions of Congress tells us something very basic and important about American government. The popular argument about gridlock is that Congress is mired in inaction. The question political scientists have addressed about divided government is "does it make a difference in Congress's ability to act?" Mayhew's approach directly addresses this. Moreover, although Congress sometimes passes superficial legislation when it can't agree on a real solution to the problem, this doesn't happen often. The historical evidence that I gathered suggests that few bills were stripped of a substantive approach to the problem at hand.

Research Design

The data used here come from a larger study of interest groups in the legislative process. This essay describes the essential elements of the research design; students interested in a more detailed description can consult *The New Liberalism*.[33] The legislative case studies come from 1963, 1979, and 1991. Using entire sessions of Congress—rather than sampling or selecting issues over a continuous time frame—facilitated measurement of how individual lobbies and interest group sectors invested organizational resources across a range of competing demands. For each of these three Congresses, case studies were developed for all domestic social and economic legislation that received hearings in either the House or Senate and received at least a minimal amount of press coverage.

The case studies relied on *Congressional Quarterly Weekly Report*, the *New York Times*, the *Wall Street Journal*, published congressional hearings, and the Congressional Information Service's indexes of congressional hearings. For a hearing to be included in the data set, there had to be at least two articles appearing in the press at different times. We had to be able to learn the legislation's basic intent and determine its final fate in Congress. We tried to answer questions about interest group participation, the nature of the interest group coalitions that emerged, press coverage of particular groups, and who won and lost in the final resolution of the bill. (A distinction between more important and less important legislation is discussed below.) Although we took hearings only from the first session of each of the three Congresses, the fate of the legislation was followed through to the end of the Congress in the following calendar year. If there were hearings in both houses on the same legislation, we used the first hearing that came up through a random selection of entries in the Congressional Information Service index.[34] The case histories, however, contain information on legislative developments in both houses.

A legitimate concern is what might be missing or how we might be misled by using hearings as the unit of analysis. Some bills proceed to the floor without a hearing, but they represent a small percentage of issues considered politically significant. Hearings on prominent issues are hard to avoid because of committee prerogatives and because committee deliberations are an efficient way of resolving disagreements within and between parties. The more controversial a proposal, the more likely it is to receive a hearing. A broader question, raised first by critics of pluralist methodology, is what about problems that don't get on the agenda?[35] Is there a bias that permits only certain kinds of "safe" issues to reach the hearing stage? This is a complicated matter, and political scientists do not have adequate methods for studying "nonissues." Problems that don't become political issues might be the ultimate form of gridlock: Congress ignoring problems altogether. Such a situation is a decision—not a lack of decision—and represents consensus rather than the divisiveness that can lead to gridlock. Still, the failure rate for legislation in any Congress may underestimate the range and quantity of problems that Congress has failed to act on.

Rates of Passage

A starting point in analyzing the data is to examine the three sessions of Congress to find evidence of increasing rates of passage or defeat of legislation. Although we cannot establish a definitive pattern because of the limited number of data points, the findings can serve as a baseline for the proportion of hearings that result in the passage of legislation. More important, these passage rates help us understand the dimensions of legislative failure and success that interest groups contend with. If, for example, most legislation passes in some form, then strategic considerations may push groups toward compromise even if they are opposed to the basic idea behind the legislation. If rates of passage are relatively low, outright opposition may be a more viable strategy.

Some hearings were held with the goal of agenda-building rather than passing a bill that session. A hearing is not truly the start of lawmaking, but it is a formal beginning of a typically lengthy and involved process. For legislators and groups alike, hearings are an opportunity to gain publicity for an issue and to begin to build a case for legislative action. Edwards and his colleagues counted a bill as seriously considered if "a committee or subcommittee in at least one house of Congress held hearings on the bill."[36]

Sometimes legislators and lobbyists recognize that legislation may be years away. In 1991 the Senate Committee on Commerce, Science, and Transportation held hearings on a business-backed bill for tort reform in product liability claims. This kind of legislation had been a priority of manufacturers for years in previous sessions of Congress, when hearings were held on similar bills that went nowhere. Again and again an alliance of trial lawyers and consumer groups and their legislative allies easily beat back the manufacturers' legislation. Yet business lobbies, particularly the U.S. Chamber of Commerce and the National Association of Manufacturers, continued to work with their Senate allies to keep the issue alive. Even though chances were slim that any bill could pass, it was important for tort reform backers to have the hearings and to try to build support for some eventual policy changes.

Given that hearings are often held without any realistic hope that a bill will be passed in that session of Congress, this method of defining the universe of legislation to be measured for rates of passage may seem to incorporate a relatively liberal standard. If we don't screen out bills that didn't stand much chance of passage in the first place, won't the resulting test bias the results toward a lower rate of passage and thus toward a misinterpretation of how much gridlock exists? It is really the opposite approach that is dangerous. If only legislation brought to the floor is used, the threshold biases the results toward passage. When whip counts indicate that a bill lacks the necessary votes for passage, it is usually held back, sometimes even after a vote has been scheduled. Moreover, a true picture of the cooperation that brings legislation to passage should include a range of bills, not just those that have the best chance of enactment. Part of the challenge of any Congress is to deal with festering problems. Likewise, part of the skill of the president and congressional party leaders is to find ways of acting on new problems and to help committees struggling to find an approach that meets the needs of both parties. Using the hearings stage as the screen ensures that such types of policy problems will be included.

The coding differentiates between bills that passed both houses and were sent on to the president for signature and bills that did not pass both houses. The set of bills that passed included those ultimately vetoed by the president, but the vetoed bills amounted to only a tiny handful. Bills that failed included those that were defeated on the floor and, much more commonly, bills that were never brought to a vote. We treated legislation that became law after the two-year session as bills that failed.

There is no clear pattern in passage rates over the three Congresses (Table 16.1). Perhaps most surprising is the relatively high rate of passage during 1979. Jimmy Carter is generally considered a weak and ineffective president, and he was widely criticized for promoting an overly ambitious agenda and for pushing for bills (like hospital cost containment) that had little chance of passing. It appears that large Democratic

Table 16.1.   Rates of Passage (in percent)

	1963	1979	1991	
All legislation	63.5	73.7	52.7	
(N)	(74)	(57)	(74)	(205)
Important legislation only	59.6	69.0	50.0	
(N)	(47)	(42)	(44)	(133)

Source: Author's data.

Note: This table shows the percentage of legislation that passed both houses and was sent to the president for approval.

majorities in the 96th Congress produced a lot of legislation that they were able to send on to Carter. Then the passage rate dropped in 1991, when President Bush faced a House and Senate firmly controlled by the Democrats. This might suggest that divided government does make a difference, but, again, with only three data points such a conclusion would be premature.

When the entire set of legislation is reduced to a smaller set of important bills, the pattern is generally the same. For a bill to be designated important, it had to have received enough press coverage for a lengthy coding sheet to be filled out, including data on a variety of questions about interest group participation. This criterion might seem arbitrary, but in relying on the judgments of reporters and editors, who determine which issues get more or less coverage, we have some confidence that these decisions reflect reasonable standards of what's important. For example, this criteria culls out bills like Potato Marketing Quotas and Coast Guard Personnel Legislation that probably can't tell us much about gridlock. Although some scholars have found that the definition of "important legislation" makes a difference, the similar findings for these two sets of bills don't support this criticism of Mayhew's methodology.

Both the results and the inherent limitations of these data fail to resolve whether government is decaying and increasingly incapable of addressing major issues. But the purpose here is to answer a more specific question about the relationship of interest groups to the passage of legislation. At first glance the data offer no clear hint that the rise of interest group politics increased gridlock. The relatively high passage rate for 1979 would suggest that the growth of interest group politics may have facilitated lawmaking. But the drop in 1991 suggests the opposite, or that by 1991 some sort of threshold was passed where the growth of groups reached a level that made lawmaking less manageable. More precise answers to these questions may come from examining groups in the specific context of the lobbying on each of these bills. Testing for a relationship between the amount or type of lobbying and legislative outcomes should tell us whether interest groups inhibit or facilitate passage.

Lobbyists and Legislators

To calculate the amount of interest group advocacy on the 205 issues, we recorded the number of groups testifying before a committee holding hearings on each of the bills. To determine what types of groups were active on each issue, we disaggregated the list of groups into five categories: corporations, citizen groups, labor unions, professional associations, and trade associations. Only a tiny percentage of groups do not fit into one of these categories (and this residual "other" category is ignored here). There is no official list of interest group participants on any individual bill before Congress, but the list of groups that testify is a reasonably good approximation of the active organizations. A survey of Washington lobbies found that 99 percent testified before Congress.[37] In reviewing press coverage over the course of the legislative process for each issue, we found the same pattern of group participation as in the hearings data.

Assessing the relative influence of any one organization's effort to push legislation toward passage, defeat, or delay is beyond the scope of our work. But applying a statistical tool (logistic regression) to this data set allows us to measure the impact of the level of group participation on legislative outcomes. For those without some background in statistics, however, the raw coefficients generated by this method are difficult to interpret.[38] Instead, those coefficients have been converted into probabilities that a bill will pass. In the accompanying tables, a figure of .60, for example, means that a bill brought to the floor had a 60 percent chance of passing.

To see if the level of interest group participation made a difference in the chances of passage, two probabilities were calculated for each of the situations analyzed. One calculation assumed that zero groups were participating; the second assumed that ten groups were participating (Table 16.2).[39] When zero groups participated the probability of a bill passing was .66. When ten groups participated the probability of passage declined to only .64. Clearly, the number of groups overall has little to do with legislative outcomes. For different types of groups, the probabilities of passage with ten groups involved were only slightly lower than with zero groups. The one exception was labor unions, where probability declined from .64 (zero groups) to .42 (ten groups).[40]

As noted earlier, the subset of important legislation was determined by a threshold of press coverage that allowed a full, narrative case study to be developed. These 133 issues received considerably more coverage in the *New York Times*, *Wall Street Journal*, and *CQ Weekly Report*, and they

Table 16.2. Probabilities of Passage

	All bills	Important bills only	All bills		
			1963	1979	1991
All interest groups	.66/.64	.61/.60	.69/.66	.78/.76	.55/.53
Citizens' groups	.64/.60	.62/.58	.64/.63	.79/.66	.56/.49
Corporations	.64/.57	.61/.57	.67/.57	.74/.73	.56/.42
Labor unions	.64/.42	.61/.47	.67/.36	.70/.75	.57/.46
Professional associations	.63/.56	.59/.60	.65/.56	.75/.69	.54/.46
Trade associations	.63/.61	.59/.60	.68/.61	.75/.71	.51/.57

Source: Author's data.

Note: The first number in each category is the result assuming zero groups are active. The second number is the result assuming ten groups are active.

warranted this attention. Because the usual criticism of Congress is that it is not addressing pressing national problems, this smaller set of important issues may be a better test of the gridlock hypotheses. But after delimiting the data set to include only these cases, no association between the number of interest groups and the likelihood of passage could be found. The aggregate measure for all interest groups and the discrete measures for types of lobbies all produce statistically insignificant comparisons. The probability of passage on important issues with zero groups is .61, as compared with .60 for ten groups. In short, using the subset of important bills yields the same results as the entire set of cases.

Because so many argue that problems with interest groups are getting worse, we repeated the statistical analysis separately for each of the three years. If things are getting worse over time, then the 1991 data set should show a different pattern from the 1963 data set. Because a rapid growth of groups was already evident by 1979, that year too could differ from 1963. Again, though, the results show no patterns. The range of probabilities between years corresponds to the variation in passed legislation shown in Table 16.1. That variation doesn't appear to have much to do with the increasing number of interest groups in Washington. For each of the three years for the aggregate "all interest groups," the probabilities for passage were never more than .03 lower for ten groups than for zero groups. In none of the paired calculations made for Table 16.2 were the differences in the probabilities between zero groups and ten groups large enough to achieve statistical significance. In other words, the numeric differences were too small to represent a meaningful differ-ence in the chances of passage.

Because citizen groups have been singled out for increasing conflict in the legislative process, a more precise analysis of their advocacy is called for. Although more conflict does not necessarily lead to more failed legislation, there may be a connection. Moreover, citizen groups seem to be at the heart of the complaint that government faces too many de-mands. By this logic, the demands of new or greatly expanded mobiliza-tion by environmentalists, consumers, women, African Americans, and other such constituencies are to blame for gridlock.

To test this overload argument we picked important issues where cit-izen groups, along with their legislative allies, initiated legislation. And the legislation had to produce a fight with at least two major sides on the issue. The fight was almost always between citizen groups and business. In some cases citizen groups were allied with one set of business groups in conflict with lobbies representing another set of business interests. In all cases citizen groups were on the offensive, trying to push legislation through and thus trying to place new demands on government. Cases in-cluded environmentalists fighting the nuclear industry (Nuclear Waste and Facility Siting Policy, 1979); the American Coalition of Citizens with Disabilities fighting the Chamber of Commerce (Equal Employment for the Handicapped Act, 1979); and the NAACP, the Leadership Confer-ence on Civil Rights, and other citizen groups against the Business Roundtable, the National Association of Manufacturers, and other busi-ness groups (Civil Rights Act of 1991).

We found no relationship between citizen group participation and legislative outcomes.[41] On important issues when citizen groups pro-posed placing more demands on government and lots of different groups were drawn into the conflict, there was no difference in legislative out-comes than when the dispute was more contained. The probability for passage if (theoretically) no citizen groups had been active was .50. For ten citizen groups it was also .50. In virtually all cases the citizen groups on the offensive were liberal groups. Outside of abortion and gun control, conservative citizen groups were inactive.

We also tested the effect of business interest participation on passage rates. A generation of scholars portrayed the interest group system as domi-nated by business and characterized by stable, cooperative relations be-tween policymakers and the industries they regulated.[42] Is an interest group universe dominated by business more likely to bring forth legislation that can pass in Congress? We tested the probabilities for passage in four combinations of citizen group and corporation activity (Table 16.3). When citizen groups and corporations are both active, they are in conflict with each other. But again the differences are statistically insignificant. The probability of passage when no citizen groups or corporate lobbies were active (.68) was only modestly higher than when both were active (.57).

Table 16.3.   Probability of Passage When Business
and Citizens' Groups Are Involved

	Zero citizens' groups active	Ten citizens' groups active
Zero corporate lobbies active	.68	.60
Ten corporate lobbies active	.55	.57

Source: Author's data.

More striking is that even when business faced no opposition from citizen groups, it was no more capable of bringing forth passable legislation (.55) than when there was conflict between the corporate sector and citizen groups (.57).

When business is active, is it unified or divided? Those who criticize the interest group system for favoring business interests generally ignore or downplay intra-industry conflict. The critics see such conflicts as insignificant in light of the greater unity of business over broader issues important to all industry sectors.[43] This rather broad question cannot be answered here, but the narrower question of whether intra-industry conflict has increased over time can be. Intra-industry conflict is defined as two or more sectors in the same industry that are openly opposed and actively engaged in lobbying Congress. Comparing intra-industry conflict in 1963 and 1991 reveals a modest (and statistically insignificant) increase, from 20.6 percent to 27.8 percent.[44] Thus it is unlikely that intra-industry conflict alone can explain why business-backed legislation without citizen group opposition doesn't do any better than when citizen groups and business are locked in conflict over legislation. In short, business-backed bills seem subject to the same complex forces that cause other groups' legislation to succeed or fail. Overall, there is scant evidence that citizen groups have pushed Congress toward gridlock or otherwise overloaded Congress with demands.

Conclusion

A variety of tests all lead to the same conclusion: interest groups are not a cause of legislative gridlock. No matter how the data are sorted, legislative outcomes barely differ. Increased levels of lobbying yield no evidence of inducing gridlock. And no one interest group sector can be linked to gridlock. Narrowing the data set to the most important bills produces the same results. The three separate sessions of Congress differed in productivity, but interest group lobbying appears unrelated to these differences.

The data set does not offer a complete set of relevant variables. Modeling the legislative process with a full array of controls would yield more definitive information about Congress, productivity, and gridlock. The question remains as to why higher levels of lobbying on bills don't appear related to legislative productivity. Should we accept Brady and Volden's contention that interest group strength is reflected in election returns and that lobbying in between elections does little to disturb legislators' policy preferences? This assumes that legislators have well-established preferences on hundreds of issues. It also assumes that when preferences are closely divided that lobbying groups don't affect the outcome through strategic efforts to sway a few votes.

These assumptions seem problematic. When a recent effort in the Senate to produce a tobacco bill fell apart on the floor after easy passage in committee, many credited the tobacco industry's broad advertising campaign against big government and new taxes. The tobacco industry's approach seems to confirm Brady and Volden's theory, because the approach reinforced the antigovernment and antitax sentiments that had led voters to elect conservative Republicans. On the other hand, what appeared to be a majority in the Senate eroded—and it didn't happen in a political vacuum.

A more likely explanation of our results is the sheer complexity of the legislative process. Although researchers focus on one or two key variables, Congress is subject to many internal and external influences. Public opinion, party strength, presidential and congressional leadership skills, presidential standing, divided or unified government, external events and crises, institutional rules, members' ideological preferences, and interest group lobbying are all factors that can influence the legislative process. So it is understandable that in isolating the role of interest groups across a large number of issues we found little evidence of an independent impact on productivity.

We may also underestimate Congress's ability to adapt to a changing external environment. As the number of interest groups in Washington skyrocketed, Congress was neither overwhelmed nor incapacitated. Exactly how Congress deals with so many more groups has never been studied. As Rauch points out, whether Congress actually solves problems is a separate issue; passing laws may be the easy part. In legislators' drive for reelection they try to demonstrate that they have spent the past two or six years fashioning important new laws. As one legislator notes, "Congress exists to do things. There isn't much mileage in doing nothing."[45]

Citizen groups have received a disproportionate amount of blame for the alleged trend toward gridlock. They are charged with generating conflict that makes it more difficult for legislative leaders to assemble winning coalitions. The data here suggest otherwise. Their levels of participation are, similar to all other kinds of groups, unrelated to legislative productivity. Even in conflict with other types of groups, citizen groups' level of lobbying made no difference in outcomes. And citizen groups have broadened the representation of chronically underrepresented interests. Huntington's argument that citizen groups have placed undue demands on the government ignores the reality of interest group politics. Business lobbies continue to dwarf citizen groups—so why are citizen groups presumed to have pushed Congress into dysfunction?

A different issue is the way citizen groups lobby, which can be pretentious and moralistic. Sympathizers might instead regard them as refreshingly stubborn in refusing to compromise their principles. There is no question that these groups' rhetoric can be harsh and uncompromising.[46] At the same time it's important to distinguish between rhetoric and reality. Some groups are particularly difficult to deal with when it comes to compromising their beliefs—Ralph Nader and the National Rifle Association come to mind—but there is no indication that citizen groups as a whole are less cooperative or less prone to compromise. Because these groups typically pursue nonmaterial goods, they use their selflessness and their broad public support to seize the moral high ground. Like any other lobby, citizen groups try to gain whatever leverage they can. In the end the evidence here demonstrates that citizen lobbies bear no special responsibility for damaging congressional productivity. Like all other types of lobbies, their participation density is unrelated to legislative outcomes.

This issue of which groups may or may not reduce the chances of legislation passing Congress is a question about representation as well as gridlock. If one sector of the interest group community has a greater capacity to stop legislation, its constituents have an advantage. There are many different types of advantages and disadvantages in interest group politics, and this study explores one source of possible bias. The absence of significant differences among the performances of interest group sectors is striking. The bills Congress considers do not seem subject to the veto power of any one lobby. Nor has Congress gotten bogged down in the demands of any one sector. These tests do not prove that all interest group sectors are equal in influence, but they do indicate that the interest group system may be more broadly representative than we think.

Notes

1. Samuel P. Huntington, "The Democratic Distemper," *Public Interest* 41 (fall 1975): 9–38; Samuel P. Huntington, "The United States," in *The Crisis of Democracy*, ed. Michel Crozier, Samuel P. Huntington, and Joji Watanuki (New York: New York University, 1975); Samuel P. Huntington, *American Politics: The Promise of Disharmony* (Cambridge: Harvard University, 1985).
2. Robert Caro, *The Power Broker* (New York: Knopf, 1974).
3. Mancur Olson, *The Rise and Decline of Nations* (New Haven: Yale University, 1982).
4. Lester C. Thurow, *The Zero-Sum Society* (New York: Penguin, 1980).

5. Jonathan Rauch, *Demosclerosis* (New York: Times Books, 1994), 158.
6. Kay Lehman Schlozman and John T. Tierney, *Organized Interests and American Democracy* (New York: Harper and Row, 1986); Jack L. Walker, *Mobilizing Interest Groups in America* (Ann Arbor: University of Michigan, 1991).
7. Kevin P. Phillips, "The 1990s' Political Upheaval and the Pressures for Reform," in *Back to Gridlock?* ed. James L. Sundquist (Washington, D.C.: Brookings, 1995), 79.
8. Vin Weber, "The Capitol Hill Perspective: A Republican View," in Sundquist, *Back to Gridlock?* 49.
9. Anthony King, "The American Polity in the Late 1970s: Building Coalitions in the Sand," in *The New American Political System*, ed. Anthony King (Washington, D.C.: American Enterprise Institute, 1979), 391.
10. David R. Mayhew, *Divided We Govern* (New Haven: Yale University, 1991).
11. George C. Edwards III, Andrew Barrett, and Jeffrey Peake, "The Legislative Impact of Divided Government," *American Journal of Political Science* 41 (April 1997): 545.
12. Sean Q. Kelly, "Divided We Govern? A Reassessment," *Polity* 25 (spring 1993): 475–484.
13. Gary W. Cox and Mathew D. McCubbins, "Divided Control of Fiscal Policy," in *The Politics of Divided Government*, ed. Gary W. Cox and Samuel Kernell (Boulder, Colo.: Westview, 1991), 155–175; Bryan D. Jones, James L. True, and Frank R. Baumgartner, "Does Incrementalism Stem from Political Consensus or from Institutional Gridlock?" *American Journal of Political Science* 41 (October 1997): 1319–1339; David W. Brady and Craig Volden, *Revolving Gridlock* (Boulder, Colo.: Westview, 1998); Keith Krehbiel, *Pivotal Politics* (Chicago: University of Chicago, 1998); Sarah A. Binder, "The Dynamics of Legislative Gridlock, 1947–96," *American Political Science Review* 93 (September 1999): 530.
14. Morris Fiorina, *Divided Government*, 2d ed. (Boston: Allyn and Bacon, 1996), 158–159.
15. One exception is Cynthia J. Bowling and Margaret R. Ferguson's study of gridlock in the state legislatures. Using various measures of interest group diversity and concentration, the authors failed to find consistent relationships between their independent variables and the probability of passage. The authors were not able to measure actual lobbying on specific issues but relied instead on population measures of interest groups. "Divided Government, Interest Representation, and Policy Differences: Competing Explanations of Gridlock in Fifty States," *Journal of Politics* 63 (February 2001): 183–206.
16. Brady and Volden, *Revolving Gridlock*, 4.
17. Rauch, *Demosclerosis*, 91.
18. Jeffrey M. Berry, "Subgovernments, Issue Networks, and Political Conflict," in *Remaking American Politics*, ed. Richard A. Harris and Sidney M. Milkis (Boulder, Colo.: Westview, 1989), 239.
19. John P. Heinz, Edward O. Laumann, Robert L. Nelson, and Robert H. Salisbury, *The Hollow Core: Private Interests in National Policy Making* (Cambridge: Harvard University, 1993).
20. Walker, *Mobilizing Interest Groups*, 62–64.
21. Mark A. Peterson and Jack L. Walker, "Interest Group Responses to Partisan Change," in *Interest Group Politics*, 2d ed., ed. Allan J. Cigler and Burdett A. Loomis (Washington, D.C.: CQ Press, 1986), 167.
22. William P. Browne, *Private Interests, Public Policy, and American Agriculture* (Lawrence: University Press of Kansas, 1988).
23. Thomas E. Mann, "President Clinton and the Democratic Congress: Promise and Performance," in Sundquist, *Back to Gridlock?* 12.
24. John B. Gilmour, *Strategic Disagreement* (Pittsburgh: University of Pittsburgh, 1995), 29.

25. Jeffrey M. Berry, *The New Liberalism: The Rising Power of Citizen Groups* (Washington, D.C.: Brookings, 1999).

26. Robert H. Salisbury, "The Paradox of Interest Groups in Washington—More Groups, Less Clout," in *The New American Political System*, 2d ed., ed. Anthony King (Washington, D.C.: American Enterprise Institute, 1990), 203.

27. David Vogel, *Trading Up* (Cambridge: Harvard University, 1995).

28. Barbara Sinclair, *Unorthodox Lawmaking*, 2d ed. (Washington, D.C.: CQ Press, 2000).

29. Brady and Volden, *Revolving Gridlock*, 4.

30. Mayhew, *Divided We Govern*, 34–50.

31. Samuel Kernell, "Facing an Opposition Congress: The President's Strategic Circumstance," in Cox and Kernell, *The Politics of Divided Government*, 87–112.

32. Rauch, *Demosclerosis*, 123–124.

33. Berry, *The New Liberalism*, 8–14 and 171–183.

34. Although hearings were selected randomly, nearly all were eventually screened. Thus the cases are not a sample of each year but represent the entire universe of hearings that met the criteria for inclusion.

35. Peter Bachrach and Morton S. Baratz, "Two Faces of Power," *American Political Science Review* 56 (December 1962): 947–952.

36. Edwards, Barrett, and Peake, "The Legislative Impact of Divided Government," 549.

37. Schlozman and Tierney, *Organized Interests and American Democracy*, 150.

38. The original statistical work can be found in Jeffrey M. Berry, "Interest Groups and Gridlock" (paper presented at the annual meeting of the American Political Science Association, Boston, September 1998).

39. Although there is an arbitrary quality to the choice of any number of groups to represent the high end of interest group participation, a qualitative review of the cases indicated that if ten groups are active, the legislation is likely to be hard-fought, involve a range of groups, and be subject to complex negotiations.

40. It's hard to know what to make of this statistical outlier. Notwithstanding the insignificance of the underlying statistical relationship, this test doesn't resonate with real-world politics. Though it is not unusual to have ten business groups active or even a large number of citizen groups, ten labor unions are almost never active on an issue. The AFL-CIO usually coordinates the lobbying and it counts here as only a single organization. In most cases labor activity involves only the AFL-CIO and one or two of its constituent unions.

41. The logit coefficient is –.017, standard error (.039), not significant.

42. See Theodore J. Lowi, *The End of Liberalism* (New York: Norton, 1969); and Charles E. Lindblom, *Politics and Markets* (New York: Basic Books, 1977).

43. Michael Useem, *The Inner Circle* (New York: Oxford University, 1984).

44. The cases included only those from the higher salience (more important) bills where there was some identifiable business lobbying.

45. John W. Kingdon, *Agendas, Alternatives, and Public Policies*, 2d ed. (New York: HarperCollins, 1995), 38.

46. Michael W. McCann, *Taking Reform Seriously* (Ithaca: Cornell University, 1986).

17

Cracks in the Armor?
Interest Groups and Foreign Policy
Eric M. Uslaner

Since the Vietnam War and the controversies in the 1980s over El Salvador, American policies abroad have caused many political conflicts at home. As a result, ethnic groups in the United States have begun to participate vigorously in domestic politics. Although the American Jewish community has long been a powerful force in both legislative and electoral politics, other groups—from Cuban-Americans to Chinese-Americans—have entered the fray.

In this chapter Eric Uslaner addresses the evolution of activity among foreign policy groups and ethnic interest groups. Sometimes, as with the American-Israeli Political Affairs Council, these two groups overlap. Indeed, Uslaner asserts that "Foreign policy interest groups began to look more and more like domestic groups. . . . And in some cases, especially where constituency groups were weak politically, foreign countries took a direct role in U.S. domestic politics." The openness of the American political process has offered great opportunities for ethnic groups, and no one would challenge the right of Arab-Americans or Greek-Americans or any other such group to lobby or fund favored candidates. But such groups must always appear more loyal to the United States than to other nations to be effective in American politics.

The author gratefully acknowledges support from the General Research Board, University of Maryland at College Park. Some data come from the Inter-University Consortium for Political and Social Research, which has no responsibility for any interpretations here.

When we think of interest group politics we generally focus on domestic policy. On foreign policy the entire country is supposed to speak with a single voice. Policy is supposed to reflect a national interest that has its roots in moral principles.

Because the stakes of foreign policy are higher than those of domestic policy—the wrong decision could lead to a nuclear confrontation—we expect foreign policy decisions to be less subject to group pressure. Instead, we make decisions based on a common interest. Foreign policy should be based on broad national principles that put American interests first when looking beyond our borders.

But foreign policy decisions increasingly reflect ethnic interests rather than some overarching sense of national interest. At least five ethnic groups saw the 2000 election as a chance to shape their foreign policy goals, even though neither major candidate nor voters showed much concern for foreign policy.[1] Two groups seeking to sway the election seem to have failed; the other three may have succeeded, at least in part.

Groups representing the Middle East conflict were at odds. American Jews welcomed and Arab-Americans worried about the nomination of the first Jewish candidate for vice president, Sen. Joseph I. Lieberman, D-Conn. Lieberman's loss pleased the Muslims, who had little else to cheer about in the 2000 elections.

Other ethnic groups had more to celebrate. Cuban-Americans, upset over the Clinton administration's handling of six-year-old refugee Elian Gonzalez, may have been responsible for the narrow Republican victory in Florida that gave the presidency to Republican George W. Bush. Other Latinos, especially Mexican-Americans, were angry at restrictive immigration legislation enacted by Republicans in Congress and in California. Latinos established themselves as a power base in California, contributing heavily to Al Gore's victory there and helping the Democrats capture several formerly Republican House seats. And Armenian-Americans claimed credit for toppling a California Republican incumbent.

American Jews have long lobbied successfully on Israel's behalf, and many groups have tried to copy the Jewish model. Irish-Americans, Greek-Americans, Cuban-Americans, Latinos, Armenian-Americans, and even Arab-Americans followed the lead of the pro-Israel lobby to gain support for their interests. Yet in the past few years we have seen cracks in the armor of powerful ethnic interests. The pro-Israel and anti-Castro lobbies still generally get their way, but their tasks are not quite as easy as they used to be, and once in a while the lobbies lose a battle.

The pro-Israel groups initially focused on the moral claims that Jews made for Israel. As the Palestinian resistance (the Intifada) developed in the 1980s, some leaders criticized Israel's military response to rock throwing by Palestinian youths. Once the pro-Israel forces lost their moral monopoly, they began to act like any other interest group—rewarding their friends and punishing their enemies. They took an increasingly active role in raising money to back candidates for office.

Foreign policy interest groups began to look more and more like domestic groups, with one key difference. It had become unclear whether some groups were more loyal to their "mother country" than to the United States. And in some cases, especially where constituency groups were weak politically, foreign countries took a direct role in U.S. domestic politics. In the 1996 presidential election, foreign interests allegedly made direct contributions to the reelection campaign of President Bill Clinton. Some of these funds may have even come from the Chinese government, which sought to protect its favored trading status with the United States.

Many people worried that decisions that ought to be made on the basis of moral concerns—what the United States's role should be in the world, especially when it is the only superpower—were being made through group conflict and campaign contributions. When does it become illegitimate for Jewish-Americans to lobby on behalf of Israel, for Cuban-Americans to lobby against the Castro regime, or for Chinese-Americans to take sides between the "two Chinas" (the People's Republic and Taiwan)? If it is acceptable for Chinese-Americans to lobby for China, why is it not acceptable for the Chinese to lobby for themselves? If the Chinese (or others) can appropriately exert pressure in Washington, should they be prohibited from influencing who gets sent to Washington?

And here is the dilemma underlying group conflict in U.S. foreign policy. When an ethnic group is united, it can take the high ground. When American Jews were single-minded in their support for Israel and when Cuban-Americans were united in their opposition to Castro, both groups could make moral arguments. As divisions grew within both communities, gaining outside support became more difficult. When a group cannot be sure of universal support, it may feel compelled to use confrontational strategies to win support. But how do others view these tactics, and how successful can they be? In an April 1997 *New York Times*/CBS News survey, 45 percent of Americans said they were bothered more by foreign government contributions to "buy influence" than by similar efforts from special interest groups (25 percent) or "wealthy people" (21 percent).[2]

Ethnic Groups in Foreign Policy

Mohammed E. Ahrari has suggested four conditions for ethnic group success in foreign policy. First, the group must press for a policy in line with U.S. strategic interests. Second, the group must be assimilated into U.S. society, yet retain enough identification with the "old country" so that this foreign policy issue motivates people to take some political action. Third, the group and its members must be politically active. Fourth, groups should be politically unified.[3] Other criteria include advocating policies backed by the larger public, having enough members to wield political influence, and being perceived as pursuing a legitimate interest.

American Jews are distinctive in their ability to affect foreign policy. They have established the most prominent and best-endowed lobby in Washington by fulfilling each of the conditions for an influential group. In recent years, however, some conditions have not been met and the pro-Israel lobby is no longer the same dominant force. Still, its rival in Washington, the pro-Arab lobby, has remained weak by failing to meet any of the conditions.

The Israel and Arab Lobbies

The most important ethnic lobby on foreign policy is the American Israel Public Affairs Committee (AIPAC). *Fortune* magazine rates AIPAC as the fourth most powerful lobbying group in Washington on any issue.[4] Jews, who dominate the pro-Israel lobby, make up 2.7 percent of the U.S. population. Yet they are strongly motivated and highly organized in support of Israel. Since the lobby's inception in 1951 it has rarely lost an important battle. In recent years Israel's policies have become more controversial in the United States—and within Israel. The splits within Israel are mirrored in the American Jewish community.

Israel receives by far the largest share of U.S. foreign aid, more than $3 billion a year. In 1985 Israel and the United States signed a free-trade pact. And Israel benefits from large tax-exempt contributions from the American Jewish community.[5] No other foreign nation is so favored.

AIPAC has a staff of 150, an annual budget of $15 million, and 55,000 members. It operates out of offices one block from Capitol Hill,[6] with considerable political acumen: "In a moment of perceived crisis, it can put a carefully researched, well-documented statement of its views on the desk of every Senator and Congressman and appropriate committee staff within four hours of a decision to do so."[7]

AIPAC's lobbying connections are so thorough that one observer said, "A mystique has grown up around the lobby to the point where it is viewed with admiration, envy, and sometimes, anger."[8] Activists can readily mobilize the network of Jewish organizations across the country to put pro-Israel pressure on members of Congress, even in areas with small Jewish populations. In 1991 the lobby organized 1,500 "citizen lobbyists" armed with computer printouts of their legislators' backgrounds. AIPAC claims to enact more than 100 pieces of pro-Israel legislation a year through some 2,000 meetings with members of Congress.[9]

The Arab lobbying effort has been far less successful. There were no major Arab organizations before 1972, and a Washington presence did not begin until 1978. The Arab lobby for many years consisted of several small organizations with differing objectives. Early Arab lobbying comprised efforts sponsored by Arab governments and oil companies and groups representing different Lebanese factions.[10] One analysis concluded, "Most Arab embassies throw impressive parties, but have little day-to-day contact with Congress, according to lawmakers and aides."[11]

The Arab uprising in the West Bank and Gaza that began in 1987 energized and united the Arab-American community. The National Association of Arab Americans now maintains a grassroots network organized by congressional district, patterned directly after AIPAC.[12] The 1990 Gulf War split Arabs once more, as supporters of Iraqi leader Saddam Hussein battled with more moderate factions. In 1988 Democratic presidential candidate Michael Dukakis rejected the endorsement of Arab-American leaders. As the Arab-American population grew—it is now estimated at 6 million, about the same size as the Jewish community—politicians began to pay more attention. All four major contenders for the Democratic and Republican nominations in 2000 addressed (either live or by satellite) the Arab American Institute national convention. Arab-Americans joined forces with the NAACP and La Raza in pressing for an end to discrimination, especially profiling at airports.

Yet Arab-Americans still find their influence limited. Jewish organizations were able to stop House Minority Leader Richard Gephardt's nomination of Salam Al-Marayati in 1999 to a counterterrorism commission. The pro-Israeli groups charged that Al-Marayati had blamed the Israeli government for inciting Palestinian violence. And Hillary Rodham Clinton returned $50,000 in contributions to her Senate campaign from the American Muslim Alliance; the leader of the alliance had also justified Palestinian violence against Israel.[13]

The Israel Advantage

Inter-Arab divisiveness thus accounts for some, but not all, of the difficulties that these Arab-American groups confront. Public opinion plays a much larger role. For a long time Americans have sympathized more with Israel than with the Arabs. Most polls show that Americans favor the Israeli position by between a three to one margin and a five to one margin. In the past few years 40–50 percent of Americans sided with Israel, about 10–15 percent with the Palestinians, 10 percent with both, and 20 percent with neither. As violence has increased in Israel, twice as many Americans blame the Palestinians as blame Israel—and public support for Israel increased to more than 60 percent.[14]

The roots of the friendship between the United States and Israel include factors such as:

- A common biblical heritage (most Arabs are Muslim, an unfamiliar religion to most Americans).

- A shared European value system (Islam is often sharply critical of the West's perceived lack of morality).
- The democratic nature of Israel's political system (most Arab nations are monarchies or dictatorships).
- Israel's role as an ally of the United States (most Arab countries have been seen as either unreliable friends or as hostile to U.S. interests).
- The sympathy Americans extend toward Jews as victims (Arabs are portrayed as terrorists or exploiters of the U.S. economy through their oil weapon).[15]

Jews benefit from a high rate of participation in politics, and Arab-Americans are not as great a political force. Jews are among the most generous campaign contributors in U.S. politics: 60 percent of individual contributions to former president Clinton's 1992 campaign came from Jewish donors. Jewish contributors, including the National Jewish Democratic Council, were among the top twenty contributors to Gore's 2000 Presidential campaign. And Jews are far more active politically than are other Americans: They are substantially more likely to vote, to try to influence others' voting choices, to attend political meetings, to work for a party or a candidate, to write letters to public officials, and to follow the campaign through television, radio, magazines, and newspapers. And they are twice as likely as other Americans to donate money to candidates for office.[16] Arab-Americans have not been very active in politics. Only 100,000 belong to any Arab-American organization, compared with 2 million Jews active in Jewish causes.

Although Arab groups are divided internally and have no common frame of reference, American Jews have traditionally been united in support of Israel. In a 1998 survey of American Jews, 58 percent considered themselves close to Israel, 41 percent had visited Israel, 42 percent had close friends or relatives living there, and 86 percent considered the fate of the Jewish community in Israel to be important to them. A 1982 poll found that three-quarters of American Jews believe they should not vote for a candidate who is unfriendly to Israel, and one-third would be willing to contribute money to political candidates who support Israel.[17]

The pro-Israel lobby before the late 1980s met all of the conditions for a group to be successful. Jews were well assimilated, had a high level of political activity, were united in their support of Israel, and had the support of public opinion. Israel was seen as a strategic asset by the American public and particularly by decisionmakers. Backers of Israel did not stand to gain from their lobbying; these backers had to contribute their own money to participate. Although not numerous compared with many other groups, American Jews and other supporters of Israel were concentrated in key states important to presidential candidates (New York, California, Pennsylvania).

The Arab-American lobby was on the other end of the spectrum. Americans have generally not seen Arab nations as strategic allies. Many Arab-Americans are not well assimilated into U.S. society and politics. The community is neither homogenous with respect to Middle East politics nor politically active. U.S. public opinion has never been favorable to the Arab (or Palestinian) cause. The financing of Arab-American organizations by Middle Eastern interests and the active pursuit of changes in U.S. policy by economic interests have weakened the legitimacy of the Arab-American cause.

In 1987 pro-Israel groups began to lose some of their clout. The Palestinian uprising against Israeli control of the West Bank and Gaza (the Intifada) raised international consciousness about the Palestinian cause and lessened U.S. public support for the Jewish state. The Jewish community began to argue about what Israel ought to do. When Israel and the Palestine Liberation Organization signed their peace accord at the White House in September 1993, a deeper schism arose among American (and Israeli) Jews. Dealing with former enemies is always difficult. Moreover, the conflict over the peace process reflected tensions within Israel over religious issues.

American Judaism is divided into three major blocs—Orthodox, Conservative, and Reform. These divisions reflect disagreements over which religious laws Jews should follow. Seven percent of American Jews call themselves Orthodox, 38 percent Conservative, and 42 percent Reform.[18] In Israel, Orthodox Jews have been prominent actors in right-wing coalition governments in Israel and largely oppose the peace process. They have pressured these governments to deny recognition to Conservative and Reform conversions conducted in the United States.

American Jews have been split in recent years over both religious issues and peace. Seventy-five percent of Reform and Conservative Jews support the peace process, with just 12 percent opposed. Almost 60 percent of Orthodox Jews oppose the peace process. A majority of Reform and Conservative Jews support the decision of most Jewish organizations (and the Israeli government) to back U.S. foreign aid to Israel, and almost two-thirds of the Orthodox oppose such assistance. Most Reform Jews say that Orthodox and non-Orthodox Jews have little in common.[19] The conflicts within American Jewry reflect similar disputes in Israel.

The power of the pro-Israel lobby rested on unity within the Jewish community and on widespread support beyond this small group. Yet conflicts over religion and peace led to fractionalization. AIPAC became increasingly linked to the more hawkish right-wing government in Israel in the 1980s. An internal power struggle within AIPAC ousted the conservative leadership and restored a liberal tilt to the organization. In turn, the (then) opposition Likud Party stepped up its efforts to discredit the peace process. The Likud supported the hawkish Zionist Organization of America, which directly competed with AIPAC for legislative support and which covertly sent its own former cabinet members to lobby on Capitol Hill.[20]

On religious issues, one group of Orthodox rabbis declared that the Reform and Conservative movements are "not Judaism." In turn, the chancellor of the largest Conservative seminary demanded the dismantling of the office of Chief Rabbi in Israel, because it was perpetuating the Orthodox monopoly on religious practice. American Reform rabbis issued a statement in January 2000 endorsing a compromise with the Palestinians over control of Jerusalem; Conservative and Orthodox rabbis took strong issue with this proposal.[21]

Jewish-American politicians have long been a bulwark of Israel's support on Capitol Hill. Most Jews are Democrats and so are most Jewish elected officials. Although Jews constitute less than 3 percent of the population, about 10 percent of the members in both the House and Senate are Jewish. They have long been a united bloc in favor of any Israeli government, but especially supportive of Labor administrations that pursue peace. And these legislators have sought positions where they could help Israel. Almost 20 percent of the Senate Foreign Relations Committee and the House International Relations Committee are Jewish and half of the members of the House Subcommittee on the Middle East, including both the chair and the ranking minority member, are Jewish. One of two Arab-Americans serving in Congress is on the House committee (and subcommittee). Despite internal divisions within the American Jewish community, Jewish members of Congress generally speak with one voice.

Pro-Israel forces in Washington were thrilled in 2000 when the Democratic Party nominated Joseph Lieberman, an Orthodox Jew and strong supporter of Israel, as its candidate for vice president. American Jews hoped that the election of the first Jewish vice president would cement American support for Israel at a time when tensions flared in the Middle East. The Democratic ticket barely lost the election. Jewish mobilization didn't make the difference in states with the largest Jewish populations: Gore carried California, Connecticut, Maryland, New Jersey, and New York by overwhelming margins—and he barely lost Florida (and the election) to Bush.

Arab-Americans are becoming a more unified and energized bloc. Arab-Americans took a much more active role in the 2000 Presidential elections, endorsing Republican candidate George W. Bush. Yet their lobbies still rank far behind the pro-Israel groups in influence, because Arab-American positions don't gather public support and Arab-Americans have not been as politically active as Jewish-Americans. Arab-American lobbies always seem to be *against* something—Israel—rather than *for* something, as the pro-Israel groups are.[22]

Sometimes Arab-American efforts appear clumsy at best. In 1999 Burger King had established a restaurant in a Jewish settlement on the West Bank, while the new Israeli exhibit at Disney's Epcot park in Orlando referred to Jerusalem as Israel's capital. Arab-American groups and Arab governments briefly boycotted Burger King and Disney until the restaurant was closed and all references to Jerusalem were excised from the Israeli exhibit. In 2001 Islamic authorities in several Arab countries issued a religious edict to all Muslims (including those in the United States) to boycott Pokemon trading cards. They charged that Pokemon translates into "I am a Jew" in Japanese (where the cards originated) and that the symbol of Pokemon characters' power was a six-pointed star, evidence that the fictional heroes are Zionist agents.[23] In the Burger King and EPCOT cases, the Arab-American groups got what they wanted, but paid a price in negative publicity. Muslim groups failed to block Pokemon sales, even in countries with overwhelming majorities of Muslims. In each case Western observers saw these activities as attacks on Western influence more generally—and this might limit the effectiveness of other lobbying activities.

Arab-Americans are becoming more active and politically sophisticated. Although American Jews are predominantly Democratic, Arab-Americans divide their loyalties almost evenly between the two parties. In principle, then, they could constitute an important swing vote in states with large Arab-American populations, such as California, Illinois, New Jersey, and especially Michigan. The Council on American-Islamic Relations in California sought unsuccessfully to tilt the 2000 Senate race to Republican challenger Tom Campbell and away from Jewish Democratic incumbent Dianne Feinstein.

A large number of Muslim groups banded together to endorse Bush over Gore, fearing that the election of Lieberman as vice president would solidify U.S. support for Israel. They focused on Michigan, a state that was expected to be close and that has the largest concentration of Arab-Americans. Many Arab-Americans stood behind Green Party nominee Ralph Nader, a Lebanese-American. Positions on the Middle East were the main motivating factor among Arab-American voters. Arab-Americans gave Bush a 46–38 percent margin over Gore, with 14 percent going to Nader, far more than his 2 percent of the national vote.[24]

Even though Bush won, Arab-Americans could hardly claim credit: Bush did not carry any of the target states. Gore not only won Michigan, but the only Arab-American senator, Spencer Abraham, R-Mich., lost his reelection bid. In California, Feinstein and the entire Democratic ticket won handily.

Neither Arab-Americans nor Jewish Americans could claim the 2000 elections as a major success. Lieberman did not become vice president. The Clinton-Gore administration was arguably the most favorable to Jews in U.S. history. Several cabinet members and many more lower level and informal advisers to Clinton and Gore were Jewish, as is Gore's son-in-law and both of Clinton's Supreme Court nominees. The Bush cabinet has no Jewish members. Yet Arab-Americans were hardly in a position to rejoice. Shortly after taking office, President Bush issued a stern warning to Palestinian leader Yasser Arafat to stop the violence in Israel and the Palestinian territories.

The balance of Middle Eastern interest groups shifted dramatically after the September 11, 2001, terrorist attacks on the World Trade Center and the Pentagon by radical Muslims. Many Americans came to identify with Israelis as victims of terror. Public support for Israel rose sharply in one month, from 41 percent to 55 percent, the highest level in a decade. A third of all Americans thought the United States should become closer to Israel, compared with 16 percent who wanted more distance. Even though more than half of Americans thought the attacks were a direct result of American policy in the Middle East, support for aid to Israel jumped while support for the Palestinians fell by nearly half.

Despite President Bush's insistence that the attacks were the work of a small group of militants, 39 percent of Americans said that they had an unfavorable view of Islam. Saudi prince Alwaleed bin Talal offered to donate $10 million to aid victims of the tragedies but linked the attacks to American foreign policy in the Middle East. New York Mayor Rudolph Guiliani quickly rejected the offer—more Jews live in New York than in any other city in the United States. African-American representative Cynthia A. McKinney, D-Ga., strongly attacked Israel's policies and praised the prince, but no other American leader joined her. Many joined the president, however, in condemning attacks on Muslims. At least one politician, Rep. John Cooksey, R-La., saw his political fortunes sink when he called for racial profiling of Arab-Americans by looking for the "diapers on their heads." [25]

Other Ethnic Interest Groups

No foreign policy interest group, and certainly no ethnic group, has the reputation for influence that the pro-Israel forces have. Even a weakened AIPAC still sets the pace—for two reasons. First, AIPAC is the model for most other successful groups. Second, like the Jewish community, other ethnic groups have been divided over the best course of action for their countries. The ethnic lobby that was poised to capture the role of "king of the Hill" from AIPAC, the Cuban American National Foundation, has been wrought with its own conflicts.

Latinos

Latinos now constitute about 12 percent of all Americans, up from 6.4 percent in 1980. The 2000 census showed that the Latino population in the United States jumped by 60 percent over ten years, so that Hispanics now have the same share of the population as African-Americans. The growth was particularly strong in California, where Latinos comprise about one-third of all residents—and among Mexican-Americans, by far the biggest immigrant group. The Hispanic Caucus in the House of Representatives has grown from five members to seventeen in 1976–2000. And the Hispanic members have gained key leadership positions, notably Rep. Robert Menendez, D-N.J., as chief deputy whip for the Democratic minority.[26]

Yet Latinos have little unity. The largest groups are Mexicans and Puerto Ricans, who are relatively poor and likely to back liberal Democratic candidates in elections. Mexican-Americans make up 60 percent of all Latinos, but many are not U.S. citizens, and those who are have ambivalent feelings toward Mexico. Until recently Mexican leaders did not encourage intervention on behalf of Mexico by Mexican-Americans. Now they do, even campaigning in the United States.[27]

Puerto Ricans are divided over the status of Puerto Rico, with some favoring statehood, others the continuation of the commonwealth status, and still others independence. For countries such as El Salvador and Nicaragua, where U.S. policy is more controversial, religious organizations with few ties to the indigenous communities dominate foreign policy lobbies, such as the Washington Office on Latin America. These organizations focus largely on human rights. Some have influence on Capitol Hill, but their lobbying tends to concentrate more on legislators already committed to their cause.[28]

Cuban-Americans are much better off financially and vote heavily for Republican candidates. Cubans represent just 5.3 percent of Latinos in this country and have the second most potent ethnic lobby in the country, the Cuban American National Foundation (CANF). Cuban-Americans are generally strongly anti-Communist. They helped fund Lieutenant Colonel Oliver North's legal expenses during the investigations into the Iran-Contra affair and a lobbying effort to force Cuban troops from the African nation of Angola.[29]

The CANF's founder, Jorge Mas Canosa (who died in late 1997), was called "the most significant individual lobbyist in the country."[30] The foundation lobbied successfully in 1985 for Radio Marti and in 1990 for TV Marti, direct broadcast stations aimed at Cuba from the United States. In 1996 Mas Canosa and the CANF were the major movers in the Helms-Burton Act that tightened the U.S. economic embargo against Cuba. The CANF runs a resettlement program for Cuban refugees funded by the federal government. The CANF claims 50,000 donors and has one hundred directors, each of whom contribute $10,000 annually. Its Free Cuba political action committee has contributed more than $1 million to presidential candidates in 1992 and $102,000 in the 2000 congressional elections, mostly to members of the foreign policy committee.[31] Two of the three Cuban-American representatives—two Republicans from Florida and a New Jersey Democrat—serve on the House International Relations Committee, compared with just one other Latino member.[32]

Ironically, the CANF may have proven too partisan for its own good. It has had close ties to Republicans, and in early 1993 it blocked a black Cuban-American nominee of the Clinton administration for the post of chief policymaker on Latin America. That tilted the administration toward a more moderate line on Cuba. Clinton invited one hundred Cuban-Americans to the White House for Cuban Independence Day, slighting CANF officeholders. A new, more moderate Cuban-American group has emerged, Cambio Cubana (Cuban Change), and the administration appeared more sympathetic to it by doing little to stop Congress from slashing funding in half for Radio Marti and from abolishing TV Marti.[33]

Fearing a loss of influence, the CANF moved to establish closer relations with Clinton. In 1994 Mas Canosa helped persuade Clinton to take a harder line against Castro when the Cuban leader put refugees on boats headed toward the United States. At Mas Canosa's urging Clinton took a tough line against the refugees, putting them in detention and sending them back to Cuba. Clinton also tightened restrictions on the amount of funds that Cuban-Americans could send to relatives in Cuba.

A Boy and a Bloc.   Yet the good relations with the Clinton administration faded as the Cuban-American community faced its biggest crisis in years. For several months in 1999 and 2000 the dominant issue in both U.S. foreign and domestic policy was what the United States would do with six-year-old Elian Gonzalez, who survived a harrowing 90-mile journey on a raft from Cuba to the Florida coast. Elian's mother drowned when the raft sank, but the boy was rescued and taken to U.S. shores. His father, who was divorced from his mother, had stayed behind in Cuba. He wanted his son back. The U.S. government agreed with the father.

So did the American public, which favored returing the boy to his father by 63 percent to 25 percent. But Latinos in Florida, especially Cuban-Americans, insisted that Elian remain in the United States. The political battle dragged on, with Republican politicians attacking the Department of Justice and the entire Clinton administration. The Democratic mayor of Miami said that he would hold the Clinton administration responsible for any unrest that occurred when the boy was finally returned to Cuba and many of the 40,000 Cuban-American Democrats changed their party registration to Republican—perhaps handing the White House to Republican George W. Bush, who carried Florida by barely 500 votes.[34]

The CANF may have won the battle and lost the war. Many in Congress were upset that the lobby "convert[ed] Elian, literally, into a poster child, distributing leaflets of him at the World Trade Organization in Seattle." And a movement emerged among farm-state legislators to weaken the trade embargo on Castro. The compromise breached the four-decades-old restriction on selling food to Cuba. Younger Cubans formed moderate groups like Brothers to the Rescue and the Bridge for Young Professional

Cuban Americans, which worked with the Clinton administration to forge a democratic opposition to Castro.

Cuban-Americans in the Miami area stand apart from the broader American public on more issues than the Elian Gonzalez case: Sixty percent of Miami-area Cuban-Americans support direct military action against the Castro regime, compared with just 18 percent of the American public. Almost two-thirds of Cuban Americans favored continuing the embargo, compared with 43 percent of Americans. Although three quarters of Cuban-Americans who came to the United States before 1985 favored military action, just 54 percent of those born in the United States did. Support for the embargo shows the same pattern—and Cuban-Americans born here were almost twice as likely to say that Elian Gonzalez should be returned to Cuba. Most critically, about 60 percent of Cuban-Americans who came to the United States before 1985 say that a candidate's position on Castro is very important to their vote; only 35 percent of Cuban-Americans born in the United States agree.[35]

The CANF was patterned after AIPAC, and it faces some of the same strains. The CANF has gone through an internal power struggle. In 1994 an employee at the Spanish-language network of Music Television (MTV) charged that the CANF pressured MTV to fire her. She had organized a private tour to Havana to see a Cuban singer in concert. The next year a federal investigation into Radio Marti charged that Mas Canosa improperly intervened in the daily operations of the station, trying to dismiss his critics. The radio station also was charged with deliberately distorting U.S. policy toward Cuba, undermining negotiations with the Castro regime. And in 1997 popular singer Gloria Estefan came under sharp attack by CANF supporters when she supported a Miami concert by Cuban musicians.[36] Today just a quarter of younger Cuban-Americans favor banning musical groups from Cuba from coming to the United States.

Like Jewish-Americans, Cuban-Americans are less united than they once were. Cuban government representatives can address audiences in Florida without being harassed, and a Spanish language radio station in Miami now airs a talk show that regularly attacks the CANF and other hard-liners. The head of Cambio Cubana even went so far as to meet with Castro in 1995.[37]

Splits in the Hispanic Community. The fragmentation of the Latino community traditionally has limited the unity and effectiveness (especially on foreign policy issues) of the Hispanic Caucus in the House of Representatives. But a new issue has brought more unity. The Republican congressional majority enacted restrictive immigration legislation in 1996. Latinos from every nationality and from both parties banded together to protest this legislation. The House Hispanic Caucus took a strong stand against the legislation.[38] California Republican Governor Pete Wilson endorsed a 1994 voter initiative that would take away the benefits of public programs, such as education, from illegal immigrants, many of whom come from Mexico. In 1998 almost 80 percent of Latinos voted Democratic in the California governor's race.

The restrictive clauses in the legislation led to a surge in naturalization rates, especially among Latinos. Latino voter registration grew by almost 30 percent in 1996 because of naturalization and increased interest in politics. Every immigrant group reported a surge in turnout and in the share of the vote they gave to Democratic candidates. Clinton's margin among Latinos rose from 60 percent in 1992 to 72 percent in 1996. The surge in Latino votes for Democrats allowed Clinton to carry two states he lost in 1992 that have large Hispanic populations: Arizona and Florida.

Despite the substantial inroads George W. Bush tried to make into the Hispanic community—he speaks Spanish and has a Latina sister-in-law—Latinos organized heavily for the Democratic ticket in 2000, especially in California. More than 70 percent of Hispanics voted Democratic for president, and the Latino vote played a big role in putting California—and five new House seats—in the Democratic column.[39] Even though Gore was not elected, Latinos confirmed their position as a key element in the Democratic constituency in California and elsewhere.

Republicans hope to shift the partisan balance of power by actively courting Hispanics. President Bush has proposed an amnesty for illegal Mexican immigrants, hoping to reverse the perception among Latinos that the Republican Party maintains a hard line on immigration. Even though the Democratic ticket did not win in 2000, Latinos demonstrated their political clout as never before. As the fastest growing group in the country, Latinos will see their power expand in the future. President Bush invited newly elected Mexican President Vincente Fox to be the first foreign head of state to visit Bush in the White House. What happens in Latin America in the twenty-first century will be of great concern to U.S. politicians.

Greeks, Turks, and Armenians

Turkish-Americans have very determined enemies. For many years Turks had to worry primarily about Greek-Americans. Now their main concern is Armenian-Americans. No wonder each of these ethnic lobbies has tried to ally itself with AIPAC.

Greek-Americans were long considered second in power to the pro-Israel lobby. The American Hellenic Institute Public Affairs Committee (AHIPAC) is modeled after AIPAC, and the two groups have often worked together. AHIPAC lobbied successfully for an arms embargo on Turkey after its 1974 invasion of Cyprus and has pressed for a balance in foreign aid between the two states. The 2 million Greek-Americans are very politically active and loyal to the Democratic Party: In 1988 they raised more than 15 percent of Greek-American Michael Dukakis's early campaign funds. In contrast, the Turkish-American community of 180,000 is not well organized. Recently it employed a Washington public relations firm to lobby the government, but it has no ethnic lobby and maintains a low profile. As one member of Congress stated, "I don't have any Turkish restaurants in my district."[40] Greek-American influence has waned as U.S. foreign policy has shifted emphasis from Greece and Turkey to other trouble spots, especially after the fall of the Soviet Union limited the strategic value of both Greece and Turkey to the United States.

Armenian-Americans are more recent entries into the ethnic group mix. For many years Armenian-Americans did not organize because there was no independent Armenia. When the Soviet Union broke up in 1989, Armenia regained its independence. Since then the Armenian-American community has become energized on two issues. One is the contested border with Azerbaijan, also formerly part of the Soviet Union. The two countries have fought over the province of Nagorno-Karabakh, an enclave of ethnic Armenians within the boundaries of Azerbaijan. Azerbaijan has imposed an embargo on Armenia, and the United States in turn imposed restrictions on aid to oil-rich Azerbaijan. The Armenian-American lobby, the Armenian Assembly of America, with 7,000 members and a budget of $2.5 million, has fought for increased U.S. aid to Armenia and for blocking assistance to Azerbaijan.

The second issue is condemnation of Turkey for its alleged genocide of 1.5 million Armenians during World War I. Armenian-Americans have pressed for a congressional resolution condemning Turkey and have mobilized considerable support in Congress. Particularly important is the Armenian-American community in southern California; Armenian-Americans make up about 20 percent of the population of the Twenty-Seventh Congressional District there. Although Armenian-Americans are often Republicans, they have been heavily courted by Democratic state senator Adam Schiff, who challenged incumbent Republican James Rogan in 2000. Rogan was facing a tough battle as a result of his role as a manager of the impeachment of Bill Clinton in the House.

The Rogan-Schiff election was the most expensive in the history of the House of Representatives, with each candidate spending about $5 million. Both candidates heavily courted the large Armenian-American bloc. But Schiff had two key advantages over Rogan: First, he had been more active in Armenian issues than Rogan had. Second, when Turkey threatened reprisals against the United States if the resolution passed—including refusing to let the United States use Turkish air space for flights over Iraq and canceling defense contracts with U.S. firms—Republican leaders in Congress refused to bring the Armenian resolution to the House floor. Rogan protested but Schiff used the issue in the campaign—with perhaps enough persuasion to tip this very close election to the Democrats.[41]

Turkish groups have been buffeted by the strong alliances between pro-Israeli forces and Turkey's historic antagonists, the Greeks and the

Armenians. But recently Turkey, even though its population is 99 percent Muslim, has forged its own links with American Jews. Turkey and Israel have military links, because both fear Syria (a common neighbor), Iraq, and Iran. In 1997 the B'nai B'rith Anti-Defamation League presented Turkish Prime Minister Mesut Yilmaz with its Distinguished Statesman Award. Yilmaz also met with leaders of AIPAC and the American Jewish Committee.[42] Recently the ties between Turkish-Americans and Jewish-Americans have frayed a bit, as Jewish groups have strengthened ties with Azerbaijan. An overwhelmingly Muslim nation, Azerbaijan has particularly warm relations with Israel.

African-Americans

African-Americans, like Latinos, traditionally have been more concerned with domestic economic issues than with foreign policy concerns. Most African-Americans cannot trace their roots to a specific African country. Until the 1960s African-American participation in politics was restricted, both by law and by socioeconomic status. There were few African-Americans in Congress, especially on the foreign policy committees, or in the Foreign Service. African-Americans contribute little money to campaigns and electorally they have been strongly tied to the Democratic Party, thus cutting off lobbying activities to Republican presidents and legislators. African-American activity on foreign policy heightened over the ending of the apartheid system of racial separation in South Africa.

The South Africa issue united African-Americans. President Ronald Reagan ultimately agreed in 1985 to accept sanctions against the South African government, pushed in that direction by public opinion, a mobilized African-American community, and a supportive Congress. The congressional Black Caucus has taken firm stands on sending U.S. troops to Somalia, lifting the ban on Haitian immigrants infected with the AIDS virus, and pushing the United States to restore ousted Haitian President Jean-Bertrand Aristide to office.

Six of the forty-eight members of the House Foreign Affairs Committee are African-American, including the ranking minority members on three of the six subcommittees (International Operations and Human Rights, Europe, and Africa). African-Americans increasingly have held key positions on foreign policy in the executive branch, including current Secretary of State Colin Powell and National Security Advisor Condoleeza Rice.

Immigration from the Carribean, especially from Haiti, has changed the dynamic of black involvement in foreign policy. Haitian immigrants in southern Florida have mobilized politically, winning a majority of seats on the city council and the mayoralty in north Miami. Haitians took strong exception to Cuban-American demands that Elian Gonzalez be allowed to remain in the United States, charging that many refugees from Haiti were turned away. The immigrants have sometimes felt that African-American politicians are not receptive to their needs, prompting an unsuccessful primary challenge in 2000 to Rep. Major R. Owens, D-N.Y., by a Jamaican-born city council member.[43]

Asian-Americans

Asian-Americans are the second fastest growing ethnic group in the United States, constituting 3.7 percent of the population.[44] Yet Asian-Americans have not been prominent in political life. Because most immigrants have not become citizens, their participation rate is substantially lower than that of other ethnic groups. There are just eight Asian-American members of Congress, six in the House and two in the Senate (both from Hawaii). The first Asian-American governor is Washington's Gary Locke.

Tensions between Japanese-Americans and Chinese-Americans stem from Japan's occupation of China during World War II. Vietnamese immigrants bear grudges against Cambodians, and Hindus and Muslims from South Asia have long-standing quarrels.[45]

Asian-Americans usually vote Republican, although Japanese-Americans are an exception. Many Asian-Americans share the GOP's priorities of family values and anti-Communism. But in 2000 Asian-Americans voted for Gore over Bush by a margin of 55 percent to 41 percent, perhaps upset over the Republicans' restrictive immigration policies.[46]

In 1994 Asian-Americans in Congress formed the Asian Pacific Caucus, admitting members without regard to race or ethnicity. Yet only one Asian-American member, the nonvoting delegate from American Samoa, serves on either the House or Senate foreign policy committee.

As with many ethnic groups, Asian-Americans are becoming more active. Asian-Americans raised a lot of money for the Clinton campaign in 1996 and are pushing for increased registration and turnout, especially in California. Yet Asian-American donations to congressional candidates have been small. The 80-20 political action committee raised $266,000 in 2000, but it donated only $500 to candidates for office, split between three Asian-American Democrats and two Anglo Republicans. Altogether three Asian-American political action committees (PACs) donated $4,131 to House candidates, most of it going to Mike Honda and David Wu, successful Democratic candidates. The Committee of 100, an antidiscrimination organization patterned after B'nai B'rith, commissioned a poll in 2001 and reported that about 70 percent of Americans hold some negative stereotypes about Chinese-Americans, limiting Chinese-Americans' political influence.[47]

The Indian-American population tripled from 1980 to 1997 and Indian-Americans have become increasingly involved in politics. Indian-Americans have the highest income of any ethnic group in the United States, yet they have not been active in politics until recently. There are no

Indian-American members of Congress—and only one Indian-American state legislator—but there is a congressional caucus on India and Indian-Americans with more than one hundred members, mostly Democrats. To combat the growing influence by Indian-Americans, Pakistani-Americans raised $50,000 for Hillary Rodham Clinton in her 2000 campaign.[48]

Are Ethnic Politics Dangerous?

Former senator Charles McC. Mathias Jr., R-Md., worried that ethnic politics might make it difficult for the nation to speak with one voice on foreign policy:

> Factions among us lead the nation toward excessive foreign attachments or animosities. Even if the groups were balanced—if Turkish-Americans equaled Greek-Americans or Arab-Americans equaled Jewish-Americans—the result would not necessarily be a sound, cohesive foreign policy because the national interest is not simply the sum of our special interest and attachments ... ethnic politics, carried as they often have been to excess, have proven harmful to the national interest.[49]

Pro-Israel groups usually place intense constituency pressure on legislators who make either anti-Israel or pro-Arab statements. Pro-Israel political action committee contributions rose from $2,450 in 1976 to $8.7 million in 1990—a higher figure than that for the largest domestic PAC, the realtors. In the 2000 election pro-Israel PAC contributions fell back to $1,907,000, still more than 10 times as much as Arab-American or Muslim-American PACs gave ($160,000). Virtually every senator and most members of the House have received support from pro-Israel PACs.[50]

Even though ethnic lobbies do not stand to benefit financially from a foreign policy that suits their preferences, many Americans are simply so skeptical of the role of money in politics that they will worry that something is not right. Legislators' support for foreign policy initiatives might be seen as open to influence from campaign contributions.

Although 61 percent of Americans believe it is acceptable for American Jews to contribute money to Israel, almost 40 percent of Americans believe that Israel has too much power in America. Yet Americans don't believe that *American Jews* have too much power: Most Americans believe that Jews have the "right amount" of power, with just 10 percent saying that Jews have "too much power." In 1984 (the last time the question was asked), 29 percent of Americans said that American Jews were more loyal to Israel than to the United States, while in 1998, 60 percent said that Arab-Americans are more loyal to Arab countries.[51]

Campaign contributions by Asian-Americans became a source of contention in the 1996 elections. Where did the money come from—Asian-Americans or Asians? What did campaign contributors want? Were the funds donated to promote good government or to buy influence for foreign interests? Asian-Americans reportedly gave $10 million or more in 1996, mostly to Democrats and especially to President Clinton. Asian-American contributions came under scrutiny when the public learned after the 1996 elections that at least $1.2 million of the donations to the Democratic National Committee (DNC) were improper. The DNC's chief fund-raiser among Asian-Americans, John Huang, appeared to have promised face-to-face meetings with the president for large contributors.[52]

James Riady, of the Indonesian conglomerate Lippo Group, made substantial contributions to the DNC and met with the president in the Oval Office six times. DNC official Huang was previously U.S. chief of the Lippo Group. Other contributors included Buddhist nuns from a Taiwan-based order who wrote checks for $140,000 at a luncheon with Vice President Al Gore. And it was alleged, though not documented, that the Chinese government tried to funnel contributions to the DNC in 1996.[53]

Conclusion

Americans worry about foreign influence in domestic politics. We have distinguished between campaign contributions and lobbying by foreign agents and governments and donations and pressures from U.S. companies with interests abroad. Our laws reflect this distinction. Yet could we have drawn the line too sharply?

One test of what constitutes an American interest, though hardly an ethical one, is what works. Perhaps there is no moral resolution to the problem of money in politics, but only a recognition that tactics that prove too heavy-handed may backfire. Pro-Israel groups were buffeted by charges that they had inappropriately mixed lobbying with fund-raising.

Charges of undue influence seem to have limited the money ethnic interests give to candidates. Now the key question seems to be how to distribute funds. Pro-Israel groups have long been associated with the Democratic Party, because Jews are among the most loyal parts of the Democratic constituency. In 2000 pro-Israel groups gave 59 percent of their contributions to the Democratic Party. Although pro-Arab groups endorsed Bush in 2000, their PACs are even more tilted toward Democrats—especially African-American Democrats (who have often been critical of Israel) but even to Jewish legislators in key positions on Capitol Hill. Even Rep. Benjamin A. Gilman, R-N.Y., former chair of the House International Relations Committee and a supporter of Israel's right wing, received $1,000 from one pro-Arab PAC (see note 49). Most other ethnic groups also favor the Democrats; Cuban-Americans are the exception.

Pro-Israel and anti-Castro groups depend on the support of public opinion and the moral force of their arguments to prod policymakers to back their causes. But as Cuban-American groups have discovered, antipathy toward the Cuban regime seems to have peaked—and the Elian Gonzalez case may have permanently damaged their cause. The pro-Israel lobby benefits from the unpopularity of its opposition. Americans now expect the Castro regime to fade away, but they are less sanguine about peace in the Middle East. Even so, there is little reason to believe that the interests in foreign policy will be restricted to moral pleadings and ethnic groups as we enter the twenty-first century. Foreign policy resembles domestic policy now more than ever. The consensus on what U.S. policy should be has evaporated and with it the argument that our international relations have a distinctive moral foundation.

Notes

1. Just 14 percent of the electorate considered any foreign policy issue (including trade and immigration) the most important problem facing the country, according to data from the 2000 American National Election Study.
2. Francis X. Clines, "Most Doubt a Resolve to Change Campaign Financing, Poll Finds," *New York Times*, April 8, 1997, A1.
3. Mohammed E. Ahrari, "Conclusion," in *Ethnic Groups and Foreign Policy*, ed. Mohammed E. Ahrari (New York: Greenwood, 1987), 155–158.
4. "The Power 25: Top Lobbying Groups," http://www.fortune.com/indexw.jhtml?channel=list.jhtml-list_frag=list_3column_power_25.jhtml-list=16-_requestid=13760, June 1, 2001.
5. Cheryl A. Rubenberg, "The Middle East Lobbies," *The Link* 17 (January–March 1984): 4. "The Power 25: Top Lobbying Groups," http://www.fortune.com/indexw.jhtml?channel=list.jhtml&list_frag=list_3column_power_25.jhtml&list=16&_requestid=13760, June 1, 2001.
6. Thomas L. Friedman, "A Pro-Israel Lobby Gives Itself a Headache," *New York Times*, November 8, 1992, E18.
7. Sanford Ungar, "Washington: Jewish and Arab Lobbyists," *Atlantic*, March 1978, 10.
8. Ben Bradlee Jr., "Israel's Lobby," *Boston Globe Magazine*, April 29, 1984, 64.
9. American Israel Public Affairs Committee, "AIPAC: About Us, Who We Are," http://www.aipac.org/documents/whoweare.html, May 31, 2001.
10. Mitchell Bard, "The Israeli and Arab Lobbies," The Jewish Virtual Library, http://www.us-israel.org/jsource/US-Israel/lobby.html, May 31, 2001.
11. Bill Keller, "Supporters of Israel, Arabs Vie for Friends in Congress, at White House," *Congressional Quarterly Weekly Report*, August 25, 1981, 1527–1528.
12. Rubenberg, "The Middle East Lobbies"; Keller, "Supporters Vie"; Steven L. Spiegel, *The Other Arab-Israeli Conflict* (Chicago: University of Chicago, 1985), 8; David J. Saad and G. Neal Lendenmann, "Arab American Grievances," *Foreign Policy* (fall 1985): 22.
13. Ted Clark, "Arab-Americans in American Politics," transcribed from National Public Radio broadcast on "Weekend Edition Sunday," October 31, 1999; Gulliaume Debre, "Arab Americans Emerge As Key Voting Bloc," *Christian Science Monitor*, April 4, 2000, http://www.csmonitor.com/durable/2000/04/04/p2s1.htm, May 31, 2001; Dean E. Murphy, "For Muslim-Americans, Influence In Politics Still Hard to Come By," *New York Times*, October 27, 2000, Washington edition, A1, C27.
14. Frank Newport, "Helping Develop Peaceful Solution to Middle East Crisis Is Important Goal to Americans," Gallup News Service, February 12, 2001, http://www.gallup.com/poll/releases/pr010212.asp, February 13, 2001; Pollingreport.com, "Israel," http://www.pollingreport.com/israel.htm, October 17, 2000.

15. John W. Spanier and Eric M. Uslaner, *American Foreign Policy Making and the Democratic Dilemmas*, 6th ed. (New York: Macmillan, 1994); Andrew Kohut, *America's Place in the World II* (Washington, D.C.: Pew Research Center for The People and The Press, 1997), 99.

16. Thomas L. Friedman, "Jewish Criticism on Clinton Picks," *New York Times*, January 5, 1993, A11; Center for Responsive Politics, "Al Gore: Top Contributors," http://www.opensecrets.org/2000elect/contrib/P800000912.htm, May 31, 2001; and the American National Election Study cumulative file, 1948–1996, made available by the Inter-University Consortium for Political Research.

17. Susan Pinkus, "Poll Analysis Part I: U.S. and Israeli Jews Have Many Common Views, Some Striking Differences," *Los Angles Times*, July 13, 2000, http://www.latimes.com/news/timespoll/special/407pa1an.htm; Leon Hadar, "What Israel Means to U.S. Jewry," *Jerusalem Post*, June 19–25, 1982, international edition, 11.

18. Executive summary of a survey of 1,198 American Jews for the Israel Policy Forum, September 1997, by Penn, Schoen, and Berland and Associates.

19. American Jewish Committee, *In the Aftermath of the Rabin Assassination* (New York: American Jewish Committee, 1996).

20. Laurie Goodstein, "Rabin Urges U.S. Rabbis to Push Peace," *Washington Post*, September 6, 1994, A1; J. J. Goldstein, "Only in America: Likud vs. Labor," *New York Times*, July 2, 1994, 19; Rowland Evans and Robert Novak, "Likud's 'Gang of Three,'" *Washington Post*, November 17, 1994, A23; Jonathan Broder, "Maverick," *Jerusalem Report*, June 16, 1994, 32–33.

21. Gustav Neibuhr, "Rabbi Group Is Preparing to Denounce Non-Orthodox," *New York Times*, March 24, 1997, A11; Gustav Neibuhr, "U.S. Jewish Leader Enters Fray over Religious Control in Israel," *New York Times*, April 17, 1997, A1; Hanna Rosin, "U.S. Rabbis Split on Future Status of Jerusalem," *Washington Post*, January 27, 2000, A16.

22. Bard, "The Israeli and Arab Lobbies."

23. Jonathan Broder, "The Arab Lobby Goes Online," *Jerusalem Report*, October 25, 1999, 32–33; Christopher Dickey and Gamel Ismail, "The Pokemon Fatwa," *Newsweek*, April 23, 2001, http://www.secularislam.org/visitors/guest67.htm, June 1, 2001.

24. James Zogby, "How Arab Americans Voted and Why," *Middle East Online*, http://www.jordanembassyus.org/121900004.htm, May 31, 2001; John Sherry, "California Muslims Flex Electoral Muscles," *The Hill*, July 12, 2000, http://www.hillnews.com/news/news9.html, July 13, 2001; Debre, "Arab Americans Emerge As Key Voting Bloc."

25. Jeffrey M. Jones, "Americans Show Increased Support for Israel Following Terrorist Attacks," Gallup News Service, September 19, 2001, http://www.gallup.com/poll/Releases/PR010919.asp; NBC News/Wall Street Journal, "Terrorism," http://nationaljournal.com/members/polltrack/2001/todays/0901918nbcwsj.htm; *Los Angeles Times*, "Poll Alert," September 16, 2001, study 462; ABC News, "66% Worry War on Terrorism Will Grow into Broader War," October 8–9, 2001, http://www.nationaljournal.com/pubs/hotline, October 12, 2001; Betsy Rothstein, "McKinney Assails Guiliani, Israel," *The Hill*, October 18, 2001, http://www.hillnews.com/101701/mckinney.shtm; Allison Stevens, "Arab-Americans Feel Bias," *The Hill*, October 11, 2001, http://www.hillnews.com/101001/bias.shtm.

26. D'Vera Cohn, "Shifting Portrait of U.S. Hispanics," *Washington Post*, May 10, 2001, A1; D'Vera Cohn and Darryl Fears, "Hispanics Draw Even With Blacks in New Census," *Washington Post*, March 7, 2000, A1; Susan Crabtree, "Hispanic Members Watch Their Political Clout Grow," *Roll Call*, September 11, 2000, http://www.rollcall.com/pages/news/00/09/news0911i.html, September 12, 2000.

27. Pam Belluck, "Mexican Presidential Candidates Campaign in U.S.," *New York Times*, July 1, 2000, A3.

28. Bill Keller, "Interest Groups Focus on El Salvador Policy," *Congressional Quarterly Weekly Report*, April 24, 1982, 895–900.
29. Robert S. Greenberger, "Right-Wing Groups Join in Capitol Hill Crusade to Help Savimbi's Anti-Communists in Angola," *Wall Street Journal*, November 25, 1985, 58.
30. John Newhouse, "Socialism or Death," *New Yorker*, April 27, 1992, 77.
31. Newhouse, "Socialism or Death," 76–81; Lee Hockstadter and William Booth, "Cuban Exiles Split on Life after Castro," *Washington Post*, March 10, 1992, A1; Peter H. Stone, "Cuban Clout," *National Journal*, February 20, 1993, 449; Larry Rohter, "A Rising Cuban-American Leader: Statesman to Some, Bully to Others," *New York Times*, October 29, 1992, A18.
32. Larry Rohter, "Jorge Mas Canosa, 58, Dies; Exile Who Led Movement against Castro," *New York Times*, November 24, 1997, A27; Center for Responsive Politics, "Free Cuba PAC," http://www.opensecrets.org/pacs/lookup2.sap?strID=C001427117, May 31, 2001.
33. John M. Goshko, "Controversy Erupts on Latin America Post," *Washington Post*, January 23, 1993, A4; Larry Rohter, "Moderate Cuban Voices Rise in U.S.," *New York Times*, June 27, 1993, A16.
34. David W. Moore, "Public: Reunion of Elian With Father Should Have Occurred," The Gallup Organization Poll Releases, April 23, 2000, http://www.gallup.com/releases/pr000425.asp, May 2, 2000; Andres Viglucci and Diana Marrero, "Poll Reveals Widening Split Over Elian," *Miami Herald*, April 9, 2000, http://content.main.40/http...hive/news/rafters99/docs/012021.htm, April 11, 2000; Katharine Q. Seeyle, "Boy's Case Could Sway Bush-Gore Contest," *New York Times*, March 30, 2000, Washington edition, A4.
35. Christopher Marquis, "Cuban-American Lobby on the Defensive," *New York Times*, June 30, 2000, Washington edition, A12; Miles A. Pomper, "Cuban-American Agenda Marked by New Diversity," *CQ Weekly*, February 27, 1999, 467–470; Cuban Research Institute, "2000 FIU/Cuba Poll: Comparison of Three Samples Frequency Tables," Center for Labor Research and Studies, Florida International University, http://www.fiu.edu/orgs/ipor/cuba2000/freq.htm, May 31, 2001. See other tables at the website ending in "cuba2000."
36. Larry Rohter, "MTV Worker Ousted over Cuba Concert," *New York Times*, June 9, 1994, A12; Steven Greenhouse, "U.S. Reportedly Finds That Head of Radio Marti Tried to Dismiss His Critics," *New York Times*, July 27, 1995, A10; Guy Gugliotta, "USIA Probes Activist's Role at Radio Marti," *Washington Post*, July 22, 1995, A1; Donald P. Baker, "Miami's Cuban American Generations Split over Anti-Castro Rule," *Washington Post*, October 18, 1997, A3.
37. Mireya Navarro, "New Tolerance Sprouts among Cuban Exiles," *New York Times*, August 25, 1995, A14; Navarro, "Castro Confers with Exiled Foe," *New York Times*, June 28, 1995, A1.
38. David Rampe, "Power Panel in the Making: The Hispanic Caucus," *New York Times*, September 30, 1988, B5; Lizette Alvarez, "For Hispanic Lawmakers, Time to Take the Offensive," *New York Times*, August 25, 1997, A14.
39. Eric Schimitt, "New Census Shows Hispanics Are Even With Blacks in U.S.," *New York Times*, March 8, 2001, Washington edition, A1; Eric Schmitt, "Census Shows Big Gain for Mexican-Americans," *New York Times*, May 10, 2001, Washington edition, A22; Steven Greenhouse, "Guess Who's Embracing Immigrants Now," *New York Times*, March 5, 2000, WK4.
40. Thomas M. Franck and Edward Weisband, *Foreign Policy by Congress* (New York: Oxford University, 1979), 191–193.
41. Miles A. Pomper, "Strong Feelings Fuel Debate on Aid to Azerbaijan," *CQ Weekly*, May 19, 2001, 1173; Steven Mufson, "Local Politics Is Global As Hill Turns to Armenia," *Washington Post*, October 9, 2000, A1; Jean Merkl, "Rogan Emphasizes 'I'

Word in Close Race With Schiff," *Los Angeles Times*, October 7, 2000, http://www. latimes.com/news/politics/calpol/todays.topstory.htm, October 7, 2000; Peter Wallstein, "Rogan's Run: The GOP Fights for a Crucial Swing District," *CQ Weekly*, June 10, 2000, 1366–1370.

42. Ted Clark, "Report on Turkey and Jewish-American Organizations," on National Public Radio's "Morning Edition," December 23, 1997, unofficial transcript.

43. Sue Anne Presley, "In Little Haiti, the Elian Fight Sheds a Painful Light," *Washington Post*, January 15, 2000, A3; Dana Canedy, "Away From Haiti, Discovering the Politics of the Possible," *New York Times*, May 19, 2001, Washington edition, A7; Jonathan P. Hicks, "Bitter Primary Contest Hits Ethnic Nerve Among Blacks," *New York Times*, August 31, 2000, Washington edition, A1.

44. United States Bureau of the Census, "Profiles of General Demographic Characteristics 2000," http://www.census.gov/prod/cen2000/dp1/2kh00.pdf, June 4, 2001.

45. Stanley Karnow, "Apathetic Asian-Americans?" *Washington Post*, November 29, 1992, C2; James Sterngold, "For Asian Americans, Political Power Can Lead to Harsh Scrutiny," *New York Times*, November 3, 1996, A36.

46. "Exit Poll Results: Election 2000," http://www.udel.edu/poscir/road/course/ exitpollsindex.html, June 4, 2001.

47. The data on Asian-American contributions come from Center for Responsive Politics, http://www.opensecrets.org, May 31, 2001. The PACs are 80-20, Asian-American Action Fund, Asian American Political Action Fund, and Coalition for Asian Political Action Fund; Committee of 100, "American Attitudes toward Chinese Americans and Asian Americans: Key Findings," April 2001, New York, typescript; Thomas B. Edsall, "25 percent of U.S. View Chinese Americans Negatively, Poll Says," *Washington Post*, April 26, 2001, A4.

48. Miles A. Pomper, "Indian-Americans' Numbers, Affluence Are Translating Into Political Power," *CQ Weekly*, March 18, 2000, 580–581; Raymond Bonner, "Donating to the First Lady, Hoping the President Notices," *New York Times*, March 14, 2000, A1.

49. Charles McC. Mathias Jr., "Ethnic Groups and Foreign Policy," *Foreign Affairs* 59 (summer 1981): 981.

50. Charles R. Babcock, "Israel's Backers Maximize Political Clout," *Washington Post*, September 26, 1991, A21; Center for Responsive Politics, "Pro-Israel," http://www.opensecrets.org/pacs/industry.asp?txt=Q05&cycle=2000; the pro-Arab PACs in the opensecrets database are the Arab American Leadership PAC, the American Task Force on Lebanon Policy, the Arab American Institute, the American Muslim Council, the Arab American PAC, and the National Association of Arab Americans.

51. Marjorie Hyer, "Tolerance Shows in Voter Poll," *Washington Post*, February 13, 1988, E18; CBS News press release, October 23, 1988; questions on Arabs and Jews from the section on polls in the reference section of Lexis-Nexis Academic Universe, accessed May 31, 2001.

52. Terry M. Neal, "Asian American Donors Feel Stigmatized," *Washington Post*, September 8, 1997, A1; Tim Weiner and David E. Sanger, "Democrats Hoped to Raise $7 Million from Asians in U.S.," *New York Times*, December 28, 1996, A1; Michael Weisskopf and Michael Duffy, "The G.O.P.'s Own China Connection," *Time*, May 5, 1997, 45–46.

53. Ruth Marcus, "Oval Office Meeting Set DNC Asian Funds Network in Motion," *Washington Post*, December 29, 1996, A1; Terry M. Neal, "Asian American Donors Feel Stigmatized," *Washington Post*, September 8, 1997, A1.

V. CONCLUSION

18

Always Involved, Rarely Central
Organized Interests in American Politics
Allan J. Cigler and Burdett A. Loomis[1]

Looking at the broad sweep of American politics at the start of the twenty-first century, we are struck by the omnipresence of interest groups. Whatever the issue, organized interests are at the table. In electoral politics groups offer tremendous financial assistance and provide increasing numbers of activists and strategists to do everything from getting out the vote to sponsoring polls. Organized interests mount highly sophisticated public relations campaigns and advertise heavily on behalf of candidates and issues. Interests consistently weigh in on judicial and administrative appointments and represent nearly all sectors of social and economic life, albeit with unequal effectiveness. Although this is especially true at the national level, all states and most large cities have their own corps of groups and lobbyists.[1]

In short, interest groups are ubiquitous. In the fifth edition of this book we argued that this ubiquity has led to a state of "hyperpluralism"— or excessive representation—in which groups protect their interests tenaciously and effectively. This makes governmental policymaking highly responsive to individual interests, but much less so to broad societal challenges. Such a conclusion might lead some to believe that organized interests lie at the center of American politics, and that some kind of group-based theory would offer a coherent way to think about our political system. But this isn't the case. Although interest groups are important across the board, no group-based theory can explain the whole of American politics. At the same time, organized interests are influential in the contexts of other political models—whether these emphasize political institutions, policymaking, or mobilization of the electorate.

In general, we see four major trends that complement one another. First, more interests are engaged in more ways to influence policy outcomes. Interests monitor more actions than they used to, and stand ready to swing into action more quickly when a red flag is raised (often by a lobbyist on retainer). Given the high stakes of government decisions, whether by a committee in the House of Representatives or a bureau of the Environmental Protection Agency, the combination of monitoring and action is a worthwhile investment for most interests.

Second, the distinction between "outside" lobbying (public relations and grassroots contacts) and "inside" lobbying (personal relationships) is blurring. Interest groups must use both to get their ideas across. To be sure, a key provision can still find its way into an omnibus bill without a ripple, but battles over most major issues are fought simultaneously on multiple fronts (see Chapter 10 in this volume). At the first sign of trouble in a committee hearing or, more likely, a casual conversation, a lobbyist can instruct influential constituents to call, fax, or email their representative. Jack Bonner and a dozen other constituent-lobbying experts can construct a set of grassroots (or elite "grasstops") entreaties within a few days, if not a few hours. And a media buyer can target any sample of legislators for advertisements that run in their districts, thus showing the legislators that their constituents and key Washington interests are watching their action on an important bill.

Third, the distinction between the politics of elections and the politics of policymaking is blurring. Though always linked in a democracy, these two phenomenons have strengthened their ties recently—in many ways reflecting the "permanent campaign" of presidential election politics that emerged in the 1970s and 1980s. Sidney Blumenthal sees this as combining "image-making with strategic calculation. Under the permanent campaign government is turned into the perpetual campaign."[2] In the 1990s many interests have come to see the combination of electoral and policy politics in much the same light, with the issue advocacy ads of 1996 serving as the initial demonstration of this new era. In addition, many interests are now viewing the "campaign" idea as one that defines their broader lobbying strategies, and the boundaries between electoral campaigns and public relations efforts are diminishing.

Fourth, political parties and organized interests are becoming increasingly integrated. The tremendous growth in soft money donations to parties and candidates makes interest groups more important to the financial viability of both. Although some interests give roughly equal amounts to Republicans and Democrats, most groups contribute heavily to one party or the other. And organized interests are now intruding directly into congressional campaigns, mounting large issue advocacy advertising campaigns as well as independent campaigns in competitive districts and states (see Chapter 7). In addition, many large membership organizations, from labor unions to the National Rifle Association to the Sierra Club, have financed sweeping get-out-the-vote drives, using both volunteers and paid staff to complement candidates' efforts. This influence is enhanced by highly partisan voting among members of many such groups. In 1998 House Minority Whip Tom DeLay publicly chastised the Electronic Industries Association for hiring former Democratic representative David McCurdy as its president rather than a more acceptable former Republican legislator.

In light of these trends organized interests can best be understood by examining their effect on parties, policymaking, and political institutions, rather than by trying to view the political process through the lens of group politics. To tease out some other implications of these trends, let us examine the role of organized interests in the two dominant contexts of post-2000 politics: partisan parity and the adjustments of organized interests in the wake of the September 11, 2001, terrorist attacks on the United States.

Partisan Parity

Although the results of the 2000 elections—for president, the Senate, and the House of Representatives—produced a snapshot of almost total partisan balance, parity between Republicans and Democrats has been a political fact of life since at least 1994, and probably since the elections of 1980. The key elements of even partisan division include divided government, narrow majorities in both houses of Congress, and a relatively small number of competitive seats in the House, as well as an overall balance in the voting public.

Parity affects interest group politics in terms of individual groups' strategies and tactics and these groups' significance in the political system. In 1990 Robert Salisbury noted that despite an increase in the number of organized interests, their overall "clout" was diminished.[3] Our take is a little different. Partisan parity may make it difficult for groups, like parties, to push through large policy changes. But parity may also mean that interest group activities will be important both in modestly adjusting policies and in protecting past gains. Moreover, partisan parity may not be a defining condition for all decisions. Some issues, like aid to farmers, have rarely reflected pure partisan divisions; others, like national security, especially in the wake of September 11, strongly encourage bipartisanship. Still, the even divisions between the parties dominate the political landscape of the post-2000 era.

Partisan parity has implications for organized interests. Above all, it means that control of Congress is always within reach of the minority party at the next election, which is never more than two years away. Organized interests know that they can "invest" in a party with the hope that it will become the majority—or retain its control.[4] Congress today has few competitive seats, perhaps twenty in 2000 and probably not more than thirty-five in the postredistricting year of 2002, so the chances for a major shift in policy direction are modest. Still, holding a majority is important for parties and groups, as was illustrated by Sen. James M. Jeffords's, I-Vt., decision to leave the GOP and become an Independent (who caucused with the Democrats). Thus a 50-50 Republican Senate (with Vice President Dick Cheney casting the decisive vote) became a 50-49-1 Democratic Senate.

Although this power shift may have altered policy outcomes only modestly (given the need for sixty votes in the Senate on many issues that attract filibusters), Democratic control enhanced opportunities for unions, environmentalists, and similar groups to affect the policy agenda. In addition, tight margins in both chambers mean that almost all legislators seek substantial funds from interest groups—both through political action committee donations and soft money contributions.

Electoral Strategies and Actions

The electoral role of organized interests has increased in recent decades as candidates and parties demand high-tech information gathering and timely communication with the electorate, activities that cost a lot of money. But interest groups are far more than financial resources during election years. The prevalence of permanent campaign politics, with its continual fund-raising and campaign-style attempts at influence, makes distinguishing lobbying from electoral activity difficult. For example, in competitive legislative races, sorting out the messages of political parties, interest groups, and candidates is next to impossible, especially for would-be voters who evince precious little interest in the campaign to begin with.

One consequence of the permanent campaign is that organizations such as the AFL-CIO, the Christian Coalition, and the National Rifle Association now participate in electoral politics full-time. Such groups have emerged as distinct electoral entities, often operating without formal cooperation or collaboration with parties or candidates. In fact, many groups operate like traditional political parties: they recruit and train candidates to run for public office, serve as advisors in primary and general elections, and communicate with voters on candidates' behalf or against their opponents.

The 1999–2000 election cycle represented a continuation of the upward spiral of interest group involvement in federal elections. Although political action committee spending and soft money contributions by organized interests garnered some attention, the major financial story of the 2000 elections was money raised and spent outside the limits of the Federal Election Campaign Act's (FECA) disclosure and expenditure provisions. Political scientist Anthony Corrado contends that campaign finance in the 2000 elections "bore a greater resemblance to campaign finance prior to the passage of FECA than to the patterns that were supposed to occur after it." That is, interest groups' activities for or against candidates running for federal office were only modestly constrained by law.[5] Much group activity occurred out of the public eye, with more and more interests learning to influence electoral politics through such devices as issue advocacy advertising.

And more groups than ever were involved early in the election cycle; a number played key roles in the 2000 presidential primaries, especially for the Republican Party. One study found that more than one hundred groups, many of which spent huge sums, were active in issue advocacy efforts leading up to the 2000 mid-March Super Tuesday primaries.[6] Interest groups were limited more by imagination and lack of resources than by federal law.

Though it is hard to say precisely how much money was invested in issue advocacy campaigns during the 2000 election cycle, estimates can be made. New York University's Brennan Center, which tracks interest group radio and television ads in seventy-five of the nation's largest media markets, found that interest groups spent $57 million on issue advocacy ads to influence races in 2000.[7] This was roughly one-tenth of all candidate-centered advertising in these markets, and it was overwhelmingly concentrated in a few competitive races.

The 2000 election also saw an escalation in interest groups' "ground war," where a few groups invested in sharply targeted get-out-the-vote efforts, direct mail, and telephone banks. If such efforts do not explicitly advocate a candidate's election or defeat and are not coordinated with either political party or candidate campaigns, they may remain undisclosed to the public and outside the confines of federal regulations. In 2000, for example, the AFL-CIO used roughly three-quarters of its $46 million in election expenses on get-out-the-vote and direct mail voter education efforts.[8] Organized labor claimed it had registered 2.3 million new union household members, had made 8 million phone calls to union households, and distributed more than 14 million leaflets at union work sites. Union get-out-the-vote efforts on election day were crucial in swing states such as Michigan and Pennsylvania. Republican Governor John Engler, explaining Al Gore's victory in Michigan, pointed to the fact that the United Auto Workers had negotiated a paid holiday in their contract, calling it the "largest soft money contribution in history." [9]

The NAACP, using its National Voter Fund as a vehicle, organized a massive get-out-the-vote campaign in forty targeted congressional districts and several key swing states like Michigan, Ohio, and Pennsylvania, spending some $9 million to boost African-American turnout. The NAACP coordinated with the American Federation of Teachers to reach young voters in Philadelphia, arranging to speak at high school assemblies and compiling lists of students eligible to vote.[10] Magleby and his associates were able to identify 211 interest groups that communicated in some way with the electorate in the seventeen competitive races the authors monitored in 2000—and 159 of these groups used telephone contacts and targeted direct mail extensively.[11] Almost all of this get-out-the-vote activity happened outside the confines of federal election law.

It is not surprising that this campaign finance environment calls for reform. But even in the wake of the most expensive election in U.S. history—and in the wake of Houston energy giant Enron's bankruptcy and its numerous campaign finance implications—meaningful reform seems unlikely.[12] There appears to be no groundswell among the public to pressure legislators to take action—even when some legislators say they would welcome reform to avoid losing control of their campaign agendas to interest groups that provide funds and issue advocacy messages (Chapter 7). But legislators understand that they generally benefit from the current system and are risk-averse as a consequence. Groups at both ends of the political spectrum, from the National Rifle Association and the Christian Coalition to the AFL-CIO and the National Education Association, are leery of changing the system of largely unrestricted issue advocacy, which they see as essential to influencing the course of public policy. Organized interests, such as Common Cause, that argue on behalf of campaign finance reform are greatly outnumbered.

The continuing parity between the two major political parties, supported by their interest group allies, also reduces the chance for change. Meaningful campaign reform might rebalance partisan strength, and both parties are wary of that risk. Continuing partisan parity may not be the first choice of either political parties or organized interests, but it is far preferable to a realignment that places one party firmly in the minority. Even more than parties, interest groups want to reduce uncertainty, and campaign reform would be a roll of the dice.

Lobbying Strategies and Actions

Despite organized interests' huge investments in electoral politics, rarely do elections produce definitive victories for a group. Indeed, having your party of choice control Congress or the presidency (or even both) does not guarantee success, as health care reform advocates discovered in 1993–1994 when President Clinton's health care reform package failed.[13] Organized interests have therefore adopted—even pioneered—many "permanent campaign" techniques to advance their own issues.[14] In the early to mid-1990s dozens of telecommunications firms used survey research, public relations campaigns, advertising, campaign contributions, personal contacts by well-paid Washington lobbyists, extensive grassroots lobbying from local and state executives, and broad coalitions to affect the content of the Telecommunications Reform Act eventually passed in 1996.[15]

But the lobbying did not stop there. The act gave continuing decision making power to the Federal Communications Commission, and so the commission—and then Congress again—became targets for further policy change. Roll Call, a newspaper that covers Capitol Hill, has been filled with advertisements for and against modifications in the Telecommunications Reform Act, and local notables have been mobilized and re-mobilized to loosen restrictions on the ability of the Regional Bell companies to offer long distance phone service.

More generally, organized interests emphasize a campaign style of lobbying dedicated to marshalling information that demonstrates the political power of an idea or proposal. For example, groups have begun to use the Internet for grassroots lobbying by identifying, recruiting, and segmenting large numbers of supporters in a fairly short time.[16] Groups from handicapped citizens to the U.S. Chamber of Commerce can encourage and provide the means for constituents to bombard their legislators with well-conceived, focused emails.

In the politics of problem definition, everyone can participate by calling a press conference, releasing a study, going on a talk show, commissioning a poll, or buying an advertisement. Nor is there any shortage in Washington of well-defined problems and potential solutions, as the capital is awash in arguments and evidence that define problems, set agendas, and suggest remedies. More difficult to understand is how certain definitions come to prevail in a system of political institutions that often, though not always, resist new—or newly packaged—ideas.

As problem definition and agenda status become increasingly important elements of policymaking, organized interests are stepping up their attempts to expand, restrict, or redirect conflict. The public interest and environmental movements of the 1960s often led the way in employing those strategies, leaving business to catch up in the 1970s and 1980s.[17] Jeffrey Berry, a long-time student of public interest groups, has concluded that citizen groups have driven the policy agenda since the 1960s, thus forcing business interests to respond to issues developed by groups such as Common Cause and environmental organizations.[18] We do not fully agree with Berry's assessment, but citizen groups have surely changed the governmental agenda in hundreds of cases.

Following on the heels of these agenda successes has been the institutionalization of interests within government, especially when broad public concerns are at stake.[19] For example, many of the 1995 battles over the Republicans' Contract with America pitted legislators against members of government agencies such as the Environmental Protection Agency. Moreover, many interests have found homes *in* Congress in caucuses composed of sitting legislators.[20]

And there's the rub. *As more interests seek to define problems and push agenda items, more messages emanate from more sources.* Threatened interests—whether corporate, environmental, or professional—compete with one another to publicize their issues and win converts. Some interests can cut through the cacophony of voices. Those in E. E. Schattschneider's "heavenly chorus" of affluent groups can—at a price—get their message across through public relations campaigns or advertisements.[21] In addition, if such messages are directed toward legislators who have received substantial campaign contributions from the sponsoring interests, the messages typically reach a receptive audience.

The emphasis on problem definition looms large when major public policy issues are on the table amid tremendous uncertainty. Lots of substantive interests are in play, many competing scenarios are put forward, legislative decisions are always contingent, and public policy outcomes are often filled with unanticipated consequences. As loose, ill-defined policy communities replace cozy policymaking triangles of interest groups, congressional committees, and administrative agencies, decision making amid great uncertainty has become the rule, not the exception.[22]

* * * * *

Partisan parity contributes simultaneously to both increased uncertainty and a greater chance for gridlock. The *Washington Post*'s Dan Balz and David Broder began a January 2002 article by saying, "Rarely has a midterm election year of such consequence begun with such uncertainty." [23] Yet they also express the conventional wisdom that only twenty-five to thirty-five House seats will be competitive in 2002, a figure that may preclude many major changes.

Organized interests react to this duality by investing in electoral politics through parties and candidates and in a range of lobbying activities. The high-tech industry's tactics (see Chapter 14) show how corporate interests seek certainty in both the electoral and legislative arenas.

The Aftermath of the September 11, 2001, Terrorist Attacks

In some profound ways the terrorist attacks on New York and Washington did "change everything." Domestic security will never be taken quite as much for granted. The role of government in regulating parts of our lives, from attending the Super Bowl to flying on airlines to crossing the Canadian border, has changed dramatically. But organized interests have altered their behavior hardly at all, save to refrain from some political giving and some face-to-face legislative lobbying, which new Capitol Hill restrictions have made more difficult.

Rather, with speed and opportunism many organized interests simply changed their pitch to incorporate terrorism and domestic security, sending a host of new messages to Congress in the days, weeks, and months after the attacks. Moreover, new groups organized to lobby on behalf of families who lost their loved ones in the attacks. Although some inside lobbying has occurred, often with representatives and senators making the case for their favored interests, the most significant efforts came as groups recast their messages in the attack's aftermath. Very few new appeals were made. Rather, organized interests dusted off dozens upon dozens of old ideas and repackaged them with a postterrorism frame of reference.

The list of reframed appeals is remarkable in both length and variety.

- "When travel sagged after the attacks, American tour bus operators . . . made two perennial issues—an exemption from the federal tax on diesel fuels and protection from public-transit competition— part of their pitch." [24]

- "Drug companies want an exemption from antitrust laws so they can work together to develop, produce, and sell drugs and vaccines against anthrax, smallpox, and germ warfare." [25]
- "[A congressional aide] heard from representatives of the travel, insurance, telecommunications, and software industries, from lobbyists for farmers, pharmaceutical companies, and manufacturers, and from several military contractors. None of them asked for anything different from what they had sought from Congress before, the aide said, but all had new pitches presenting their cases as responses to the attacks." [26]

Finally, our particular favorite. Borrowing the words of that astute political analyst Dave Barry, we are not making this up: "Ever since lawmakers did away with the full tax deduction for business meals and entertainment in 1986, the [restaurant] industry has been trying to get it restored. After September 11, the restaurateurs declared eating out 'the cornerstone of the economy,' and their campaign for the full write-off began anew." [27]

To be sure, the events of September 11, 2001, did change some priorities. President Bush in his 2003 budget requested an extra $50 billion for defense spending—a potential windfall for defense firms and hundreds of subcontractors.

Groups produced new studies, new surveys, and new rationales for the same old policies they had long sought. Should we be surprised? No. Groups seek to protect their own interests. For many large membership groups, the terrorism context offered few opportunities for new gains. But groups of seniors, consumer activists, and environmentalists might benefit from an increased sense that government plays an important role in protecting its citizens from harm. And the collapse of Enron—another kind of disaster—demonstrated a similar need for controls. With both more government spending and increased regulation, most organized interests could find positive aspects of the postterrorism context in which all their skills at lobbying and campaigning could be put to work. And the political system need not suffer. As Berry argues in Chapter 16, group activity across the board does not have to produce policy gridlock.

Always at the Table

Organized groups are integral to American politics, as they have been for a century (see Chapter 9), and they represent a wide variety of interests in electoral campaigns, agenda setting, decision making, and policy implementation at all levels of government. Whether forging breast cancer victims into a formidable political force (Chapter 4), reasserting the power of a traditionally strong group (the National Rifle Association, Chapter 3), or embarking on sophisticated media lobbying campaigns (Chapter 12), organized interests demonstrate their resilience in a political system that affords multiple points of access and influence.

However important money may be in American politics, useful information is usually worth more. Much of this information is technical, and group representatives provide reams of data and analyses to elected and appointed officials. Increasingly, however, the information comes with explicitly political overtones from constituents activated with breathtaking efficiency and armed with well-tested messages tailored to each legislator. Chapters 10 and 11 demonstrate the continuing relevance of inside lobbying, but much of this complements constituency-based efforts that employ highly sophisticated campaign techniques.

So, interest group activity is vigorous. But is it effective, too? Success and failure can be difficult to assess; political parties, individual legislators, and the media come into play, as does competition among interests. In the end organized interests have their say on almost all issues, yet they rarely dominate the process. Nor can we explain all outcomes on the basis of their activities. As the articles in this book and other studies demonstrate, the politics of organized interests is messy, frustrating, and fully integrated into our system of checks and balances. In that sense, there are few permanent victories and even fewer unassailable generalizations. Rather, groups interact with government officials, sometimes influencing outcomes, sometimes not, and sometimes operating at the direction of elected officials rather than the reverse. Things do change, from the increasing use of telephones at the turn of the twentieth century to the growth of the Internet at the advent of the twenty-first. But much remains the same as legislators and lobbyists combine to represent constituents and interests in distinct, but overlapping, ways.

Notes

1. On state lobbying, see Alan Rosenthal, *The Third House*, 2d ed. (Washington, D.C.: CQ Press, 2000); for cities, see Tony Nownes, "Lobbyists in the Metropolis" (paper presented at the 2001 Midwest Political Science Association meetings, Chicago, April 19–22).
2. Sidney Blumenthal, *The Permanent Campaign* (New York: Touchstone, 1982), 23.
3. Robert H. Salisbury, "The Paradox of Interest Groups in Washington: More Groups, Less Clout," in *The New American Political System*, 2d ed., ed. Anthony King (Washington, D.C.: American Enterprise Institute, 1990), 203–229.
4. See Thomas Ferguson, *Golden Rule* (Chicago: University of Chicago, 1995) for a thorough articulation of an "investment theory" of political parties.
5. Anthony Corrado, "Financing the 2000 Election," in *The Election of 2000*, ed. Gerald Pomper (New York: Chatham House, 2001), 95.
6. David B. Magleby, *Getting Inside the Outside Campaign* (Provo, Utah: Brigham Young University, Center for the Study of Elections and Democracy, 2001).
7. "2000 Presidential Races Were First in Modern History Where Parties Spent More on TV Ads than Candidates," http://www.Brennancenter.org/presscenter/ pressrelease 2000/1211cmag.htm, March 23, 2001.
8. AFL-CIO, http://www.aflcio.org/Labor/2000/election.htm, May 21, 2001.
9. Joseph Serwack, "Day Off Helps UAW Flex Muscle; Union Turnout Boosts Democrats," *Crain's Detroit Business*, November 12, 2000, 1.

10. Robert Dreyfuss, "Rousing the Democratic Base," *The American Prospect* 11 (November 2000): 20–23.

11. A range of interest groups used targeted direct mail in competitive electoral contests in 2000. See, for example, the case studies in Magleby, *Election Advocacy*, especially Craig Wilson, "The 2000 Montana At-Large Congressional District Race," 206–216 and Todd Donovan and Charles Morrow, "The 2000 Washington Second District Race," 261–276.

12. Enron's Chapter 11 filing in December 2001 decimated the retirement savings of thousands of employees whose 401k holdings were in company stock. The Securities and Exchange Commission began investigating Enron's accounting procedures after the company admitted to overstating revenue and understating debts for several years. Enron contributed significantly to George W. Bush's presidential campaign and to many congressional campaigns in 2000.

13. For an excellent analysis of organized interests in the health care battle, see David Broder and Haynes Johnson, *The System* (Boston: Little, Brown, 1997).

14. Burdett Loomis, "The Never Ending Story: Campaigns without Elections," in *The Permanent Campaign and Its Future*, ed. Norman Ornstein and Thomas Mann (Washington, D.C.: American Enterprise Institute, 2000), 162–184.

15. Darrell West and Burdett Loomis, *The Sound of Money* (New York: W.W. Norton, 1998).

16. From a presentation by Peggy Crawley of Issue Dynamics, Inc., at Public Affairs Institute, American University, Washington, D.C., January 10, 2002.

17. David Vogel, *Fluctuating Fortunes* (New York: Basic Books, 1989), 295–297.

18. Jeffery Berry, *The Power of Citizen Groups* (Washington, D.C.: Brookings Institution, forthcoming).

19. See Gary Mucciaroni, *Reversals of Fortune* (Washington, D.C.: Brookings Institution, 1995).

20. Susan Webb Hammond, *Congressional Caucuses in National Policy Making* (Baltimore: Johns Hopkins University, 1998).

21. E. E. Schattschneider, *The Semi-Sovereign People* (New York: Holt, Rinehart, and Winston, 1960); West and Loomis, *The Sound of Money*.

22. See William P. Browne, *Cultivating Congress* (Lawrence: University Press of Kansas, 1995); John Wright, *Interest Groups and Congress* (Boston: Allyn and Bacon, 1996).

23. Dan Balz and David Broder, "So Much to Win—or Lose—in 2002," *Washington Post National Weekly Edition*, January 14–20, 2002, 12.

24. Christopher H. Schmitt, Julian E. Barnes, and Douglas Pasternak, "Bellying Up to the Antiterrorist Bill," *U.S. News and World Report*, December 31, 2001, 18.

25. Robert Pear, "Lobbyists Seek Special Spin on Federal Bioterrorism Bill," *New York Times*, December 11, 2001, A1.

26. David Rosenbaum, "A Nation Challenged the Interests," *New York Times*, December 3, 2001, B1.

27. Schmitt, Barnes, and Pasternak, "Bellying Up to the Antiterrorist Bill," 18.

Index